THE UNITED STATES OF AMERICA
New England
Middle Atlantic
Midwest
South
Southwest
West
CANADA
MEXICO
USA
PACIFIC OCEAN
ATLANTIC OCEAN
GULF OF MEXICO
Gulf Stream
Gulf Stream
AK
HI
WA
OR
CA
ID
NV
MT
WY
UT
CO
AZ
NM
ND
SD
NE
KS
MN
IA
MO
WI
IL
MI
IN
OH
OK
TX
AR
LA
MS
AL
TN
KY
GA
FL
SC
NC
VA
WV
PA
NY
NJ
DE
MD
VT
NH
MA
CT
RI
ME
Seattle
San Francisco
Los Angeles
San Diego
Phoenix
Denver
Topeka
Dallas
Houston
Chicago
Detroit
New Orleans
Miami
Philadelphia
Washington D.C.
New York City
Boston
Augusta

LEARNING ENGLISH

GREEN LINE NEW 3

Ausgabe für Bayern

von

Stephanie Ashford
Rosemary Hellyer-Jones
Marion Horner

Ernst Klett Verlag
Stuttgart Düsseldorf Leipzig

LEARNING ENGLISH GREEN LINE NEW 3
Ausgabe für Bayern

von
Stephanie Ashford, Brigachtal; Rosemary Hellyer-Jones M.A., Ehingen (Donau);
Marion Horner M.A., Cambridge; sowie Raimund A. Mader M.A., Eschenbach (i.d.Opf.)

Beratende Mitarbeit
Dr. Thomas Becker, Nürnberg; Anne Marie Deißenböck, München; Harald Fischer, Nürnberg;
Waltraud Gschwendner, München; Renate Leive, Sonnefeld; Gerhard Nickl, Nürnberg

Illustrationen
Elsie Lennox, London (Zeichnungen); Christian Dekelver, Weinstadt (Grafik);
Dorothee Wolters, Köln (Zeichnungen im Vokabular)

CDs

1 Begleit-CD zum Schülerbuch für zu Hause und für den Unterricht mit Texten, Liedern, Ausspracheübungen (Klettnummer 547238)

1 CD mit den Hörtexten für den Unterricht (Klettnummer 547239)

Lernsoftware

Zu diesem Band gibt es ein multimediales Lernprogramm. Dieses Programm bietet abwechslungsreiche Übungsformen zu Vokabular und Grammatik, Leistungs- und Lernzielkontrollen und ein Lexikon mit dem Wortschatz des Lehrwerks.

1. Auflage 1 11 | 2015 2014

Alle Drucke dieser Auflage sind unverändert und können im Unterricht nebeneinander verwendet werden. Die letzten Zahlen bezeichnen jeweils die Auflage und das Jahr des Druckes.

Internetadresse: www.klett.de

Redaktion: Peter Cole M.A., Monique Kunhar M.A.
Herstellung: Marietta Heymann

Umschlaggestaltung: Christian Dekelver, Weinstadt
Reproduktion: Meyle + Müller, Medien-Management, Pforzheim
Druck: Firmengruppe APPL, aprinta druck, Wemding
Printed in Germany
ISBN-13: 978-3-12-547230-3
ISBN-10: 3-12-547230-X

9 783125 472303

Hallo und herzlich willkommen
bei LEARNING ENGLISH GREEN LINE NEW 3, Ausgabe Bayern!

Die vertraute Grundstruktur eures Englischbuchs mit **Units, Focus on, Revision, Extra Line, Mediation** und nicht zu vergessen den wichtigen Nachschlageseiten am Ende, nämlich **Grammar, Vocabulary, Dictionary, Classroom phrases** und **Irregular verbs** ist gegenüber dem Vorjahr unverändert geblieben. Wo ihr die einzelnen Abschnitte findet, steht genau im Inhaltsverzeichnis.

Doch in diesem Band gibt es auch einige Neuerungen:
1. In jeder **Unit** gibt es eine **Skills page.** „**Skill**" bedeutet Fähigkeit oder Fertigkeit. Hier lernt und übt ihr besonders intensiv, wie man eine komplexere Aufgabe durchführt, z. B. wie man ein Referat hält oder zielgerichtete Lesetechniken anwendet.

2. Die **Revisions** bestehen immer aus vier Seiten: zwei Seiten für die Wiederholung aus der 5. und 6. Klasse, zwei Seiten für die Wiederholung aus Band 3. Jede **Revision** enthält eine **Test yourself page** zum selbstständigen Üben. Die Lösungen für diese Übungen findet ihr auf den Seiten 194/195. Ihr könnt also auch selbstständig überprüfen, ob alles richtig ist. Für den Fall, dass bei diesen Übungen noch Fehler vorkommen, hilft euch **Doctor G** mit gezielten Übungen im **Workbook,** selbstständig an der Verbesserung eurer Leistungen zu arbeiten.

3. Die **Classroom phrases** auf den Seiten 196/197 enthalten vermehrt nützlichen Wortschatz für Diskussionen und Präsentationen in der Klasse. Es lohnt sich in jedem Fall hier nachzuschlagen, wenn Diskussions- und Präsentationsaufgaben anstehen.

Wenn auch ansonsten vieles ähnlich ist wie in den ersten beiden Bänden, merkt ihr sicher schon, dass in der 7. Klasse auch etwas Neues auf euch zukommt: Es geht vermehrt um Arbeitstechniken und um selbstständiges Lernen. Mit **Green Line NEW Bayern** werdet ihr mit diesen neuen Aufgaben sicher gut zurechtkommen.

Weiterhin also viel Freude am Unterricht und viel Erfolg beim Lernen!

Zeichenerklärung

1 Alle Texte und Übungen, die auf der Begleit-CD zum Schülerbuch aufgezeichnet sind, erkennst du an diesem grünen Zeichen. ■ Hier beginnt ein neuer Track auf der CD.

1 Übungen mit diesem blauen Symbol verweisen auf die CD zum Hörverstehen. Die Hörtexte sind nicht im Schülerbuch abgedruckt.

Übungen mit diesem Symbol löst du am besten in Partnerarbeit.

Alle Übungen mit diesem Symbol könnt ihr gemeinsam in Gruppenarbeit lösen.

⟨ ⟩ Diese Klammern zeigen an, dass die Übung fakultativ ist.

G10 Dieses Symbol verweist auf den Grammatikteil.

Inhaltsverzeichnis

unit 1 intro

London

A punk

Tower Bridge & the Tower of London

Oxford Street

The Natural History Museum

West End theatres

Camden Market

1 What do you know?

a) What do the photos tell you about London and the people there? What can you see or do in London?

b) What else do you know about London? What famous sights have you heard of or seen?

2 Listening: The Morgans

1

a) The Morgans from Seattle, USA, have arrived at their hotel in London. Listen, and find out what kind of things each of them is interested in.

b) Make a grid with these names:

Oxford Street • the National Gallery • Tate Modern • the Millennium Bridge • the Tower of London • the London Dungeon

Then listen again. Take notes about the places.

c) Say what you would like to do or see in London. Try to explain why.

Buckingham Palace

A homeless person

The Notting Hill Carnival

3 Using the Underground

a) The quickest way to move around London is on the Underground. The nearest station to the Morgans' hotel is Swiss Cottage, and Ceri and Gareth have made a list of other stations near places they want to visit. Look at the map at the back of your book and read the dialogue. Whose route do you think is best?

UNDERGROUND

Ceri: For the Natural History Museum, we take the train from Swiss Cottage. Then at Baker Street we change to the Circle Line. And we get off at South Kensington.

Gareth: Yeah, but we can also stay on the Jubilee Line as far as Green Park. Then it's three stops to South Kensington on the Piccadilly Line.

Place	Station
the Natural History Museum	South Kensington
Oxford Street	Oxford Circus
the National Gallery	Leicester Square
the Tower of London	Tower Hill
Camden Market	Camden Town
Buckingham Palace	Victoria

b) Work out the routes to the other places on the list. You can start at Swiss Cottage, or you can go straight from one sight to another.

A The river Thames

A good way to see London's sights is from the river. There are lots of different boat services. The commuter service is used by some Londoners on their way to work. During trips on tourist boats the sights are described over a loudspeaker.

On your left is the London Eye – one of the new projects which were chosen to celebrate the millennium. It took six years to build the huge wheel. In fact it wasn't finished in time for the celebrations and in the end it was opened in March 2000. Now it's one of London's most popular tourist attractions. You're taken up to a height of over a hundred and twenty metres, and you get fantastic views over the whole city. You can book in advance. Tickets are sold over the phone and online, too.

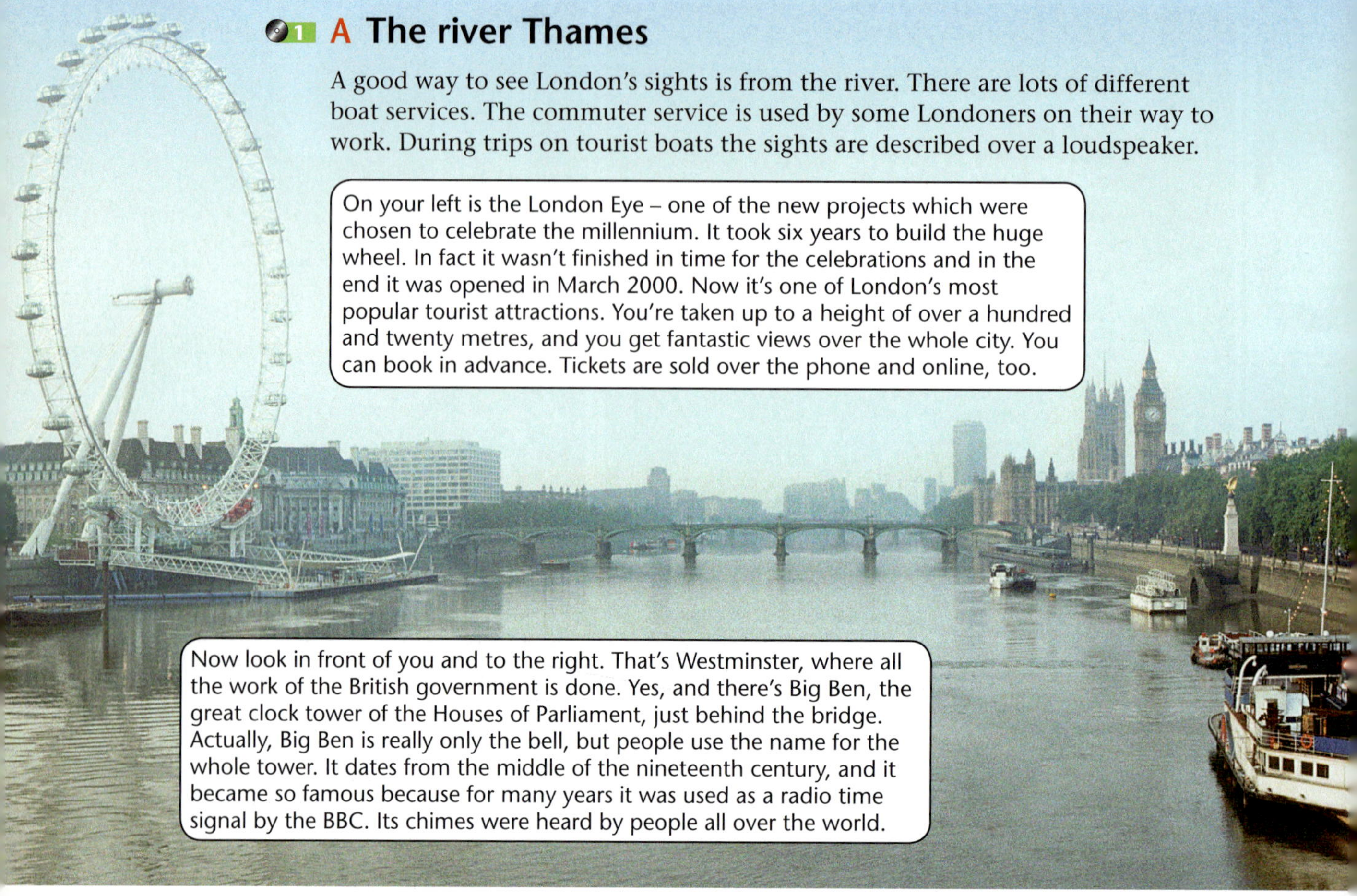

Now look in front of you and to the right. That's Westminster, where all the work of the British government is done. Yes, and there's Big Ben, the great clock tower of the Houses of Parliament, just behind the bridge. Actually, Big Ben is really only the bell, but people use the name for the whole tower. It dates from the middle of the nineteenth century, and it became so famous because for many years it was used as a radio time signal by the BBC. Its chimes were heard by people all over the world.

1 Tourist information

a) 1. What boat services are there on the Thames? 2. What information is given about the London Eye? 3. What happens in Westminster? 4. Why did Big Ben become so famous?

b) Have you ever been on a boat trip on a river? Or on another kind of sightseeing trip? Talk about when and where it was, and what you saw during the trip.

c) Role play: You want to go on the London Eye, but your friend wants to go on a boat trip. Try to persuade each other. Say what it will be like. Explain what you will be able to see or do.

2 New forms

a) Look for passive forms in the text, and collect them in two lists. Find the rule about how the passive is made. What verb forms do you use?

present tense

subject	?	?
the commuter service	is	used
the sights	are	…

past tense

subject	?	?
the new projects	were	chosen
…	…	…

tip
The passive is often used to give information. In passive sentences the focus is more on the action than on who does it.

b) In a passive sentence, which preposition is used to show who does (did) the action?

3 The Globe Theatre

a) Another sight near the river is the Globe Theatre, where the plays of William Shakespeare (1564–1616) are performed. One of his most famous plays is *Romeo and Juliet*.

Use the present passive to explain what is done at the Globe.
Example: 1. Shakespeare's work **is celebrated.**

1. celebrate Shakespeare's work
2. perform his plays there
3. keep up old theatre traditions
4. show visitors around the theatre
5. explain the history of the building
6. do a lot of work with schools and colleges
7. invite students to take part in drama classes

b) Write a short text about the history of the Globe Theatre. Use the past passive.
Start: The first Globe Theatre **was built** in 1599. …

The first Globe Theatre **(build in 1599)**. Many of Shakespeare's plays **(write for the Globe)**. However, over the years many changes **(make in London)**. In the end the old theatre **(lose and forget)**. Then in 1989 parts of it **(find under newer buildings)**. A project to build it again **(start)**. The new Globe Theatre **(open in 1997)**.

c) Put the correct present and past passive forms into this text from a brochure.

play | invite | kill | act out | add | experience | wear | present

Don't miss **Shakespeare's Globe Exhibition!**

You'll find it in a room under the Globe Theatre.

- Learn how the theatre ___ by Londoners 400 years ago. A lot of the information ___ inter-actively.
- See the kind of costumes that ___ in those days, and listen to the musical instruments that ___ then.
- Watch while fighting ___ in front of you, and find out how characters ___ on stage in the past.
- You ___ to join the action, too! When you read a part, your voice ___ to a video scene of the play.

4 More about the Thames

Put these sentences into the passive.
Example: 1. London **is divided** into north and south **by** the river Thames.

1. The river Thames divides London into north and south.
2. Once there were buildings on London Bridge. The Great Fire of London of 1666 ruined them.
3. Today lots of bridges join the two parts of the city.
4. In the past smugglers often used the river.
5. Fog often hid the smugglers from the police.
6. Now tourists from all over the world enjoy attractions on the river.
7. Stupid people sometimes throw rubbish into the river.
8. In 1953 high water levels from the North Sea hit London badly.
9. Today the Thames Barrier protects the people and the buildings.
10. Queen Elizabeth II opened the Thames Barrier in 1984.

G1,2

5 The Notting Hill Carnival

The Notting Hill Carnival takes place during the last weekend in August every year.

a) Read the newspaper article. Then write Mel's notice and draw a picture of the costume.

b) You already know how to make the passive in the simple present and simple past. Find the passive forms of two other tenses in the article. Make a grid for each tense to explain the forms.

c) Write a story. Say how the costume was stolen and why.

CARNIVAL COSTUME MYSTERY

A fourteen-year-old girl's costume has been stolen from a garage – just days before this year's Notting Hill Carnival.

"I feel devastated," Mel Christie told our reporter. "My costume was for a competition at the Carnival. Making it has taken months. Even if we try to make another one, it won't be finished in time. I hope the person who took it will be found and punished!"

It is a mystery to Mel's mother why anyone would want the costume. "It's no good to anybody else. If they wear it at the Carnival, it will be recognized," she says. The costume looks like a huge gold sun. A full description of it has been given to the police, and notices have been put up in the area by Mel. Anyone with any information should report to the police immediately.

6 Changes in the East End

Mr Morgan is comparing the East End of London now with what it was like when he visited London many years ago. Use the passive to give the same information in written form.

Start: A lot of changes **have been made** in the East End. The whole Docklands area **will be** …

"Hey, what a lot of changes they've made in the East End since I was here last time. Wow! If they go on like this, they'll tidy up the whole Docklands area soon. Look at all those expensive new apartments they've built! And they've opened lots of health clubs and restaurants, too. Yeah, I can see they've spent a lot of money, and it looks like they'll do even more in the future. I guess they've improved the area. It'll make life better in some ways. But – well, they'll lose the old friendly neighbourhoods, won't they? I mean, they'll push poorer Londoners out of this part of the city. I'm sure people have already forgotten a lot of the traditions of the East End. Over the years they'll change the character of the place completely!"

7 Information from signs

Look at the examples of the passive infinitive in the box. Then explain what these signs tell you.
Use: **must (not) / can / should + the passive infinitive**

grammar
Tickets can **be bought** here.
Animals must not **be fed** by visitors.

1

2

3

4

5

6

B In Covent Garden

Ceri didn't want to visit Tate Modern with the others. She decided to go to Camden Town, but promised to meet the others in Covent Garden at one o'clock.

Dad: Well, if my watch isn't fast, it's one fifteen already. So where's Ceri?

Mom: Oh, I hope she isn't lost. I knew we shouldn't allow her to go off alone!

Gareth: Hey, I can see a stupid hairstyle in that crowd over there. It must be Ceri's – yeah, she's coming now.

Ceri: Hi, guys! Sorry I'm late. I was watching some buskers – two guys on guitar and bass. They could really sing – and without microphones, too! Did you see them?

Gareth: No, we didn't – because we had to wait here for you!

Ceri: Oh, sorry! But there are some great street shows here in Covent Garden. I saw some fantastic acrobats, too.

Dad: And how was Camden Town, honey?

Ceri: Oh, really interesting! The markets there have all kinds of funky things. Just look at these earrings I got.

Mom: Oh yes, dear. Very – er – funky.

Ceri: Don't worry, Mom. You don't have to wear them. They're a present for me, not for you. – Hey, and I even made friends with an English guy there. We crashed into each other!

Gareth: You never look where you're going!

Ceri: Actually, it wasn't my fault. He was having a skateboard race – and he didn't see me! Anyway, his name is Darren. His people have a food stall there, with Caribbean food. I tried some of their rice. It was delicious.

Dad: Oh, so you've already had your lunch? Well, that's fine. But we haven't, and we're hungry. Come on, let's get something to eat.

1 Talking about the text

1. Whose morning do you think was more interesting: Ceri's or her family's? Why?

2. What do you learn about Ceri from the text?

2 Sound practice

a) Say these words and find the odd one out.

[ʃ] crash, delicious, national, sugar, stall
[ɪ] visit, guitar, kind, chicken, give
[ʊ] look, put, lunch, shouldn't, push

b) How are these words stressed? Make four lists.

[●••]	[•●•]	[●•]	[•●]
…	…	…	…

acrobat, anyway, delicious, earring, expensive, fantastic, guitar, hairstyle, important, interesting, microphone, palace, persuade, (a) present, (to) present, police

c) Put these words in the right list.

[ʌ]	[iː]	[e]	[eɪ]
…	…	…	…

already, bass, busker, dead, each, even, friend, funky, great, honey, hungry, jealous, late, people, street, wait

Souvenirs of London

Sometimes things happen that you'll never forget. Like last Saturday. I was with my new American friends, Ceri and Gareth. Ceri is cool, but her brother seems a bit odd at first. He reads history books and doesn't talk much, but he's OK really. They were buying souvenirs and Gareth wanted to have another look at a computer game in Oxford Street. Outside the store we saw Steve, one of my friends from school.
He grinned and said, "Hi, Darren! What are you doing here? And who are your friends?" So I introduced them. Steve seemed to like Ceri. Anyway, he decided to come with us, so we went in together and headed straight for the games department.

Gareth soon found the CD-ROM he was interested in. It was a detective game about Sherlock Holmes. He looked at it for ages.
"Well, are you going to buy it?" I asked.
"No," Gareth sighed. "I'd like to. I want to give it to – er – somebody. But it's too expensive. I don't have the money."
I looked at the others. Steve was talking to Ceri. They weren't listening to us.
"Who's the somebody? A girl?!" I said.
That hit the bull's-eye! Gareth went bright red and turned away. I could see he felt really embarrassed, so I just suggested, "Why don't you look for something else for her? How about a T-Shirt with a map of the Underground on it, that kind of thing?"
Then I turned back to the others.

Ceri was showing Steve one of the souvenirs she had in her bag. It was a clock that looked like Big Ben.
"It's for my grandma," she told him. "It's her birthday when we get back from Wales."
"Wales? Sorry, Ceri, but you're in England here!" Steve corrected her.
"She knows that, you idiot! But they're off to Wales on Monday," I explained.
Next Ceri showed Steve a little teddy bear – a present for a friend of hers. She pulled a string, and the bear began to sing. Then she held it up and danced around with it.

While she was dancing, I suddenly noticed we could be seen on the CCTV monitor above us. Ceri saw it, too.
"Hey, we're on TV!" she laughed. "Everyone in the store can see us!"

When Steve asked about Gareth's souvenirs, Gareth didn't seem to hear him. He was still looking at the computer game.
"I can show you what he's bought," said Ceri. "It's in my bag, too."
But Steve didn't want to be watched on TV all the time. So we moved away, and Ceri got Gareth's souvenir out of her bag. It was a hat like the ones that are worn by the Beefeaters at the Tower of London.
"Beefeaters! What a crazy name for those guards!" laughed Ceri.
"Well, they eat lots of steaks," Steve joked. His jokes are sometimes a bit weak.
Anyway, that was all the souvenirs, and Ceri decided it was time to go.
"We've given Gareth enough time. We can't stay in this computer store all day," she said.

While she and Steve were putting the things back in the bag, I looked over to where Gareth was standing. He had his back to us, but I could see that he was still holding that CD-ROM. When I saw what he did with it, my heart jumped into my mouth.
He suddenly put it under his jacket.
I went over to him. "Gareth! Are you crazy?" ...

When we tried to leave the store, we were stopped by a man and woman who were waiting for us at the door. The man put his hand on Gareth's shoulder. Oh damn! I knew it! "Excuse me, young man," he said. "You'll have to come with us. We think you've got something you haven't paid for."
Store detectives! Everybody in the store was looking at us again, but now it wasn't funny. Gareth's face went bright red again.
I felt terrible. "Why didn't I stop him?" I thought.
Ceri got really angry. "Are you calling my brother a thief?" she protested. "You –"
"We saw it on our CCTV system," the woman interrupted. "You'll all have to come with us."
"It's nothing to do with me! I don't even know those bloody Americans," Steve shouted and tried to get away. But the man grabbed him by the arm. "Do what we tell you, or you'll make everything worse."
Poor Steve, he doesn't want to get into trouble because his brother was caught once when he tried to steal a CD.

■ All four of us were taken to a room where there was a table and chairs, and a row of monitors on the wall.
"Sit down," the man ordered. "I want you to watch this video."
First came the scene with Ceri's souvenirs and her dance with the teddy bear. However, nobody was laughing now. Then the scene with Gareth was shown.
"There. He's putting it under his jacket!" said the man, and paused the video. "Look, it can be seen quite clearly."
I looked at the others. Steve was shaking his head, and I could see the shock in Ceri's eyes. She was looking at Gareth, but his eyes were on the floor.
"Show us what you've got in your bags and your pockets," the woman ordered.
Everything had to be put on the table. The clock, the teddy bear, and the hat. It was like a bad dream, but I couldn't wake up from it.
"Why didn't he listen?" I kept thinking.
Next all our money, then a map, two biros and some keys. I waited for the worst.
At last everything was on the table. I was amazed. There was no CD-ROM.
The store detectives checked all our bags and pockets again, but they were empty now.
There was definitely no computer game.
The woman and the man looked at each other. Nothing was said for a time. Then the man stood up and opened the door.
"You can go, kids. Sorry about the mistake."

■ At last we were out of the store and in the street again. Boy, was I happy!
But Ceri was really angry with Gareth. "That was no mistake! I saw you with my own eyes! How could you do a thing like that?" she shouted at him.
"I don't get it. Where's the game now? What happened to it?" Steve wanted to know.
It was all too much for Gareth, and he started to cry.
"I'm so sorry," he said. "I was an idiot. Darren warned me, but I didn't listen. I really wanted that game. But then, on the way out, I got scared and put it down somewhere."
"Lucky you did. But why didn't you tell them that?" I asked.
"I don't know," he replied.
Ceri was still angry. "You must be out of your mind! All that for a stupid game!"
I felt sorry for the poor kid. "It wasn't for him," I told Ceri.
I didn't expect Ceri's reaction. She suddenly threw back her head and started to laugh.
"Not Angela Spencer?! You *are* out of your mind, Gareth! She's fifteen and you're twelve!" Then she looked at her watch.
"Oh my God, is that the time? We have to go! Our parents are waiting for us at the London Dungeon," she explained. And they quickly said goodbye.

As usual, Steve had the last word.
"The London Dungeon?" he shouted after them. "That's just the place for Gareth!"
Gareth didn't smile. I'm sure that experience will be a souvenir of London he'll never forget.

1 An important scene

a) One important scene is missing (between lines 78 and 79). Talk about what you think happens.

b) Do you think leaving this scene out makes the story better or worse?
Try to explain your answer.

c) Creative writing:
Write your own version of the scene. (It can help to look at exercise 3 first.)

2 Words in context: Explain these phrases in other words

1. That hit the bull's-eye! (line 27)
2. My heart jumped into my mouth. (line 75)
3. His eyes were on the floor.(line 117)
4. I don't get it. (line 142)
5. You must be out of your mind! (line 153)
6. All that for a stupid game! (line 154)

3 The characters in the story

1. Talk about Gareth's feelings at different points in the story.
2. What is your opinion about Gareth and what he does?
3. What kind of friend is Darren?
4. What do you think of Steve? Explain.
5. What happens when Ceri and Gareth have gone? Write a dialogue between them.

4 Word power: Don't always use *said*

When you write dialogue in a text, it is boring always to repeat 'said'. Look in the text for other verbs you can use. Make a list, then choose the best verb for each of these sentences.

1. "Let's wait for the gang at the door," **said** one of the store detectives.
2. "I met Ceri while she was walking round the markets in Camden," Darren **said.**
3. "Ha ha! That's a brilliant joke!" they all **said.**
4. "Oh dear, it's school again tomorrow," Steve **said.**
5. "Careful, Ceri! You're going to crash into that guy behind you!" **said** Darren.
6. "Come with us! Now!" the woman **said.**
7. "But we –" "Be quiet! We know you've got the CD," he **said.**
8. "No! Stop! You can't do that!" they **said.**

5 Statements for discussion

Below are two statements you can discuss in groups or in class. Before you start, prepare for your discussion. Collect reasons for your opinion and organize your arguments. (The list of discussion phrases on page 197 can also help you.)

- "If one of your friends does something wrong, you should tell an adult."
- "You should behave even better in another country than in your own country."

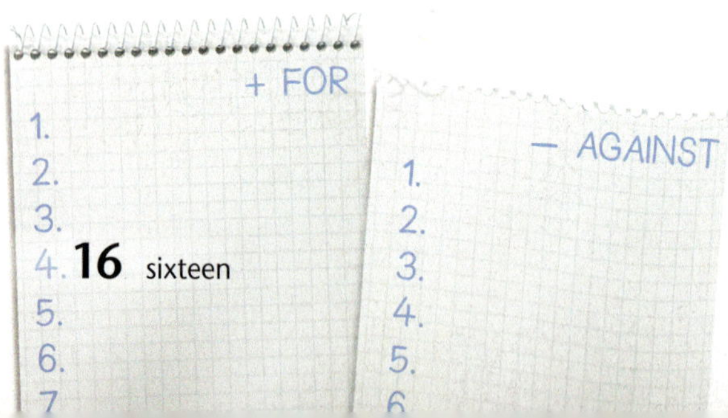

6 Sound practice: Strong and weak forms

In English some short words have strong and weak forms. Usually the weak form is used. However, if a word is especially important or if it comes at the end of a sentence, the strong form must be used. Listen, and say these sentences.

1. There are **some** great computer games, but **some** can be boring, too.
2. Who's the hat **for**? Is it **for** you?
3. **Your** pockets, too, young lady! Take everything out of **your** pockets.
4. He wants **to** go to London, but I don't want **to.**
5. It **was** a stupid thing to do – it really **was!**

8 7 A song

a) Look at the title and say what you think the song will be about. Then listen and find out if you are right.

b) Listen to the song again, and then discuss these questions.

1. What feelings does the song express? How are these feelings shown? (In the words / the music?)
2. Make a grid and fill in the information about the two opposite 'worlds' that are described in the song:

homeless people	rich people
– sleep in cardboard boxes	– …
– …	– …

3. Do you know any other songs about social problems? Say what they are about.

[1]cardboard box – Pappkarton • [2]to beg – betteln • [3]verschieden • [4]Ausreißer(innen) • [5]I don't care for your opinion – deine Meinung ist mir egal • [6]some day – eines Tages • [7]to bet – wetten • [8]Abfall • [9]used to sail – segelten früher • [10]Preis • [11]a couple of – ein paar • [12]Blöcke mit Eigentumswohnungen • [13]for sale – zu verkaufen • [14]drunk to hell – sturzbesoffen • [15]to scream their minds to the heavens – sich die Seele aus dem Leib schreien • [16]Steuern • [17]to line – hier: füllen • [18]Lohn • [19]ausgefallen • [20]to moor – anlegen • [21]Kai

Cardboard Box[1] City (The Levellers)

Have you seen them in Euston Station
Begging[2] in their separate[3] ways
Some of them no more than children
Some of them are runaways[4]
I don't care for your opinion[5]
I've seen you turn your face away
You say to me, Son, what's your problem
Let's talk about this over lunch some day[6]

And I bet[7] you've never walked south of the river
Down the Old Kent Road or down Southwark way
I bet you've never never seen them lying in the litter[8]
In the cardboard boxes where you make them stay

In the Docklands of East London
Where those great tall ships used to sail[9]
For the price[10] of a couple of[11] hundred thousand
I've seen your condominiums[12] for sale[13]
While in the north at the Archway Tavern
You can see them lying there every day
They're drunk to hell[14], they'll scream their minds
to the heavens[15]
My God, why did it have to be this way

And I bet …

I worked my time, I paid my taxes[16]
I lined[17] your pockets with my pay[18]
And you said you'd take my money, you said
you'd help them
Ah, but in your pockets it just seems to stay
I've seen your fancy[19] house in Richmond
I know where you moor[20] your boat, Kingston quay[21]
Every week you take the wife and children sailing
Try taking them down to South London some day

And I bet …

Words: Mark Chadwick, Simon Friend, Jonathan Mark Sevink, Charles Kenton Heather, Jeremy James Cunningham

Skills: Giving a talk about London

1 Choosing a subject

Choose a subject that has something to do with London – places, events, people, sport etc.

Madame Tussaud's
The London Dungeon
Wimbledon
Sherlock Holmes
Hyde Park
Rock Circus

2 Looking for information

Use different sources: books, the Internet, travel brochures etc. Look for facts that will be interesting for your audience. Maybe you can find pictures or maps you can show during your talk, but don't use too many figures. Check that you know (and can explain!) all the English words you need.

3 Organizing your information

a) First note down the most interesting points and the material you want to show.

HYDE PARK
- lake called the Serpentine: (photo)
- Rotten Row: path for horse riding
- 1536 the king's deer park: from 1635 open to everyone
- Underground: Hyde Park Corner, Marble Arch (map)

b) Make a plan for your talk. Check the points on your list. What is the best order? How can you start and end your talk?

Introduction:	Why I chose Hyde Park
Main part:	Information about a) how to get there b) history c) park today d) activities
Conclusion:	Summary (great place!)

Introduction:	sightseeing hard work – Hyde Park good place to relax
Main part:	a) how to get there – Underground: Hyde Park Corner or Marble Arch b) history: …

c) Write notes you can use during your talk. Follow your plan, and take the information from your list. Don't write complete sentences. Key words are often enough.

4 Giving your talk

Take turns to give your talk in groups or in front of the whole class. First look at these tips.

➜ Use your notes, but speak freely.
➜ Try to look at your audience as often as you can.
➜ Speak clearly and not too fast.
➜ Don't be too serious. Relax – and don't stop if you make a mistake.
➜ Be ready to answer questions at the end of your talk.
➜ Practise your talk at home before you actually give it.

1 Word power

Explain the difference between these pairs of words. You can give definitions, or you can show the meaning in example sentences.

1. millennium • century
2. clock • watch
3. stall • store
4. department • apartment
5. community • commuter
6. guide • guard

2 Helping homeless people

Read what Darren tells Ceri. Put in passive forms in the correct tense.

"I'm already looking forward to a big concert that **(give)** at my school in December. Events like this **(organize)** every year by the pupils. Tickets **(sell)** to parents and friends, and over the years a lot of money **(raise)** for different charities. Last year, for example, the money **(give)** to a project in Camden that helps homeless people. It's a centre where food **(cook)** for them, and where they can get a bed for the night. I was really happy when the project **(choose)** as our special charity for the year. If places like that don't get enough money, their doors **(shut)** sooner or later. And what will happen to those people then? Most of us **(treat)** well by life so far, but not everybody is so lucky."

3 Scenes in London

Read what the people say. Then complete the information in the passive.
(Be careful with the last sentence. Think how the negative form should be shown.)

1. "They had to open Tower Bridge!" – The ship was too tall. Tower Bridge had to be ...
2. "I couldn't persuade the guard." – The tourist didn't get into the palace. The guard couldn't ...
3. "They had to pick up all the rubbish." – The streets looked terrible after the Carnival. ...
4. "We couldn't hear the pilot's words." – The plane made a terrible noise. ...
5. "They didn't have to take the drivers to hospital." – It wasn't a serious accident. ...
6. "They couldn't play any matches." – It rained all day at Wimbledon. ...

4 Mixed bag: Lunch in the park

1 the Morgans came out 2 Buckingham Palace, it was time for lunch. " 3 buy sandwiches," suggested Gareth. "Yes, that's quicker 4 going to a restaurant. That's a good 5, Gareth," Mr Morgan said. "It's much cheaper, 6," added Mrs Morgan, 7 job it was to look after the money for the family. "London is 8 expensive place for tourists." They went to the nearest shop 9 sandwiches could 10 bought and taken away, and they all chose what 11 wanted. "12 sandwich has cheese and tomato in it," Gareth told Ceri. "Well, I 13 egg with salad," she replied. The Morgans 14 and walked down 15 St James's Park. There were lots of people in the 16. The Morgans had to sit on the grass 17 there were no empty seats, but they 18 mind. "This is a beautiful place for lunch, 19 it? Look at 20 sweet little ducks over there on the lake," smiled Mrs Morgan. She took the 21 of her two sandwiches out of the box they 22 packed in and started to eat it. The second sandwich was left in the open box on 23 of her bag. Nobody noticed the little duck 24 came from behind them until it was too late. The duck stole Mrs Morgan's second 25 and ran away. "Hey, that's my lunch!" she 26 angrily. "Not 27 more," the others laughed. "Now it's the sweet little 28 lunch!"

focus
Focus on British history

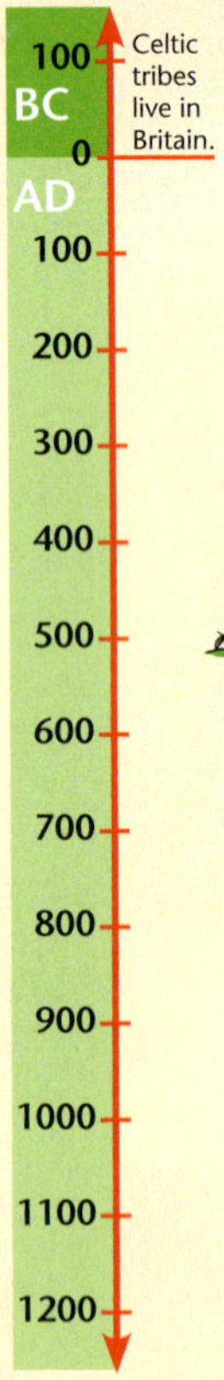

1 From the Romans to the Normans

a) Match the pictures above to the paragraphs on the next page. Explain which words or sentences give you the clues.

b) Copy the time line (above left) into your exercise book and put in the important events from this double page.

2 Listening: Hadrian's head

The Morgans are in the British Museum.

a) Look at the plan and talk about what you expect to see in the museum.

b) Now listen, and find out about:

1. Hadrian (Who was he? Where and when was his head found? What did he build and why did he build it?)
2. Roman roads in Britain (What is special about them?)

c) Imagine you are a Roman soldier in Britain. Write about your day in your diary.

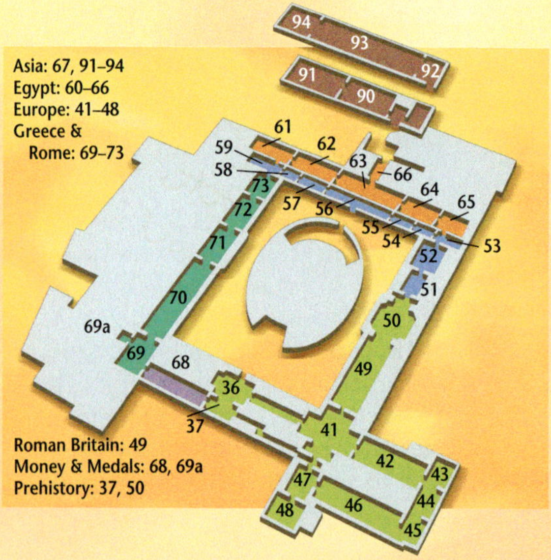

a The last time Britain was invaded was in 1066, when William of Normandy brought an army from France. He defeated King Harold of England at the Battle of Hastings. The Normans immediately started to build castles from where they could control the country. One of the first of these was the Tower of London. For the next two hundred years all the kings of England were Normans. They helped to make England strong, but life for the Anglo-Saxon people was very hard. (Remember Robin Hood?!)

b The Romans left soon after AD 400 when their own country was attacked. After that Angles and Saxons from Germany invaded the east coast of Britain. Gradually they moved across the country and pushed the Celts north to Scotland and west to Wales. While the whole island got its name from a Celtic tribe called the Britons, the new land of the Angles and Saxons was known as England, and their language was English. Over the years, the separate Anglo-Saxon kingdoms joined together and became one country with one king.

c Although the Romans were strong, the Celts didn't give up easily. The most famous Celtic leader was Queen Boudicca. In AD 60 she started a rebellion against the Romans. She and her army of 100,000 fought their way to London and were even able to set fire to the new town. In the end, however, they were defeated, and Boudicca took her own life so that the Romans could not take her prisoner. Her statue can be seen near Westminster Bridge in London.

d Like many other English cities London has a name of Latin origin. In AD 42 Britain was invaded by a Roman army that was too strong for the native Celtic tribes. Most of what is now England was conquered, and became part of the huge Roman Empire. London was founded soon after the Romans arrived. At first it was not much more than a bridge over the Thames, but it soon became a busy river port and an important trading centre.

3 The Bayeux Tapestry

a) Look on the Internet for websites about the Bayeux Tapestry, and find out: how old the tapestry is; how big it is; what story it tells; where the original tapestry can be seen today.

b) Look at the scene on the right and write a sentence about what is happening in it.

c) Draw a picture of an important event from the tapestry that happens before or after this scene. Write a sentence about your picture.

4 Language links

The Normans brought their language, French, to England. Gradually lots of French words were added to English. Look at these French words and say what they are in English. Then put them into four groups and find headings for them:

acteur • arriver • changer • cousin • danse • départ • dialogue • discuter • excuser • famille • grands-parents • histoire • musique • poème • répéter • station • théâtre

A holiday in Wales

Snowdonia National Park

Conwy Castle

1 The Morgans in Wales

a) It is now September 2nd, and the Morgans are in Wales. Here are some clues to where they have been. Look at them carefully to find out:

1. how they are travelling
2. where they have been so far and what they have done
3. what they are going to do – and why

b) What else can you say about Wales?

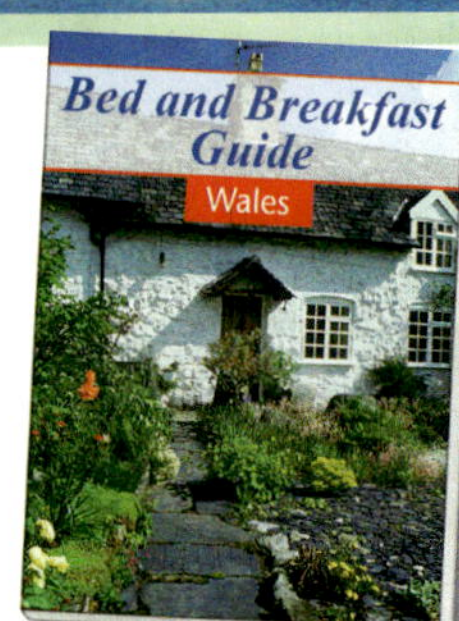

Shopping centre in Cardiff

FAX

From: Owen Morgan, 29 Cardiff Rd, Pontypridd, Glamorgan CF37 5RF, South Wales

To: Evan Morgan, Park Hotel, Belsize Rd, London NW3 5HH

Dear Evan,
We can hardly believe you're all coming! It's hard for us to realize that our American relatives are coming to visit us after all these years! And we're so pleased you've managed to arrange the dates so that you'll be here for my mother's 80th birthday.

You'll find Pontypridd very small after Seattle, and we only hope you won't be disappointed. But Wales is a beautiful country, and the scenery in our area is magnificent.

We're looking forward to seeing you, your wife Pam and the children on September 3rd.

We all send our love,

Owen, Mari and Bronwen

RENT-A-CAR- agency London
August 28th •••••••• **£50.00**

2 Listening: The Morgans' family history

a) Mr Morgan is telling Ceri and Gareth something about their family history. Listen and take notes. What do you find out about:

- Mr Morgan's father? • the valleys of South Wales? • Owen?

b) Your turn: Tell your partner about your family history. What would you like to know about your grandparents?

A The Welsh Morgans

The American visitors have arrived. They are in the Welsh Morgan family's living room.

Mari: Well, this is great! Our American relatives, here at last!

Pam: It's great to be here in Wales. Thank you for the invitation – and thanks for a wonderful lunch.

Owen: Don't mention it, Pam! Now, are you all interested in rugby? If you're really Welsh, you should be.

Gareth: Rugby? Oh sure. It's played in the States, too, but not as much as American football.

Owen: Well, there's a match on TV this afternoon, Wales against New Zealand. Would you like to watch it?

Evan: Yeah, sounds like a good idea.

Bronwen: OK, I'll switch it on, Dad.

Owen: It hasn't started yet. But listen to the singing. We Welsh love singing!

Ceri: Hey, the words don't sound English.

Mari: Because they're not. They're Welsh!

Ceri: You guys have your own language here in Wales, right? I forgot that.

Gareth: Oh, Ceri! We've been driving around Wales since Monday. Didn't you see all the road signs in two languages?

Mari: Welsh is a Celtic language. It's much older than English, actually. People have been speaking Welsh here since King Arthur's time. Or even earlier.

Ceri: Wow! And do you learn it at school?

Bronwen: Yes, I've been learning it for four years now.

Pam: This is a nice home you've got. How long have you been living here?

Owen: We've been living in this house for about two years. And we moved to Pontypridd ten years ago. My mother still lives up in Aberfan.

Evan: Do you and Mari both work here in Pontypridd?

Mari: I work at the post office here, and Owen works at one of the new factories in Cardiff.

Owen: Yes, I've been working in Cardiff since last year. The job is OK …

Bronwen: Hey, Dad. The match is starting. *(to Ceri)* He's been looking forward to this for ages!

Owen: You bet! If we win, I'll take you all down to the pub for a drink.

Evan: Hey! Well, come on, Wales!

1 Some facts

a) Put the sentences together correctly. Then write them down.

1. The Welsh have been speaking	around Wales	for four years.
2. Bronwen has been learning	their own language	for ages.
3. The Morgans have been living	in Cardiff	since King Arthur's time.
4. Owen has been working	Welsh at school	since Monday.
5. The American visitors have been driving	to the rugby match	for ten years.
6. Owen has been looking forward	in Pontypridd	since last year.

b) Look at the examples of the present perfect progressive in these sentences and in the text. How are the forms made?

G4,5

2 *For* or *since?*

a) Look at the sentences with **for** and **since** from Exercise 1. Then complete the diagram (with the words in the blue box) and use it to explain when we use **for** and when we use **since**.

b) Now make two lists of words or phrases you can use with **for** or **since**. Example: **for** four years

grammar

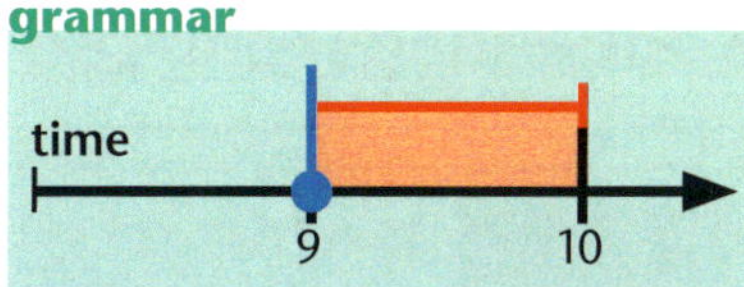

since (9 o'clock) • for (an hour) • past • now • point in time • period of time

3 Down at the Red Dragon

Owen and his family are telling the American Morgans some more about their life in Wales. Fill in the verb forms and decide which is correct: **for** or **since**?

1. *Owen:* I **(work)** in a factory that makes DVD players **(?)** almost nine months now. But a lot of people around here **(look)** for a job **(?)** years, and they still haven't found one. So I'm lucky.

2. *Mari:* Most of the people in our family still live here. But my sister got married last year and moved away. She **(live)** up in Caernarfon **(?)** last Easter, so I can't see her so often. Owen's mother still lives in Aberfan, as you know. She **(talk)** about moving **(?)** Owen's father died two years ago. But I think she's too old to move now.

3. *Bronwen:* I **(learn)** Welsh **(?)** a long time now. And I'm beginning to find it useful! I've got a new friend that **(speak)** Welsh at home **(?)** she was a kid. So she can teach me a lot, of course. And **(?)** the last two or three months I **(listen)** to more Welsh on TV and radio. My friend's aunt **(work)** for Welsh radio **(?)** a year or so.

4 Getting to know each other

a) Read this information about the American Morgan family. Then work with a partner. One of you asks questions, and the other gives answers. Start your questions with 'How long ...?' and use **for** and **since** in the answers.

1. The Morgans live in Seattle now. They moved there six years ago.
2. Evan works in the computer industry. He started work in computers 14 years ago.
3. Pam is a teacher. She started teaching when she was 26.
4. Ceri and Gareth both take French classes at school. Gareth started French last year, while Ceri started three years ago.
5. They both play an instrument. Ceri started the piano when she was ten, and Gareth started the guitar last April.

b) Collect topics and phrases from the text which you can use to talk to people you meet for the first time. Invent a character for yourself (name, age, where you live, what you do, etc.). Then start a dialogue with your partner. These ideas will help you:

What ...? | When ...? | How long have ...? | When did you start ...? | Why do you like ...?

10 B An e-mail from Ceri

Hi Tricia!

Wales is great! Even the weather has been OK so far. We've been here since Monday and it has only rained once. Welsh is really funny – you should see the road signs!

Gareth is in his element here – because of all the medieval castles. We've visited five already! He's been interested in history for a long time, and the castles here are really old – not like in Disneyland!

Today we visited the old Roman camp at Caerleon. Some old Welsh stories say that this was where King Arthur had his castle, Camelot, centuries ago. You have heard of it, haven't you? Of course Gareth had to buy a book about it, and he's been reading parts of it to us since then. But even I have to admit it's all quite interesting!

Seeing our Welsh relatives has been the real highlight of this trip. I've known about them for ages, and now we've actually met them! We've been staying with Dad's cousin Owen and his family since Saturday. Their daughter Bronwen and I are already best friends. We both feel we've known each other for years. It was Owen's mother's 80th birthday yesterday, so we all went to the party in Aberfan. All the cousins, aunts and great-uncles were there. I still haven't been able to work out who is who! But it was quite sad, too. We visited the graves of Owen's two sisters. They were killed in the Aberfan disaster of 1966, when they were only children.

Bye now, Ceri

1 Ceri's news

Look at the text carefully to answer these questions.

1. How long have Ceri and her family been in Wales?
2. What has the weather been like so far?
3. How long has Gareth been interested in history?
4. How many castles have they visited?
5. What kind of book did Gareth buy?
6. What has he been doing since he bought it?
7. How long has Ceri known about her Welsh relatives?
8. How long have she and the others been staying with cousin Owen?
9. What happened yesterday?

2 The present perfect

a) Find all the present perfect forms (simple and progressive) in the text.
Write them down in two lists, and mark any signal words you find in a different colour.

present perfect simple	present perfect progressive
Even the weather **has been** OK so far.	…
…	…

tip
Some verbs (like **be** and **know**) cannot be used in the progressive form.

b) Now look at your sentences. Which ones stress the result of an action? Which ones stress how long the action lasted?

3 Simple or progressive?

Make sentences with the **present perfect** (simple or progressive?) with **for** or **since**.
Example: 1. What a wet day! **(rain • hours)** → It's been raining for hours!

2. When does the rugby match end, Dad? **(they • play • ages)**
3. My cousin Gemma is also my oldest friend. **(know • we were little)**
4. Waiter! What's happened to my soup? **(sit here • half an hour)**
5. Isn't that Mr Jones, our new neighbour? **(only • live • in our road • April)**
6. Oh, come on, Ceri! **(write • e-mails • ages)**
7. Life isn't easy for my uncle. **(be • out of work • months)**
8. Haven't you got anything better to do? **(watch • TV • tea time)**

4 At the 80th birthday party

It's Gwen's (Owen's mother's) 80th birthday party. Complete what these people are saying. Choose between the **present perfect simple** and the **simple past**.

1. *Gareth:* We **(be)** in Britain for ten days now. We **(spend)** a few days in London, then we **(take)** a car and **(drive)** to Wales.
2. *Gwen:* **(visit)** you Caerleon yet? You **(hear)** about the Roman camp, I expect?
3. *Evan:* Sure. When Gareth **(see)** pictures of Caerleon in our guide book, he **(want)** to go there immediately! But no, we **(not be)** there yet. On our first day in Wales, we **(visit)** Conwy Castle. That **(be)** great! And since then we **(see)** four other castles.
4. *Pam:* When **(start)** the people here in Wales to speak Welsh?
5. *Gwen's sister:* Well, the Celts **(come)** to Wales before the Romans **(invade)** Britain, so Welsh must be a very old language. But it **(change)** a lot since then.
6. *Mari:* At one time we **(be)** afraid our language would die out, but I don't think it will now. There **(be)** TV programmes in Welsh since 1982, and children **(have)** lessons in Welsh for some years now.

11 5 A song: Shiny happy people (REM)

Words: W. T. Berry, P. L. Buck, M. E. Mills

Shiny happy people laughing
Meet me in the crowd
People people
Throw your love around
Love me love me
Take it into town
Happy happy, put it in the ground[1]
Where the flowers grow
Gold and silver shine

Shiny happy people holding hands
Shiny happy people laughing
Everyone around love them, love them
Put it in your hands
Take it take it
There's no time to cry
Happy happy, put it in your heart
Where tomorrow shines
Gold and silver shine

[1] Boden

a) Like a poem, a song can have words that sound the same at the end, words that begin with the same sound and words that are repeated. Find examples in the text.

b) It can also have words that express a special kind of feeling. What kind of feeling is expressed here? Which words in the song prove it?

Skills: Skimming and scanning

Skimming and scanning are important reading skills. Both will help you to read quickly – and save time.

1 Skimming: Getting the gist

'Getting the gist' of something means understanding the main ideas. You can often find out what a text is about before you start to read it.

tip
Don't read every word. Just look out for
- headings, pictures and key words
- the beginnings and ends of paragraphs

a) Look at this information from the Internet for one minute. Then cover it up and tell a partner in two or three sentences what the text is about.

b) Now say where your information came from (which points from the tip helped).

The Aberfan Disaster (1966)

The coal tip[1]

Everyone knows that coal tips move. Everyone fears that one day the tip above their village will come rumbling down into the valley. ***(Merthyr Express newspaper)***

It started to move slowly at first, then it got faster and turned into a wave; down it went, down towards Aberfan village. There was nothing we could do. We had no telephone to give an alarm. I shouted, but it was no good. ***(Tip worker)***

In Aberfan

I heard a noise, a big rumbling noise … I saw a tree coming towards me first, then I saw a big black mass of stuff. ***(Schoolboy, 13)***

Pantglas Junior School

I was just going to start the lesson when there was a terrible noise. So I said, "Get under your desks quickly and stay there." Nothing actually happened, just this dreadful noise. Then there was silence … When I got outside, I just couldn't believe it. The end of the school where a hundred or more children were – well, it was all gone. ***(Teacher)***

I was thrown across the classroom. … I woke to the sound of rescuers breaking a window, then I saw my friend. Blood was coming out of his nose and I knew he was dead. If I close my eyes, I can still see his face. ***(Pantglas pupil, 9)***

The rescue

On each side of the school, bulldozers worked at the muck, and lorries carried it away. At regular intervals work stopped and rescuers listened – for a cry, the sound of a movement, anything that would give hope to the mothers and fathers. ***(Journalist on the scene)***

No one was brought out alive after eleven o'clock. ***(Police officer)***

144 people lost their lives. 116 of them were children. ***(Official report)***

Bereavement

In the night we had to go and see if we could identify her in the chapel. I've never forgotten that. All those little bodies wrapped in blankets. ***(Bereaved father)***

Years later

It gives you a respect for living. You're thankful just to be here. All my friends seem to be very quiet. We seem to be different … ***(Pantglas pupil)***

[1]tip – Kohlenhalde

2 Scanning: Reading for details

To find out more from a text, you must look for the details you need – and ignore the rest.

tip
- Stop when you find a key word and read that part carefully.
- Read it again and make notes.
- Headings will help, too.

a) Look at the page from the book Gareth bought. Look for information and make notes about:
1. the legend of King Arthur
2. how people became knights in those days
3. why castles were important in the Middle Ages.

b) Write down questions and test your partner's scanning skills.

The Medieval World of Knights and Castles

Who was King Arthur?

There are many stories about King Arthur and his knights, but no actual facts. If King Arthur ever existed, it was probably in the 5th or 6th century, after the Romans left Britain. The Angles and Saxons were trying to conquer the country, but the Britons were not strong enough to keep them out. So as the Angles and Saxons moved further inland, a lot of Britons moved west. Many of them settled in the hills of Wales and South West England, where they felt safer.

The beginning of the Arthurian legend was in Wales. Arthur was probably a leader of the Britons. It was said that he never lost a battle against the Saxons! The stories about him and his knights of the Round Table lived on, and when they were told, new ideas were often added. In time Arthur and his knights' courage, honour and noble ideals became more and more important in the stories. Films and books about their adventures are still popular today.

The role of knights

A thousand years ago, knights were simply men who fought in battle on horseback. But later they played an important role in society. They fought for their king, and in return for this the king gave them land. A knight also had to protect the peasants who lived and worked on his land.

Training to become a knight started at the age of seven. A boy began as a page in a noble household. Pages learned how to serve a knight, and how to use weapons.

Then, at the age of 15 or 16, a page became a squire, the personal servant of his master, and learned how to fight on horseback. Five years later, a squire could become a knight – if he was good enough.

Medieval castles – symbols of power

Many of the castles in Wales were built by the English King Edward I, who conquered Wales in the 13th century (and whose son became the first Prince of Wales). The strong walls and towers of a castle were designed so that enemies would not be able to destroy it. But they also had a symbolic importance. Castles were built by rulers – kings and queens, barons, bishops and knights. They were built (often on hills) to dominate the land around, so that their owners could 'look down' on the peasants below them, and so that the peasants would not forget the people who had power over them.

How Percival became a Knight of the Round Table

Stop when you see this sign and go to Exercise 1 on page 32.

Until Percival was sixteen years old, he knew nothing at all about King Arthur. He didn't even know what knights were – or what they looked like! Percival lived with his mother in the quiet forests of Wales. Apart from his mother, he knew only the wild animals of the forest, the birds and the sound of the wind in the trees.

One day, while he was hunting in the forest, five knights in armour came through the trees on horseback. In the light of the summer sun, their armour shone like gold.

"Hello, young man!" called one of the men. It was Sir Lancelot, one of King Arthur's knights. But the boy did not answer, he was so surprised. He went down on his knees and looked up at the knights without a word.

"What's the matter, boy? Get up now!" said another of the knights. "Don't worry, we won't hurt you."

"Are you angels?" said Percival. "My mother has told me about angels."

"Angels?" laughed the knight. "Oh, no! We're only men! On our way to Camelot."

"Camelot? I've been living here all my life – but I've never heard of Camelot. Where is it? Somewhere in the forest?"

"Never heard of Camelot?" said a third knight in amazement. "That's where King Arthur has his castle. We're his knights. Knights of the Round Table!"

"Perhaps you will be a knight one day, too," said Lancelot kindly. The others laughed.

"But how?" asked Percival eagerly. "How can I become a knight?"

"You must love adventure," said Lancelot, "and you must prove that you are brave."

"Come to Camelot one day, boy," said another knight. "Why not? Perhaps you'll even be able to meet King Arthur."

And they rode off together through the forest.

Percival lost no time. As soon as the men were gone, he hurried straight home to his mother and told her about the wonderful men in armour.

"I want to be a knight, too, Mother," he said. "Tell me the way to Camelot and I'll go there tomorrow!"

He looked at his mother. Her face was white now, and he could not understand why.

"What's the matter, Mother?" he asked her. "And why have you never told me about King Arthur and his knights?"

His mother began to cry.

"Oh, Percival!" she said. "For years now I've been wondering if I should tell you this – but now I know I must. Your father was one of King Arthur's knights, and your two older brothers were knights, too. You never knew them, they left home so many years ago! And now they're dead. They all lost their lives in battle!" She looked at him. "Percival, must you go to Camelot? Must I lose you, too? And live in the forest here alone?"

But she could see that it was useless. She had to let him go. So the next day Percival said goodbye and set off, armed only with his hunting spear, on his way to Camelot.

It was a long way through the deep forest. But at last, when he came to the top of a hill, he could see the tall white towers of Camelot. Suddenly, a knight in beautiful red and gold armour appeared through the trees.

"Hello!" said Percival when he saw him. "Are you one of the Knights of the Round Table? I'm just on my way to Camelot!"

But the knight only laughed. He held up a big gold cup and showed it to the boy.

"See this cup? It's King Arthur's – and I've stolen it! Taken it from his great Round Table! Ha!"

"Stolen it?" said Percival, horrified. "King Arthur won't like that. When he hears what's happened, he'll ..."

"Now listen to me, boy," said the knight. "Go to Camelot and tell Arthur I've got his cup. Tell him the Red Knight has got it. The Red

Knight, understand? Give him this message: If he wants the cup back, one of his knights must come and fight me for it!"

When Percival arrived at the castle, he was very excited. Outside the main gate, he was able to join a small group of servants who were just going in. A few minutes later he was in the Great Hall. Some knights who were there with their ladies, all in beautiful clothes, looked at him in surprise.

"What's that farmer's boy doing in here?" said one of the ladies, and held her hand to her nose.

"Where's King Arthur?" Percival shouted. "I've got an important message for him!"

Some of the knights laughed. When they heard the message, they laughed even more.

"Go back home and look after the pigs!" said Sir Kay, the king's brother.

"Wait!" said Lancelot. "Isn't this the boy we met in the forest? – Let me take you to King Arthur, boy. Who knows? Perhaps this is the chance you've been waiting for – the chance to become a knight!"

King Arthur spoke to Percival – and saw at once how eager the boy was. "All right, young man," he said. "If you manage to get my gold cup and come back here with the red and gold armour on, I'll make you a knight! – Give him a horse, Lancelot!"

In a moment, Percival was riding down the road through the trees.

Soon he found the Red Knight, in the same place as before.

"Give me that gold cup!" Percival shouted. "And take your armour off, I need that, too!"

But the Red Knight only laughed. "Are you crazy, boy?"

"Take your armour off!" Percival repeated. "I must take it to King Arthur!"

"If you want my armour, you'll have to kill me first!" shouted the Red Knight, angry now.

"All right then, let's fight for it!" said Percival, and he tried to push the Red Knight off his horse.

"Enough!" shouted the Red Knight, and hit Percival with his lance. Percival fell off his horse. It was a bad fall, and the nasty blow from the lance made his shoulder hurt badly. His face hurt, too, and when he looked down, he saw blood on his clothes. This made him angry. He took his spear and threw it.

"Aahh!" Percival watched in amazement as the Red Knight fell off his horse. He tried to stagger to his feet, but then he fell heavily to the ground, and a moment later his body was quiet.

When Percival took the Red Knight's armour off, he looked at the dead man's body. How white it looked! How small now, without the heavy armour! When Percival rode away, he was crying. But he was wearing the red and gold armour – and he was carrying the king's cup.

1 How does it feel?

Talk about the characters' thoughts and feelings at these points.

- Percival
- Percival's mother
- Sir Kay, Sir Lancelot, Percival
- The Red Knight, Percival
- Percival

2 The Red Knight

The Red Knight says:
"See this cup?" (line 80) • "Taken it from his great Round Table!" (line 81) • "The Red Knight, understand?" (line 88)

What do you notice about these sentences? Why do you think he speaks in this way?

3 Just for fun

4 Listening: More scenes

a) You will hear three scenes from the CD. They are between different characters from the Percival story. When you listen to the recording, find out …
1. who is talking
2. where the scene is
3. when it takes place.

b) Now write another scene that isn't in the text.

1. The knights talk about Percival after he has gone to fight the Red Knight. **Or:**
2. Percival gives the gold cup back to the king.

5 Word power: How to be a good knight

Collect words and phrases in a grid to describe what is expected of a knight. Use the new words and what you already know.

What is he like?	What is he good at?	What does he need?
…	…	…

6 Your opinion

a) Can you imagine why stories, films and games about knights are still popular today? What do/don't you like about them?

b) Percival has to kill someone to become a knight. What do you think of this?

7 What now, Percival?

Young Sir Percival would like to tell his mother about his new life, so he writes her a letter. He tells her …

• what has happened so far • how he feels • what the people at Camelot are like • what he is going to do next.

Write the letter.

1 Saying it differently

Change these sentences so that you use **since** instead of **for** – and **for** instead of **since**.
What else do you have to change? Imagine the people are speaking at this moment in time.

1. We've been living in Munich since 1998.
2. You've been playing computer games for three and a half hours!
3. I've been working on this project for ten days now.
4. We haven't seen our American cousins since they came to Germany in 2001.
5. I've been able to swim since I was six.
6. My sister and her boyfriend have known each other for three months.

2 What's the situation?

Use the present perfect to explain the situation. Sometimes you will need the progressive form.

Example: 1. Percival is riding back to Camelot in the red and gold armour. **(kill)**
➜ He has killed the Red Knight.

2. The Morgans arrived in Wales five days ago. **(be)**
3. After four years of Welsh at school, Bronwen is quite good at it now. **(learn)**
4. Gareth is coming out of the visitors' shop with a book about Caerleon. **(buy)**
5. The Welsh Morgans moved into their new house two years ago. **(live)**
6. Evan is looking for his map of Wales in the back of the car. **(lose)**
7. It is 10 o'clock and the two Morgan families are still at the Red Dragon. They went in at 6.30. **(sit and talk)**
8. Soon the American Morgans' holiday in Britain will be over. **(The time – go so quickly!)**

3 Mixed bag: An interview

Back home, Ceri is listening to an interview she did with Gwen. She wants to use it in an article for her school magazine. Put in the missing words and the correct verb forms.

Ceri: Here I am in Aberfan and I **(talk)** to Gwen Morgan, our oldest **W** 1 relative.

Gwen: Hello, Ceri. I'm so **p** 2 that our American **r** 3 **s (manage)** to be here today!

Ceri: I'd like to **b** 4 with a question. **(Wales change)** much **s** 5 you were young?

Gwen: Oh yes! When I **(be)** a girl, these valleys were famous for their **c** 6 . But now the **m** 7 **s (nearly all close)**. And lots of people are **o** 8 . My **s** 9 Owen is lucky – he **(find)** work at a **f** 10 in Cardiff at last. But what **a** 11 you? I **w** 12 what *you* think of Wales?

Ceri: Me? I love it! We **r** 13 a car in London last Monday, and we **(drive)** all over Wales 14 then. We **(see)** some **m** 15 scenery and lots of medieval **c** 16 .

Gwen: Yes, Wales **(have)** lots of interesting **s** 17 that you could **m** 18 in your article. But I **(love)** Aberfan best. The people here **(be)** so **k** 19 to us when we **(lose)** our little **d** 20 **s** Glenda and Jill in the **d** 21 of 1966.

Ceri: The poor girls! We **(visit)** their **g** 22 **s** this afternoon. That was so **s** 23 .

Gwen: It still hurts. Owen wants me to live in Pontypridd **i** 24 of Aberfan. But I **(live)** here 25 80 years and I **(not want)** to **m** 26 !

Ceri: Right! Well, here's another question. Why **(the Welsh love)** rugby so much ?

Gwen: I must **a** 27 I've no idea.

Ceri: Well, thanks for this interview.

Gwen: Don't **m** 28 it! I'd like to read your article. **P** 29 you can **(send)** it to me.

Ceri: I **(do)** that as **s** 30 as it **(appear)**.

1 revision Books 1+2

1 A quiz on the UK

a) Copy the puzzle grid in your exercise book. (Be careful to put in the correct number of boxes for each word!) Then write in your answers.

Clues

1. one of the countries in the UK
2. one of Robin Hood's outlaws (2 words)
3. a famous English football team
4. the sea between the British Isles and America
5. a special day at the end of October
6. a mountain in the Lake District (2 words)
7. the capital of Northern Ireland
8. the first thing on the timetable every day at British schools
9. a part of the UK that is good for surfing

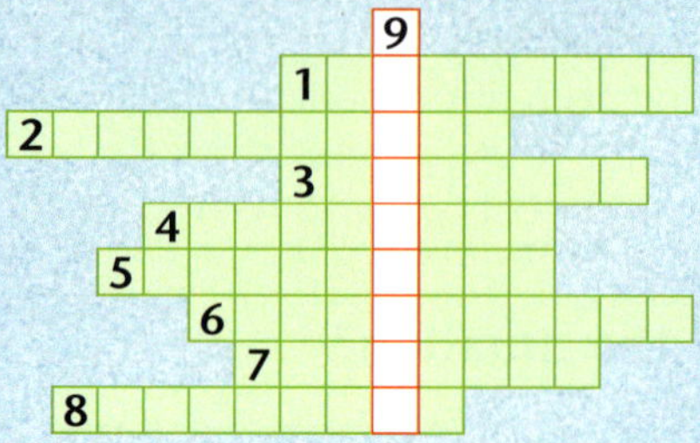

b) Make your own quiz! Then find a partner and work out answers to each other's quizzes.

2 Word power

a) Can you explain what these are?

1. a bully
2. a show-off
3. a competitor
4. a waiter
5. a traffic jam
6. a rainbow
7. wildlife
8. a target

b) What's the difference between …

1. a card and a ticket?
2. a sea and a lake?
3. a bag and a pocket?
4. wearing and carrying?
5. jam and marmalade?
6. standing up and getting up?
7. a blanket and a ceiling?

c) How many of these can you think of? Make lists. Start like this: 1. chicken, …

1. animals you can find on a farm
2. different jobs
3. buildings you find in a town
4. means of transport
5. adjectives that describe how people feel
6. verbs that describe movement

Now choose two words from your lists and use them to write a story. Then work in groups and read each other your stories.

d) Adjectives and adverbs. Complete the text. Use your own ideas here.

A __1__ lion[1] was walking __2__ through the jungle[2] when it saw a __3__ deer. "Who is the King of the Animals?" asked the lion in a __4__ voice. The deer felt __5__ and answered __6__: "You are, Mister Lion!" The lion felt __7__ when it heard this. Soon it met a zebra[3] and asked the zebra the same question. The __8__ zebra – who was __9__ of the lion – answered: "You are!" "That's __10__!" thought the lion __11__. Then it met a __12__, __13__ elephant[4]. "Who is the King of the Animals?" the lion shouted __14__. Without a word the elephant came up to the __15__ lion and jumped on it. The lion – who was very __16__ – stood up again __17__ and said, "OK, OK, you needn't get __18__ just because you didn't know the answer!"

[1]['laɪən] • [2]['dʒʌŋgl] • [3]['zebrə] • [4]['elɪfənt]

Test yourself!

3 The mouse and the cheese

Complete the text with the right verb forms. Use the past and present tense – simple and progressive. Write down your answers, then turn to page 194 to check them.

Once there **1 be** a mouse that **2 live** in a hole[1] in the kitchen of a big old house. When it **3 wake** up one morning, it **4 notice** that a delicious smell **5 come** in through the hole. "Cheese!" it **6 think**. "That **7 smell** good! I **8 begin** to feel really hungry now!"
But just before it **9 run** out of its hole, it suddenly **10 think**: "Maybe it **11 be** a trap! Once my father **12 warn** me about traps. Maybe it's OK – but how **13 I know**? There **14 be** lots of people who **15 not like** mice in the house. Everybody **16 know** that."
The mouse **17 not want** to do anything silly, so it **18 sit** down and **19 wait**. While it **20 sit** there, it **21 hear** a cat's "Miaow!"
"Aha! The cat **22 wait** for me somewhere in the kitchen!" it **23 think**. "Lucky I **24 not go** out!"
The next day when it **25 get** up, it **26 smell** cheese again! "Perhaps the cat **27 sit** in the kitchen again," it **28 think**, "you **29 never know**!" So it **30 lie** down with its ear near the hole.
While it **31 listen** this time, it **32 hear** a little "Woof! Woof!" "That's good!" it **33 say** quietly. "The dog probably **34 chase** the cat away while I **35 sleep**. Yes, I **36 not think** there'll be any trouble if I **37 leave** my hole now."
So it **38 go** out and **39 run** to the cheese. Just as it **40 start** to eat it, the cat **41 jump** on it, **42 kill** it and **43 eat** it for breakfast. This all **44 happen** so quickly, the mouse **45 not have** a chance to escape.
"Mmm, delicious!" **46 say** the cat. "A cat **47 not get** a breakfast like that every day! Well, lucky I **48 do** what my father **49 tell** me all those years ago and **50 learn** a second language. Today I **51 find** it very useful!"

[1] [həʊl] – Loch

4 Before a trip to London

Decide which verb form is correct. Write down your answers, then check them on page 194.

1. What are your plans for the holidays? **(Will you/Are you going to)** do anything special? – Yes, **(we're going to/we'll)** go to London for a long weekend.
2. The weather forecast sounds OK. **(It isn't/It won't be)** very warm on Friday, but **(there's/there'll be)** lots of sunshine on Saturday and Sunday.
3. **(It'll/It's going to)** be Dad's birthday when **(we're/we'll be)** in London. **(He'll/He's going to)** get tickets for a musical, and after that **(we probably go/we'll probably go)** to an Indian restaurant.
4. I can't find the Dominion Theatre on this map! – Give it to me. **(I'm going to/I'll)** show you where it is.

5. Come on, you two! If we **(won't/don't)** hurry, **(we'll miss/we miss)** our train! Just look how late it's getting – I'm sure **(we miss/we're going to miss)** it now!
6. That's a nice camera. **(Are you going to/Will you)** take it with you? – Yes, I'm sure **(I'll take/I take)** lots of photos in London.
7. **(Do you/Will you)** send me a postcard when **(you'll be/you're)** in London? – OK, **(I'm going to/I'll)** get you one with a photo of Tower Bridge on it. **(I won't/I'm not going to)** forget, I promise!

5 What has happened?

throw away

pick up

shut

mend

put back

collect and take away

Lots of visitors come to Wales – but some of them don't behave very well …
First describe what has happened. Then explain what will have to be done.
(Remember: when nobody knows who exactly has done something, we often use the passive.)

Example: 1. A lot of rubbish has been thrown on the grass in this park.
It will have to be picked up.

6 London in the early days

Fill in the verbs – in the passive. Be careful with the forms.

Soon after Britain **(invade)** by the Romans in the first century AD, the city of London – or Londinium as it **(call)** in those days – **(found)**. It was very small at first, but its position was important, and soon Roman roads **(build)** in all directions[1] from London, so the new Roman towns and camps could **(connect)** together.
A thousand years later, when England **(conquer)** by the Normans, about 20,000 people lived in London. Today, a place of that size would **(call)** a small town. But in those days there was no other town in England in which more than 5,000 people lived, so London **(see)** as a huge city! The Tower of London, which today **(visit)** by many thousands of tourists from all over the world, **(build)** by William of Normandy, and it **(make)** larger by later Norman kings. Since those early days, it **(use)** as a castle, a palace, a prison[2] – and even a zoo! Now, of course, it **(see)** mainly as a tourist attraction.

[1][dɪˈrekʃn] – Richtung; [2][ˈprɪzn] – Gefängnis

7 Word power: Anagrams[1]

a) Do you know these adjectives from Units 1 and 2? They can all be used to describe people.

1. People sometimes go bright red when they feel ___.
2. If you want to do something very much, you're very ___.
3. If you hear that something really terrible has happened, you'll probably feel ___.
4. If you're happy about something, you naturally feel ___.
5. Somebody who is good and friendly to others is ___.

deepsal · firedrioh · dreambasser · geera · dink

b) Think of five other adjectives that can describe a person's character or feelings. Write them down. Then make anagrams – like the ones in **a)** – and write your own clues. Find a partner and test each other.

1 ['ænəgræm] – Anagramm: durch Umstellung von Buchstaben aus einem Wort entstandenes neues Wort

8 At a big hotel in Llandudno

It is Saturday – and some of the hotel guests aren't happy. Why not? Make little dialogues (between the guests and the manager or a waiter or one of the other people that work at the hotel).

Example: 1. This guest is annoyed because he's been waiting at the table for ages/because the waiter hasn't brought his food.

Guest: Waiter! Where's my steak? I've been sitting here since half past twelve/for a whole hour!
Waiter: Sorry, sir. Your steak will be ready in a few minutes now.

9 Mixed bag: Gareth remembers his time in London

London is a great 1, even 2 exciting than I expected. I loved the boat 3 on the River 4 on 5 first day. Big 6 and the Houses of 7 looked fantastic, and I'll 8 forget the 9 of those chimes! The Tower 10 London was one of my favourite 11, because I'm so 12 in history. The 13 parts of it date 14 the time of William of 15; they were 16 in the 11th 17 soon after the 18 of Hastings. The London Eye is 19 popular, so we had to 20 tickets 21 advance. The 22 over the city (from a 23 of over 120 metres!) were fantastic, and I 24 lots of photos. But there's one day in London I'd 25 to forget – when we 26 to that 27 in Oxford Street 28 Darren and Steve. Ceri and I already had the souvenirs 29 wanted to 30 back home – Ceri's was a teddy 31, and I had a Beefeater's 32. So I didn't have 33 money left for the present I wanted to 34 for Angela. What I did was 35, I see that now. Although I put that game 36 somewhere 37 the way out, I still went bright 38 when the store 39 stopped us, I felt so 40. Ceri got really 41 with me, but she didn't 42 Mom and Dad 43 it.

unit 3 intro

Living history

The Battle of Hastings 14/15 October

Workshops and activities

Fighting & weapons
- archery
- sword fighting
- sword making
- shield painting

Arts & crafts
- making clothes
- pottery
- working with leather and wood

Other
- camp building
- cooking
- music
- medieval dancing

1 History – live!

Historical re-enactments are role plays of famous events from the past. They are very popular. Most of the time battles are acted out, but often there are also workshops and other activities which can be fun, too. You can find a lot more information about re-enactments on the Internet.

a) Look at the photos and the list of activities above. What do you know about the historical event?

b) What can you see in the pictures?

c) Make a grid and collect words you can use when you talk about re-enactments. Put them in these groups: people, things, activities.

d) Which activities would you like to take part in and why? What kind of character would you like to play? What could you do?

e) What needs to be done before an event like this?

f) Can you imagine why re-enactments are so popular?

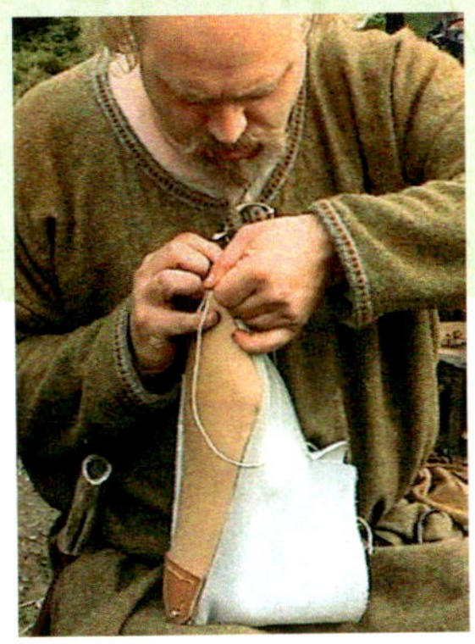

7 2 Listening: A history class

Mr Eden is a new history teacher at Darren's school in London.

a) Listen, make notes and say
- what the situation is at the beginning
- what Darren thinks about history
- what Caroline suggests
- what plans are made at the end.

b) Imagine you are in Mr Eden's class. Write an e-mail to your French exchange partner. Tell him or her what the class decided during Mr Eden's lesson and say what you think of the idea.

3 Your turn: A discussion

What do you think of living history events? Find arguments for or against them. Choose a discussion leader and someone who will take notes on the blackboard, and start a discussion in class. These ideas will help you:

fun • learning about … • dangerous • time • prepare • money • exciting • another world • boring • work • people • place • help • …

17 A An e-mail to Ms Deneuve

Dear Ms Deneuve (or may I call you Michelle?),

Many thanks for your e-mail and that wonderful photo of you and your 'Normans'.

I had a meeting with my 'Saxons' yesterday, but things went a bit wrong. I was late for the meeting because I had been very busy. When I arrived, the pupils had started without me, apart from two girls who had already gone home. Since no instructions had been given, there was complete chaos. One group had made Norman shields by mistake. Some others who were making soldiers' uniforms had added pockets for their mobile phones!

Then Alex, the boy who is going to play 'brave' King Harold, ran up to me close to tears. He couldn't remove an arrow that had been stuck onto his head! The school nurse had already gone home so I dealt with the problem myself. But as soon as I had pulled the arrow off, he started to get a headache. I hope he'll be OK on the day of the battle.

When it was time to go, we couldn't get out of the school building. The cleaning staff had locked the main door, and I had left my school keys in the staff room. Of course, that door had been locked, too! It was lucky Darren had brought his mobile with him. He called the caretaker, Mr Griffiths, and asked him to come and open the door for us. When the phone rang, Mr Griffiths was watching a football match and France had just scored a goal, so he wasn't very pleased!

Anyway, that's enough from me. I'll be there to meet you when your train arrives.

I look forward to getting to know you.
'Au revoir' – Martin Eden

1 Reasons for the chaos

Are the statements true or false? Explain how you know, with examples from the text.

1. Mr Eden was late for the meeting because he had forgotten about it.
2. Mr Eden's pupils were already busy when he arrived.
3. Not all of the pupils were at the meeting.
4. The pupils hadn't made the right shields.
5. Pockets for arrows had been added to the soldiers' uniforms.
6. Alex's headache had started before Mr Eden pulled the arrow off his head.
7. The cleaning staff had forgotten to lock the staff room.
8. Mr Eden knew where his keys were.
9. Darren had forgotten his mobile.
10. Mr Griffiths was pleased when Mr Eden rang him.

2 Looking at language

a) Collect examples of the past perfect from the text. (Remember the passive forms, too!) Explain how to form the past perfect in the active and passive forms.

b) Draw a diagram to explain the tenses in this sentence:
When Mr Eden **arrived** at the meeting, two girls **had** already **left.**

c) The conjunction **when** is often used with the past perfect. Find more conjunctions from the text and make your own sentences with them. Use the past perfect together with the simple past tense.

3 Why Mr Eden was late

Put in the **simple past** or **past perfect.**
Use the passive when the verb has a '**P**' in front of it.

I **(be)** in the gym that afternoon because I **(have)** a basketball class. After the lesson **(finish)**, I **(go)** to the staff room to make a phone call. I **(order)** some wood for the shields, but since it **(not arrive)**, I **(need)** to find out why. But I **(cannot)** find the phone number because I **(put)** my address book in my sports bag, which I **(left)** in the changing rooms. So I **(run)** back, but when I **(get)** to the changing rooms, the bag **(already go)**! Maybe someone **(take)** it by mistake. Then I **(run)** back to the staff room, and I **(see)** that a note **(P put)** on my table. It **(say)** "Dear Mr Eden, the wood **(P bring)** to the school this morning, so we can make our shields now. And we've got your sports bag, too. Someone **(find)** it in the changing rooms. Yours, Darren." I was pleased that my sports bag **(P find)** and that the wood **(arrive)**, but now I **(be)** late for my meeting with the Saxons!

4 The bone and the key

Look at the pictures below. Think of the order of events and write the story. To link the events better, use the past perfect where you can and the conjunctions on the right.

after • but • because • since • when • then • which • so

18 B On the way

On the day of the battle, the coach with Mr Eden, Ms Deneuve and the pupils left Camden on time. The sun was shining brightly from a blue sky and everyone was talking excitedly.

Steve: You'll never believe what happened yesterday after you and Marie left!
Caroline: Yes, we had to be home by 5.30.
Steve: We'd all been working hard since about 3 pm, and everything was OK until Darren caused chaos!
Caroline: Oh no! What happened?
Steve: Well, he'd been painting a yellow background on his shield for about half an hour. You know he always does things slowly and carefully.
Darren: Shut up, Steve. I can hear you!
Caroline: No, go on, Steve. Don't stop until we've heard all the details!
Steve: Then he wanted to paint a red lion on top and he was just fetching a big pot of paint from the cupboard when he decided to go past that French girl – you know, the one with the really long hair –
Caroline: Valérie?
Steve: Yeah. The one Darren fancies.
Darren: I'm warning you, Steve!
Steve: Anyway, Valérie had been working on this medieval dress for ages. And when Darren came past, he stopped and said something like "Wow, that's *fantastique,* Valérie!" And then he bent over to see the dress better and guess what happened!
Caroline: He spilt paint all over it? Oh no!
Darren: It was an accident, Caroline!
Caroline: Well, let's hope there won't be any accidents at the battle this afternoon.
Alex: A-a-a-a-tishoo!
Ms Deneuve: One of your boys is sneezing badly. Is he all right?
Mr Eden: Hm. It's our King Harold. His mum says if it rains, he must stay inside all afternoon. Oh dear! And just look at those dark clouds over there.

1 Getting the word order right

a) Put these adverbs / adverbials in groups.

1. **Manner (how)**: brightly, …
2. **Place (where)**: from a blue sky, …
3. **Time (when)**: on time, …
4. **Frequency (how often)**: never, …

on time • brightly • from a blue sky • excitedly • never • yesterday • home • by 5.30 • hard • since about 3 pm • on his shield • always • slowly • on top • for ages • better • at the battle

b) Look at the position of the adverbs and adverbials in the sentences below. Then work out some rules. Are they the same for German sentences?

1. The sun was shining brightly from a blue sky and everyone was talking excitedly.
2. Darren had been painting a yellow background on his shield for about half an hour.
3. He always does things slowly and carefully.
4. Let's hope there won't be any accidents at the battle this afternoon.
5. Mr Eden looked nervously at the dark clouds in front of them.

c) Put the words in the right order.

1. at school • has • usually • at 12.30 • Darren • lunch
2. quietly • but today • since 12 o'clock • he's been eating • in the coach • his sandwiches

2 Looking back at the text

a) Explain in your own words how Darren caused chaos.
Start: The day before the battle, the pupils were working hard on their costumes. Darren …

b) What do Darren and Valérie say to each other? Write a dialogue. Put in these words:

Oops! • all over my dress • ruin • idiot • for hours • my mum • wash • carefully

3 When things started to go wrong, …

… the pupils **had been working** hard **for two hours**. What had these people been doing – for how long (or since when)?

tip
Use the progressive form of the past perfect to stress how long the action had lasted before another action started.

Valérie – two days

Darren – 4.30

Tim – an hour

Mr Eden – 3 pm

4 The battle plan

This is what Mr Eden told the pupils when they were all standing on the battlefield.
Put in the correct forms of the past perfect (**simple** or **progressive**).

"Listen please, everybody! This is where the Battle of Hastings was fought on October 14th, 1066. William of Normandy **(land)** near here a few days earlier. He **(wait)** over there on the French coast for weeks – without much luck. But then the wind, which **(be)** against him for so long, suddenly changed. Harold, however, wasn't so lucky. His soldiers were tired because they **(march)** for ages. Remember, they **(just fight)** a battle in the North of England and then they **(hurry)** straight down here. And Harold wasn't very clever. His Saxons **(stand)** up on that hill since the battle started. A brilliant position! But then they came down off their hill, the idiots! That was because the Normans **(start)** to run away, you see – but it was a trick! Well, the battle went on for a while, but the Saxons **(make)** their big mistake by then. And after that arrow **(land)** in Harold's eye and **(kill)** him, they soon gave up. OK? So I want you Normans over here, *s'il vous plaît …*"

5 Mr Eden remembers

Rewrite the sentences. Change the parts in blue and use **until, not … until** or **by**.

Example: 1. In the morning we had our usual lessons, **but we finished at** 11 o'clock.
➜ In the morning we had our usual lessons **until** 11 o'clock.

2. We had hoped to be at the battlefield **not later than** 1 pm.
3. But there was heavy traffic and we **arrived late – at** half past one.
4. Then we had to wait **because the tents hadn't been put up yet.**
5. But everything was ready **at** two o'clock **or maybe even before.**
6. **"Start the battle when I give the signal and not before!"** I told everybody.

19 Memories of the battle

"Wake up, Darren," the nurse smiled. "It's ten o'clock and you've got visitors."
Darren groaned and opened one eye. The hospital room was very bright. All the curtains had been opened to let the sunshine in. Then he opened both eyes and saw his parents at the end of the bed.
"Oh my poor boy," said his mother. "Don't worry. We've spoken to the doctor and he says everything will be all right."
"You've had a heavy blow on the head," his father explained. "But the doctor tells us that your memory will be OK in a few days. The arm will take a bit longer," he sighed. "Really! Boys!"
Darren looked at his right arm, and groaned again. It was covered in white plaster and he couldn't move it.
"We'll visit you every day," promised his mother. "Look, I've brought you a big bowl of fruit. The nurse says you must eat to get strong again."
"Do what the nurses tell you," said his father. "And be careful with that arm."
Darren kept his arm still while his father wrote a message on the plaster. Then his mother wrote her message next to it.

After Darren's parents had gone, the nurse brought him a pill for his headache.
"Your friends have come to see you," she said. "But they can only come in two at a time. It looks like there's an army out there!"
Darren hadn't asked for visitors, but he was pleased when he saw Tim and Alex.
"Hey, look at the injured soldier," said Tim. They sat down on the bed and started to eat the fruit.
"How are you feeling now?" asked Alex.
"Dizzy," replied Darren.
"I'm not surprised," laughed Tim. "It's a pity you missed the party. That was the best part!"
"Party? What party?" Darren couldn't remember anything.
"At the local school. We were all muddy after the battle so we had to go there to get clean. That was after you'd had your little accident."
"What little accident?"

"Don't you remember anything? Well, Alex can tell you all about it."
"Yes, I was in the tent when it happened," Alex explained. "The battle had ended, and everyone was having a big mud-fight. Do you remember that? I couldn't play King Harold because I had a cold and it had started to rain. So I was helping in the 'Saxon Snacks' tent. Then you came in. You were waving your sword and shouting 'Free food for Saxons!' It was brilliant! Especially when you jumped onto that table and it fell down. You hit the ground and that huge bowl of apples landed on your head! It knocked you out."
Darren groaned again. He was beginning to remember. But why had it happened to him? Tim and Alex wrote something on his arm and then left. When they had gone, Darren noticed that they had eaten all the grapes.

■ "Hi Darren!" said a voice. It was Caroline and a girl whose name he had forgotten.
"You remember Marie, don't you?" said Caroline. "She's my exchange partner."
"Yeah, sure. Hi, Marie. How are you?"
"I'm fine, thanks!" the girl smiled.
"We all had great fun yesterday," Caroline said, "even if things went a bit wrong."
Darren tried to smile bravely. "You mean, my little accident?"
"No, I mean the rain. It ruined the battle. Don't you remember? The Saxons were on top of the hill and the Normans had to attack from below. But when it started to rain, it got really muddy and slippery. So when they ran up the hill, it was a disaster."

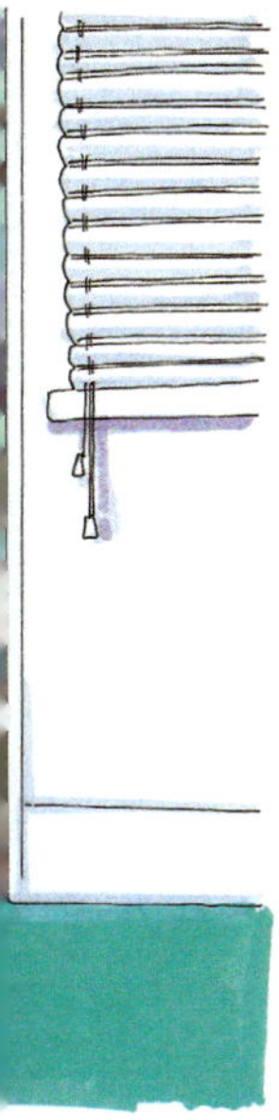

Now Darren began to remember more. There was mud everywhere. Bodies were rolling on the ground. People were shouting and cheering … It was just like rugby.
"And at first we didn't have a King Harold," said Caroline. She helped herself to an apple. "That was because Alex wasn't allowed to get wet. Can you believe it? Then you wanted to be the king and you grabbed Alex's crown. Mr Eden had to take it away from you!"

The two girls laughed. Then they wrote something on the plaster.
"Hey! I remember that!" cried Darren. "I wanted the Saxons to win!"
"Exactly!" laughed Caroline. "But you can't change history, Darren. In the end Mr Eden decided to play the part of Harold himself. He looked a bit strange in Alex's costume."
"It was too small for him!" cried Marie.
"Even Ms Deneuve had to laugh when she saw him," Caroline added. "She was helping us in the Saxon Snacks tent because she didn't want to fight. Do you remember what happened in the tent, Darren?"
The girls laughed, and Darren thought of what Alex had told him. It was so embarrassing. And now Caroline and Marie were eating all his fruit.
"We've got to go, Darren," Caroline said. "Get well soon. By the way, you've got a royal visitor next!"

■ The nurse looked in and said, "You've got five more minutes of visiting time, Darren."
Then Steve came in, with another boy.
"Hello, Darren," said Steve. "Thank God you're all right. When I saw you I thought 'Oh, no! He's dead! Who's going to help me with my homework now?' Well, you looked dead when they put you in the ambulance!"
"Thanks a lot, Steve," said Darren. Steve was OK, but this was not the right moment for one of his jokes.
"Oh, this is Serge, my exchange partner," Steve went on. "You'll have to be nice to him. He's your new king."
Serge was big and strong, but quiet. He smiled at Darren, said 'Hello' and then began to eat a banana.
"Serge was William of Normandy, and he won the Battle of Hastings so he's King of England now. Ah, but we gave them a good fight, didn't we Darren?"
"I don't remember," said Darren.
"If you ask me, we were actually winning," said Steve. "But then Mr Eden stuck the arrow onto his own head and the battle was over. I think he'd had enough. It wasn't exactly his lucky day, was it?"
Serge laughed.
"Because it rained so much?" Darren said.
"Not just that!" Steve replied. "There was the rain. Then there was your accident in the tent. And then his big moment arrived …"
"What do you mean?"
"When he carried you out of the tent."
"Mr Eden carried me out of the tent?"
"Like a baby," said Steve.
Darren went red and covered his head with a pillow.
"But then he slipped in the mud. He landed on your arm and hurt his back, too! The poor man couldn't move, so you were taken away in the ambulance together."

Serge and Steve were writing messages on Darren's arm when a young blonde woman came in. She was carrying a big box of sweets. It was Ms Deneuve.
"Oh, – um, hello!" She looked embarrassed. "It's Darren, isn't it? I hope you're better now. Can I write on your arm, too?"
She wrote something quickly, and then began to look around the room.
"I think I'm in the wrong place. I'm looking for poor Mart… um, I mean, Mr Eden."
She went out again with the box of sweets.
Steve looked at Serge and grinned. Then he looked at Darren. Darren grinned, too, but he was disappointed because the sweets weren't for him.

"Alone at last!" he sighed when the two boys had left. He turned towards his bowl of fruit – but it was empty.

1 What happened when?

Put the pictures in the order of events as they happened. Then tell the story in your own words.

2 Graffiti

Who wrote these things on Darren's arm? Say how you know.

3 Creative writing

Choose one of these topics.

1. Caroline (or Steve) writes an article for the school magazine.
2. Someone walks past the field where the re-enactment is taking place. Later they tell their friends about the strange sights they have seen.
3. Ms Deneuve visits Mr Eden in hospital.

4 Word power

a) Give definitions of these words: Then make a sentence with each word.

caretaker • crown • historical • injured • instruction • memory • pillow • to remove • to shut up • shield • snack • sword

b) Start with the word 'hospital' and make a mind map.

c) Have you ever been in hospital or visited someone there? Write about it.

Skills: How to use an English-German dictionary

1 Getting the gist

First read the text without a dictionary.
Explain in your own words what the problem is.
Then look up any words you don't know.

Lost in translation

Travellers abroad are often amused to see how efforts to give information in English can lead to mistakes in translation. These are often found in hotels, restaurants and shops around the world. For example, a sign in a Nairobi restaurant says: "Customers who find our waitress rude should see the manager." Then there is the notice in a Bucharest hotel which reads: "The lift is being fixed. We regret that you will be unbearable." And the following sign was found outside a Hong Kong tailor's: "Ladies may have a fit upstairs."

Such examples show what can happen when words are translated literally or if a dictionary isn't used with care. So can technology help? There are computer programs which can change a text from one language into another, but results can be just as disastrous. For example, a program to translate English into Russian produced this wonderful mistranslation. The phrase "The spirit was willing, but the flesh was weak" was first translated into Russian and then back into English. It ended up as "The vodka was good, but the meat was bad."

Once more, this shows that translations are dependent on context and situation and that language is made up of more than just individual words.

2 Mistranslations

Use your dictionary to explain how the mistranslations in the text happened.

3 One word – many meanings

How do you translate these expressions with **to have**?

a) to have a baby
b) to have a drink
c) to have to go
d) to have a bath
e) to have a look
f) to have lunch

4 Pronunciation

Check the pronunciation of these words:

a) road, abroad, coat, board
b) Russian, lesson, dessert, discussion
c) laugh, height, ought, enough
d) bear, gear, break, learn

5 Word building

The prefix **mis-** means that something is done badly or wrongly. In which of these words is **mis-** not a prefix?

a) mistranslation **b)** miss **c)** mistreat
d) mistake **e)** mistrust **f)** mister
g) misunderstand

6 More mistranslations

Try to translate these German phrases correctly.

Es ist mir Wurst. (≠ "It is me sausage.")
in die Hose gehen (≠ "to go in the trousers")
unter vier Augen (≠ "under four eyes")

7 Using a dictionary

What information does a dictionary give you? Make a list.

1 Word power: What goes together?

Match each verb with three expressions from the box.

1. to feel 2. to go 3. to have 4. to take

to sleep • a cold • place • ages • to hospital • angry • a meeting • to school • part • cold • a headache • sorry

2 The trip to France

Put in the missing verb forms. Use the simple past or the past perfect (simple or progressive).

1. One morning I **had** an important meeting with B, my boss. She **wanted** me to go over to Paris. Agent D **had agreed** to talk to us.
2. I **(must)** go. I **(be)** the only one in our office who **(ever meet)** Agent D. Actually, I **(only see)** her a few times.
3. When I **(tell)** B about my car – I **(have)** a crash in it the day before –, she **(throw)** a plane ticket at me and **(say)**, "Good luck!" Her assistant **(already book)** a flight for me.
4. But things **(not go)** well. When I **(arrive)** at the airport, my plane **(already take off)**. Just my luck! My taxi **(get stuck)** in a big traffic jam.
5. Then it **(take)** ages to get through check-in. There **(be)** a man in front of me who **(be)** nervous and slow because he **(never fly)** before.
6. When it **(be)** my turn, I **(find)** that I **(leave)** my ticket in the taxi! In the end I **(not arrive)** in Paris until late afternoon. The journey **(take)** ages!
7. Sometime later I **(get)** to D's place, but she **(not be)** there. Maybe I **(just miss)** her? How annoying! I **(be)** tired because I **(travel)** for ages, but I **(wait)** outside.
8. When D **(finally return)** hours later, I **(not recognize)** her because she **(change)** completely!
9. "This is a trap!" I **(think)**. I **(try)** to get out my gun, but I **(can't)**. Then I **(wake up)** in the middle of the night in bed. I **(dream)** the whole time. "Are you OK, Mr Eden?" said the nurse.

3 Word order: Exchange partners

Complete the sentences. Choose the best place for the adverbs or adverbials on the right.

1. The French group arrived.	last month • in Camden
2. Marie has been staying.	for four weeks • at Caroline's house • happily
3. She plays tennis.	after school • often • with Caroline
4. They are allowed to go.	sometimes • at the weekend • to the cinema
5. When Serge met Steve, he looked at him.	at first • nervously
6. Serge is quiet.	in the company of others • always
7. But the two boys do lots of things.	now • together
8. Staying has been fun for the French group.	with their partners • for so long • in London
9. But they are going back.	tomorrow morning • to France • early

4 Using a dictionary

a) You already know more than one translation for these German words.

Use your dictionary to explain when you use each one.

1. bis
2. bringen
3. Decke
4. eng
5. Fahrt
6. Geschichte
7. Gesundheit
8. halten
9. Himmel
10. Kartoffelchips
11. Marmelade
12. scheinen
13. Schloss
14. spielen
15. Tafel
16. während

b) Use your dictionary to explain the cartoon. Imagine what happened to the man before he went to see the doctor.

5 Word power: A competition

Work in groups. How many words can your group write down for each of these headings in one minute? You can complete the lists later in your exercise book.

school	fighting	fruit
…	…	…

6 Mixed bag: Mr Eden writes to his head teacher

Choose the right words or phrases.

Dear Mrs Batty,
I know you **(would like / had liked / will like)** a short report on our Third Year History **(subject / object / project)**. I **(write / am writing)** this from my hospital bed – I hope you don't **(mind / hate / dislike)**. The **(nurse / cleaning staff / doctors)** say I should be back at school **(by / since / until)** the end of the month.
The re-enactment **(go / went / had gone)** very much as I **(have planned / had planned / was planning)** – **(until / because / apart from)** one or two small problems!
The weather was a **(disaster / mistake / accident)**! It was **(embarrassing / lucky / happy)** that only one other person got **(injured / muddy / headache)**. But Darren Taylor's arm **(gets / is getting)** better and his **(memories / memory / remember)** will **(soon / in a few days / the day after tomorrow)** be OK again.
The pupils from our French partner school **(already did / have already done / had already done)** a lot of work before they **(went / got / arrived at)** here. Their teacher, Ms Deneuve, **(was organizing / had been organizing / had organized)** her side of things **(since / for)** two weeks. She helped me **(much / lots / a lot)** while she **(was / had been)** here.
Please thank the **(caretaker / staff)** for the nice **(fruit and sweets / arts and crafts)** they **(sent / were sending / had sent)** me.
Yours **(clearly / dearly / sincerely)**,
Martin Eden

focus 2 The United Tastes of America

1 Buy buy buy!

Look at the pictures and texts above.

a) Collect words that can be used to describe food.
- **How it is prepared:** to grill, …
- **What it tastes like:** tasty, …
- **What it feels like in your mouth:** crispy, …

b) Which of these products do you like best? Say why.

8 2 Listening: Gareth and Ceri go shopping

a) Gareth is shopping for his birthday party with Ceri. Compare the shopping list with what they actually buy. Make a grid like this:

bought		not bought
on the list	not on the list	…
…	…	

b) Which of the things are they going to have at the party? What about the rest?

c) Discuss these statements in class:
- Shopping for food is boring.
- You should eat and drink only what you like.

3 Facts and figures: What American teenagers eat

About 42% of US teenagers eat five or more times a day. A typical teenager visits fast food restaurants more than twice a week and spends an average of $5.72 per visit. Most of that money is spent on hamburgers, and then pizza, Tex-Mex and chicken. Lunch is usually eaten away from home. Most teenagers (58%) buy something at school. About 28% bring something from home. After school, a typical teenager spends $1.25 on snacks.

a) True or false? Correct the false statements.

1. About two-fifths of America's teenagers eat at least five times a day.
2. American teenagers spend an average of $5.72 a week on fast food.
3. They spend less money on pizza than on burgers.
4. A typical teenager eats lunch at home.
5. Less than a third of American teenagers bring a packed lunch from home.
6. The average American teenager spends $1.25 on snacks at school.

b) What questions do you think the American teenagers were asked? You and your partner can use them to interview each other. Compare your answers with those of the typical American teenager.

c) What do you think 'slow food' is? How is it different from 'fast food'?

4 Planning a birthday meal

Plan a surprise birthday meal for a friend. Think of a menu (starter, main course, dessert and drinks) and make a shopping list. Decide who is going to do what (shopping, cooking etc.). Then present your plans to the class.

unit 4 intro

Living together

1 Many people are born with a disability while others become disabled as a result of illness or an accident. There are lots of different kinds and levels of disabilities – and also lots of ways to try and overcome problems so that everyone can live a full life in the community …

1

There are lots of activities which disabled and able-bodied people can take part in together. Sailing is very popular not only because it is a great experience but also because everyone in the boat can work as equals. They all learn different skills from each other, too.

2

Although illness took away the power of his body, Professor Stephen Hawking became one of the greatest names in the world of science. His famous book *A Brief History of Time* explains the origins of the universe. Even losing the ability to use his voice did not stop his work as a teacher. Instead he found a new way to communicate with a speech synthesizer.

3

Some children with physical or mental disabilities improve through special therapies with animals. Swimming with dolphins can make them stronger or help them to form relationships. While they are having fun, they learn to try new things, and they begin to feel more positive about life.

1 Collecting information

a) Talk about the information in the pictures and texts.
What different kinds of disability are there?
What problems can disability cause?
How can these problems be overcome?

b) What is the situation where you live? Give examples of what has been done for people with disabilities. What still needs to be changed?

2 Who am I?

Imagine you are one of the people in the pictures above, but don't tell your partner who you are.
Think about the situation you're in and start to talk about your thoughts and feelings.
As soon as your partner can guess who you are, it's his or her turn. Otherwise, go on until he or she finds out.

4

For disabled people who love sport the Paralympics offer competition at the highest international level. Athletes from six different disability groups do all kinds of sports, from running and archery to judo and wheelchair basketball. Some athletes – like South African swimmer Natalie du Toit, who lost part of her left leg in an accident – are so good that they also take part in the Olympics for able-bodied people.

5

Blind people can enjoy art if instead of their eyes they use their hands. So in many art galleries they are allowed to hold and to feel sculptures. Some works of art are made especially for people who cannot see.

6

Rules for the whole community can help everyone to live as equals in society. For example, since 1993 all televisions that are made in the US have had caption decoders for deaf people. And new buildings must be designed so that wheelchairs can go in and out. However, much more still has to be done before everyone can use their abilities and not be held back by their disabilities.

10 3 Listening: A radio interview

a) Listen, and answer the questions according to what Barbara Hudson says.

1. Why can helping someone in a wheelchair be dangerous?
2. Why do some disabled people get annoyed when help is offered?
3. Why do many able-bodied people grow up with negative feelings about disabled people?

b) Divide the class into two groups. Listen again. One group collects ideas about how able-bodied people should behave, and the other group collects ideas about how disabled people should behave. Make a list of 'Dos and don'ts' for both sides. Maybe you can add your own ideas.

dos	don'ts
…	…

A Online

When Gareth Morgan needs some information from deaf people,
Ceri advises him to try a deaf people's discussion forum on the Internet.

Author	Posted	Topic: Useful devices
Gareth e-mail	14 March 19.32	Hi! Anybody out there? I'm doing a school science project and would like to find out about devices that have been invented to help deaf people. Which are most useful or have made the biggest difference to you? It would be great if I got some answers from you. Thanks in advance!
Jerome e-mail	14 March 20.05	Hi, Gareth. If a hundred people answered your question, you'd probably get a hundred different opinions! But the device that helps me most is my wake-up alarm. If it didn't vibrate under my pillow every morning, I'd never get to college on time. Actually, since last month it has also been my favorite device for another reason. After I'd dropped it while I was making my bed, it had to be repaired. And the assistant at the place where I took it is now my girlfriend! :-)
Grace e-mail	15 March 14.49	I love movies, but I wouldn't enjoy them so much without the caption decoder for my TV. Lip-reading only works when you can see people's faces, but in every movie there are scenes where you can't. I wouldn't be able to follow the dialogue if there was no help on the screen. I once did a funny experiment with a friend who can hear. I played her a scene from a video with the sound and the decoder both switched off, and made her write captions for the characters. I thought it would be interesting if we compared her ideas with the real captions. And it was. She'd imagined a completely different story!

Internet

1 Discussing ideas

a) 1. What sounds are important in your daily life? What kind of signals can be used by deaf people instead of sounds?
2. Have you ever watched a movie with captions? Explain why captions can be useful.
3. If you posted a question on a discussion forum for deaf people, what would you ask?

b) Do an experiment that is similar to Grace's. Watch a scene from a DVD or video with no sound. Write down what you think the characters are saying. Then play the scene again and find out if you were right.

2 Sentences with *if*

a) Look for the sentences with 'if' in the text. Which tense is used in the if-clause?
How do you make the conditional tense in the main clause? (Do you use the same tenses in German?)

b) You now know two kinds of sentences with 'if'. Look at the examples below.
Talk about when you can use type I and type II.

grammar

Type I: If you **go** online,
you**'ll** find lots of discussion forums.

Type II: If there **wasn't** an Internet,
it **would be** more difficult to make contact.

3 More statements from the discussion forum

Complete these **type II** sentences with the correct verb forms.

1. If I **(have to)** choose my favorite thing, it **(be)** my computer.
2. If my telephone **(not allow)** me to use text, I **(not be able to)** communicate with it.
3. If my doorbell **(not be)** connected to a light signal, I **(not notice)** when it rang.
4. More deaf people **(go)** to the movies if there **(be)** captions on the screen.
5. If people **(not speak)** so fast, I **(find)** it easier to lip-read.
6. I **(not feel)** so safe if my house **(not have)** a special fire alarm.
7. If I **(not have)** my hearing aid, I **(not hear)** anything at all!
8. Life **(be)** more difficult if we **(not get)** so much help from modern technology.

4 Just imagine!

Discuss with a partner what you would do if these things happened. (They probably won't!)

Example: 1. "If I saw a ghost, I would run away." – "Oh, I wouldn't do that. If I saw a ghost, I would ask its name."

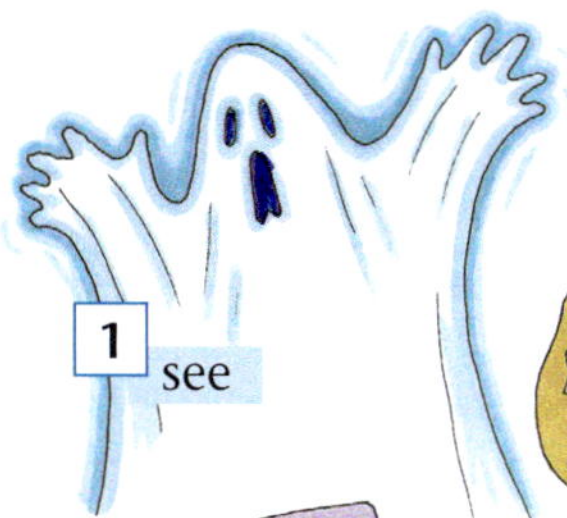
1 see

2 find

3 win

4 meet

5 learn

6 become

5 Only if ...

Talk in groups or in class. Would you ever do these things? In what situations?

Example: I would only miss school if I was ill.

miss school • jump from a bridge • break a window • copy another student's work • run out of a lesson • live without television • ask to change schools • kill an animal

6 If I were you

a) What advice would you give these people?
Example: 1. If I were you, I'd look on the Internet.

tip
When you want to give advice in English, you often start with 'If I were you, ...'.
(After 'if' you can use 'were' instead of 'was'.)

1. "I'd like to find out how I can help disabled kids."
2. "I had an argument with my boyfriend, and now he doesn't phone me any more."
3. "My friend wants me to go to judo classes with her, but I'm not sure about the idea."
4. "My parents are annoyed with me because my grades at school aren't very good."
5. "Another student at school keeps saying nasty things about me."

b) Think of more problem situations. Explain your problem to your partner. What advice does he/she give you?

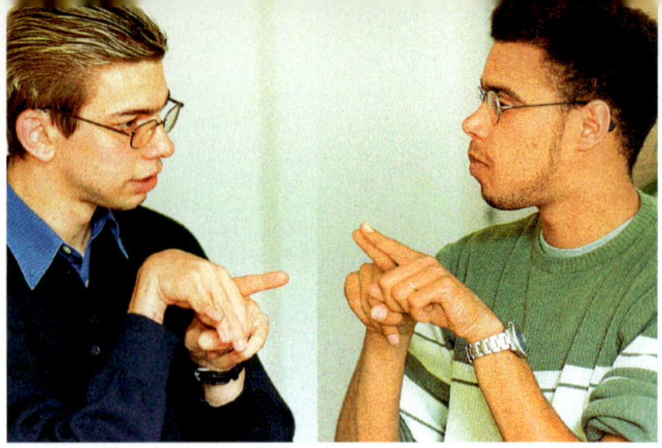

7 Jerome

Complete what Jerome thinks with the correct verb forms. (Think carefully! Are the if-clauses type I or type II?)

1. If deafness could be cured, of course I **(be)** happy.
2. But it would be stupid if I **(allow)** my disability to ruin my life.
3. I'm sure that if I **(get)** a good education, I'll have a better chance of a good job.
4. Being deaf **(not hold)** me back if I can work with computers.
5. If my college **(not have)** a center for deaf students, it would be much harder for me.
6. It's good to know that someone will always give me help if I **(need)** it.
7. I really believe that if more people with disabilities can overcome their problems, it **(mean)** a better future for the whole community.
8. If only other people learned to look at us with open minds, they **(see)** we have great abilities, too.

8 What would you do?

Look at the situations and the people's reactions. Would you do the same or not? Explain your answer.

Example: 1. If someone fell into a river, I would try to rescue them, too. I would feel terrible if I didn't do anything and the person died.

or: I wouldn't jump into a river because I'm not a good swimmer and I wouldn't be able to save the person. Somebody else would probably have to rescue me, too!

Skills: Listening and understanding the gist

11 1 Listening for key words

A team of British athletes is taking part in the Paralympics. There's an assistant who helps with any problems they have.

a) First look at the pictures and say what words you think of.

b) Listen to what some athletes tell the assistant and match the pictures with the speakers. (There is one extra picture without a text.) Which key words or phrases help you to decide?

12 2 Understanding announcements

a) In airports you often hear announcements for passengers. You want to be able to understand them because they could be important for you! Collect ideas about what announcements in an airport can be about.

b) Listen to the announcements. Say who each of them is for. What should these people do?

tip

Listen for the key words like names, times, numbers and places.
The main information is often repeated, so don't worry if you don't get everything the first time.

13 3 American or British?

People from different English-speaking countries have different accents. You can recognize American English if you know which sounds are pronounced differently from British English.

a) Listen to what an American wheelchair basketball player says after a game with the British team. Which words sound typically American?

b) Now listen to some more athletes who are interviewed during the Paralympics. Do they come from the US or Britain?

American pronunciation

- Words like 'aunt', 'half' or 'after' are pronounced with the sound [æ:] (BE: [ɑ:]).
- You can hear the 'r' in words like 'sure', 'car' or 'work'. (In BE you can't.)
- 't' in the middle of words like 'beautiful' or 'British' often sounds like a 'd'.

4 Project: 'Real' English

a) How can you listen to 'real' English where you live? Talk about what sources you can use.

b) Keep a 'listening diary' for a week. Listen to some English every day (pop music, TV or radio news, movies, commercials, ...) and try to get the gist. Write down what you listen to.

c) Record examples of English that you find interesting / useful / funny / ... .
Make a class 'listening library' – and use it!

B Party clothes

Ceri Morgan is in her favorite clothes store in Seattle with her friend Naomi.

Ceri: See, Naomi? Like I told you, they have all kinds of funky clothes here. I'm sure **you'll be able to** find something you can wear at Pete's party next week.

Naomi: Yeah. Pants, I think. **I could** get a dress, of course. A long one would look OK. But pants are usually more comfortable for me.

Ceri: You should try on a few different pairs. How about these? Or these? Hey, and what do you think about these white ones?

Naomi: I like them all! But **they might** be too big.

Ceri: Well, **why don't you** take the next size down, too? Here we are. Two sizes of each.

Naomi: **You don't have to** carry them. **I can** put them across my wheelchair. Now, what else is there? Wow! Look at these green ones. They're really cool, aren't they?

Ceri: The green ones? You must be out of your mind, Naomi!

Naomi: **You needn't** worry about me, I'll try them on anyway! Oh, and here are some real party pants. Or shouldn't I wear glitter?

Ceri: Why not? You know, **if I were you, I'd** look for a new top, too.

Naomi: Hm. **I may not** have enough money for that. But – it doesn't cost anything to try on a few. I'll take these. And also this red one.

Ceri: Yes, red really suits you. Blue, too – here you are. Hey, and my new earrings would look great with this top here.

Naomi: You mean the ones you got in London?

Ceri: Yeah. **You can** borrow them for the party if you decide to buy the top.

Naomi: Oh, thanks, Ceri. Now **can you** just look on that high shelf there for me, please?

Ceri: Yes, but – er – **maybe it would be better not to** collect any more clothes at the moment.

Naomi: You're right. I already have a mountain here! I'll just ask this assistant. – Excuse me. **Is it OK if I** try on these pants and tops?

Assistant: But **you're only allowed to** take three things at a time into the changing rooms.

1 Talking about the text

a) What does the dialogue tell you about Ceri and Naomi, and about their relationship?

b) Why do you think customers are usually only allowed to take three things into the changing rooms?

c) How could the dialogue go on?

d) Do you prefer to go shopping for clothes alone or with somebody else? Explain your answer.

2 Looking at language

a) Find examples of **one** and **ones** in the text. What nouns do these words stand for? Why is it better to use **one / ones** here instead of the nouns?

b) Put the phrases you found in **a)** into German and compare the two languages. What do you notice?

3 Shopping

Finish the answers with an **adjective + one / ones.**

1. "Are you going to buy an expensive watch?" – "No, I just want a cheap ..."
2. "Which jeans should I buy?" – "I think you look best in the ..."
3. "This music shop isn't very good." – "You're right. Let's look for a ..."
4. "I like your sunglasses." – "They're boring. I want some ..."
5. "Can you carry some of these bags, please?" – "OK, but don't give me the ..."
6. "Oh no! We've just missed a bus." – "Well, we'll have to wait for the ..."

4 What's different?

Work with a partner. One of you looks at picture **A,** the other one looks at picture **B.** Talk about the pictures and find out what is different.

Example:
A: How many bears are there in your picture?
B: There are three – two black ones and a brown one.
A: Well, in my picture there are two black ones.

5 Words in context: Different words for different people

a) Which of these phrases can you say to friends, which of them to adults or strangers?

1. "Please can you give me some advice?"
2. "You must be out of your mind!"
3. "Here – can you hold my bag for a minute?"
4. "Thank you, but I think I'll be able to manage alone."
5. "Hey, it's my turn first."
6. "Excuse me. Could you give me space to come past with my wheelchair, please?"
7. "You're late, as usual!"

b) Imagine the speakers in a) are talking to different people. Make the formal words more informal, and the informal words more polite.

6 Role play: Talking about the party

a) Look at the dialogue again and put the phrases in **blue** into a grid.

possibility	advice	permission	ability	obligation
I could	...	...	...	...

b) Now work with a partner. Choose one of the situations and act out a dialogue. Think about the relationship between the people and choose the right kind of words. Use phrases from **a).**

1. Pete asks his mother for permission to have a party for his friends. She isn't happy with the idea, but he is able to persuade her.
2. Pete discusses his party with Naomi. He wants to make it the best party ever and would like to hear Naomi's advice.
3. Pete warns the old man in the apartment upstairs about his party. (You can decide if the neighbor's reaction is positive or not.)

G12

Helpless

Before you read: Have you ever felt completely helpless? Describe what happened and how you felt.

At Sheremetyevo airport in Moscow, two men stood and waited for their flight to New York. "Try not to look so nervous," the taller one said. "You'll make people notice us." "But I am nervous. What if it goes wrong?" his friend answered. "It won't go wrong. Trust me. Ah! I've just seen the right person. That's exactly what we need when we get to the other end."

"There she is! Hi, Susie! We're here!" Susie O'Brien was really happy when she heard her parents' voices at JFK airport. Although she had enjoyed her college exchange trip to Moscow, it was good to be back home again. Susie thanked the woman who had helped her from the plane to the arrivals hall. Then she took her mother's arm and they walked together through the crowd of people while her father came behind with her suitcase. "Hey!" Suddenly Mr O'Brien shouted angrily, and at the same time Susie felt a tug on her shoulder bag. "What's going on?" she wanted to know. "Some guy tried to put his hand into your bag. It's lucky I was behind you and saw him. I've told you before, Susie. It'd be better if you used a bag with a zipper. Your things aren't safe in that one."

■ An hour later, after a slow journey through the New York traffic, the O'Briens arrived at their house in Brooklyn. None of them noticed the other car that went past and then stopped on the other side of the street. Susie's parents went into the house with her, but they didn't take off their coats. "It seems terrible that we both have to rush away to work before we have a chance to hear about your trip," said Mrs O'Brien. "Don't worry," Susie answered. "It isn't your fault my flight arrived in the morning. It was great you could at least pick me up from the airport. Anyway, I'm really tired, so I'm happy just to sleep right now. We can talk this evening when you get back home."

Before Susie's parents left, her father carried her suitcase down to the basement. The apartment which had been made there for Susie was a good solution for her. Her own place in her parents' house meant that she could be independent like other young adults, but she could also easily get help when she needed it. Because she was blind it was no problem for her that there was no natural light in the basement. She was too tired to unpack her suitcase before she slept. So she pulled it off the bed where her father had put it and left it on the floor in her bedroom. Then she remembered that her cellphone was still switched off. If her parents tried to call her later, she wouldn't know. So she picked up her shoulder bag and felt for the phone in it. The bag was especially full, with all the extra things Susie had needed for her journey. While she was searching for the phone, she touched a small package which didn't seem familiar. However she didn't have time to stop and think what it was because at that moment she heard the door at the top of the stairs to the basement.

■ At first Susie thought her mother or her father had returned to the house. However, she knew their footsteps, and these were different ones. She could hear that there were actually two men, one of them quite big,

and they were coming downstairs. Susie felt scared, but she came out of the bedroom into the hall.
"Who's there? What do you want?" she called out.

Now she could feel that the two men were close to her. One of them was so close that she could smell his aftershave.
"Who are you?" Susie asked again. When there was still no answer, she got nervous and tried to push past the men to the stairs, but the bigger one grabbed her arm and pulled her back. What was happening? They still didn't say a word. She was terrified. The man pulled her into the living room and made her stand in a corner far away from the door. She could hear that the men were searching the room. She also knew that if she tried to escape again, they would see her and easily be able to stop her. There was nothing she could do. She felt dizzy with fear. However, she suddenly realized that she was standing next to the fuse box for the apartment.

■ When all the lights went out, there were angry shouts from the men. Then they both went quiet again. Susie listened. One of the men was coming towards her. He was trying to move quietly, but she could hear him. She waited until she was sure which side he was coming from, then she moved to the other side and started to make her way carefully to the door. Behind her the man suddenly cursed loudly as in the darkness he bumped into a chair. Susie was still scared, but now she felt that at least she had one advantage over the men. She was in her own home and she didn't need light to find her way around in the apartment. Her only problem now was that she didn't know where the second man was. Was he anywhere near the living room door? Would he catch her if she tried to go through? If only she could get into the hall, she would be able to escape. She took one step, then another. She was through the door and almost safe.

"Oh no, you don't!" The other man was there in the hall, between her and the stairs. He tried to grab her again, but she was too quick for him. She turned and ran into the bedroom. But in the bedroom Susie felt as if she was in a worse trap than before. It was a very small room. Even in the darkness, it wouldn't be easy to escape. As she crept quietly around the bed, she could hear that the man had managed to find the door. He felt his way into the room. Her heart beat faster. Crash! When the man fell over Susie's suitcase, she quickly took her chance. She climbed over the bed and ran out of the room, through the hall and up the stairs. She shut the door behind her and locked it. Then she ran out into the street and shouted for help as loudly as she could.

"It's a Russian icon. A very small one, but very valuable," the police officer told the O'Briens. "Those guys wanted to smuggle it into the country. But they didn't want to be found with it. So they looked for somebody else who could carry it through for them. Of course they planned to take it back again right away at the airport."
"But I stopped them," said Mr O'Brien.
"Right. So they followed you back here and waited until Susie was alone. They thought she would be helpless. How wrong they were!"

1 Reading and thinking

a) In some stories you don't always get all the information you want right away.

1. After you have read the story, say what happens between lines 9 and 10?

2. Look again at lines 10 to 70. There are three clues that something might happen to Susie. Can you find them?

3. Add an extra part to the story. Use your own ideas to describe what happens between lines 138 and 139.

b) Some stories have a 'turning point', when something important suddenly changes. What is the turning point in 'Helpless'? What changes?

tip

When you are dealing with a new text, it always helps to divide it into parts and look for the key words and sentences. It's useful to make a copy of the text and mark these things on it.

2 Susie

Write a short description of Susie. Include the facts that are given about her in the story, and also the ideas you get about her character.

3 Word power

Explain the difference in meaning between these pairs of words or phrases.

1. to go wrong – to be wrong
2. a bag – a suitcase
3. a step – a footstep
4. to search something – to search for something
5. to shut the door – to lock the door
6. her only problem – only her problem

9 4 A song: In the shadows[1] (The Rasmus)

No sleep – no sleep until I'm done[2] with finding the answer.
Won't stop – won't stop before I find the cure[3] for this cancer[4].

Sometimes I feel like going down, I'm so disconnected[5].
Sometimes I know that I am haunted[6] to be wanted.

I've been watching, I've been waiting
In the shadows for my time.
I've been searching, I've been living
For tomorrows all my life
In the shadows, in the shadows.

They say that I must learn to kill before I can feel safe
But I, I'd rather[7] kill myself than turn into[8] their slave[9].

Sometimes I feel that I should go and play with the thunder[10].
Somehow[11] I just don't wanna stay and wait for a wonder[12].

Lately[13], I've been walking, walking in circles,
Watching, waiting for something.
Feel me, touch me, heal[14] me, come take me higher.

Words: Yloenen, Johannes Lauri

[1]Schatten • [2]fertig • [3]Heilung • [4]Krebs • [5]isoliert • [6]ruhelos • [7]I'd rather – ich würde lieber • [8]to turn into – werden • [9]Sklave • [10]Donner • [11]irgendwie • [12]Wunder • [13]in letzter Zeit • [14]to heal – heilen

a) What do the words and the music tell you?

1. The person in the song feels

- **A** important
- **B** alone
- **C** nervous
- **D** bored
- **E** nasty
- **F** lazy
- **G** happy
- **H** sad

2. The person wants

- **A** to do what other people tell him / her to do.
- **B** to do nothing.
- **C** to do something to change the situation.
- **D** someone to help him / her.
- **E** to do the same thing again and again.

b) Which words and phrases prove that you are right?

1 Word power

a) Which words have the same (or a similar) meaning? Find seven pairs.

equal • suggestion • mend • solution • short • the same • brief • expensive • test • repair • valuable • experiment • advice • answer

b) Write the sentences again with only one word in place of the blue words.

1. Hey, that color really **is a very good color for** you!
2. I hope the movie has got **the words on the screen**.
3. I talked to one of the **people who were traveling** on the plane.
4. Some people find it difficult to form **links with other people**.
5. You should**n't** speak **rudely** to your teachers.
6. E-mail is a good way to **give and get information**.
7. If you like, you can **take** my CD **and give it back tomorrow**.

2 If

Match the if-clauses and the main clauses to make sentences.

1. If the doors here **(not be)** wide enough,
2. I **(feel)** very weak
3. It **(be)** easier to learn how to live together
4. If there **(be)** more contact between disabled and able-bodied kids,

- they **(find)** it easier to understand each other.
- people in wheelchairs **(cannot)** get in.
- if I **(have)** to ask other people for help.
- if disabled and able-bodied kids **(go)** to the same schools.

3 Everyday English: Situations

What would you say **a)** to your friend or **b)** to your friend's mother or father?

1. It's very cold, so you want someone to shut the window.
2. You want to borrow a book.
3. Someone has dropped some money.
4. You want to take the last sandwich.
5. Someone doesn't know how to get to the Chinese restaurant. You offer your help.
6. Someone has had an accident and is hurt.
7. Someone wants to go to London on a sightseeing tour and asks you for advice.

4 Mixed bag: An interesting experience

Mark, a boy in Gareth's class, is talking. Put in the missing words.

"Three years **1**, before my family came **2** Seattle, I had **3** illness **4** made my legs really weak. So **5** almost three months I **6** use a wheelchair. It **7** a hard time, but an interesting **8**, too. I experienced life **9** a disabled person. That taught **10** a lot. There were so **11** problems. Of course one of the biggest **12** was that I wasn't **13** to run around any more. But I also learned **14** when you're physically disabled, some people **15** treat you like you expect. They seem **16** think you must **17** mentally disabled, **18**. And there are other people **19** aren't sure how they **20** behave, so **21** just ignore you. I was lucky **22** my illness **23** last forever. But I think **24** I had to spend my whole life in a wheelchair, it **25** be very difficult for me. I think it's great **26** people with disabilities manage to stay as positive **27** most of them do."

2 revision Books 1+2

1 Role play: Conversations with new friends

a) Prepare for the situations on the right. Write down ten things you could say about yourself, and ten questions you could ask a new friend. Think about personal and family information, where you live, hobbies and interests etc.

b) Practise conversations with a partner in two of the situations. Take turns to be yourself and to act the other person. Remember to listen carefully and try to use your voice and face and feedback phrases to keep up the conversation.

You meet:

1. a young Londoner on a beach in Spain.
2. a young American from Billings, Montana, in a park in your town.
3. a young Russian (who speaks English but not German) at JFK airport in New York.

You can start like this:
Excuse me. ... • Hello. ... • Do you speak English? • Is this seat free? • This is a great place/..., isn't it? • Would you like to join our game? • ...?

2 Word power: Expressing ideas exactly and correctly

a) Find pairs of words with similar meanings. Which of the two has the stronger meaning?
Example: angry – annoyed:
'Angry' has the stronger meaning.

angry • good • amazed • bad • large • scared • huge • hot • terrified • fantastic • warm • surprised • terrible • annoyed

b) Write sentences or draw pictures to show the difference between the words. Examples:
I get a bit annoyed when people are late.
I got really angry and started to shout.

c) Write down a full and exact description of one of the boys in the picture. Can your partner guess which one it is? Find a partner whose description is of a different boy. Check your partner's description. Are any details missing?

d) Complete the text with prepositions. (Sometimes more than one preposition can be correct.)

Once I travelled **1** London **2** Edinburgh **3** train. Just before the train left, a young man and woman sat down **4** me. They started to talk **5** each other, so I just looked **6** the window. Soon we had left London **7** us, and were going **8** open country. I wasn't listening **9** the man and woman. I wasn't interested **10** their conversation. Anyway, I was tired, so I closed my eyes and slept **11** a while. I dreamt that someone was talking **12** a gun. Then I suddenly realized **13** a shock that I wasn't dreaming. "How are you going to get rid **14** the gun?" the man was asking. "I'll throw it **15** the river," the woman said. "All you have to do is wait **16** me **17** the airport. Then we'll be **18** our way **19** a new life **20** a bag full **21** money!" Oh no! The two of them were making plans **22** a crime! Did they have the gun **23** them now? I was horrified, and this clearly showed **24** my face because suddenly they both started to laugh. I opened my eyes and looked **25** them. "You needn't be afraid **26** us," the woman told me. "We're taking part **27** a drama festival in Edinburgh next week. We've been acting out a scene **28** our play!"

Test yourself!

3 An e-mail from Denver

Lewis from Nottingham is travelling around the US with his friend Jason.
Complete the text with the right forms of the present perfect or simple past.
Write down your answers, then turn to page 194 to check them.

Hi, Kim!
I (1 **just arrive**) in Denver. My plane only (2 **land**) a few hours ago, but as you can see, I (3 **already find**) an Internet café. (4 **get**) you my e-mail from New York on Friday? You (5 **not answer**) it yet! Jason and I (6 **spend**) three fantastic days there last week. New York is the most exciting city I (7 **ever visit**), with the friendliest people I (8 **ever meet**). Don't worry – I (9 **not get**) too friendly with the girls! I really (10 **not want**) to leave, but in the end Jason (11 **persuade**) me to move on to Denver today. The flight here (12 **be**) cool! (13 **ever fly**) you over high mountains? We (14 **have**) a fantastic view of the Rockies – I (15 **never see**) anything like it! Anyway, what's the news back in England? I (16 **not have**) time to check the football results yet. (17 **win**) Forest at the weekend? They (18 **not lose**) many games so far this year, but of course so far I (19 **always be**) there to bring them luck! (20 **tell**) I you on Friday about the American football game I (21 **go**) to in New York? I (22 **not think**) it (23 **be**) nearly as exciting as our football, but of course I (24 **not say**) that to any Americans! I must go now because we (25 **not organize**) a place to stay yet. Please answer this e-mail. I hope you (26 **not forget**) me already!
Love, Lewis

4 Parents and kids

a) Choose the correct modal verbs. Write down your answers, then turn to page 195 to check them.

can | can't | must | mustn't | needn't

1. "You 1 wash up, Dad. I 2 do it for you." – "Thanks. But please be careful with those valuable glasses. You 3 drop them."
2. "I 4 stand the mess in your room any more. Come on, let's tidy it up together." – "No, Mum! You 5 touch my things. When you tidy up for me, I 6 never find anything!"
3. "Mum, 7 I have a party for my friends, please?" – "OK. But you 8 clean the house after the party. I don't want a mess."
4. "It 9 be nice to have kids who don't fight their parents all the time!" – "We 10 fight, Dad, if you just let me do what I want."

b) Complete the dialogue with the correct past or future substitute forms.
Careful with **can**! Does it express ability or permission?

Daughter: Er – Mum – I hope I (1 **can**) have my pocket money a bit earlier than usual. OK? If not, I (2 **can't**) buy a present in time for Dad's birthday.
Mother: But I (3 **must**) give you your money early last month, too. Actually, because you got good grades at school you (4 **can**) have a bit more than usual. Where has it all gone?
Daughter: I wanted a new T-shirt, didn't I? And the only nice one I (5 **can**) find was very expensive.
Mother: You (6 **needn't**) buy that T-shirt. When I was your age, I (7 **mustn't**) spend so much money. Anyway, I never had much, so I (8 **can't**) throw it away like that. I think you (9 **must**) look for a Saturday job. If you earn your own money, you (10 **can**) understand at last that it doesn't grow on trees!
Daughter: But Dad says I (11 **mustn't**) get a Saturday job until I'm older. Anyway, I must get his present now. Please! You (12 **needn't**) help me ever again, I promise!

revision 2
Units 3–4

5 A report about the school play 'Tom Sawyer'

Use the connecting words and the past perfect to give the same information in one sentence – and improve the style. Think which action comes first. The order of the clauses might have to be changed, too.

Example: 1. The drama group wrote their play after they had all read the book.

1. The drama group all read the book. Then they wrote their play. **(after)**
2. They worked hard for many months. They performed the play last Friday. **(before)**
3. Hundreds of people bought tickets. The school hall was full. **(because)**
4. Alex Brown broke his leg the day before. He wasn't able to play Tom. **(because)**
5. Will Nevin didn't expect to take part. He acted the role very well. **(although)**
6. He forgot a few words. He only had to be helped once. **(when)**
7. Friends and families waited eagerly to see the play. They enjoyed it very much. **(who)**
8. The drama group wrote jokes into the dialogue. Everyone laughed at them. **(which)**
9. The play finished. The audience clapped and cheered. **(after)**
10. The actors came back onto the stage five times. Then the audience stopped clapping and cheering. **(not until)**

6 All for charity

Sometimes people do things to make money for charity. They keep doing it until something stops them. Look at the pictures. Why did these people stop? What had they been doing, and for how long or since when had they been doing it?

Example: 1. She stopped because she was tired. She had been swimming for over an hour.

7 A girl from our street

Make sentences. Think carefully where the adverbs and adverbials should go.

1. Cindy • now • known • for a long time • I've
2. moved • seven years ago • her family • to a house in our street
3. has always • brilliantly • been able to • tennis • Cindy • play
4. after school • practiced • at a local club • she • every day • hard • in the neighborhood
5. I • in the street • for the last year or two • haven't seen her
6. in Florida • she's training • at the moment • with a group of top young players
7. see • on TV • maybe • one day • I'll • my friend

8 Word power: 'Body' verbs

a) Collect 'body' verbs in a mind map. The example below shows you how you can start. Use one colour for the body parts and a different colour for the verbs. Add as many ideas of your own as you can – especially all the new 'body' verbs you learned in Units 3 and 4.

⟨**b**⟩ Work in groups. Take turns to act the 'body' verbs you collected in a). Can the others in your group guess what the verb is? (If someone acts a verb you didn't write down, add it to your mind map.)

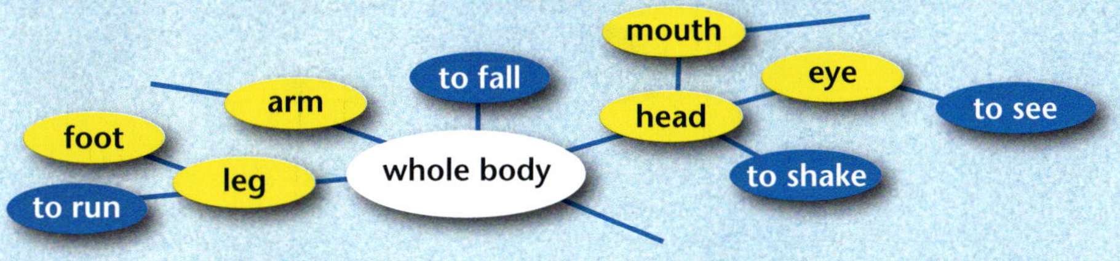

9 Our city would be a better place

a) Put the correct ideas together and make type II if-sentences. Decide which idea you should use for the if-clause and which idea should be in the main clause.

Example: If neighbours talked to each other, not so many people would feel lonely.

neighbours • talk to each other ✔	there • be more parks
there • not be a traffic problem	the city • look nicer
the streets • look cleaner	people • needn't worry about thieves
more trees • be planted	not so many people • feel lonely ✔
all buildings • be designed for wheelchairs	idiots • not drop rubbish on the ground
kids • not have to play in the streets	everyone • use buses
doors and windows • can be left open	it • help many disabled people

b) What about where you live?
Use your own ideas to say what would make it better for everyone.

10 Mixed bag: A TV program

Naomi: Hi, Ceri. 1 you see that new TV program last 2 ?

Ceri: 3 program are you talking 4 ?

Naomi: It's the 5 I mentioned 6 the phone the other day. It's 7 'New Look'.

Ceri: Oh, I 8 now. They take someone 9 looks terrible and 10 them look great, right? No, I 11 see it. Sorry, but 12 was busy with 13 assignment I have to finish 14 Friday.

Naomi: Oh, I'd hoped you 15 watch it, too, so we 16 talk about it. I 17 believe what they did with a poor girl yesterday. 18 they'd finished with her she looked 19 instead of better! I 20 , the hairstyle they gave her didn't 21 her at all. And the clothes she'd been 22 at the beginning of the program were much funkier 23 the 24 they chose for her. Of course she wasn't 25 to see her 'new look' until the 26 of the program.

Ceri: And what was her 27 then? Did she like what they 28 done?

Naomi: No, she really 29 it! At first she was 30 to tears. But then she suddenly 31 angry and started to shout. She 32 stop 33 they'd promised to give 34 another 'new look' next week. I 35 wait to see it. And you 36 watch next week, too, Ceri!

intro **unit 5**

In and around Seattle

YOUR WORLD – INTERNET GUIDE

Welcome to SEATTLE

Seattle fans say this is the best place in the world to live. There's something for everyone, from **sightseeing** and **shopping** to some of the most magnificent scenery in **nature**. In the summer, water **sports** such as windsurfing, sailing and rowing are only a 10-minute drive from Seattle, and you can hike on wilderness trails or go camping only 45 minutes away in the Cascade Mountains, where winter sports are also possible. There's great **music** in Seattle. Grunge rock was born here, and there are lots of exciting new museums, funky coffee bars and fun places to hang out. So if you're looking for **lifestyle** and a full calendar of **events**, Seattle is the place to be!

Our website has **maps** of the city and lots of interesting **facts and figures**.

1

2

3 **Area:** 83.9 square miles (217.3 square km)
Population: 563,400
State: Washington
Time Zone: Pacific Standard Time
Weather: Cool winters, mild summers
Sunshine: 55 days a year

4 Your adventure in the Space Needle begins with a 41-second journey up one of the three glass elevators. You'll get fantastic views from the restaurant at the top.

5

Whale watching on Puget Sound

6 One of Seattle's great summer festivals is Seafair, a celebration in July and early August with seaplane races on Lake Washington, a downtown carnival with parades and music, an air show, a Milk Carton Derby and lots of other fun things to do.

1 Links

a) Which picture / text goes with which link in the introduction of the Internet guide?

b) What's special about Seattle? Take notes and say what you think.

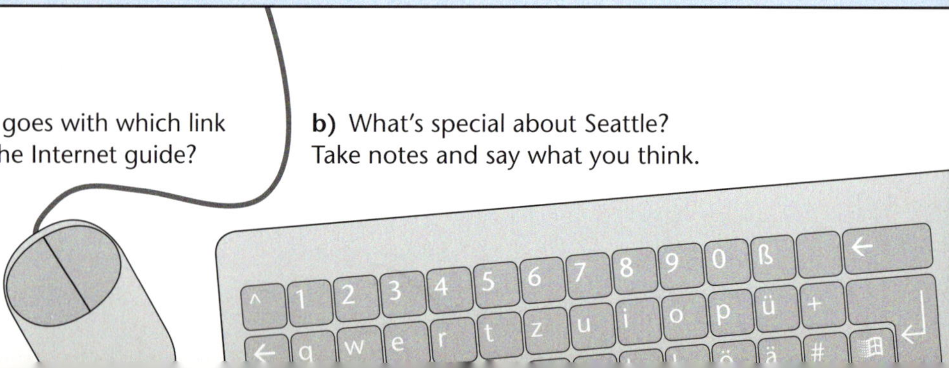

The Space Needle with Mount Rainier in the distance – one of the many active volcanoes in the Pacific Northwest.

7

10

8 For a hungry visitor there's no better place than Pike Place Market. Nearly a century old, it's one of Seattle's most popular attractions. The best time to enjoy the market is during the week, where you'll find fewer people but lots of flying fish. The fishmongers throw huge salmon between their stalls – so watch out!

9

11

12 **Experience Music Project**

EMP is an interactive museum that tells the story of American popular music, from its roots in jazz, soul, gospel, country and the blues, to its influence on hip-hop, punk and other styles. Visitors of all ages come to discover and enjoy the power of music.

sightseeing | shopping | nature | sports | music | lifestyle | events | maps | facts & figures

15 2 Listening: Visitors to Seattle

Listen to these four scenes and say where the people are and what they are doing.

3 A step further

Think of places of interest and things to do where you live. Write a guide to your town.

10 A Preparing for a trip

This is a handout Ceri's geography teacher, Mrs Baxter, gave her students in order to prepare them for a camping trip to the Cascades.

INFORMATION

I'd like you to read this information carefully. We'll discuss the details at our next meeting.

Safety in numbers: Always hike with me (your group leader). Stay on the trail and stop regularly to wait for others. It's best to carry a map and a loud whistle for emergencies.

How to stay fit: Do some exercises before you start. It's important to drink lots of water during the hike and to carry dried food in case you get hungry. But don't eat wild fruits or mushrooms.

What to take: I'll give you a list of basic camping gear (tent, sleeping bag, change of clothing etc.) Don't take any unnecessary extra stuff, like laptops! Remember to pack a waterproof jacket in case it rains, and a water bottle. If you aren't sure what else to bring, ask me.

Where to camp: When we reach our campsite, find an open, flat and dry area to put up your tent. Then look for a place to have our campfire. There are special areas for this. It's important not to wait too long as we need time to collect wood for the fire.

Cooking: Put food in aluminum foil and grill it slowly. You can use water from a stream to make soup and hot drinks, but boil it first. Any fish we catch must be cleaned, cooked and eaten immediately. (Don't expect me to clean your fish, but I'd be happy to show you how to do it.)

Protecting nature: Don't break branches or pick flowers. Fishing is OK, but leave other wildlife alone. Leave your campsite clean and free of trash, and don't throw anything into rivers or lakes. Paper can be burned in the campfire. Other kinds of waste should be taken away with you.

Bears: If you want to keep bears away from the campsite, don't leave food in or near your tent.

1 What to pack

a) Look at the text and say what Mrs Baxter wants the students to bring. Make a list.

b) Work in a group. Talk about the things on the list. Explain why they are necessary.

Examples: – A tent and sleeping bag are necessary **because** it gets cold at night.
– You should have a waterproof jacket **in case** it rains.
– You need a whistle **(in order) to** call for help in an emergency.

c) Imagine you are going on a camping trip and can only take five things in your backpack. What would you take? Discuss this in your group and make a 'hit list' of the five most important things.

2 Looking at grammar

a) Find examples of **to + infinitive** in the text. Put them into four groups:

purpose	question word + to	verb + object + to	other phrase
… in order to prepare …	…	…	…

b) Which of these can you translate by ***um … zu + Infinitiv*** in German?
Which can you translate by ***zu + Infinitiv?*** What about the others?

c) Put these sentences together with the infinitive forms you have collected.

1. I'm going into town. I want to buy a tent.
→ I'm going into town **(in order) to** buy a tent.
2. Buy a waterproof jacket. Remember that!
3. Find an open, flat and dry area.
You can put up your tent there.
4. Don't leave food in your tent.
That's very important.
5. If you get lost, use your map.
With the map, you'll find the trail again.
6. Don't take a laptop. It won't be necessary.
7. But you can bring your cellphones.
That's a good idea.
8. The water from the rivers isn't safe.
You can't drink it.

3 Camping tips

Make sentences.

The handout gives tips about …
It tells you …

what who when where how	(not) to	eat and drink • hike • put waste • take in a backpack • go hiking with • put up a tent • collect wood • cook food • do with fish • keep bears away

4 Plans for the trip

Ceri is telling her parents about the plans for the trip. Use the information from the handout and the verbs **want, allow, would like, expect + to.** You may need some negative forms.

Example: Mrs Baxter wants us to read this carefully. She'd like us to … /
She won't allow us to …

11 5 A song: I want you to want me (Letters to Cleo)

Words: Richard A. Nielsen

I want you to want me.
I need you to need me.
I'd love you to love me.
I'm beggin'[1] you to beg me.

I want you to want me.
I need you to need me.
I'd love you to love me.

I'll shine up[2] the old brown shoes, put on a brand-new[3] shirt.
I'll get home early from work if you say that you love me.

Didn't I, didn't I, didn't I see you cryin'?
Oh, didn't I, didn't I, didn't I see you cryin'?
Feelin' all alone without a friend, you know you feel like dyin'.
Oh, didn't I, didn't I, didn't I see you cryin'?

[1]to beg – anflehen, bitten • [2]to shine up – blank putzen • [3]brandneu

a) What are the three things the singer would do for love?

b) Now talk about what else she could do and why.
(For example, she could write a card to express her love, or invite the person she loves to a disco to be near him, etc.)

G13,14

B Chatroom messages

Can you put these messages in the right order and say who wrote which one?

A No idea – I must be crazy! Mrs Baxter, our teacher, wants to take us on a hike near Mount St. Helens (a volcano that erupted in 1980). She's already done it twice herself. But it won't all be bad. A cool new guy in my class is going to be there. His name is Ben. I got a Valentine's card today, and I'm sure it was from Mr Cool Guy ☺ himself. Did you get lots of Valentine's cards, Bronwen?

B Well, don't eat all those cookies yourself, Ceri, or you'll get *fat*! That camp sounds interesting. How many people are going to go with you? If there aren't enough insects for everyone, you could always go out and catch a whale together and cook it yourselves. ☺

C Hi Ceri,
When was the last time we mailed each other? RUOK??????

D No, I didn't get any Valentine's cards. Now I'm feeling really sorry for myself ☹☹☹. Next year I'm going to write hundreds of cards and send them ALL to myself!

E Can't wait to see the pictures. I hope you and Ben enjoy yourselves on your trip!

F I'm a *vegetarian* whale-watcher, remember! I'm not looking forward to this camp. We'll have to do everything ourselves – cook for ourselves, put up our tents, wash our clothes, carry all our stuff, etc. And I'll miss all my favorite TV shows.☹

G Hi Bronwen!
Yes, I'm still alive, but I cut myself with a knife this morning, so I'm typing with one hand. It's hard! If you're wondering how it happened, it's because I'm off to camp with my geography teacher tomorrow. I'm worried we'll have to eat insects, so I've baked a ton of cookies – all by myself!

H Never mind, Bronwen. Buy yourself some flowers and RELAX! By the way, I'm going to take my cellphone so that I can take pictures of myself and Ben, and then mail them to you.

I Don't worry, Ceri. I'm sure you'll find ways to amuse yourselves. You could tell each other ghost stories around the campfire! But tell me – why are you going on the trip if you hate camping?

1 Questions and answers

myself • yourself (yourselves) • itself • herself • himself • ourselves • themselves

a) Use information from the text to find answers to the questions.

Example: *Ceri:* Who's going to put up our tents, Mrs Baxter?
Mrs Baxter: You're going to put them up yourselves, guys!

1. *Ben:* Did your mom bake these cookies?
   Ceri: No, I …
2. *Mari:* Who gave Bronwen those flowers?
   Owen: Nobody! She …
3. *Principal:* Are you going to carry the food?
   Mrs Baxter: No, the students …
4. *Ben:* Would you wash my socks for me?
   Ceri: What?! Sorry, Ben, but you …

b) Look at the pictures and captions.

1. Translate the word **myself**.
2. Which picture is still correct if you leave out **myself**?
3. In which sentence is **myself** the object of the verb?

I baked the cookies myself.

I cut myself with a knife.

2 At the camp

Complete the sentences using a verb and a reflexive pronoun.

buy • cut • enjoy • amuse • teach • hurt • record
+
-self / selves

1. Ceri and Ben had great fun at the camp. They really ___.
2. Ben ___ a book called *Camping Skills* to prepare for the trip.
3. He ___ how to make a fire from the book.
4. "Be careful with that knife, Ceri! Don't ___ again!"
5. In the evening they ___ with stories and songs around the campfire.
6. "We also played games and ___ on video."
7. Once Ceri tripped while she was hiking, but she didn't ___.

3 The Seafair Milk Carton Derby

After the trip, Ceri and Ben built a boat out of milk cartons and took part in Seattle's traditional Seafair Milk Carton Derby.

Look on the right to see the difference between **themselves** and **each other.** Then look below and use **each other** or **themselves** to describe what happened.

Start like this: Ceri and Ben met every evening to prepare for the derby. They got to know … better.

They looked at themselves.

They looked at each other.

get to know | teach | help … to carry | save | take photos of

4 News from Ceri

Put in a reflexive pronoun or **each other** where necessary. Be careful! A lot of verbs are reflexive in German, but not in English, for example: *sich vorstellen* = to imagine.

Hi Bronwen,
You're probably wondering (1) if our trip was OK. I can't complain (2)! I felt (3) good because Ben and I were able to see (4). Ben helped (5) to most of my cookies, but apart from that he behaved (6) well. After the camp was over, we even prepared (7) for this year's Milk Carton Derby together. Did I mention that before? I can't remember (8). Anyway, we didn't borrow (9) our boat, we made it (10)!

Can you imagine (11) what it looks like when empty milk cartons change (12) into a boat? Actually, it didn't move (13) very fast and we didn't win the race, but we really enjoyed (14)! Our relationship is improving (15) all the time. I must hurry (16) up now. We're going to meet (17) at a disco tonight and I haven't decided (18) what to wear yet.
Bye for now. Love, Ceri XXX

G15

A day to remember

I still remember that day. Well, maybe not all of it, but I'll never forget that clear, bright Sunday morning of May 18th, 1980. I was camping up in the Cascades with my cousin Rob and his friend Marty. We got up early because Rob wanted to take some pictures of Mount St. Helens in the morning light. He was a really great photographer and he loved taking pictures. So after breakfast we packed our backpacks and set off on our hike. We moved slowly and carefully because we hoped to see wildlife on the trail. The forest was quiet, with only the trees around us, and the blue sky above.

After half an hour we were on top of a ridge. The view was magnificent. The lakes and the Green River were far below, and Mount St. Helens was shining in the sunlight. I could almost touch it. Apart from the call of a bird, everything was quiet.

Suddenly there was a crash. A small, dark animal ran across our path.

"Raccoon," said Rob. Then a bigger animal followed, very near.

"Hey, look over there, you guys. That's a deer!' said Marty in a loud voice.

"Ssh, you'll frighten it away," whispered Rob. And then, as we stood very still, we saw more deer. It was strange; they were all heading north. Rob took pictures of them as they moved around us through the trees.

"What's happening?" I asked. "Do you think there's a cougar around here?"

"I don't know," Rob replied. "But a cougar wouldn't make them behave like this."

Suddenly a bear came out of the trees not far from where we were standing. I had only seen bears at the zoo before, and my heart was beating fast.

"Don't move, and it won't attack us," said Rob quietly. He took a picture and then it was gone. It was heading north, like the other animals. "Hey Laura, did you see the size of that bear!" laughed Marty. "He'd eat you for breakfast!" Marty could be so annoying. It was best to ignore him.

■ Soon everything was quiet again. But now it felt spooky. I looked at my watch. It was still only 8:30. Then there was the sound of a small plane above us. It was flying towards the mountain.

A few minutes later, we heard a sound like a train and the ground began to move.

I was trembling, too. I touched Rob's arm.

"Is that an earthquake?"

"Yeah, a strong one. I think it's coming from Mount St. Helens."

"Hey Laura, isn't this great!" shouted Marty. He stood in front of us and did a stupid wild dance. What a jerk!

"Stop it, Marty!" I said. "This is serious. If you could see yourself in the mirror, ..."

Suddenly there was a terrible explosion. We looked up at Mount St. Helens and couldn't believe our eyes. A huge rock avalanche was coming down the mountain towards us. And behind it, a thick cloud of smoke and steam was coming out of the top of the mountain. The clear blue sky was turning black. As I stood there, unable to move in shock and fear, two strange things happened that I still remember clearly. First the top of the

mountain disappeared. Then, like a terrified bird, the small plane we had seen minutes earlier shot away from the clouds of ash towards safety. But we were trapped.

Now there was a second earthquake, even stronger than the first. Something black began to spill out of the mountain. It rushed towards us like a wave. I looked around for the others. Marty wasn't playing the jerk any more. He was already running away, in a panic. And he was taking the only direction possible – back down the steep trail into the valley. I wanted to run too, but then I remembered Rob.

"Come on, Rob!" I shouted to him. He was still taking pictures of the eruption. He looked back at me for a moment and smiled. He seemed more excited than scared. I ran up to him and grabbed his arm.

"Don't just stand there, Rob! Run!"

"Don't worry about me, Laura! I'll be OK! I'm taking some fantastic pictures!"

He shook off my arm and turned away from me. I didn't know what else to do so I began to run myself. I looked back one last time. Rob was still standing there. Then a cloud of ash came between us and he was gone.

Now I could only think of one thing. I had to escape from this mountain and reach the safety of the valley. But how can you run away from a volcano? The air was getting hotter. I had to run faster, so I threw down my backpack, and then my jacket. But I felt weak and my lungs were full of smoke. I heard crashing sounds around me. Burning rocks were falling from the sky, and exploding on the dry leaves of the forest floor. Trees were burning and falling around me. As I ran, I came to a place I recognized – our campsite! So at least I was on the right trail.

I knew the trail followed a stream down into the valley. But the stream was gone – it was now just a bed of dried mud. Thinking of water made me thirsty. I had nothing to eat or drink, but the sky was getting darker and I knew I had to go on. A black cloud of ash was chasing after me. Soon I was covered in it. It was burning my clothes and my hair. When I breathed, the ash filled my mouth and burned my throat. Then something fell on the path in front of me and made me stop. I was sure it was a rock or lava from the volcano. But it was just a bird, and it fell dead at my feet.

The cloud was thicker now, but the black ash had turned white like snow and was turning everything white. It wasn't as frightening as the black cloud because it didn't burn, but it was so thick that I could hardly see or breathe. I tried to concentrate on the trail, but the white ash became so heavy that I couldn't move. I was turning into stone. I was becoming a statue. Then everything went black.

The next thing I remember was a voice.

"She must be dead."

I felt something cold and hard on my face, but it was helping me to breathe. I tried to say Rob's name, but I couldn't.

"Let's get her into the helicopter and get out of here. We won't find anyone else alive."

Then someone spoke to me: "Everything's going to be OK."

1 The story

Look at the text again and write down the main points of the story:

- where and when it takes place
- who the characters are, and who is telling the story
- the main events

Now talk about them in class.

The 1980 eruption of Mount St. Helens Facts & figures

Date: May 18, 1980

Reason: earthquake near the volcano

Height before: 9,677 feet

Height after: 8,363 feet

Size of the crater:
1.2 miles east-west,
1.8 miles north-south,
2,084 feet deep

Ash fall area: 22,000 square miles

Damage: enough wood to build 300,000 small houses, nearly 7,000 big animals, all birds and nearly all small animals, thousands of young fish, 27 bridges, nearly 200 homes, 185 miles of roads, etc.

Deaths: 57

2 Reading between the lines

Writers sometimes give clues about their characters, for example the way they speak or behave.

a) How would you describe Laura, Rob and Marty, and the way they feel at different times? Use the words below and give examples from the story.

afraid • angry • annoyed • annoying • brave • clever • crazy • cruel • gentle • kind • lazy • mischievous • nervous • a show-off • silly • ...?

b) Did Laura do the right thing? What about Rob and Marty? Explain what you would do in Laura's situation.

3 Creative writing

a) Laura meets Marty again twenty years later. Write the dialogue between them.

b) Look at the cartoon and write a story to go with it.

"It's not a bear, sweetie. It's the pizza."

Skills: Saying the right thing

15 1 Reacting

Sometimes there's a standard phrase or a more polite way to say something.
Two tourists from Scotland, Nick and Lucy, are at the Seattle Tourist Information Office.

Nick: Excuse me.
Clerk: Yes, how can I help you?
Nick: We'd like some information about whale watching. Do you have any brochures?
Clerk: Yes, but I'm afraid it's the wrong time of year for whales. Sorry about that.
Nick: Oh, I see. What a pity.
Lucy: Never mind! There are lots of other interesting things to do.
Nick: But I was looking forward to whale watching!
Lucy: I know. I guess we could go to the Space Needle instead.
Nick: What is that, exactly?
Lucy: It's a tower. You can go to the top in an elevator. The view is fantastic.
Nick: That sounds interesting.
Lucy: OK, let's do that.
Clerk: Space Needle. Here it is on the map. It isn't far from here. Would you like tickets?
Lucy: Yes, please. Can we buy them here?
Clerk: Of course you can! That's twenty-five dollars, please. Oh, and the map is free.
Lucy: Hey! Thanks a lot.
Clerk: You're welcome. Have a nice day.

a) How could people react to these sentences? Use expressions from the dialogue.

1. I'm afraid I can't come to your party.
2. Thanks for carrying my bags for me.
3. May I use your cellphone?
4. Here – have a cookie.
5. Why don't we go to Pike Place Market?
6. Excuse me, is this store open?
7. I'm building a boat out of milk cartons.
8. Sorry, I've spilt tea on your foot.
9. The watch I got from you doesn't work.
10. Have you been to the Arboretum yet?

b) Think of three everyday situations. Collect useful phrases for these situations, then write a short dialogue for each one. You could record yourselves.

19 2 Listening: Heard in Seattle

a) Listen to three reactions to each of these questions. Which reaction do you like best?

1. Excuse me, do you have the time, please?
2. Can I look at your map for a moment?

b) You are going to hear some short dialogues. For each one, listen to the first person and say how you would react. Then listen and compare.

3 Taking part in conversations

a) Work with a partner.
Write short dialogues for these situations:

in a restaurant • at a train station • asking the way

b) Act out your dialogues to the class.

1 Words in context: Saying the right thing

Which is the best, or most polite, reaction?

1. Excuse me.
a What do you want?
b How can I help you?
c Yeah?

2. I'm sorry. I can't find your CD anywhere!
a You've lost my CD? How typical!
b I won't give you any of my things again.
c Oh dear. Well, let's look for it together.

3. Thanks for all your help.
a You're welcome.
b Yes, of course.
c Please.

4. I'm afraid there won't be any seaplane flights today. It's too foggy.
a Damn! But we've booked!
b Thanks a lot! And what do you expect us to do all afternoon instead?
c What a pity! We were really looking forward to our flight.

5. If you'd like to go kayaking, I'll drive you down to Lake Washington.
a Yes, I enjoy kayaking.
b Oh, that's nice of you. What a great idea!
c OK, why not?

2 Word power: Find the odd one out

a) There is one 'wrong' word in each group. Put them in the right groups and explain what the words in each group have in common.

Examples: They are all wild animals: bear – …
This comes out of a volcano: smoke – …

1. river • lava • lake • sea
2. avalanche • stream • storm • eruption
3. bear • deer • cougar • whistle
4. jazz • blues • hip-hop • raccoon
5. mouth • trail • lungs • eyes
6. street • path • road • throat
7. smoke • steam • ash • grunge
8. backpack • earthquake • sleeping bag • water bottle

b) Give the noun forms of these verbs and adjectives.

1. to explode
2. natural
3. active
4. safe
5. to erupt
6. dead
7. muddy
8. to react
9. trapped
10. to pronounce

3 At Pike Place Market

Complete the text. Put in a reflexive pronoun, **each other** or nothing.

Dear Diary,
I'm in bed and feeling very sorry for 1. This morning Dad and I were at Pike Place Market and the fishmongers were throwing salmon at 2. That's how they amuse 3, I guess. Then suddenly I noticed a thief who was helping 4 to a woman's handbag. While I was wondering 5 what to do, a huge fish hit me on the head and I fell to the ground. When I picked 6 up, I couldn't remember 7 who or where I was. A fishmonger hurried 8 over to me. "I'm so sorry," he said, "but I tried to hit the thief with the fish and got you instead." "Never mind," I said. "Relax 9, I haven't hurt 10." We shook hands with 11, and I went to look for Dad. I soon found him. He'd caught the thief all by 12, but had got a blow on the head, too! When we got home and saw 13 in the mirror, we had to laugh. But now I can't concentrate 14 any more, so good night, Diary.

4 Mrs Baxter gives her students some advice

a) Make one sentence from two. Use **so that** or **in case**, as in the examples.

1. You'll need to take a map. You might get lost.
   ➜ You'll need to take a map in case you get lost.
2. Of course, you'll need a map anyway. Then you can find the way.
   ➜ Of course, you'll need a map anyway so that you can find the way.
3. You should take a waterproof jacket. It might rain.
4. Please wear warm clothes. You don't want to get cold.
5. Remember to bring a water bottle. You could get thirsty.
6. Always carry a whistle. Maybe there'll be an emergency.
7. We'll need to collect lots of wood. Then we can make a really nice campfire.
8. You may want to phone home. That's why you're allowed to take your cellphones.

b) Put in **to** and a verb.

show climb hear camp buy discuss catch

1. Let's have a meeting … the camping trip.
2. Ceri went shopping … things for the trip.
3. Mount St. Helens isn't easy …
4. I know of a great place …
5. I'm sorry … that you can't come with us.
6. Would you like me … you how … a fish?

c) Complete the questions with **do you want me to …?** or **would you like me to …?** and the verbs.

1. Can I go now, or …
2. Do you know how to make a fire yourself, or …
3. Did you hear what I said, or …
4. Do you know what to pack, or …
5. Can you carry all that gear, or …

show you stay repeat it help you give you a list

5 Mixed bag: A postcard from Ceri

Hi Bronwen,
I'm really **e** 1 myself on this trip. I wasn't looking **f** 2 to the long **h** 3 because I didn't **e** 4 them to be fun. But I don't have any **u** 5 things in my **b** 6, so it isn't too heavy **t** 7 carry. We've **d** 8 lots of ways to amuse **o** 9 around the campfire. From our **c** 10 we can see Mount St. Helens in the **d** 11, a big **v** 12. There was a huge **e** 13 there in 1980 that did a lot of **d** 14 to the area, but there are now trees and **f** 15 again, and the wildlife that had **d** 16 is now coming back.
My hand is better, so I'm **a** 17 to write again. I can even **p** 18 up a tent by **m** 19.
I'm **g** 20 to know Ben better. I'll tell you more when we mail **e** 21 **o** 22 again!
Love, Ceri

Focus on regions of the USA

Amelia Earhart

THE MIDWEST
Where is the Midwest?
Landscape:
Main products:
Another name for the Midwest:
What Midwesterners are like:

KANSAS
Capital:
Where its name comes from:
Climate:
Flower:
Animal: Buffalo
Song: Home on the range
Famous people: Amelia Earhart

The Midwest

New England

NEW ENGLAND
Location: Northeast
States:
Origin of name:

MAINE
Capital:
Biggest city:
Landscape:
Economy/products: lobsters, …
State fish:
State animal: moose
Nickname: Pine Tree State

30

1 Listening: Regions of the USA

a) Three new students in Ceri's class are talking about where they lived before they moved to Seattle. Copy the notes. Listen and look at the map at the front of your book to complete the missing information.

b) Discuss whether these regions would be good places to visit or to live.

c) Jerry and Vicky both ask a question at the end of their talk. Can you find out the answers?

d) Project: Work in a group. Choose one of the regions / states below and prepare a presentation together:

Alaska | Florida | the Rocky Mountains | the Great Lakes

Redwood trees are the biggest in the world. The tallest ones (up to 367 feet or 111 meters) only grow on the west coast of the US. They have existed for about 160 million years (since the age of dinosaurs). They usually live up to 600 years, but some even reach an age of 2,000 years.

16 2 A song: This land is your land

Well, I rode that ribbon[1] highway[2].
I saw above me the endless[3] sky.
I saw below me the golden[4] valley.
This land was made for you and me.

I've roamed[5] and rambled[6] and followed my footsteps
Through the sparkling[7] sands of her diamond[8] deserts[9]
And all around me a voice was calling
This land was made for you and me.

This land is your land,
This land is my land,
From California
To the New York island,
From the Redwood Forest
To the Gulf Stream[10] waters.
This land was made for you and me.

Well the sun came shining and I was strolling[11]
Through wheat fields waving and dust[12] clouds rolling
And a voice was sounding as the fog was lifting[13],
Saying this land was made for you and me.

[1]hier: schnurgerade • [2]Fernstraße • [3]endlos • [4]golden • [5]to roam – umherziehen • [6]to ramble – umherstreifen • [7]glitzernd • [8]Diamant • [9]Wüste • [10]Gulf Stream – Golfstrom • [11]to stroll – schlendern • [12]Staub • [13]to lift – sich heben

Words: Woody Guthrie

a) Use your map to follow the singer on his journey from coast to coast.

Which regions does he travel through? Suggest a route and say what he can see or do in the states he goes through.

Use ideas like these:
His journey begins in California.
There he can see …
Then he goes on to Arizona. It's …
He reaches the east coast in …

⟨b⟩ Get information on Germany. Use a map and imagine a journey from the south to the coast. What can you see or do in the regions you pass through?

⟨c⟩ Work in groups and make a poster of the different regions of Germany or the US with photos and English texts.

unit 6 intro — Sports in the US

c

helmet

d
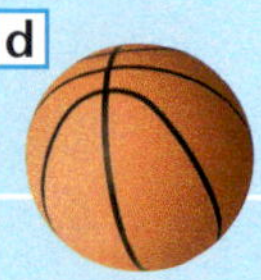

e

golf ball

f

bowling ball

g

1

basketball court

2

baseball field

a

b

h
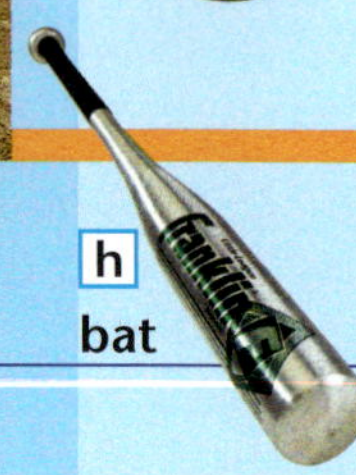
bat

33 1 Listening: Which sport?

Look at the pictures and listen to the sounds on the CD, and say which sports they go with. What can you say about each sport? (Say where you can play it, what you need etc.)

34 2 Listening: In the sports shop

a) Listen to the dialogue. What is the problem? Now imagine you are the father. What do you decide to do? Give reasons.

b) Work with a partner. Make a similar dialogue and act it out.

i

l

3

bowling alley

4

golf course

j

glove

k

club

5

football field

3 My favorite sport

Work with a partner. Tell each other about your favorite sport. Make notes and tell the class about your partner's sport.

4 Just for fun

Referee: I'm sending you off.
Player: What for?
Referee: For the rest of the game.

I played soccer at school until I couldn't see the ball any more.

That's when I became interested in track and field.

I've been working really hard since then.

I'm preparing for my second Olympics at the moment.

I had trained too hard and my body wasn't able to recover.

I forced myself to finish.

I was really disappointed with fifth place.

I've studied to become a teacher of deaf and blind children. That's what I'm going to do when I retire from running.

You may want to look at my website. There you'll find more about me, and you can look up all my results, too.

17 A A top athlete

Marla Runyan is one of the top US track and field athletes. Although she is nearly blind, she takes part in races from 1500 meters to the marathon. After she had given a talk at Gareth's school, Gareth told his mother all about it.

Mom: So how was Marla Runyan's talk, honey?
Gareth: Oh, really interesting, Mom! She told us that she had played soccer at school until she couldn't see the ball any more because of her illness. Isn't that sad?
Mom: How awful!
Gareth: But she said that was when she'd become interested in track and field. She's a great example to other people. She told us that she had been working really hard since then and that she was preparing for her second Olympics at the moment.
Mom: What a success story!
Gareth: But she didn't only talk about the good things. She also described the pain she felt during the Boston Marathon in 2003. She said she had trained too hard and her body hadn't been able to recover. She'd forced herself to finish in spite of terrible muscle problems in her arms and legs. And then she'd been really disappointed with fifth place! Imagine it!
Mom: Wow! Fifth is still really good! But she won this year's Boston Marathon, didn't she? So what else did she tell you?
Gareth: Oh, a lot about herself. She told us that she'd studied to become a teacher of deaf and blind children and that was what she was going to do when she retired from running. And she thought we might want to look at her website. There we would find more about her and we could look up all her results, too. Let's do that now, Mom!

1 Looking at the text

What do you find out about Marla Runyan's life?

2 Looking at language

a) Compare the things Marla Runyan actually said with what Gareth told his mother. What differences in language can you find? Make a list.

b) How do tenses change when you report what somebody said?

grammar

direct speech		indirect speech
I	➜	she
played	➜	had played

3 What did they say?

Use the rules you have written down to report what these people said about Marla Runyan's visit.
Example: Mrs Kershaw said that the talk **had been** a great success.
She added / explained / pointed out that …

Mrs Kershaw, Principal: The talk was a great success. Sports are an important part of the life of the school, so the students will always want to see a well-known sportsman or sportswoman.

Jim Lewinsky, 7th grade: I'm really interested in track and field. That's why I was looking forward to her visit. I wasn't disappointed. I learned a lot from her. One day I want to run a marathon, too.

Cathy Lo, 9th grade: Sports are not my thing, but I actually enjoyed the talk. I think Marla's cool because she can describe her feelings so well. I'm definitely going to look up her website.

35 4 Listening: Messages

When Gareth is alone at home, the telephone keeps ringing. Each time it's for somebody else, so he has to take a message.

a) Read the first call and think what Gareth's message would be. (Start: "Ed Walters called, Dad. He said …") Then listen and compare the call with Gareth's message.

Gareth: Hello.
Caller: Hello. Can I speak to Evan Morgan please?
Gareth: My dad? Sorry, I'm afraid he's out. Can I take a message?
Caller: Yes, please. This is Ed Walters. Evan and I arranged to play golf today. Evan is going to pick me up. Can you tell him I won't be ready by four? I'll be an hour late, OK?
Gareth: OK, Mr Walters. I'll tell him.

b) Now listen to two more calls and make notes. Play Gareth's part. What messages do you pass on?

5 A postcard from Uncle Frank

Help Gareth to tell Ceri what Uncle Frank wrote. (She's too busy to read the card herself.) Use indirect speech.

Start: "He wrote that he'd arrived in Bermuda …" Change the tenses and pronouns where necessary. Choose the words in the box instead of the words in **blue**. Why do these have to be changed, too?

Hi everybody,
I arrived in Bermuda **yesterday** and I'm really enjoying myself **here**. They had some rain **last week**, but it's hot and sunny **today** so I'm glad that I **brought** a good sunhat. I spent **this** morning on the golf course and I've already played two hours of tennis **this** afternoon! That's why I'm going to relax **tomorrow**. A day on the beach would be just the thing. You guys should **come here** for a vacation sometime. You'll love it!
See you,
Frank

• there (2x) • that day • go • that (2x) • had taken • the week before • the day before • the next day

G16–18

B Cheerleaders

Ceri is talking to her friend Angela Spencer on her cellphone.

Ceri: Hi Angie! **How's it going?**

Angela: Oh, not too good, Ceri.

Ceri: Why, **what's the problem?**

Angela: It's Ms Snyder, our cheerleading coach. She told me to get my act together. She said if I didn't, I might find myself off the team!

Ceri: **Did she really say that?** That's awful! But don't forget, you were late for last week's football game. She just wants all her cheerleaders to arrive on time. What's wrong with that?

Angela: OK, OK, that was really dumb of me. But then she wanted to know why I hadn't concentrated on the game. It wasn't my fault that I got a call on my cellphone and missed the half-time cheer.

Ceri: Oh, come on, Angie! What do you expect? Cheerleaders can't stand around and talk all the time.

Angela: I guess you're right. But Ms Snyder asked me in front of all the others whether I really wanted to be a cheerleader. Of course I do! Some girls would give anything to be in my place. Anyway, I didn't want her to kick me off the team. So I said I was sorry and I asked if I could have one more chance.

Ceri: And what did she say?

Angela: She said I could – Saturday's basketball game.

Ceri: Well, don't ruin it, OK?

Angela: Of course I won't! My brother Bobby's on the team. He told me it was going to be a really important game and everybody should come. He more or less ordered all his friends to be there! But I don't have to tell you, Ceri – you're going to come anyway. You're Dave Mitchell's biggest fan, right?

Ceri: What do you mean? I think he's a really good team captain. That's all.

Angela: Oh, yeah?

1 Expectations

a) Look at the text and find …

1. what Ms Snyder told Angela.

→ She told her to get her act together.

2. what Ms Snyder wanted to know from her.
3. what Angela asked Ms Snyder.
4. what Bobby told his sister.
5. what he told his friends.

b) Compare the sentences below with the questions in the text in **blue**. Work out rules for indirect questions with or without question words. Then say what else Ceri asked Angela.

1. Ceri asked Angela how it was going.
2. She asked what the problem was.
3. She wanted to know if Ms Snyder had really said that.

c) What should a good cheerleader be like?

d) Can you imagine why it is so important for high school girls to be on their school's cheerleader team?

2 Indirect questions

Put these questions into indirect speech. Start: Ceri asked when …

1. *Ceri:* When do the cheerleaders practice?
2. *Angie:* What can I do to stay on the team?
3. *Bobby (to Gareth):* Are you and your friends going to watch the game?
4. *Gareth:* Is it an important game?
5. *Ceri:* Should I wish Dave good luck?
6. *Angie (to Ceri):* Are you Dave's biggest fan?
7. *Bobby:* How can we win the game?
8. *Angie:* Bobby, do you want everyone to come and cheer for you?

3 What the coach told them

How do you make indirect commands?
Put these examples into indirect speech.

1. Come to our practices on time.
➜ She told the cheerleaders to come to their practices on time.
2. Please bring your uniforms and pompoms.
3. Don't be late!
4. You should practice your cheers at home.
5. Don't leave the group during the game.
6. Watch the game carefully.
7. Don't miss the half-time cheer.
8. Always keep a smile on your face!

4 Useful verbs

If you want to report what someone said, you might not want to use "say" all the time. You can use these verbs. Complete the grid with more verbs you already know.

statement	question	command
to point out	to ask	to want
to explain	…	to tell
to report	…	…

5 An interview

Angela's little sister Bessy interviews her about the cheerleading team.

Bessy: Please sit down. I want to ask you some questions about cheerleading.
Angela: Yes, I'm looking forward to the interview.
Bessy: How long have you been a cheerleader?
Angela: I've been on the team since January.
Bessy: What do you cheerleaders do?
Angela: Well, we do everything to help our team during a match.
Bessy: How do you do that?
Angela: We shout and cheer and dance and jump in the air. Or we make a big V with our arms.
Bessy: What does that mean?
Angela: Don't you know? V is for victory.
Bessy: I see. How do you stay fit?
Angela: I play sports and I try to eat healthy food mainly. I drink a lot of water because it's good for my voice. It has to be loud, you know.
Bessy: What is the most important thing for a cheerleader?
Angela: You should keep smiling!
Bessy: Thanks for the interview. I think this will be very interesting for anyone in my class who wants to become a cheerleader.

a) After Bessy has recorded the interview, she listens to it and thinks about everything that happened: First I asked Angela to sit down. Then I said that I wanted to ask her some questions … Go on.

b) Now she has to write a report of the interview for homework. Of course she doesn't write down everything that was said. Can you help her? Think of a title and give the basic ideas.

G19–21

19 The big game

Saturday was *it* – the big game. Ballard against Franklin High. Just a basketball game between two schools. To anyone else nothing special, but to me it meant everything. The last game of the season, against our biggest rivals. Franklin High had beaten us earlier in the year so we were eager for revenge. And I was the captain of our team. I really wanted to finish the season well.

"Good news for you, Dave," said our coach on Friday afternoon when I arrived at the gym for training.

"Oh, yeah?" I replied. I tried not to seem too excited. "So they kicked Marvin Grimson off the team?"

Our coach laughed and shook his head. Grimson was Franklin High's star player. He was a really big guy and their top scorer. And very mean as well. If he didn't play, we would definitely have a better chance.

"No, but I hear that scouts from Washington State are going to be at tomorrow's game," our coach said. "And they've got their eye on you, Dave!" And on Marvin Grimson, I thought bitterly.

"I don't know about college, Coach," I said. "I just want to win this game."

Actually I wanted to play college basketball more than anything else in the world. But I knew how much money you needed to go to college. Dad had had an accident at work and was in a wheelchair, while Mom worked as a cleaner. We had enough to live on, but no more. And nobody in our family had ever been to college.

"Look, Dave," he went on. "It's OK, I know the story. But if you play well on Saturday, those scouts could send you to college on a scholarship. I hear that they have one position to fill."

■ Saturday finally arrived and the gym was full of noise and color. The fans of both teams filled the seats and cheerleaders marched up and down the court. Our coach gave us the best pep talk I'd ever heard and we were really motivated when the game started. But we were probably trying too hard. Or we were too nervous. I don't know what it was, but we had a terrible start. A few early mistakes gave Marvin Grimson two easy baskets, while our guys missed three or four shots from right under the hoop. Before we knew it, we were ten points behind.

After that both sides scored freely. The score went from 0-10 to 48-58, but all the time we stayed ten points behind Franklin High. Grimson was scoring most of their points, and their fans were shouting out his name, while I was having a quiet game. Then I had a bit of luck with a long throw and we were

now only seven points behind. 51-58.

"Come on, guys," I shouted to my team-mates. "It's not over yet!"

But I now found myself in a new situation. The Franklin High coach had told Grimson to stay with me and he was doing his best to make things difficult for me. Wherever I went, there he was, with his long arms and legs, his spiky blond hair and his cold blue eyes. He held me and pushed me and the referee let it happen. One time we both jumped for the ball and I felt a blow to my head. I landed hard on the floor and everything went black.

■ "Are you OK, Dave?" said a voice. I opened my eyes. I was still lying on the floor and our coach was standing over me. I could hear that the game had stopped. When I touched my head, there was blood on my hand.

"He did that on purpose!" our coach said angrily. "It looks bad, Dave. You'll have to come off." He and one of my team-mates helped me off the court.

"Hmm," said our coach when he had looked at my head again. "We can send on somebody else. Maybe you should lie down a bit."

"No way, Coach!" I cried. "Put a bandage on it – I'm captain and I'm going back out there!"

When I got back into the game, I had a bandage above my left eye. There were two minutes left and we were four points behind at 60-64. Then Grimson held me when I was trying to jump for the ball. It was a crazy thing to do because we were right in front of the referee. This time he had to blow his whistle! Suddenly it was quiet in the gym.

As I waited to shoot the two free throws, I told myself not to get nervous: "Relax! You can do it with your eyes shut. You've done it a thousand times in practice."

My knees were shaking, but I took a deep breath and – plop! – the ball disappeared through the hoop. Plop! The same again.

■ Our fans cheered loudly. 62-64! We were two points behind with twenty seconds left, but Franklin High had the ball. They began to pass it around to give us no chance to get it back. But suddenly they made a mistake and we had the ball again. We got it down the court fast and Bobby stopped near the hoop and got ready to shoot.

"Go on, Bobby!" I cried. Two points for a tie. But Bobby paused and then turned back, saw me over behind the three-point line and threw me a long pass. "Oh, no!" I thought. "He won't take two points for a tie. He wants three to win." On the clock there were four seconds to go. The orange ball felt heavy in my right hand. As Grimson came at me, I jumped up and pushed the ball towards the hoop. I watched as it flew through the air. It seemed to stay there for ages. Then it came down, rolled twice around the hoop and dropped off the side. The game was over. The Franklin High fans cheered. We had lost again.

With my head down I walked off the court. I didn't know what to say to my team-mates, I was so disappointed. To make things worse, Marvin Grimson was jogging around the gym with his arms in the air and waving at the crowd. I felt sick. That was it! I didn't want to play basketball ever again.

But you learn how to lose. That game was last year. This year I'm in college and I'm really enjoying my new basketball team. Yes, I got to college! Believe it or not, they gave the scholarship to me. They didn't give it to Grimson, although his team won and he scored more points than I did! Our coach said it wasn't just a question of skill, but of character, too. He said they were looking for team players. I don't know. I guess they saw things in Grimson that they didn't like. Well, I certainly did.

1 Words in context: What it means

Look at what the characters said. Decide what it means in the context and say why you think so. Sometimes more than one answer is possible.

1. "And they've got their eye on you, Dave!"
A They are going to watch you carefully.
B Be careful. They don't like you.
C You've got a chance to win a college scholarship.

2. "So they kicked Marvin Grimson off the team?"
A Is Marvin Grimson not allowed to play?
B It would be much easier to win if Marvin Grimson didn't play.
C So Marvin Grimson is going to play?

3. "Look, Dave. It's OK, I know the story."
A I can tell you a story about someone who has been in a similar situation.
B I know what you mean.
C I know what the problem is.

4. "I hear that they have one position to fill."
A I know that they are looking for someone.
B They want to give you a scholarship.
C One person is missing from their team.

5. "It's not over yet!"
A I hope it will be over soon.
B We mustn't give up.
C We still have a chance to win.

6. "He did that on purpose!"
A It wasn't an accident.
B He should be punished.
C It's your fault.

7. "I'm captain and I'm going back out there!"
A I don't feel well, but I'm going to go on.
B I must be a good example to the others.
C I'm the boss. You can't tell me what to do.

8. "Relax. You can do it with your eyes shut."
A You'd better close your eyes.
B It can't go wrong.
C You can't see well with the bandage above your eye.

9. "Go on, Bobby!"
A Run away!
B Give me the ball!
C Go for the hoop!

2 The story

a) The game: What is special about it?

b) Dave: What are Dave's feelings before, during and after the game?

c) The ending: What are the reasons for the scouts' decision? Do you agree with them?

d) Write a dialogue between the scouts and Dave after the game.

or

e) Write a dialogue between Marvin and his coach after the game.

3 Word power: Word families

What other words from the same word family do you know?
Examples: sport – sportswoman, guitar – guitarist, to score – scorer, different – difference etc.

1. to study
2. to cheer
3. to expect
4. to decide
5. to react
6. to explode
7. to clean
8. to pass
9. to act
10. to live
11. to build
12. dark
13. family
14. culture
15. element
16. to express
17. foot
18. head
19. to help
20. home
21. wild
22. to pack
23. real
24. to serve

Skills: Creative writing

This song may make you remember one very special day in your own life, or it may make you think about your general idea of a perfect day, or a person you want to spend a day with. If you want to write about one of these topics, steps 2–5 are important.

23 1 A song: Perfect day (Lou Reed)

Just a perfect day,
Drink sangria[1] in the park,
And then later, when it gets dark,
We go home.
Just a perfect day,
Feed animals in the zoo
Then later, a movie, too,
And then home.

Oh it's such a perfect day,
I'm glad[2] I spent it with you.
Oh such a perfect day,
You just keep me hanging on[3],
You just keep me hanging on.

Just a perfect day,
Problems all left alone[4],
Weekenders on our own.
It's such fun.
Just a perfect day,
You made me forget myself.
I thought I was someone else,
Someone good.

You're going to reap[5] just what you sow[6].
You're going to reap just what you sow …

Words: Lou A. Reed

[1]Getränk • [2]froh • [3]to hang on – dranbleiben • [4]beiseite • [5]to reap – ernten • [6]to sow – säen

a) What idea of a perfect day does the singer have? Use your own words.

b) How does the singer change during the perfect day? Say why.

c) Explain the meaning of the sentence: You're going to reap just what you sow.

2 What do you know about the topic?

Collect ideas and vocabulary that are connected with the topic.

You can make a simple list or try to organize your thoughts while you write them down, for example in a grid or a mind map. Your mind map could look like this:

3 What kind of text are you going to write?

There are three main points you have to think about before you start:	This could be your decision:
1. What is the main purpose of the text? A story should be interesting. It can also be exciting or funny. What about a newspaper article? A comment? A poem? A text for a diary? A letter? A dialogue? An advertisement?	You want to write a story which concentrates on one event, like a football game. Everyone expects one team to win easily, but then something happens …
2. Who do you expect to read it? A diary is usually for yourself. What about other kinds of text?	Your story is for your classmates. They know the same things as you, they know the same words, and they can understand your feelings. You don't want to just give them information, you want them to enjoy your story.
3. How are you going to write it? When you have decided what kind of text you want to write, you can think about things like perspective and style (words, tenses, direct speech etc.).	You write in the past tense about something that is over. You use the first person ("I") because it is easier for people to understand your feelings from your perspective.

4 How do you build up your text?

Think of:

1. a good **title**,
2. an **introduction** that makes your readers want to read on,
3. a **main part** with everything that is important,
4. a **conclusion**.

t e x t

Examples:

Title: A perfect day?

Introduction: The day seemed perfect. The sun was shining, but nobody really noticed it because we were all too excited before the big game. It meant everything to us …

Conclusion: Nobody had expected that to happen. In fact it wasn't a perfect day, really. When everyone had recovered from the shock, we realized how lucky we had been.

5 Now write your own text

a) Work with a partner. Collect ideas together. Then each of you chooses a different kind of text about a perfect day. Try to make your text typical of its kind. Read each other's texts, compare them and say what you think about them.

b) Here are some more ideas for creative writing with a partner:

1. A thief has been caught by store detectives. Partner A writes a **story** from the perspective of the thief. Partner B writes a **newspaper article** about what happened.
2. Partner A is a house. Partner B is a window in the house. Write **letters** to each other.
3. Write a text that goes with the picture below. Then compare your texts.

1 What did they actually say?

There may be more than one answer.

1. Ms Snyder expected them to arrive on time.
→ *Ms Snyder:* You should arrive on time. I want / expect you to arrive on time.
2. She wanted to know why Angela had missed the half-time cheer.
3. She said that Angela should get her act together or she might find herself off the team.
4. The coach ordered Bobby to get back into the game.
5. Angela's mom didn't want her to go to the game in that dress.
6. The referee warned Marvin not to do it again, otherwise he'd send him off.

2 Reporting what they said

After the game, the coach talked to Bobby and Dave. Report what they said to each other.

Coach: Why didn't you go for the two points, Bobby? → The coach asked Bobby why ...
Bobby: I'm sorry, Coach. I didn't want a tie. I wanted to beat them.
Dave: Don't be too hard on Bobby, Coach. It's not his fault. My throw didn't go in. That's why we lost.
Coach: OK, but don't worry, Dave. Anyone can miss a long shot like that!
Dave: Yeah, but I'm still really disappointed. Actually, I've had enough. I don't want to play basketball ever again.
Coach: But Dave – you should think hard before you make that kind of decision.
Bobby: I agree with the coach, Dave.
Coach: Apart from that shot you had a good game. The scouts saw that, too. I'm sure you'll get that scholarship.

3 Word power: Explain the difference

Look at the cartoon and say what differences there are between football in the USA and football in the UK.

[1]['tɔːnəmənt] – Turnier

4 Mixed bag: An exciting game

Complete this part of an e-mail. Then say who it is from and who it is to. How did you find out?

I must tell you **a** 1 the exciting game we had on Saturday – our basketball team **a** 2 Franklin High, our big **r** 3. They'd **b** 4 us earlier in the **s** 5, so we wanted **r** 6. Did I **m** 7 my friend Angela before? Well, she's a **c** 8 and her **c** 9 had told her to get her **a** 10 together **o** 11 she'd be **k** 12 off the team. Cheerleading is really **i** 13 over here, so you can **i** 14 how **h** 15 she tried this time. In **f** 16, all the girls were great, and when the game **s** 17, our team was really **m** 18. But I guess our **e** 19 were too high, because soon we were ten points **b** 20. Then Dave, our **c** 21, was knocked over **b** 22 one of their players. I'm **s** 23 the guy did it on **p** 24. Dave was hurt, but he came back onto the **c** 25 and played well in **s** 26 of the **b** 27 over his eye. Then, when the **s** 28 was 62-64 with only four **s** 29 to go, he tried a long **t** 30 for three points to win the game! The ball rolled around the hoop but **d** 31 go in! It was **a** 32! Now I know how you feel when Wales **l** 33 at rugby!

3 revision Books 1+2

Modern times

Making predictions about the future has always been difficult. Some of the most famous inventions of the last 200 years were regarded as unimportant initially. Here are some of the most astonishing examples.
In 1894 Lord Kelvin predicted that radio had no future. The first radio factory was opened 5 years later, and today there are more than a billion[1] radio sets in the world, tuned to more than 33,000 radio stations.
In the early 20th century a small world market for automobiles was predicted because "the world will run out of chauffeurs." Today more than 70 million motorcars are produced every year.
Even the telephone received little appreciation during the first 15 years or so after its appearance in 1875. In the British parliament it was said that there was no need for telephones because "we have enough messengers here." Today a world without telephones would be unimaginable.
In 1943 Thomas Watson, the head of IBM, prophesied a world market for "maybe only five computers." Since then, of course, computers have revolutionized our lives.
The head of the US Patent Office topped it all in 1899 when he declared: "Everything that can be invented has already been invented."

[1] ['bɪliən] – Milliarde

1 Dealing with new words

a) Read the text and collect all the new words in a grid. Try to guess the German meaning of each word, and note what helped you. Use a dictionary to check your list when you have finished all the parts of this exercise.

English	German	word family	German / French / …	context
invention	Erfindung	to invent	–	–
to regard	betrachten	–	French	✗

b) Words sometimes have more than one meaning. Which is correct in this context?

1. set (line 9): Satz? Garnitur? Reihe? Gerät? Bühnenbild?
2. to tune (l. 9): stimmen? einstellen? tunen?
3. appreciation (l. 17): Einschätzung? Verständnis? Anerkennung? Wertzuwachs?

Now look up **run out of** (l. 13) and **need** (l. 19) and decide which is the correct meaning here. What other meanings do these words have?

c) Explain in English what these words mean – with a definition, or with words / phrases of similar meaning:

1. initially (l. 4)
2. astonishing (l. 5)
3. automobile (l. 12)
4. chauffeur (l. 13)
5. to receive (l. 16)
6. to revolutionize (l. 26)

d) Look at the words you wrote under 'word family' in a) and think of more words in these word families. Then use your dictionary to find more words which are related[1] to **to produce** and **unimaginable**.

[1] [rɪ'leɪtɪd] – verwandt

2 Understanding and talking about the text

Make a list of the inventions that are mentioned in the text. Try to imagine what life today would be like without them.

Test yourself!

3 Telephones

Complete the sentences – with adjectives or adverbs. Sometimes you will need comparative or superlative forms (+). Write down your answers, then turn to page 195 to check them.

1. The telephone was one of the **(important+)** inventions ever. It's **(hard)** to believe that so many people thought it would never be **(useful)**.
2. "My phone's making a **(terrible)** noise! There's something **(wrong)** with it, I think – so I can't hear you very **(good)**. Can you speak **(clear+)**, please? OK, it's **(good+)** now!"
3. "I talk to my friends **(regular)** on the phone. But if I call someone's mobile number, it's **(good+)** not to have a **(long)** conversation, because it's much **(expensive+)** than a **(normal)** phone."
4. "I'm never without my mobile for **(long+)** than a few minutes. I wouldn't feel **(safe)** without it!"

4 Add the adverbs

Find the best place for the adverbs and adverbials in these sentences. Then turn to page 195 to check your answers.

1. I switch the radio on when I get up. **(usually / in the morning)**
2. Do you listen to music? **(often / in the car)**
3. Sally bought a new CD. **(yesterday / at Martins Media)**
4. Tim plays the piano. He practises, of course. **(well / regularly)**
5. Did you watch that programme? **(last night / on TV)**
6. The best films are on TV. **(always / late at night)**

5 A long way home

Put in the correct verb forms: Present or past tense (simple / progressive)? Present perfect? Will? Going to? Write down your answers, then turn to page 195 to check them.

Last summer a British family (1 **enjoy**) a holiday in France when their car suddenly (2 **break down**[1]). They (3 **not be able to**) get the spare part[2] they (4 **need**), so they (5 **have to**) leave the car where it (6 **be**) – in a small French village. They (7 **not speak**) French – so they (8 **feel**) very pleased when they (9 **meet**) another Briton – called Tom. "We (10 **not know**) what to do!" they (11 **tell**) Tom. "Our holiday here (12 **be**) over tomorrow, but now our car (13 **break down**). If we (14 **not get**) to Boulogne in time, we (15 **miss**) the boat back to England! The children (16 **be**) in trouble if they (17 **miss**) the first day back at school. And our bosses (18 **be**) angry if we (19 **not appear**) at work!" Tom (20 **offer**) to help them. "I (21 **take**) you to Paris in my car! I'm sure we (22 **get**) there in a few hours. Then you (23 **be able to**) take the train to Boulogne!" – "But we (24 **not want**) you to change your plans," they (25 **protest**). "No problem!" he (26 **laugh**). "I (27 **spend**) a week in Paris anyway." So Tom (28 **take**) them to Paris. When they (29 **get**) to a big station, he (30 **go**) to the ticket office with them. Then he (31 **ask**) a guard[3] – in French! – for the right platform to Boulogne. The train (32 **wait**) at the platform when they (33 **arrive**). What luck! "Thanks!" they (34 **cry**). "We (35 **never forget**) the help you (36 **give**) us today!" The train (37 **just leave**) the station when Tom (38 **notice**) the departure board: the British family (39 **be**) now on their way to Bologna – a town in Italy!

[1][ˌbreɪk ˈdaʊn] – eine Panne haben • [2][ˌspeə ˈpɑːt] – Ersatzteil • [3][gɑːd] – Schaffner

6 Hiking and camping

Try to express ideas differently – with the help of infinitives.

1. I need your help with my tent!
   ➜ I'd like …
2. We must drink lots of water on the hike.
   ➜ It's important …
3. Have you brought your waterproof jacket?
   ➜ Did you remember … ?
4. How should I clean this fish?
   ➜ I've no idea …
5. I'm not going to collect firewood!
   ➜ Don't expect …
6. You can easily call for help if you've got a whistle. ➜ Use a whistle …
7. Don't leave food near your tent.
   ➜ It's best …
8. What do we do if a bear comes?
   ➜ We don't know …
9. Should I put the food in foil first?
   ➜ Do you want … ?
10. I can't decide about my camera.
    ➜ I'm still wondering …

7 Disappointed!

People sometimes promise something – and later change their minds …
How would you react to these annoying situations? Tell people how you feel – and use indirect speech to explain the reasons.

1. *Dad:* We're going to have a great vacation this year. I've been to a travel agent's, and I'm wondering about a trip to Florida. I found a hotel in one of their brochures which really isn't expensive.
(*Later:* Sorry, all of you, but I don't think we can manage a vacation this year …)

Example: But Dad! You can't be serious! **You said we were** going to have a great vacation this year. **You told us …**

2. *Friend:* I definitely want to see the Yankees on Saturday. My mom'll take us in the car – I've already asked her. It's not too late to get tickets. Sue can come, too, if she likes. Will you ask her?
(*Later:* Sorry, I can't come at the weekend. My mom'll be away, and it's too late to get tickets now anyway …)

3. *English teacher:* Right.You've all worked really hard today. Next time we won't do any grammar! I'll bring my guitar and we'll sing English songs instead.
(*Next time:* In today's lesson I want to see if you really understand indirect speech. …)

4. *Shop assistant:* Oh yes, we'll be able to order the Big Slugger bat for you. Don't worry. It may take a few days, that's all. Come in again at the end of next week, and we'll have it for you, OK?
(*Later:* Sorry about the baseball bat, but the Big Slugger is no longer available[1]. …)

[1] [ə'veɪləbl] – erhältlich, lieferbar

I can't believe it! • You can't be serious! • But why? • I feel so disappointed! • Do you really mean it? • Oh no!

8 Words in context: Replying politely

How would you reply?

1. Are there any more cookies?
2. Thanks for the advice!
3. Oh, hello! How are you?
4. I'm afraid there isn't enough snow for skiing just now.
5. Would you like some more mushrooms?
6. Have a chocolate!
7. May I borrow your pen?
8. Sorry, I've lost your magazine.
9. You can borrow my backpack if you like.
10. The coffee you gave me wasn't very hot.

Thanks a lot!
You're welcome!
What a pity!
Never mind!
I'm afraid not.
Yes, please!
Sorry about that.
That's nice of you!
Yes, of course.
Fine, thanks.

9 Mixed bag: Marty's memories

Complete the text. Be careful! Sometimes there is nothing missing.

1 course I remember 2 the day it happened 3 as clearly as if 4 was yesterday.
Rob 5 looking 6 forward 7 the views of 8 St. Helens so he could 9 pictures.
Laura and I just wanted 10 enjoy 11 in the forest, and we wondered 12 if we 13 see any bears or cougars or other 14 on the 15.
We saw lots! They 16 all heading 17 north, and we couldn't imagine 18 why they 19 behaving 20 so strangely. They had 21 the earthquake before we did!
When it came, Rob and Laura looked at 22 in amazement. I could see Laura felt 23 scared, but I didn't realize 24 it 25 serious 26 first.
I was 27 a stupid wild dance and generally amusing 28.
When the explosion came, the situation suddenly changed 29. I looked 30 Rob, and saw he was still 31 photos. I 32 believe it!
I shouted, but he turned 33 away from me.
Then I started 34 run back 35 the trail.
I didn't know it 36 the time, but the truth was, Rob and I 37 never see 38 again.
I hurried 39 away as 40 as I could. Laura wasn't with me, I was all by 41. Soon the ash was 42 thick that I couldn't 43 the trail any more. Now I had no idea 44 way to go. 45 the end, I couldn't even move 46 any more …
When we 47 rescued, Laura and I were 48 to different hospitals, so we didn't see 49 until some time later. When we finally met 50 again, we had so much to tell 51. We were the lucky 52; fifty-seven people 53 died in the disaster – and 54 of them was Rob.

10 Word power: What goes together?

Which of the words or phrases on the right go together with the verbs on the left?

1. to boil — a car • an egg • grass • a taco • a steak
2. to recover — from hard work • a trick • to France • at work
3. to discover — from a shock • an old friend • at home • a secret
4. to reach — a hand • with a train • an argument • the station • a dessert

Focus on the small screen

1 TV commercials

Of all the media TV plays the biggest role in most people's lives, and with satellite and cable TV there are a huge number of channels to choose from. These days most TV is paid for by the commercials that are shown every 15 or 20 minutes. Often these commercial breaks interrupt movies, quiz shows or other programs at a particularly exciting point.

a) What do you think of TV commercials?

b) Do you ever want to buy something because you have seen it on TV?

2 Reacting to the texts

a) Look at the photos. Which of these TV programs would you want to watch? Say why or why not.

b) Now read the texts and compare the three kinds of program. (When are they shown? What do they show? Who are they aimed at? etc.)

c) Try to explain what these TV words mean: 1. commercial break; 2. video clip; 3. sitcom; 4. prime-time audience; 5. viewer.

Since MTV (Music TeleVision) was first shown in the US in 1981, it has become more and more popular. Now the 24-hour music channel is watched in more than 406 million homes in 164 countries and is presented in 18 different languages. The programs are aimed at a young audience. Music is the main focus, of course, with video clips of the latest hits, but there are also news stories about media events and lots of competitions with exciting prizes. Some lucky viewers have even won the chance to meet their favorite stars.

d) Imagine you and a partner run a fashion company. You want to put a new commercial for jeans on TV. Look at the diagram below and decide together which of the possibilities you would choose. Compare your decisions in class.

Channel	MTV	Family Channel	CNN	ABC
Program	Top twenty show	Tom & Jerry	Business news	Who wants to be a millionaire?
Time	SAT 10.25 am	MON 5.10 pm	TUE 6.40 am	THUR 8.20 pm
Cost	$20,000	$8,000	$10,000	$50,000

38 3 Listening: A new reality show

a) First look at the notice on the right. Would you like your family to take part in this reality show? Why or why not?

b) Now listen to the Morgans. Take notes while you listen.
1. What other information do you learn about the show?
2. Explain why each person wants or doesn't want to be on the show.

c) Why are reality shows popular? What do you think of them?

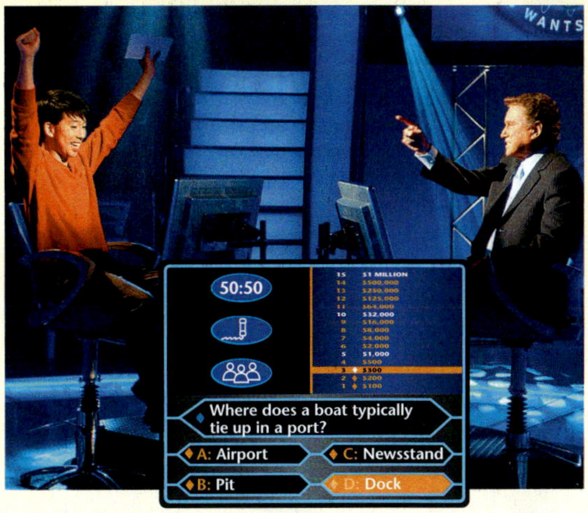

Sitcoms (situation comedies) have always been a big part of TV entertainment. They show funny stories about a group of characters and each episode is usually complete in itself. Although most sitcoms are filmed with actors, one of the most popular shows is the cartoon series *The Simpsons,* about Homer and Marge Simpson and their children Bart, Lisa and Maggie. The series makes fun of different aspects of American life and manages to be attractive to children and adults.

Quiz shows are popular with TV companies because they are cheap to produce and can attract huge audiences, so the costs are easily paid for by the very expensive prime-time commercials. In *Who wants to be a millionaire?* it's exciting to watch as the contestants try to take the fifteen steps that will lead to the million-dollar prize. (Will they take risks? How much help will they get?) As the first few questions are relatively simple, most viewers believe that they, too, could play the game and win a lot of money.

4 Talking about TV

a) Explain the idea behind the cartoon.

b) Work in groups and do a class survey about TV.

1. First decide what you want to find out (how much TV you all watch; what channels or programs you like best; how many of you have your own TV etc.). Then prepare a questionnaire.

2. Compare your questionnaires in class. Choose the best questions to make a final version. Give copies of it to everyone to fill in.

3. Collect and organize the information from the answers. Then present the results in class.

ARD	game show
ZDF	quiz show
RTL	cartoon
SAT 1	documentary
PRO 7	sitcom
...?	movie
	...?

extra line

A Jimmy's travel diary (after Unit 2)

We've come to pick up the campervan from the Cliftons. Mum and Dad aren't too happy about it, but it's comfortable enough for me!

This is my room. I always leave things until the last minute. How can I get everything into one suitcase?

We're getting ready to leave. Mum has just found a dead mouse in one of the beds.

Off we go! Mum is driving and Dad is reading the map. We go round and round for an hour before we leave London.

We've stopped at this motorway café for a sandwich. A typical English castle.

All the campsites are full. It's raining cats and dogs. Our campervan hasn't got a toilet. Help!

We've decided to camp in this wood. Let's hope nobody sees us. Water is coming into the van. Dad is trying to find the hole. Mum is going crazy inside.

Dad has mended the hole, but we can't make tea because there aren't any matches. Dad is rubbing sticks together to start a fire and imagining he's an American pioneer like Daniel Boone. The rain has stopped – but too late for the sleeping bags.

Dad's famous last words before he gets on: "Maybe I shouldn't eat a third hot dog after all!"

Cycling and walking in the Yorkshire Dales: My bike has got a flat tyre AGAIN! All this healthy activity is a bit too much for Dad.

This is one of Dad's famous 'short-cuts'. I've never seen so many sheep – but where's the sheepdog?

Snowdonia: A 'traditional English breakfast' – in a Welsh B&B! Fried bacon, fried eggs, fried sausages, fried tomatoes and fried bread. Mum calls it a 'heart attack on a plate'.

One whole week without photos – no film in the camera!

The Bradens' new house in Penryn. The campervan has broken down again, but they've invited us to stay with them as long as we like!!! So Mum gets her 'hotel', Dad is having a nice rest, and Liz and Liam have lent me their tent. We go swimming and surfing every day, so it's a perfect holiday!

1 As fast as you can

Work in pairs. Read the texts and see how fast you can find:

five animals | six things to eat | four places to sleep | four hobbies

2 Good or bad?

a) Look at the pictures and say who says what, and when.

b) Think of things they can say for the other pictures.

1. This is just like the Wild West!
2. Look what I've just found.
3. This isn't my idea of a relaxing holiday.
4. Maybe it isn't healthy, but it's good!
5. I can't wait much longer!
6. Go left. No! Go right!

3 Creative writing

Write about a funny, fantastic or terrible holiday. It can be a true story, a fantasy story, or a bit of both. Add photos or draw pictures to go with the text if you want.

B Poetry page (after Unit 3)

Acrostic poems

You can make acrostic poems with names or other words.
Each line may contain one or more words. Here are some examples:

Always
Nice
Never
Annoyed

Blue
Eyes –
Nice

Shiny
Weapon
Or
Royal
Disaster

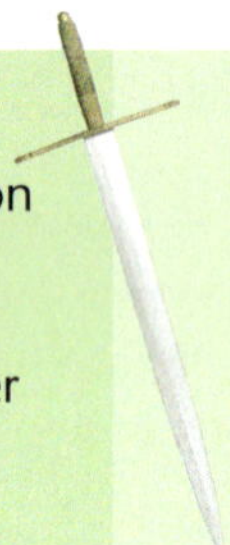

Game
Over
All's
Lost

Sun
Now
On
White

So many
Teachers
All
Feeling
Fantastic

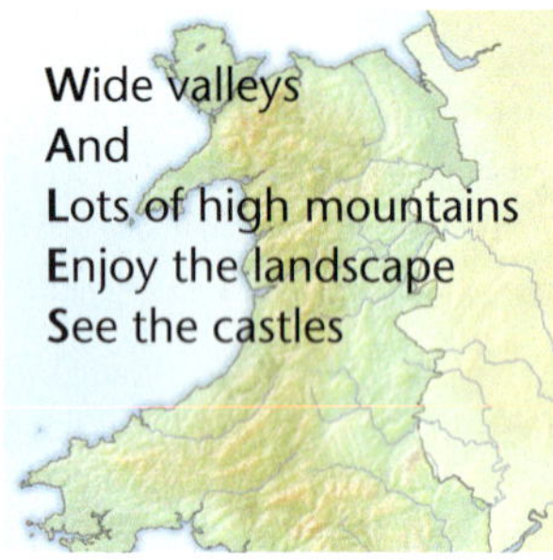

Wide valleys
And
Lots of high mountains
Enjoy the landscape
See the castles

Fried eggs are nice
Omelettes, too
Or what's your favourite
Dish?

Every day
New words
Get the gist
Listen and find out
It's not easy
Sound practice
Helps me to learn

a) Can you make your own acrostic poems? You can use your dictionary if it's hard for you to find the right words. Try to complete these first:

Laughing
In the sun
F ...
E ...

People
Are dancing
R...
T...
Y...

When snow falls
In the
Night
T...
E...
R...

b) Here is another suggestion for creative work with words. Collect words in a special alphabet, for example a holiday alphabet.
Try to find a word for each letter of the alphabet (Never mind letters like 'X'!).

Adventure
Bed and Breakfast
Camping
Drink
Eat
Fun
G...
...

C Communication: Sign systems (after Unit 4)

People communicate to share information and experiences. Forms of communication are for example speaking, writing and gestures. When we speak, meaning is transported by sounds, which form words and sentences. Spoken language is represented by written language in different ways. While in German one sign (letter) or a combination of signs stands for one sound, in Chinese, however, one sign can represent a whole word or idea. There are sign languages which use gestures instead of sound and are usually developed in deaf communities. But there are also sign languages which are used by people who can hear, for example by some native American tribes who do not speak the same language, or in situations where people have to be quiet or where they can't hear each other because there is a loud noise.
Before devices like mobile phones existed, sign systems like the morse code or an alphabet that used flag positions were very important.

Sign systems are the basis of all communication.

It is not possible not to communicate, even if we don't really want to. For example, our eyes and body show other people how we feel. And if we don't speak, it usually means something, too. Even animals use sign languages. Honey bees for example show each other in a special kind of dance where the best food can be found.

1 Questions on the text

a) Why is communication so important?

b) Where speaking or writing isn't possible, other sign languages are used. Give examples.

c) Do you know more examples of sign language?

2 A quiz on signs

Look at the pictures and say what the signs mean.

A My finger hurts.
B One beer, please.
C Well done!

A Don't write back.
B I feel sad.
C See you soon.

A We are going to win!
B You look like a rabbit.
C Give me two minutes.

A Wait.
B Leave immediately!
C What you did wasn't good.

3 A sign system: The torch telegraph

Look at the pictures and read the text about the torch telegraph.

A	F	K	P	U
B	G	L	Q	V
C	H	M	R	W
D	I	N	S	X
E	J	O	T	Y
				Z

In the second century BC the Greek Polybios invented a system of torch signs to communicate over some distance. The number of torches above the wall on the left gives you the column of the letter in the code table, and the number of torches above the wall on the right gives you the line.

a) What was good about this system? What could you do with it? What was not so good?

b) Use the code table to find the word that is shown below. You can make more words or a complete text for your partner. Then find solutions to each other's puzzles.

D A sketch: George's first computer (after Unit 5)

George: Hey, Billy!
Billy: Yes, George?
George: I just got my first computer.
Billy: That's great, George. What did you get?
George: A Pentium IV-3.2 Gigahertz, with 512 Megs of RAM, a 180-Gig hard drive, and an 8X DVD writer.
Billy: That's terrific, George.
George: But I don't know what any of it means!
Billy: You will in time.
George: That's exactly why I'm here to see you.
Billy: Oh?
George: Yes! I heard that you're a real computer expert.
Billy: Well, I don't know …
George: Yessir-EE. You know your stuff. And you're going to train me.
Billy: Really?
George: Uh huh. And I am here for my first lesson.
Billy: OK, George. What do you want to know?
George: I am having no problem turning it on, but I heard that you should be very careful how you turn it off.
Billy: That's true.
George: So, here I am working on my new computer and I want to turn it off. What do I do?
Billy: Well, first you go to the 'Start' button, and then …
George: No, I told you to turn it off.
Billy: I know, you click on 'Start' …
George: Wait a second. I want to turn it *off*. I know how to start it. So tell me what to do.
Billy: I did.
George: When?
Billy: When I told you to click on 'Start'.
George: Why should I click on 'Start'?
Billy: To shut off the computer.

George: I use the 'Start' button to stop?
Billy: Well, 'Start' doesn't actually stop the computer.
George: I knew it! So what do I use?
Billy: 'Start'.
George: Start what?
Billy: 'Start' button.
George: 'Start' button to do what?
Billy: Shut down.
George: You don't have to get rude!
Billy: No, no, no! That's not what I meant.
George: Then say what you mean.
Billy: To shut down the computer, use …
George: Don't say, 'Start'!
Billy: Then what do you want me to say?
George: Look, if I want to turn off the computer, I am willing to use the 'Stop' button, the 'End' button and 'Cease and Desist' button, but no one in their right mind uses 'Start' to stop.
Billy: But that's what you do.
George: And you probably go at stop signs, and stop at green lights.
Billy: Don't be ridiculous.
George: I'm being ridiculous? Well, I think it's about time we started this conversation.
Billy: What are you talking about?
George: I am starting this conversation right now. Good-bye.

E A story: Nathan and Lara (after Unit 6)

In the dark assembly hall, almost every eye was on the young actors on the stage. They were in the middle of a funny song. Every year, a group of pupils did a play for other pupils and for parents, and this year it was a musical. It was very good. Only Lara and Nathan at the back of the hall were not interested in the play. These two pupils were too busy with their plans. “Well, I'd like to, Nathan,” Lara whispered. “Really, but I just can't – I'm sorry.”

Nathan was a pupil at Nelson Comprehensive in Watford. Lara was not. She was from Nelson's partner school in Germany and was on a short visit with 32 other pupils.

“It's OK, no problem,” Nathan said. But he wasn't happy. He liked Lara and he knew that she liked him, too. They were good friends already, even after just a week.

Their problem was the next day. Saturday was the German group's last day in England. “We're going to visit Stratford-upon-Avon,” Lara explained in a quiet voice, “and nobody must miss the trip. We all have to go. I'd like to stay here in Watford with you but I can't. It isn't just a holiday, you know. We have to answer more questions on worksheets. About Shakespeare this time, of course.”

“It's OK, I understand,” Nathan said.

But Lara wasn't so sure. Did he understand? “He probably thinks I don't care for him,” she thought.

“Some English pupils are going to come with us tomorrow,” she said. “Did you know that? We're going to use two buses. Both are full or almost full, I think, but perhaps somebody will be ill. Can you be at the school car park at 8 o'clock?”

Before Nathan could say anything, the musical finished and everybody clapped. He and Lara started to clap, too. Then suddenly the lights were on again and everybody got up. After the musical, Nathan, Lara and Susan Fox walked to Susan's house where Lara was a guest for the week. Susan soon said, “Good night.” Then she went inside.

“Well?” Lara asked.

“I can't. I'm playing in a football match in the morning. The team needs me. It's an important game,” Nathan said. “Are you sure you can't spend the day here, Lara? Perhaps you can get up late and miss the bus? Then you can watch our football match and after lunch we can go for a walk by the river. Or we can meet my friends and listen to music. What do you think?”

Nathan waited for Lara's answer. Lara thought for a moment. She needed a good idea now. She wasn't very interested in football – but the river was pretty, and of course she wanted to see Nathan again.

But then, school was important to her, too. That was why she was here. She wanted to find out more about England. She really wanted to visit Stratford.

And she didn't want to get into trouble with her teachers. “No, I can't,” Lara said. “I don't usually miss lessons at home and I'm not going to start now, I'm sorry.”

“Then I won't see you again?” Nathan said. “It will be late when you get back from Stratford tomorrow. And your bus back to

Germany leaves early on Sunday morning, doesn't it?"

Lara laughed. Or she tried to laugh. "Well, you might get up early and come to the bus and say goodbye to me. And you can see me in Germany when your group comes to our school."

"Mm," Nathan said.

After Lara had gone inside, she thought of an excuse for not going to Stratford. She called a friend and told her that she didn't feel well and couldn't go on the trip.

She felt terrible because she didn't usually tell lies, but all she could think about was seeing Nathan on her last day in England.

So the next morning she didn't go to the buses but went to watch the football match.

It was an exciting game, but Nelson lost 4-3. Worse still, she didn't see Nathan. He wasn't in the team.

"Where's Nathan?" she asked one of the players right after the game.

"Don't ask me, I don't know and I don't want to talk about him," was the answer.

Lara asked another boy. "I'm looking for Nathan. Have you seen him?"

"Perhaps he's still in bed. He hates getting up early in the morning. He likes playing football in the afternoon. We had to play with ten men."

Lara had a lot of free time now, so she went to Nathan's house. Perhaps he was ill?

"No," his mother said. "He left the house this morning without any breakfast. He said he was late for a bus to Stratford."

Nathan's mother was right. That morning he had run to the school car park and got there just in time. He had jumped on the nearest bus and hoped that Lara was on the other which was just leaving.

A week later, Lara got a postcard from England. On one side, there were pictures of Shakespeare's Stratford-upon-Avon. On the other side, it said:

mediation

1 Zwei Londoner Sehenswürdigkeiten

Unit 1

Eure Klasse geht auf Klassenfahrt nach London. Ihr habt im Internet recherchiert, um euren Aufenthalt vorzubereiten. Dabei hast du folgendes Material gefunden. Deine Oma sieht die Bilder und fragt dich, was dort zu sehen ist und was du darüber weißt. Erzähle ihr das Wichtigste.

Madame Tussaud's

Madame Tussaud came to England from France in 1802 and opened her famous wax figure collection in London. Since then, more and more figures have been added.
Today you will find models of well-known sports personalities, musicians and film stars, statesmen from around the world, and even the Royal Family.
Have fun in the new Superstars and Legends section by searching for your personal hero or heroine, or find your favourite film star and tell them you are their greatest fan ... only don't be disappointed if you do not get an answer! Enjoy a visit to the Garden Party, where you will meet stars of sport and television.
What everyone comes to see is the Chamber of Horrors. Scared, horrified or frightened you may be, but you will not be disappointed, so be brave and enter! Murderers from down the ages await you; some of the serial killers have a whole section of their own. Watch out for the guillotine – it is authentic!
Complete your tour of Madame Tussaud's with a ride in a miniaturised London taxi cab. This will take you through London's past history from the time of the first Queen Elizabeth bringing you right up to date in today's London.

St. Paul's Cathedral

St. Paul's Cathedral is a famous landmark on the skyline of the City of London. It was designed by Sir Christopher Wren and built between 1675 and 1710. Rising up to 365 feet (111.3 metres) and weighing 65,000 tonnes, its dome is one of the largest cathedral domes in the world.
The left of the two baroque towers houses the largest bell in England, 'Great Paul' made in 1882, weighing 17 tonnes.
Around the Dome there are three galleries. The most famous is the Whispering Gallery, 259 steps from ground level. Words that are whispered to the wall there can be heard 100 feet away on the opposite side. The Stone Gallery, 378 steps from ground level, is on the outside of the Dome, from where you have a good view of the city and the River Thames. You get the best views from the Golden Gallery, 530 steps from ground level, the highest point of the outer Dome.
Inside the cathedral, in the crypt which is probably the largest in Europe, there are a lot of graves where some famous dead people are buried. One of them is Sir Christopher Wren.

2 Im Schilderwald

a) Dein amerikanischer Freund Jim ist zum ersten Mal in Deutschland. Ihr macht einen Ausflug mit deiner großen Schwester Tina, die am Steuer des Familienautos sitzt. Als Jim die deutschen Verkehrsschilder sieht, müsst ihr ihm einiges erklären.

Jim: 'Einbahnstraße'? What's that? Isn't 'Bahn' the word for 'train'?
Du: No, not here. It means …
Jim: There's a 'no entry' sign. But two cars just drove through.
Du: Well, the sign says …
Jim: Look, you can park here at the station, Tina. There's a 'P' sign.
Tina: Yes, but …
Jim: I guess 'privat' means private, so we can't park here, can we?
Tina: That's right. If you …
Jim: Is it OK here? What's a 'Parkscheibe'?
Tina: Look, …
Jim: This looks like a nice little coffee bar. Let's go in and have a drink.
Du: Oh no, it's Monday. …

Tipp

Diese Situation soll eine echte Alltagssituation nachbilden. Solche Übungen helfen dir zu lernen, wie du am besten im Dialog handeln und sofort reagieren kannst.

Halte dich nie an einzelnen Wörtern auf, die du nicht kennst und nicht übersetzen kannst, z. B. "kostenpflichtig" (d.h. du musst dafür bezahlen, und das verstehst du). Das Ganze ist mehr als die Summe seiner Teile. In Wirklichkeit weißt du viel mehr als nur die Übersetzung einzelner Wörter, denn du verstehst den Sinn ganzer Aussagen. Gib immer den Sinn dessen wieder, was gemeint ist. Drücke dich ganz einfach mit den Mitteln aus, die du kennst. Es funktioniert. Du musst es nur immer wieder üben.

b) Erklärt euch diese Schilder gegenseitig auf Englisch.

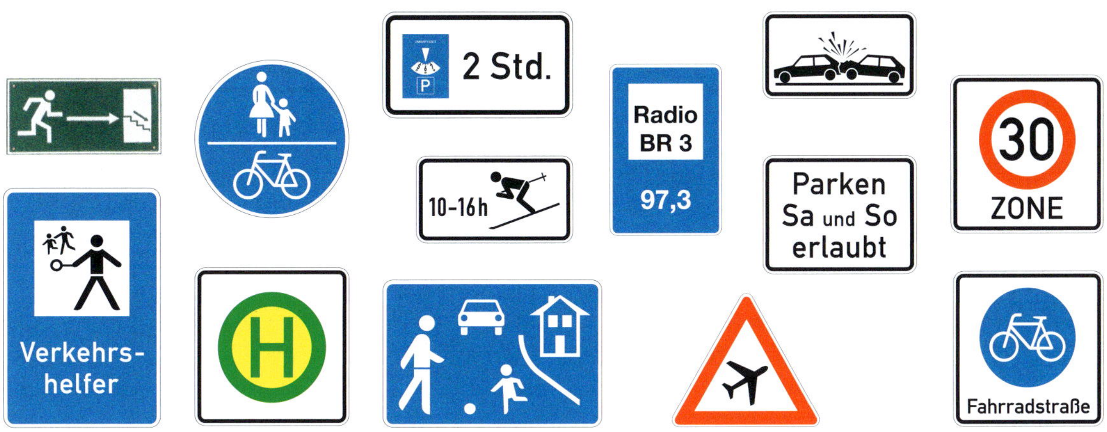

3 Ein weltberühmtes Schloss

Eine befreundete englischsprachige Familie (Vater, Mutter, zwei Schulkinder und ein Hund) wird euch im Juni besuchen. Du möchtest mit ihnen das Schloss Neuschwanstein besichtigen. Verwende die nachstehenden Informationen von der Internetseite der Bayerischen Schlösserverwaltung www.neuschwanstein.de und schreibe der Familie einen Brief, in dem du begründest, warum du Neuschwanstein ausgewählt hast und was man bei der Planung eines Besuchs beachten muss.

▶▶ Neuschwanstein

▶ Neuschwanstein heute

Besucherrekorde und Erhaltungsprobleme

Sieben Wochen nach dem Tod König Ludwigs II. wurde Neuschwanstein 1886 für das Publikum geöffnet. Der menschenscheue König hatte das Schloss erbaut, um sich aus der Öffentlichkeit zurückzuziehen – jetzt wurde sein Refugium zum Publikumsmagneten. Neuschwanstein gehört heute zu den meistbesuchten Schlössern und Burgen Europas. 1,3 Millionen Menschen jährlich besichtigen „das Schloss des Märchenkönigs". Im Sommer drängen sich im Durchschnitt täglich mehr als 6000 Besucher durch Räume, die für einen einzigen Bewohner bestimmt waren.
Die idyllische Lage von Neuschwanstein ist einmalig. Allerdings müssen Bewegungen im Fundamentbereich ständig überwacht und die steilen Felswände immer wieder gesichert werden. Ebenso greift das raue Klima die Kalkstein-Fassaden stark an, die daher in den nächsten Jahren abschnittsweise saniert werden müssen.
Seit 1990 hat der Freistaat Bayern für die Sanierung und Instandhaltung des Schlosses sowie für die Verbesserung des Besucherservices etwa 11,2 Millionen Euro ausgegeben.

▶ Führungen

Sie können Schloss Neuschwanstein nur geführt besichtigen. Die Führungen in den Sprachen Deutsch und Englisch dauern ca. 35 Minuten. Während der Führung müssen Sie insgesamt 165 Stufen aufwärts und 181 Stufen abwärts zurücklegen.
Sie können Ihre Führung direkt beim Ticketcenter Hohenschwangau reservieren.
Zusätzlich können Sie das Schloss mit einer Führung mittels Audio-Guide besichtigen. Diese Führungen dauern ebenfalls ca. 35 Minuten und werden in den Sprachen Japanisch, Französisch, Spanisch, Italienisch, Tschechisch, Slowenisch, Russisch, Polnisch, Chinesisch (Mandarin), Portugiesisch und Ungarisch angeboten.

▶ Innenräume

In den Wandbildern des Schlosses werden Geschichten um Liebe, Schuld, Buße und Erlösung thematisiert. Könige und Ritter, Dichter und Liebespaare bevölkern die Räume. Drei Figuren sind von zentraler Bedeutung: der Dichter Tannhäuser, der Schwanenritter Lohengrin und dessen Vater, der Gralskönig Parzival (Parsifal). Für Ludwig waren sie Vorbilder und Seelenverwandte.

Tipp

Erinnerst du dich ans *Scanning*? Meist enthalten Texte mehr Informationen als die, die du gerade suchst. Lies deshalb erst jeden Abschnitt gründlich durch und mach dir Notizen zu den wichtigsten Dingen, die darin stehen. Schreibe nur die Details auf, die wirklich von Bedeutung sind. Es ist z. B. nicht wichtig für die Aufgabe, dass das Schloss am Faschingsdienstag nicht geöffnet ist, da die Familie im Juni zu Besuch kommt. Du wirst sehen, dass du keine Wörter nachschlagen musst, wenn du nur die wesentlichen Dinge herausfilterst. Überlege erst, nachdem du den Text verstanden und diese Vorauswahl getroffen hast, wie du die Information auf Englisch formulieren kannst.

▶ Neuschwanstein

▶ Eintritt & Tickets

Eintrittskarten erhalten Sie nur im Ticketcenter im Ort Hohenschwangau unterhalb des Schlosses. Sie müssen daher Ihre Eintrittskarte kaufen, bevor Sie den ca. 30 Minuten langen Fußweg zum Schloss antreten. Eine Reservierung von Eintrittskarten ist gegen einen Zuschlag zum Kartenpreis möglich. Eine Umbuchung oder Stornierung kann nur bis zu 2 Stunden vor der Einlasszeit erfolgen (auch telefonisch).
Ticketcenter Neuschwanstein – Hohenschwangau
Alpseestr. 12, 87645 Hohenschwangau
Tel.: (0 83 62) 9 30 83-0,
Fax: (0 83 62) 9 30 83-20
Internet:
www.ticket-center-hohenschwangau.de

▶ Preise

Regulärer Preis: 9 Euro
Ermäßigter Preis: 8 Euro
Verbundkarte „Königsticket“ für Schloss Neuschwanstein und Schloss Hohenschwangau am gleichen Tag:
17 Euro bzw. 15 Euro ermäßigt

▶ Öffnungszeiten von Schloss Neuschwanstein

April–September:	9–18 Uhr
Kassenöffnung:	8–17 Uhr
Oktober–März:	10–16 Uhr
Kassenöffnung:	9–15 Uhr

▶ Geschlossen am

1.1., Faschingsdienstag, 24.12., 25.12., 31.12.
Schlosswirtschaft, Tel.: (0 83 62) 8 11 10
Kein Ruhetag

▶ Besucherinformationen

Das Mitnehmen von Hunden in das Schloss ist nicht erlaubt. Kinderwagen und sperrige Gegenstände (Rucksäcke etc.) bitten wir an der Garderobe abzugeben. Im Schloss besteht grundsätzlich Rauch- und Fotografierverbot. Die Besichtigung ist nur im Rahmen einer Führung möglich.
Bei weiteren Fragen wenden Sie sich bitte an die Schlossverwaltung Neuschwanstein.

4 Eine Ballonfahrt

Du bist mit deiner Familie in Wales im Urlaub und schaust dir mit deiner kleinen Schwester eine Broschüre über Ballonfahrten an. Sie ist ganz begeistert und möchte gerne einmal mitfahren. Kannst du ihre Fragen mit Hilfe der unten stehenden Auszüge beantworten?

When can I fly?
Flying takes place throughout the year in the early morning and the evening. We do not fly in wet or windy conditions, so please be patient with the British weather.

What should I wear?
Comfortable outdoor clothing suitable for the time of year is recommended, preferably made of natural materials. As the balloon moves with the wind, there is no 'chill' factor.

How long will the flight last?
The flight itself will last approximately one hour. You should allow at least three hours for your adventure.

Who can fly?
There are no age restrictions on who can fly. Passengers should be fit enough to climb in and out of the basket and to stand for about an hour.

Do I need a 'head for heights'?
No. Dizziness seems to be associated with tall buildings, mountains, bridges etc. which are connected to the ground.

Can I help?
You are more than welcome to help if you wish. The pilot and crew will give you instructions.

Is it safe?
Ballooning has the best safety record of all air sports.

- Kann ich helfen, den Ballon für den Start vorzubereiten?
- Ist Ballonfahren gefährlich?
- Was passiert, wenn es regnet?
- Wird es in dem offenen Korb sehr zugig sein?
- Wie lange dauert so ein Ausflug?
- Können wir nach dem Mittagessen losfliegen?
- Oma ist 67. Kann sie im Ballon mitfahren?
- Kann man sich in dem Korb hinsetzen?
- Wird mir schwindelig werden?

39 5 Eine Unterhaltung mit einem Fußballfan

Dein örtlicher Fußballverein hat Gäste aus England. Unter ihnen ist auch Kevin, ein junger Mann im Rollstuhl. Beim Straßenfest sitzt dein kleiner Cousin Rico mit euch am Tisch. Er ist sehr neugierig und hat einige Fragen an Kevin. Da er noch kein Englisch kann, bittet er dich, als Dolmetscher zu fungieren.

Rico: Wie lange bist du schon Liverpool-Fan? Liverpool ist mein Lieblingsverein.
Du: *My cousin wants to know …*
Kevin: *I've been a fan for ages! I try to go to their matches with my friends as often as I can.*
Du: …
Rico: Ist es ein Problem, mit dem Rollstuhl zu einem Spiel zu kommen?
Du: …
Kevin: *No, not really. My friends usually go with me and help me to get on and off the coach. When the accident happened, I thought that was the end and I could never be happy again. I loved playing football before the accident. Now I can only watch. But it's great fun, too.*
Du: …
Rico: Wie lange sitzt du denn schon im Rollstuhl?
Du: …
Kevin: *About eight years. Yes, it happened eight years ago. Before that I was running around and playing football like you. Then I had a car accident, you know.*
Du: …
Rico: Warst du lange im Krankenhaus?
Du: …
Kevin: *I spent eight weeks in hospital. The doctors tried everything. But in the end they couldn't help. So they gave me a wheelchair and I practised moving with it every day. That wasn't easy at the beginning.*
Du: …
Rico: Durftest du den Rollstuhl mit nach Hause nehmen?
Du: …
Kevin: *Yes, I used the wheelchair from the hospital during the first few weeks. But I had to give it back. They needed it for someone else. I was lucky. My parents bought a new wheelchair for me. It's much better than the one from the hospital.*
Du: …
Rico: Wie schnell kannst du mit deinem Rollstuhl fahren?
Du: …
Kevin: *I can move around really fast with it. At home I even play basketball.*
Du: …
Rico: Darf ich ihn mal ausprobieren?
Du: …
Kevin: *Well, if you like. Maybe tomorrow.*
Du: …
Rico: Au ja. Du interessierst dich ja sehr für Sport. Was machst du sonst so? Hast du Arbeit? Oder noch irgendwelche anderen Hobbys?
Du: …
Kevin: *I work in a call center three times a week. And sometimes friends come over to my house and we talk about sports or we play computer games. Once a week my parents take me to basketball practice. I also read a lot, and I love drawing. My best friend and I draw comic figures. We've invented whole stories. Do you want me to draw something for you?*
Du: …
Rico: Oh ja, super! Kannst du uns eine von deinen Geschichten zeichnen? Hier sind Stifte.
Du: …
Kevin: *Yes, of course. I'd love to do that.*
Du: …

6 Ein Filmabend

Du hast Besuch von einem entfernten Verwandten, Robert, der in Singapur aufgewachsen ist und kein Deutsch kann. Ihr möchtet euch einen Film ausleihen und blättert zusammen im Katalog der Videothek. Das Bild des Vulkanausbruchs macht euch neugierig.

a) Fasse für Robert auf Englisch zusammen, worum es in dem Film geht und ob du denkst, dass er für euch geeignet ist.

Mount St. Helens – Der Killervulkan

(USA 1981)

Originaltitel: St. Helens
Regie: Ernest Pintoff
Darsteller: Art Carney, David Huffman, Cassie Yates

Dieser Film ist aus dem Jahr 1981 und beruht auf einer wahren Begebenheit.

Bundesstaat Washington. Leichte Erdstöße erschüttern die Gegend um den Mount St. Helens. Die Tiere der Region verhalten sich äußerst merkwürdig, spielen teilweise verrückt. Alles Zeichen dafür, dass der Vulkan Mount St. Helens kurz vor einer gewaltigen Eruption steht. Als der Geologe David Johnston davon erfährt, beschließt er, umgehend dorthin zu reisen, um auf keinen Fall einen Ausbruch zu verpassen. Dort angekommen, muss er allerdings entsetzt feststellen, dass die Menschen dort in keinster Weise auf eine bevorstehende Naturkatastrophe vorbereitet sind.
Das Interessante an diesem Film ist, dass er keine billigen Trickaufnahmen verwendet, sondern echte Aufnahmen vom Ausbruch, die sehr überzeugend in die Geschichte eingefügt sind.

Die deutsche DVD von Marketing-Film präsentiert den Film in Deutsch und Englisch. Als Extras zum Film gibt es *Deleted Scenes* (0:50 Min.), eine *Artwork* Galerie (1:29 Min.) und Filmographien der Hauptdarsteller und des Regisseurs.

b) Schreibe auf Englisch eine ähnliche Zusammenfassung deines Lieblingsfilmes für einen englischsprachigen Freund.

40 7 Ein Interview mit Anna Jones

Anna Jones ist eine sehr gute Basketballspielerin, die aus den USA nach Deutschland gezogen ist und ab diesem Schuljahr eure Schulmannschaft verstärken wird.

Ihr macht ein Interview mit ihr, das im freien Radio eurer Stadt gesendet wird. Die auf Deutsch an sie gestellten Fragen müssen ins Englische übertragen werden, ihre Antworten für die Zuhörer ins Deutsche.

Frage: Hallo Anna, willkommen an unserer Schule. Wir freuen uns, eine so gute Spielerin in unserem Team zu haben. Anna, wo hast du gelernt, Basketball zu spielen und wie lange spielst du schon?

Du: *Hi Anna, …*

Anna: *I started to play when I was about seven years old. My dad was crazy about basketball and whenever he went to the gym he took me with him. There I played with a bunch of guys who were much older than me and that was pretty hard, you know. I learnt a lot from them though. But then I really got started when I went to high school …*

Du: Anna sagt, dass sie …

Frage: Stimmt es, dass du mit deiner Schulmannschaft in der NJB, der National Junior Basketball League, trainiert hast?

Du: …

Anna: *Yes, and I have to thank that organization a lot for what they did for me and other young players.*

Du: …

Frage: Was genau ist die NJB?

Du: …

Anna: *The NJB is a national youth league with over 25,000 young players in 6 states. The program is directed at boys and girls up to 12th grade. Its aim is to prepare athletes for high school competition.*

Du: …

Frage: Wie ist dein Eindruck von deiner neuen Mannschaft? Und hast du schon etwas von der Gegend und der Stadt gesehen?

Du: …

Anna: *I think the team is very talented. Their technical skills are on a high level, and I like the way they work during practice. – Uh, what was the other question?*

Du: …

Anna: *OK. No, I haven't seen a lot of the area so far. I went to the shopping center yesterday, but that was it.*

Du: …

Frage: Deine neue Trainerin sagte neulich in einem Interview, dass sie großen Wert darauf legt, mannschaftsdienliche Spielerinnen zu gewinnen. Wie siehst du deine Rolle innerhalb der Mannschaft?

Du: …

Anna: *Well, I think with basketball it's always the team that wins games, never the individual player.*

Du: …

Frage: Vielen Dank für das Interview und viel Glück mit deiner neuen Mannschaft!

Du: …

Anna: *Thank you.*

Du: …

grammar

Grammar

In jeder Unit gibt es wieder Verweise auf die mit G1, G2 etc. durchnummerierten Grammatikkapitel, in denen du wie gewohnt Regeln und Beispiele zum neuen Grammatikstoff findest.
Die Seitenangabe rechts neben der Überschrift zeigt dir, auf welcher Seite der Grammatikstoff in der Unit eingeführt wird.

Wo ein ! steht, musst du wieder besonders aufpassen.

Der Grammatikteil fasst die Regeln zusammen, die du aus dem Unterricht kennst. Er kann dir auch beim selbstständigen Lernen zu Hause helfen, z.B. wenn du für eine Schulaufgabe übst oder wenn du etwas nicht verstanden hast und noch einmal wiederholen möchtest. Im Folgenden findest du eine Liste der grammatischen Begriffe aus diesem Buch.

Die Angabe G… zeigt, wo du im Grammatikteil zu dem Begriff etwas findest.

Grammatical terms

Englisch	Englisches Beispiel	Deutsch
adjective after verbs	He **looks good** in his new coat.	Adjektiv nach Verben
adverb/adverbial G10		Adverb / adverbiale Bestimmung
adverbs/adverbials of manner	**quickly, easily, in a friendly way** etc.	Adverbien / adverbiale Bestimmungen der Art und Weise
adverbs/adverbials of place	They play **in the park**.	~ des Ortes
adverbs/adverbials of time	We're going to meet **at ten o'clock**.	~ der Zeit
adverbs/adverbials of frequency	I **always** get up early.	~ der Häufigkeit
auxiliary	**to be, to do, to have**	Hilfsverb
modal auxiliary	**can, may, might, must, need, should**	modales Hilfsverb
substitutes for modal auxiliaries:		Ersatzformen für modale Hilfsverben
to be able to	Sarah **won't be able to** come at eight.	
to be allowed to	Becky **is not allowed to** go outside.	
to have to	**Do** you really **have to** leave?	
comparative	old**er**, **more** beautiful etc.	Komparativ, 1. Steigerungsform
comparison of adjectives	small, small**er**, small**est**	Steigerung der Adjektive
comparison of adverbs	slowly, **more** slowly, **most** slowly	Steigerung der Adverbien
comparison with more/most	**more** expensive, **most** expensive	Steigerung mit more / most
conditional clause		Bedingungssatz
conditional clause type I	**If they leave,** we'll go with them.	
conditional clause type II G11	**If I were you,** I wouldn't complain.	
connective	**and, or, because, when** etc.	Konjunktion / Bindewort
contact clause	That's the film **I like best.**	Relativsatz ohne Relativpronomen
defining relative clause	Tom was the boy **who phoned me.**	notwendiger Relativsatz
future		Futur
going-to future	We're **going to** have fun.	going-to-Futur
will future	It **will** be a big hit.	will-Futur
if and when	**If** it rains, we'll go to the cinema. **When** Mum comes, she'll cook for us.	konditionales *wenn* temporales *wenn*

Englisch	Englisches Beispiel	Deutsch
indirect speech G16–21		indirekte Rede
expressions of time **G18**		Zeitangaben
indirect commands, requests and advice **G20**	Our teacher **told us to listen.**	indirekte Befehle, Bitten und Ratschläge
indirect questions **G19**	She asked me **why I had left.**	indirekte Fragen
introductory verbs **G21**		Einleitungsverben
indirect speech with tense shift **G17–19**	He said the film **was** great.	indirekte Rede mit Zeitverschiebung
indirect speech without tense shift **G16**	He says the film **is** great.	indirekte Rede ohne Zeitverschiebung
infinitive constructions G13–14	**I'd like you to look** at my picture.	Infinitivkonstruktionen
object	Jenny is buying **a pen.**	Objekt
one, prop-word G12	I like the **green one** better than the **red one.**	Stützwort *one*
passive voice G1–3, G8		Passiv
active and passive voice **G1**		Aktiv und Passiv
by-agent **G2**	The wall was built **by the Romans.**	Verursacher einer Handlung
passive infinitive **G3**	Changes will **be made.**	Infinitiv des Passivs
past perfect passive **G8**	Trees **had been planted.**	Plusquamperfekt im Passiv
past participle	**walked, done, eaten** etc.	Partizip Perfekt
past perfect G7–9		Plusquamperfekt
past perfect passive **G8**	One of the windows **had been broken.**	Plusquamperfekt im Passiv
past perfect progressive **G9**	They **had been singing** for over an hour.	Verlaufsform des Plusquamperfekts
past perfect simple **G7**	He **had** already **left** when I arrived.	einfaches Plusquamperfekt
past tense		Vergangenheit, Präteritum
past progressive	We **were dancing** when Kim came in.	Verlaufsform der Vergangenheit
simple past	I **went** to a party last night.	einfache Vergangenheit
possessive determiner	**my, your, his, her** etc.	Possessivbegleiter / besitzanzeigendes Fürwort
present perfect G4–6	We **haven't done** it yet.	Perfekt
present perfect progressive **G4, G6**	**I've been watching** the birds for a long time.	Verlaufsform des Perfekts
present perfect with for and since **G5**		Perfekt mit *seit*
present tense		Präsens / Gegenwart
present progressive	Look, he**'s playing** football.	Verlaufsform des Präsens
simple present	I often **go** to school by bus.	einfaches Präsens
pronoun		Pronomen
object pronoun	**me, him, us** etc.	Personalpronomen im Objektfall
personal pronoun	**he, she, it, we** etc.	Personalpronomen
reflexive pronoun **G15**	**myself, yourself, himself, herself, ourselves, yourselves** etc.	Reflexivpronomen
relative pronoun	**who / which / that / whose / whom**	Relativpronomen
reported speech G16–21	**= indirect speech**	indirekte Rede
sentence with comparison	Tim is **nicer than** his sister. He's **not as old as** Tom.	Vergleich im Satz
subject	**The book** is on the table.	Subjekt / Satzgegenstand
superlative	old**est**, **the most** difficult	Superlativ / 2. Steigerungsform
word order G10		Wortstellung

unit 1

G1 The active and the passive voice Aktiv und Passiv

page 10

	subject	verb		
active	Somebody	stole	my bike yesterday.	Jemand hat … mein Fahrrad gestohlen.
passive	My bike	was stolen	yesterday.	Mein Fahrrad wurde … gestohlen.

- Passivsätze stellen Handlungen aus einer anderen Sicht dar als Aktivsätze. Anders als in einem Aktivsatz tut das Subjekt eines Passivsatzes nichts, sondern etwas „geschieht" mit ihm.
- Im Passivsatz liegt daher die Betonung auf dem, **was** gemacht wird, und weniger darauf, **wer** etwas tut. In Passivsätzen sind die Verursacher der Handlungen entweder nicht bekannt oder unwichtig oder so offensichtlich, dass sie nicht genannt werden müssen.
- Passivsätze findet man vor allem in Zeitungsberichten, historischen Texten und technischen Beschreibungen. Oft lässt sich ein englischer Passivsatz auch mit einem deutschen „man"-Satz übersetzen: Man hat mein Fahrrad gestohlen.

passive tenses		
simple present am/is/are + past participle	The London Eye **is visited** by thousands of tourists every year. Tickets **are sold** over the phone or online.	… wird … besucht. … werden … verkauft.
simple past was/were + past participle	The first plans **were drawn** in 1993. The huge wheel **wasn't built** in a few weeks. It took six years.	… wurden … gezeichnet. … wurde nicht … gebaut.
present perfect has/have been + past participle	**Have** any new attractions **been opened** this year?	Sind … eröffnet worden?
future passive will be + past participle	I don't know, but there's a new museum which **will be completed** next month. But it **won't be opened** immediately.	…, das … fertig gestellt (werden) wird. … wird nicht … eröffnet (werden).

- Das Passiv wird mit einer Form von ***to be*** und dem ***past participle*** gebildet.
- Passivsätze können in verschiedenen Zeitformen vorkommen. Dabei wird die Form von ***to be*** der jeweiligen Zeitstufe angepasst.
- Passivsätze kann man nur mit Verben bilden, denen ein Objekt folgt (transitive Verben), z. B. ***to build (a house), to visit (a museum), to serve (a customer)***.

G2 The *by-agent* Passivsätze mit einem *by-agent*

page 10

- Möchte man dennoch in einem Passivsatz sagen, von **wem** etwas gemacht wird (also den Verursacher der Handlung nennen), kann man ihn mit Hilfe der Präposition ***by*** (auf Deutsch: **von**) am Satzende anfügen. Dieser Verursacher der Handlung wird ***by-agent*** genannt.
  "Romeo and Juliet" was written by William Shakespeare.
  „Romeo und Julia" wurde von William Shakespeare geschrieben.
- Man kann den gleichen Inhalt in einem Aktivsatz vermitteln. In diesem Fall wird der ***by-agent*** zum Subjekt des Satzes:
  William Shakespeare wrote "Romeo and Juliet".

William Shakespeare

G3 The passive infinitive Der Infinitiv des Passivs

page 12

Um auszudrücken, dass etwas gemacht (oder nicht gemacht) werden muss, kann, soll, darf etc., braucht man ein **modales Hilfsverb** *(modal auxiliary)* oder dessen **Ersatz** *(substitute)* und einen ***passive infinitive***.

	auxiliary or substitute + to	passive infinitive (be + past participle)		
Something	must	be done	to the Docklands.	... muss ... getan werden.
The place	can't	be left	like this.	... kann ... nicht gelassen werden.
How	can it	be improved?		... kann ... verbessert werden?
Those buildings	should	be pulled down.		... sollten abgerissen werden.
But the area	mustn't	be ruined	by skyscrapers.	... darf nicht ... ruiniert werden.
A lot of money	will have to	be spent.		... wird ausgegeben werden müssen.

- Der ***passive infinitive*** wird mit ***be*** + ***past participle*** gebildet.
- Bei Hilfsverben ***(can, may, must, needn't, should*** etc.*)* wird er unmittelbar daran angehängt. Bei den Ersatzverben ***(have to, be able to, be allowed to)*** steht dagegen immer ein ***to*** vor dem Infinitiv. Deshalb lernst du das ***to*** immer gleich mit.
- Auch in Sätzen mit einem ***passive infinitive*** kann der Handlungsträger durch einen ***by-agent*** ausgedrückt werden.

unit 2

G4 The present perfect progressive Die Verlaufsform des Perfekts

page 24

- Das Perfekt hat wie alle englischen Zeitformen eine ***simple form*** und eine ***progressive form***. Die einfache Form des ***present perfect*** kennst du bereits aus dem letzten Jahr. Man verwendet das ***present perfect (have/has + past participle)*** für Handlungen, die in der Vergangenheit stattgefunden haben und in der Gegenwart noch von Bedeutung sind, z. B. weil ein Ergebnis vorliegt: *"I've made breakfast." – "Mmm! It smells good."*
- Man verwendet das ***present perfect progressive*** dagegen, um die Dauer einer Handlung zu betonen.

- Das ***present perfect progressive*** wird gebildet aus ***have/has been*** und der ***-ing***-Form.
- Mit dem ***present perfect progressive*** kann man ausdrücken, dass ein Vorgang in der Vergangenheit begonnen hat, bis jetzt andauert und unter Umständen noch weitergehen wird.

! Im Deutschen benutzen wir dafür das Präsens und unterstützen die Dauer des Vorgangs oft mit dem Wort **schon.**
It has been raining for hours. – Es regnet **schon** stundenlang.

G5 *For and since* *For* und *since*

page 24

For und ***since*** werden häufig mit dem ***present perfect progressive*** verwendet. Mit ihnen werden Zeitangaben ausgedrückt.

How long?	I**'ve been living** here **for ages.** She **has been learning** Welsh **for two years.** **Have** you **been waiting** here **for hours**?	...wohne schon ewig lange ... ... lernt schon seit zwei Jahren ... Wartest du schon stundenlang ...?
Since when?	Dad **has been working** there **since last year.** We**'ve been travelling** around **since Monday.** You**'ve been watching** TV **since 5 o'clock!**	... arbeitet (schon) seit letztem Jahr ... ... reisen (schon) seit Montag ... ... siehst (schon) seit 5 Uhr fern!

- *Since* bezieht sich auf den **Zeitpunkt,** an dem die Handlung begann:

since	ten o'clock last Sunday I was ten	2004 July

- *For* bezieht sich auf den **Zeitraum,** den eine Handlung andauert:

for	two hours a long time twenty minutes	ages a few months

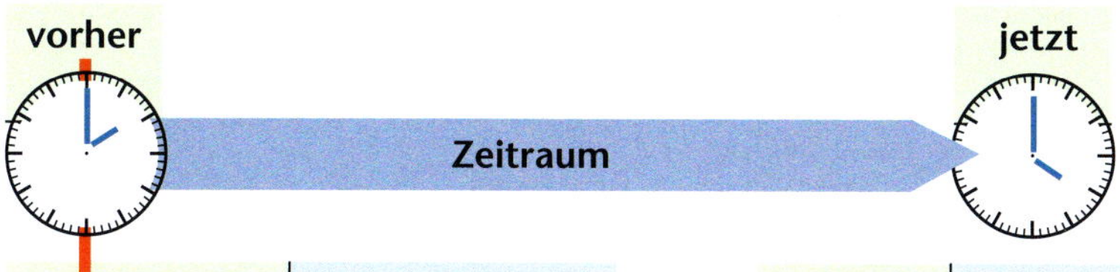

Zeitpunkt des Beginns:	***Since when?***
	***since** two o'clock* seit zwei Uhr

Zeitraum:	***How long?***
	***for** two hours* seit zwei Stunden

! Mit ***since*** stehen Uhrzeit, Datum, Wochentage, Monatsnamen, Jahreszahlen.

! ***For*** und Zeitraum – beide Male ein „r"!

G6 The present perfect: simple or progressive form?

Das Perfekt: einfache Form oder Verlaufsform?

page 24

simple	present perfect progressive
"I'**ve just made** some coffee. Would you like some?" – "Yes, please." "What **have** you **done** in Wales **so far**?" "Well, we'**ve seen** a lot of castles." "**Have** you **been** to Caerleon **yet**?" "No, we **haven't.** – Actually, **I've never** even **heard** of it!"	"We'**ve been looking** forward to your visit **for weeks.**" "Oh yes, Mum **has been cooking all morning.**" "**Have** you **been travelling** much **since you arrived in Wales**?" "Sure. We'**ve been driving** around **since Monday.**"

- Mit dem *present perfect (simple)* drückt man die Wirkung einer vergangenen Handlung auf die Gegenwart aus. Das Ergebnis dieser Handlung ist spürbar (z. B.: Der Kaffee ist fertig).
- Signalwörter wie *just, so far, yet, never, ever, already* unterstreichen den Bezug zur Gegenwart.

- Das *present perfect progressive* bezeichnet einen Vorgang, der in der Vergangenheit anfing und noch nicht beendet ist oder eben erst zu Ende gegangen ist.
- Die Dauer dieses Vorgangs wird betont, vor allem durch Zeitangaben mit *for* und *since.* oder Ausdrücke wie *all day, the whole week* etc.

! Verben wie ***to be, to know, to forget, to like*** und ***to love*** kommen nicht in der *progressive form* vor, weil sie keine Handlung, sondern einen Zustand bezeichnen.

*They'**ve been** in Wales since Monday.*
*I'**ve known** her for years.*
*He'**s loved** her since the day they met.*

unit 3

G7 The past perfect Das Plusquamperfekt

page 40

Für Handlungen und Ereignisse, die in der Vergangenheit stattgefunden haben, verwendet man meistens das ***simple past:***

*Tom **left** the party when I **arrived.***

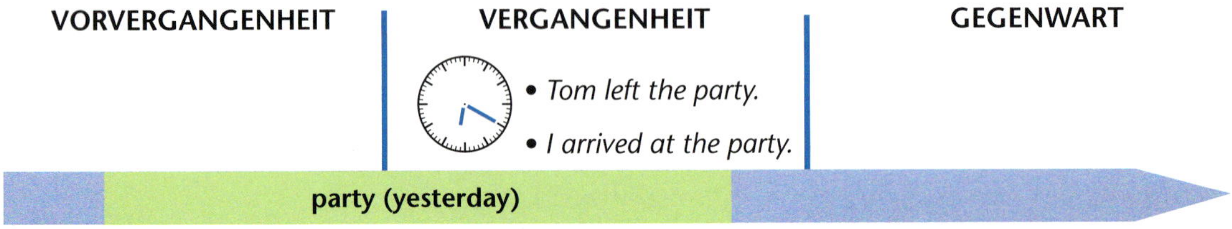

Hier treten die Ereignisse kurz nacheinander (oder sogar gleichzeitig) ein. Tom verließ die Party, und ich kam dazu. Für beide Ereignisse verwendet man das ***simple past.***

Ich habe Susan auf der Party nicht mehr angetroffen. Sie war schon vorher gegangen.

*Susan **had** (already) **left** the party when I **arrived.***

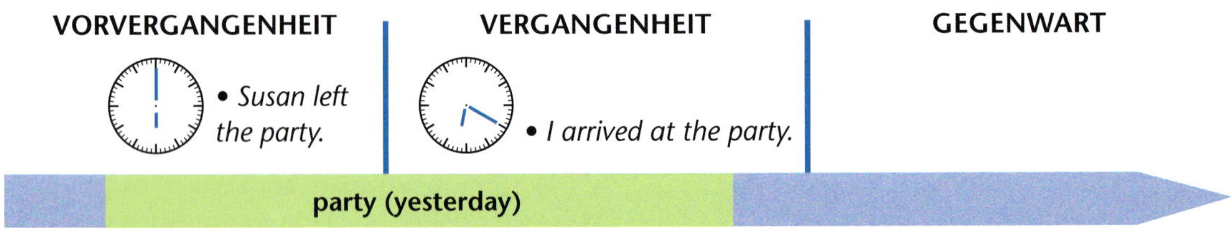

Um diese Situation zu beschreiben, verwendet man das ***past perfect*** (und das ***simple past***).

(simple past)	past perfect		
I **was** late for the party because I	**had been**	busy.	... weil ich ... gewesen war.
I **couldn't** find the present that I	**had got**	for Sally.	... das ich ... besorgt hatte.
When I **arrived**, the others	**had eaten**	all the food!	... hatten ... (auf)gegessen.

- Das ***past perfect*** drückt Vorzeitigkeit aus; man gebraucht es für Handlungen oder Zustände, die **vor** einer anderen Handlung (oder einem anderen Zustand) der Vergangenheit stattfanden.
- Das ***past perfect*** wird mit ***had*** + ***past participle*** gebildet.
- Die Formen sind für alle Personen gleich.

G8 The past perfect passive   Das Plusquamperfekt: Passiv

page 40

Jede Form des Passivs wird durch die entsprechende Form von ***to be*** und das ***past participle*** gebildet. Daraus folgt, dass das ***past perfect passive*** in allen Personen aus ***had been*** + ***past participle*** gebildet wird.

When I arrived, the classroom was a terrible mess!

	past perfect passive		
The blackboard	**hadn't been cleaned.**		... war nicht sauber gemacht worden.
And my name	**had been written**	on it.	... war ... geschrieben worden.
Rubbish	**had been thrown**	on the floor.	... war ... geworfen worden.
Two windows	**had been broken.**		... waren zerbrochen worden.

G9 *The past perfect progressive*   Die Verlaufsform des Plusquamperfekts

page 42

- Wenn man beschreiben möchte, wie lange eine Handlung schon dauerte, bevor eine andere Handlung eintrat, verwendet man im Englischen das ***past perfect progressive.*** (Im Deutschen: Das Präteritum oder das Plusquamperfekt.)
- Oft wird das ***past perfect progressive*** von Zeitangaben mit ***for*** oder ***since*** oder von ähnlichen Ausdrücken (***all day, the whole time*** etc.) begleitet. Dabei werden der Ablauf und die Dauer der Handlung betont.

	past perfect progressive		
When we arrived,	**they had been waiting**	for an hour.	... warteten ... schon ... (... hatten schon ... gewartet.)
When we got there,	**we had been travelling**	all day.	... waren ... unterwegs gewesen.
I was tired because	**I'd been driving**	the whole time.	... gefahren war.

! Das ***past progressive*** benutzt man, um eine Hintergrundhandlung in der Vergangenheit zu beschreiben. Tritt eine neue Handlung ein, so steht diese im ***simple past***:

*I **was watching** TV when the phone **rang.***

! Das ***past perfect progressive*** benutzt man, um zu betonen, wie lange eine Handlung bereits dauerte, als eine neue Handlung begann. Auch hier steht die neu eintretende Handlung im ***simple past***.
*I**'d been watching** TV for an hour when it **rang.***

G10 The position of adverbs and adverbials

page 42

Die Stellung von Adverbien und adverbialen Bestimmungen

Adverbien und adverbiale Bestimmungen können an verschiedenen Stellen im Satz stehen:

Front position: vor dem Subjekt
Mid position: entweder zwischen Subjekt und Vollverb oder hinter ***to be*** (als Vollverb) oder zwischen Hilfsverb und Vollverb
End position: hinter dem Vollverb und (falls vorhanden) dem Objekt

	Front position	Subjekt	Hilfsverb	*Mid position*	Vollverb	Objekt	*End position*
			to be			Subjektergänzung	
1.		Valérie			plays	the piano	**brilliantly.**
		Ceri		**slowly**	left	the room.	
2.		The boy	is		drawing	a red lion	**on his shield.**
		We			live		**in Camden.**
3.		My uncle			wants	to visit us	**tomorrow.**
		We			hope	to finish	**by 5 o'clock.**
4.	**In Britain**	it		**often**	rains		**in April.**
	At night	they	are	**never**		alone.	
		Martin	has	**always**	liked	vegetables.	

Die Adverbien und adverbialen Bestimmungen in der Tabelle oben bilden vier Gruppen:

- **1. Adverbien der Art und Weise**
  (adverbs / adverbials of manner) stehen meist in ***end position***, manchmal in ***mid position.***
  Examples: brilliantly, slowly, excitedly, brightly, hard.
- **2. Adverbien des Ortes**
  (adverbs / adverbials of place) stehen meist in ***end position.*** Zur Betonung können sie auch in ***front position*** stehen.
  Examples: on his shield, in Camden, everywhere, over there, on top, at the battle.
- **3. Adverbien der Zeit**
  (adverbs / adverbials of time) stehen meist in ***end position.*** Zur Betonung können sie auch in ***front position*** stehen.
  Examples: yesterday, today, tomorrow, now, by 5 o'clock, for two days, since Monday.
- **4. Adverbien der Häufigkeit**
  (adverbs / adverbials of frequency) stehen in der Regel in ***mid position.***
  Examples: often, never, always, sometimes, usually, ever.

! Wenn Adverbien der Zeit und Adverbien des Ortes am Satzende stehen, dann
ORT vor ZEIT *(PLACE before TIME)*
*Let's meet **at the cinema** **this afternoon.***

Im Deutschen ist die Stellung solcher Adverbien meist umgekehrt:
Ich werde **um 5 Uhr** **dort** sein.

Trifft auf die ***adverbs of place and time*** noch ein ***adverb of manner,*** dann gilt: ***MPT***

	Manner	*Place*	*Time*
Valérie played	***brilliantly***	***at the concert***	***on Tuesday.***

unit 4

G11 Conditional sentences type II   Bedingungssätze Typ II

page 54

Der Bedingungssatz besteht aus einem ***if***-Satz (Nebensatz) und einem Hauptsatz.

a) Den Bedingungssatz **Typ I** kennst du bereits. Zur Erinnerung:

If it rains, we'll go to the cinema. Wenn es regnet, gehen wir ins Kino.	Der ***if***-Satz drückt eine Bedingung aus, der Hauptsatz drückt aus, was passiert, wenn diese Bedingung erfüllt wird. Das ***simple present*** drückt aus, dass die Bedingung erfüllbar ist, im Hauptsatz folgt meistens das ***will future.***

Der Bedingungssatz **Typ I** drückt eine erfüllbare oder realistische Bedingung aus.

b) Der Bedingungssatz **Typ II** dagegen drückt eine unwahrscheinliche oder unerfüllbare Bedingung aus.

If-Satz: ***simple past***	Hauptsatz: ***conditional (would + infinitive)***
If I **won** a million,	I **would travel** around the world.
If the alarm clock **didn't ring** every morning,	I **would** never **get** to school on time.
If there **was** no Internet,	pupils **wouldn't be able to get** information so quickly.
If I **were** you,	I **wouldn't trust** these people.

- Im ***if***-Satz steht das ***simple past*** und im Hauptsatz das ***conditional (would/wouldn't + infinitive).***
- Das ***simple past*** im ***if***-Satz drückt eine Bedingung aus, die unwahrscheinlich oder sogar nicht erfüllbar ist.
- Bedingungssätze (Typ I und Typ II) können entweder mit dem ***if***-Satz oder mit dem Hauptsatz beginnen:
  If I was ill, I'd stay in bed. → Komma vor Hauptsatz!
  I'd stay in bed if I was ill. → kein Komma vor ***if!***
- Statt ***If I was …*** wird oft ***If I were …*** gebraucht.
- Im Deutschen verwendet man sowohl für die Übersetzung des ***if***-Satzes als auch des Hauptsatzes den Konjunktiv: *If she was my friend, she wouldn't say nasty things about me.* Wenn sie meine Freundin **wäre, würde** sie nichts Gemeines über mich **sagen.** *If I had a computer, I would write e-mails all day.* Wenn ich einen Computer **hätte, würde** ich den ganzen Tag E-Mails **schreiben.**

! In der Regel kein ***would*** im ***if***-Satz!

G12 Prop-word one / ones Das Stützwort *one/ones*

page 58

I bought two dresses, **a short one** and **a long one.**	... ein kurzes und ein langes (Kleid).
Which pants did you buy? – **The cheaper ones.**	... – Die billigere (Hose).
Which songs do you prefer? – **Slow ones.**	... – Langsame (Lieder).

- Durch ***one*** (im Plural ***ones***) kann man ein zählbares Substantiv ersetzen. Oft steht ***one/ones*** nach Adjektiven und dem Komparativ. Es ist nötig, da ein Adjektiv im Englischen nur in Ausnahmefällen allein stehen kann. Nach dem Superlativ ist ***one/ones*** nicht zwingend nötig. *Which tickets did you buy? The cheapest (ones).*
- Auch nach ***the, which*** und ***this*** kann ***one/ones*** stehen.
  Look at these rings. Which one do you like? – This one. The one with the red heart.

unit 5

G13 The infinitive with *to* Der Infinitiv mit *to*

page 70

Der Infinitiv mit ***to*** hat verschiedene Funktionen. Er wird verwendet:

a) um eine Absicht auszudrücken.

I went on the trip	**to have**	a good time.	... um mich zu amüsieren.
She gave us the handout	**in order to prepare**	us for the trip.	... um uns ... vorzubereiten.

- Es gibt keinen Bedeutungsunterschied zwischen ***to*** und ***in order to.***
  Letzteres wirkt jedoch etwas formeller.

b) um ein Fragewort, ein Substantiv oder ein Adjektiv zu ergänzen.

	question word	**to + infinitive**		
The list told us	**what**	**to take.**		... was wir mitnehmen sollten.
I wondered	**whether**	**to buy**	a map.	... ob ich ... kaufen sollte.
I wasn't sure	**where**	**to get**	one.	... wo ich ... bekommen konnte.
	noun			
We found a	**place**	**to put up**	our tents.	... Stelle, wo wir ... aufschlagen konnten.
There was	**time**	**to start**	a fire.	... Zeit, ein Feuer anzuzünden.
	adjective			
Firewood was	**easy**	**to find.**		... leicht zu finden.
It's	**important**	**not to wait**	too long.	... wichtig, dass man nicht zu lange wartet.

- Nach Fragewörtern kann der Infinitiv mit ***to*** einen Nebensatz mit einem Modalverb ersetzen *(... what to take* statt *... what we should take).* Die Infinitivkonstruktion ist kürzer und eleganter. Im Deutschen muss man einen Nebensatz verwenden.
- Der Infinitiv mit ***to*** wird auch nach Substantiven und Adjektiven verwendet. Manchmal ist im Deutschen eine ähnliche Konstruktion möglich. Oft muss man aber im Deutschen einen Nebensatz verwenden.

G14 The infinitive with *to* after certain verbs

page 70

Der Infinitiv mit *to* nach bestimmten Verben

a) Du kennst schon einige Verben, die mit einem Infinitiv + ***to*** verbunden sind.

Nobody ***remembered to*** *bring a map, so we* ***decided to*** *go back for one.*

to hope to • to arrange to • to try to • to want to • to decide to • to plan to • I'd like to • to prefer to • to forget to • to remember to	+	do something

b) Es gibt Verben, die mit einem direkten Objekt und einem Infinitiv + ***to*** verwendet werden. Sie drücken eine Aufforderung, eine Bitte, eine Erlaubnis oder einen Rat aus.

	verb + object	to + infinitive		
Mrs Baxter	**expected us**	**to read**	the handout.	… erwartete (von uns), dass wir …
She	**asked us**	**to stay**	on the trail.	… bat uns … zu bleiben.
She	**didn't allow us**	**to hike**	alone.	… erlaubte uns nicht … zu wandern.
She	**advised us**	**not to leave**	food in our tent.	… riet uns, keine Lebensmittel …

- Den Verben ***to expect, to tell, to ask*** (bitten), ***to allow, to advise, to want*** und ***to need*** kann ein Objekt + Infinitiv angeschlossen werden.

! Im Deutschen sagt man „Ich möchte, dass …" und „Ich will, dass …" und verwendet dabei einen Nebensatz. Im Englischen dagegen steht nie nach ***want*** oder ***would like*** ein Nebensatz mit ***„that"***. Man verwendet immer eine Infinitivkonstruktion:
Sandra, **ich will, dass** du mir hilfst. — *Sandra,* ***I want you to*** *help me.*
Ich möchte, dass du mir diesen Satz erklärst. — ***I'd like you to*** *explain this sentence to me.*

G15 Reflexive pronouns Reflexivpronomen

page 72

Singular	
I –	**myself**
you –	**yourself**
he –	**himself**
she –	**herself**
it –	**itself**

Plural	
we –	**ourselves**
you –	**yourselves**
they –	**themselves**

a) Verstärkender Gebrauch

It's OK. I can put up this tent	**myself.**
Ceri baked all those cookies	**herself.**
I won't clean their fish for them. They must do that	**themselves.**

- Mit dem Reflexivpronomen kann man betonen, dass jemand etwas **selbst** tut.
- Das Reflexivpronomen steht am Satzende.

b) Reflexiver Gebrauch

I think	**I**	'll buy	**myself**	an ice cream.	... mir ...
Did	**she**	really teach	**herself**	to read?	... sich ... selbst ...
Are	**you**	enjoying	**yourselves?**		... euch ...
Have	**they**	hurt	**themselves?**		... sich ...

- Mit dem Reflexivpronomen kann man auch ausdrücken, dass jemand sich etwas antut oder für sich etwas tut.
- Das Reflexivpronomen ist dann meist Objekt im Satz und bezieht sich reflexiv (rückbezüglich) auf das Subjekt.
- In diesem Fall entspricht es den deutschen Pronomen „mich / mir (selbst), dich / dir (selbst), sich (selbst)" etc.

! Verben, die im Deutschen mit „sich" gebildet werden, werden nicht automatisch im Englischen von den Reflexivpronomen ***-self/-selves*** begleitet.

sich (ver)ändern	*to change*	sich bewegen	*to move*	sich treffen	*to meet*
sich etwas ausleihen	*to borrow sth*	sich entscheiden	*to decide*	sich verbessern	*to improve*
sich beeilen	*to hurry*	sich erinnern	*to remember*	sich vorbereiten	*to prepare*
sich beklagen	*to complain*	sich fragen	*to wonder*	sich vorstellen	*to imagine*
sich benehmen	*to behave*	sich setzen	*to sit down*	sich waschen	*to wash*

unit 6

G16 Direct and indirect speech — Direkte und indirekte Rede

page 84

Wenn man weitergeben möchte, was ein anderer gesagt hat, verwendet man meistens nicht die direkte, sondern die indirekte Rede. Vergleiche:

direct speech	indirect (or reported) speech
Ceri: (on the phone to Mrs Morgan) "**I'm** going to be home late, Mom. **I'll** be with **my** friend Angela. **We** want to go shopping together."	*Mrs Morgan tells Gareth about Ceri's phone call:* "Ceri says that **she's** going to be home late. She says **she'll** be with **her** friend Angela. **They** want to go shopping together."

- Die indirekte Rede besteht aus einem Einleitungssatz *(Ceri says ...)* und einem Folgesatz *(... that she's going to be home late.).*
- Anders als im Deutschen steht zwischen Einleitungssatz und Folgesatz kein Komma.
- Das einleitende ***that*** kann weggelassen werden.
- Wie im Deutschen müssen Personalpronomen und Possessivbegleiter verändert werden, wenn sie dem neuen Standpunkt nicht mehr entsprechen:
  I → she, my → her, etc.
- Steht das einleitende Verb im Präsens *(says),* so wird in der indirekten Rede die gleiche Zeitform verwendet wie in der direkten Rede.
  *Gareth: "Marla Runyan is really nice." → Gareth **says** (that) Marla Runyan is really nice.*

G17 Indirect speech with tense shift Indirekte Rede mit Zeitverschiebung

page 84

Wenn eine Äußerung nicht sofort wiedergegeben wird, sondern erst später,

- steht das einleitende Verb in der Vergangenheit;
- kommt es zu einer Zeitverschiebung im folgenden Satz.

direct speech	indirect speech
"I run 10 miles every day." **simple present →**	She said that she ran 10 miles every day. **simple past**
"I'm preparing for the Olympics." **present progressive →**	She told us she was preparing for the Olympics. **past progressive**
"I've worked out a new training schedule." **present perfect →**	She explained that she had worked out a new training schedule. **past perfect**
"Boston in 2003 was a terrible experience for me." **simple past →**	She said Boston in 2003 had been a terrible experience for her. **past perfect**
"I had trained too hard for it." **past perfect →**	She said she had trained too hard for it. **past perfect**
"I'll never make that mistake again." **will (future) →**	She said she'd never make that mistake again. **would (conditional)**
"You may not believe me, ... **may →**	She said we might not believe her ... **might**
... but I can laugh about it now." **can →**	... but she could laugh about it now. **could**

- Die Verbform in der indirekten Rede wird gegenüber der in der direkten Rede um eine Zeitstufe in die Vergangenheit zurückversetzt. Aus ***present*** wird ***past,*** aus ***past*** wird ***past perfect*** etc.
- Verbformen, die unverändert bleiben, weil sie nicht weiter in die Vergangenheit zurückversetzt werden können, sind Verben im ***past perfect*** sowie ***could*** (könnte), ***would, should*** und ***might.***

G18 Expressions of time in indirect speech
Zeitangaben in der indirekten Rede

page 85

Tuesday, May 10th (morning) **Tuesday, May 10th (afternoon)** **Friday, May 13th**

- Zeitangaben wie ***today, this month, next year*** etc. werden in der indirekten Rede beibehalten, wenn man noch am gleichen Tag, im gleichen Monat oder Jahr berichtet, was jemand gesagt hat. Wenn der Tag (der Monat, das Jahr) vorbei ist, verändern sich diese Zeitangaben in der indirekten Rede:

today	→ that day	tonight	→ that night
tomorrow	→ the next/following day	this evening	→ that evening
yesterday	→ the day before	three days ago	→ three days before/earlier
next year	→ the next/following year	last week	→ the week before

! Neben den Zeitangaben müssen eventuell auch andere Wörter verändert werden, wenn sie dem neuen Standpunkt nicht mehr entsprechen.
Einige Beispiele: ***here*** → ***there, to come*** → ***to go, to bring*** → ***to take.***

Ceri's text message (from the Cascades): It's cold **here.** If I ever **come** back to **this** place, I'll **bring** warmer clothes!	*Gareth (looks at his cellphone) to Mom:* Ceri says it's cold **there.** If she ever **goes** back to **that** place, she'll **take** warmer clothes.

G19 Indirect questions Fragen in der indirekten Rede

page 86

direct speech	indirect speech
Angela: "**What's** the problem, Ceri?"	Angela asked Ceri **what** the problem **was.**
Ceri: "**Why didn't** Ben call me?"	Ceri wondered **why** Ben **hadn't called** her.
Mom: "**Where were** you, Gareth?"	Mom asked Gareth **where** he **had been.**
Ms Snyder: "**Do** you really **want** to be a cheerleader, Angela?"	Ms Snyder asked Angela **if** she really **wanted** to be a cheerleader.
Bobby: "**Are** you **going** to the game?"	Bobby asked **whether** I **was going** to the game.

- Steht in der direkten Rede **ein Fragewort *(what, when, who, why, how, where)***, so wird es in der indirekten Rede beibehalten.
- Steht in der direkten Rede **kein Fragewort,** so wird der Nebensatz in der indirekten Rede mit ***if*** oder ***whether*** eingeleitet. (Im Deutschen: **..., ob ...**)
- Die Wortstellung in indirekten Fragesätzen ist dieselbe wie in Aussagesätzen:

subject verb object.

*"Why does Angela like cheerleading?" – I asked why **Angela liked cheerleading.***

G20 Indirect commands, requests and advice

Aufforderungen, Bitten und Ratschläge in der indirekten Rede

page 86

direct speech	indirect speech	verb	object	to + infinitive	
Ms Snyder: "Practice every day."	She	**told**	the girls	**to practice**	every day.
	(She	**wanted**	the girls	**to practice**	every day.)
"Please don't arrive late."	She	**asked**	them	**not to arrive**	late.
	(She	**didn't want**	them	**to arrive**	late.)
Coach: "Get back onto the field, Jim!"	He	**ordered**	Jim	**to get back**	onto the field.

- Mit den Verben ***to ask, to want, to tell*** und ***to order*** (immer mit einem direkten Objekt!) kann man berichten, dass jemand etwas wünscht oder fordert.
- Aus dem Imperativ *("Practice ...")* wird in der indirekten Rede ein **Infinitiv** mit ***to*** bzw. ***not to.***

direct speech	indirect speech	verb	object	to + infinitive	
Ms Snyder: "You should try harder, Angela."	Ms Snyder	**advised**	Angela	**to try**	harder.
Coach: "You mustn't eat too much before the game."	The coach	**warned**	the team	**not to eat**	too much before the game.
"I'm sure you'll win!"	He	**expected**	them	**to win.**	

- Man kann diese *Objekt + Infinitiv*-Konstruktion auch nach Verben wie ***to advise, to warn*** und ***to expect*** verwenden. (Siehe **G14 b**)
- Damit kann man Ratschläge oder Warnungen *("You should/shouldn't ... / You mustn't ... / If I were you, I wouldn't ...")* sowie Erwartungen *("I'm sure you'll ...")* in der indirekten Rede wiedergeben.

! Bei dem Verb ***warn*** muss man aufpassen.
Auf Englisch sagt man: *"He warned them not to eat too much."*
Im Deutschen heißt es: *„Er warnte sie davor, zu viel zu essen."*

G21 The introductory verb in indirect speech

Das einleitende Verb in der indirekten Rede

page 87

- Für das einleitende Verb in der indirekten Rede gibt es viele verschiedene Möglichkeiten. Es muss nicht immer ***said, told*** oder ***asked*** heißen.

statements			questions		commands, requests etc.	
to say **to tell sb** **to explain** **to point out** **to inform sb**	**to add** **to admit** **to reply** **to report** **to mention**	that ...	**to ask** **to wonder** **to want to know**	if ... why ... when ... where ... how ... who ...	**to tell** **to ask** **to want** **to advise** **to expect** **to order** **to warn**	sb to ...

vocabulary

Aufbau des Vokabulars

Im ***Vocabulary***-Teil sind die Vokabeln dieses Bandes in der Reihenfolge ihres Vorkommens aufgelistet und erklärt. **Fett gedruckte Wörter** kommen häufig vor, so dass du sie verstehen und verwenden können musst. Normal gedruckte Wörter sind zur Behandlung bestimmter Themen und Texte notwendig. Die mittlere Spalte kann verschiedene Dinge enthalten, die dir beim Lernen helfen: Bilder, Beispiel- oder Erklärungssätze und Hinweise auf Besonderheiten. Die rechte Spalte enthält deutsche Übersetzungen oder Erklärungen. Außerdem gibt es im ***Vocabulary*** wieder Lerntipps, nützliche Zusammenstellungen und Übungen.
Im Anschluss findest du wieder einen alphabetisch geordneten ***Dictionary***-Teil, in dem du die Wörter aller Bände noch einmal nachschlagen kannst.

Abkürzungen und Zeichen

pl. = Plural, Mehrzahl
sg. = Singular, Einzahl
sb = somebody
sth = something
jmdm = jemandem
jmdn = jemanden
etw. = etwas
AE = Amerikanisches Englisch
BE = Britisches Englisch

e.g. = zum Beispiel
• Wort, das im Deutschen sehr ähnlich ist oder leicht aus bereits bekannten Bestandteilen erschlossen werden kann
* unregelmäßiges Verb (siehe S. 198)
↔ ist das Gegenteil von
→ ist verwandt mit
= entspricht; ≠ entspricht nicht
! Achtung!

Lautschrift

Hier seht ihr noch einmal die Erklärung der Zeichen, die in der Lautschrift verwendet werden:

Konsonanten
[ŋ] morni**ng**
[r] **r**ed
[s] thi**s**
[z] i**s**
[ʒ] televi**s**ion
[dʒ] pa**ge**
[ʃ] **sh**e
[tʃ] lun**ch**
[ð] **th**e
[θ] **th**anks
[v] **v**ideo
[w] **w**ow, **o**ne

Vokale
[ɑː] f**a**ther
[ʌ] b**u**t
[e] p**e**n
[ə] **a** sist**er**
[ɜː] g**ir**l
[æ] fl**a**t
[ɪ] **i**t
[i] happ**y**
[iː] t**ea**cher, sh**e**
[ɒ] g**o**t
[ɔː] b**a**ll
[ʊ] b**oo**k
[u] Jan**u**ary
[uː] t**oo**, tw**o**

Doppellaute
[aɪ] **I**, m**y**
[aʊ] n**ow**, h**ou**se
[eə] th**ere**, p**air**
[eɪ] n**a**me, th**ey**
[ɪə] h**ere**, id**ea**
[ɔɪ] b**oy**
[əʊ] hell**o**
[ʊə] s**ure**

Zusätzliche Zeichen
[ˈ] Hauptakzent auf der nachfolgenden Silbe
[ˌ] Nebenakzent auf der nachfolgenden Silbe
[‿] Bindebogen zwischen zwei Wörtern

Alle anderen Zeichen werden genauso ausgesprochen, wie sie geschrieben werden, z. B. [b], [j], [l] usw.

unit 1 London

In den ersten zwei Bänden hast du schon einige Vokabellerntipps kennen gelernt, die dir auch in diesem Schuljahr eine Hilfe beim Wörterlernen sein können.

Also, denk daran:

Kleine Lernportionen von 10–15 Wörtern lernen sich am besten, wenn du dir diese Portionen **mehrmals am Tag** zwischen anderen Aufgaben vornimmst und sie **nur jeweils 5–10 Minuten** „bearbeitest".

Die **Vokabelkartei** hilft dir dabei, die schwer zu lernenden Wörter herauszufinden und gezielt zu wiederholen. Genauso können **Lernplakate** mit „schwierigen Fällen" dich beim Hinsehen immer wieder daran erinnern.

Versuche, für jedes neue Wort **Zusammenhänge** herzustellen, die das Erinnern erleichtern.

Falls du jetzt anfängst, weitere Sprachen zu lernen, solltest du versuchen, Verwechslungen zwischen den Sprachen zu vermeiden. **Halte sie auseinander!** Also erst die neuen Englisch-Vokabeln, dann die Mathematik-Hausaufgaben und dann erst die neuen Wörter für Französisch oder Latein lernen. Und dazwischen sind auch die **Lernpausen** wichtig.

Intro

• **punk** [pʌŋk]		Punk
natural history [ˌnætʃrl ˈhɪstri]	history → *natural history* If you're interested in facts about animals, birds, flowers and trees, you'll enjoy the *Natural History Museum* in London.	Naturgeschichte
• **natural** [ˈnætʃrl]	! Achtung Aussprache!	natürlich, Natur-
palace [ˈpælɪs]	A *palace* is usually finer than a castle, but not so strong.	Palast
• **homeless** [ˈhəʊmləs]	home → *homeless*	obdachlos
• **carnival** [ˈkɑːnɪvl]		Karneval
2 • **gallery** [ˈgæləri]	A room or building where you can look at pictures and other forms of art.	Galerie
• **millennium**, *pl.* **millennia** [mɪˈleniəm]	A thousand years; *here*: the year 2000.	Jahrtausend
two thousand [ˌtuː ˈθaʊznd]		zweitausend
dungeon [ˈdʌndʒn]		Verlies
3 **Underground** [ˈʌndəgraʊnd]	Going by *Underground* can be quicker than going by bus, but you don't see so much of London.	Londoner U-Bahn
• to **change** [tʃeɪndʒ]	Does this train go all the way to London? – No, it only goes *as far as* Birmingham. Then we have to *change*.	umsteigen

• **as far as** [əz 'fɑːr‿əz]		bis
• **stop** [stɒp]	to stop → a *stop*	Haltestelle
to **work out** [ˌwɜːk‿'aʊt]	to work → *to work out* If you don't know the answer to a problem (for example in Maths), it's often best to *work* it *out* on paper.	herausbringen, herausfinden; ausarbeiten

Language A The river Thames

• **service** ['sɜːvɪs]	to serve → *service* There's a good bus *service* into town, so we don't often go by car.	Service, Dienst
commuter [kə'mjuːtə]	Sb who travels a long way from home to work, usually by train.	Pendler(in)
• **Londoner** ['lʌndənə]		Londoner(in)
during *(+ noun)* ['djʊərɪŋ]	! Compare the two: – while we were travelling – *during* the journey	während *(+ Nomen)*
• loudspeaker [ˌlaʊd'spiːkə]	speaker → *loudspeaker*	Lautsprecher
• *to **build** [bɪld]	building → *to build*	bauen
in fact [ɪn 'fækt]	fact → *in fact*	tatsächlich; eigentlich
in time for [ɪn 'taɪm fə]	We'll be just *in time for* the beginning of the film. = We won't miss the beginning of it.	rechtzeitig zu
• **height** [haɪt]	high → *height*	Höhe
in advance [ɪn‿əd'vɑːnts]	If you want to be sure you'll get a ticket, book one *in advance.*	im Voraus
government ['gʌvnmənt]	A group of people whose job it is to 'look after' a country and deal with its problems.	Regierung
clock [klɒk]	o'clock → *clock* A *clock* tells you what time it is.	Uhr
• clock tower ['klɒk taʊə]	tower → *clock tower*	Uhrenturm
• **parliament** ['pɑːləmənt]	! The spelling is different from German.	Parlament
• to **date from** ['deɪt frəm]	date → *to date from*	zurückgehen auf
century ['sentʃri]	We live in the 21st *century.*	Jahrhundert
• **for many years** [fə ˌmæni 'jɪəz]		viele Jahre lang
the BBC [ˌbiːbiː'siː]	British Broadcasting Corporation. There are a lot of programmes on BBC television and radio.	*britische Rundfunkanstalt*
chime [tʃaɪm]	The sound of church bells or clocks, especially to show what time it is.	Glockenspiel, Glockengeläut
1 to **persuade** [pə'sweɪd]	If you want to *persuade* sb to do sth, it's important to find good arguments.	überreden
2 • **passive** ['pæsɪv]		Passiv
3 to **perform** [pə'fɔːm]	If you *perform* a play, you act it in front of people who come specially to watch it.	aufführen, auftreten
• *to **show sb around** (a place) [ʃəʊ]	to show → *to show sb around*	jmdn (an einem Ort) herumführen
• **musical** ['mjuːzɪkl]	music → *musical* Sue is very *musical.* She plays three different *musical* instruments.	musikalisch, Musik-

4 • **barrier** ['bæriə]	A kind of wall or fence that is put somewhere to protect sth or to keep things or people out.	Barriere, Sperre
5 *to **take place** [teɪk 'pleɪs]	! *to take place* = stattfinden to sit down = Platz nehmen	stattfinden
notice ['nəʊtɪs]		Anschlag, Notiz
• **mystery** ['mɪstri]	Sth that people can't understand; a puzzle.	Mysterium, Rätsel, Geheimnis
devastated ['devəsteɪtɪd]	Very unhappy, for example after a terrible shock.	niedergeschmettert
even if [ˌi:vn‿'ɪf]	We'll never be able to beat their team, *even if* we play really well.	auch wenn
• **area** ['eəriə]	The Notting Hill *area* is the part of London in and around Notting Hill.	Areal; Fläche; Gebiet
to **report** [rɪ'pɔ:t]	If you *report* a thing to the police, you give the police information about it.	berichten; (sich) melden
6 the Docklands ['dɒklændz]		Docklands *(Hafengebiet in London)*
• **they** [ðeɪ]		*hier:* man
• **health club** ['helθ klʌb]	health → *health club*	Fitnessklub
7 • **sign** [saɪn]	! Achtung Aussprache: *sign* [saɪn] → signal ['sɪgnl]	Zeichen; Schild
• **infinitive** [ɪn'fɪnətɪv]		Infinitiv

London sights and places

Buildings
The Archway Tavern [ðiˌ‿ɑ:tʃweɪ 'tævn]
Big Ben [ˌbɪg 'ben]
Buckingham Palace [ˌbʌkɪŋəm 'pælɪs]
The Globe Theatre [ðə 'gləʊb ˌθɪətə]
The Houses of Parliament [ðə ˌhaʊzɪz‿əv 'pɑ:ləmənt]
London Bridge [ˌlʌndən 'brɪdʒ]
Marble Arch [ˌmɑ:bl‿'ɑ:tʃ]
The Millennium Bridge [ðə mɪˌleniəm 'brɪdʒ]
The Thames Barrier [ðə ˌtemz 'bæriə]
Tower Bridge [ˌtaʊə 'brɪdʒ]
The Tower of London [ðə ˌtaʊər‿əv 'lʌndən]

Museums
The British Museum [ðə ˌbrɪtɪʃ mju:'zi:əm]
The London Dungeon [ðə ˌlʌndən 'dʌndʒn]
Madame Tussaud's [ˌmædəm tu'sɔ:dz]
The National Gallery [ðə ˌnæʃnl 'gælri]
The Natural History Museum [ðə ˌnætʃrl 'hɪstri mju:ˌzi:əm]
Rock Circus [ˌrɒk 'sɜ:kəs]
Tate Modern [ˌteɪt 'mɒdn]

Other places
Baker Street ['beɪkə ˌstri:t]
Camden Market [ˌkæmdən 'mɑ:kɪt]
Camden Town ['kæmdən ˌtaʊn]
Covent Garden [ˌkɒvnt 'gɑ:dn]
The Docklands [ðə 'dɒklændz]
Euston Station [ˌju:stn 'steɪʃn]
Hyde Park [ˌhaɪd 'pɑ:k]
Leicester Square [ˌlestə 'skweə]
Notting Hill [ˌnɒtɪŋ 'hɪl]
The Old Kent Road [ðiˌ‿əʊld ˌkent 'rəʊd]
Oxford Circus [ˌɒksfəd 'sɜ:kəs]
Oxford Street ['ɒksfəd ˌstri:t]
South Kensington [ˌsaʊθ 'kenzɪŋtən]
Southwark ['sʌðək]
Tower Hill [ˌtaʊə 'hɪl]
Victoria Station [vɪkˌtɔ:riə 'steɪʃn]
The West End [ðə ˌwest‿'end]
Westminster [west'mɪntstə]
Wimbledon ['wɪmbldn]

Language B In Covent Garden

watch [wɒtʃ]	A clock:  A *watch*: 	Armbanduhr
*to **be fast** [bi: 'fɑ:st]	"Hurry up, it's five to two!" – "No, it's only ten to. Your watch must *be fast*."	vorgehen
• **hairstyle** ['heəstaɪl]	hair → *hairstyle*	Frisur
busker ['bʌskə]	Sb who plays music or sings for money in busy city streets or stations.	Straßenmusikant(in)
honey ['hʌni]	*AE*: "Hello, *honey!*" *BE*: "Hello, dear!"	Honig; Schätzchen *(AE)*
funky ['fʌŋki]	Young people usually like *'funky'* clothes more than their parents do.	irre
*to **make friends (with)** [ˌmeɪk 'frendz]	To meet a person who becomes a friend.	Freundschaft schließen (mit)
(my) fault ['maɪ ˌfɔ:lt]	It wasn't *my fault*. = I didn't do anything wrong.	(meine) Schuld
stall [stɔ:l]	On market day, people sell different things at different *stalls*.	Stand, Bude
Caribbean [ˌkærɪ'bi:ən; kə'rɪbiən]		karibisch
2 to **stress** [stres]	If you *stress* sth, it shows that you think it is especially important.	betonen

Text Souvenirs of London

• *to **have a look (at)** [ˌhæv‿ə 'lʊk]	to look → *to have a look* Let's *have* another *look* at it. = Let's look at it again.	anschauen
store [stɔ:]	Another word for a shop.	Laden, Geschäft
• to **grin** [grɪn]	To smile (with a big smile).	grinsen
to **head (for)** [hed]	If you *head for* a place, you move towards it.	zusteuern auf
department [dɪ'pɑ:tmənt]	The games *department* is the part of a shop that sells games.	Abteilung
• **CD-ROM** [ˌsi:di:'rɒm]		CD-ROM
• **detective** [dɪ'tektɪv]	! Achte auf die Betonung: [-'--]	Detektiv(in)
for ages [fr‿'eɪdʒɪz]	age → *for ages* For a very long time.	ewig lange
to **sigh** [saɪ]	People often *sigh* if they feel disappointed or tired.	seufzen
embarrassed [ɪm'bærəst]	When you're *embarrassed*, you often feel stupid and don't know what to say. ! Achtung Schreibung!	verlegen
• **idiot** ['ɪdiət]	! It's very rude to call sb an *idiot*.	Idiot(in)
• **teddy bear** ['tedi ˌbeə]	black bear → *teddy bear*	Teddybär
string [strɪŋ]	You can tie things together with a piece of *string*.	Schnur
CCTV (closed-circuit TV) [ˌsi:si:ti:'vi:]		Fernsehüberwachungsanlage
• **monitor** ['mɒnɪtə]		Monitor
Beefeater ['bi:fˌi:tə]		Beefeater, königlicher Leibgardist

guard [gɑ:d]	Sb whose job it is to watch and protect a person or a place (often a building).	Wache; Wächter(in)
My heart jumped into my mouth. [maɪ ˌhɑ:t dʒʌmpt‿ɪntə maɪ ˈmaʊθ]		Das Herz schlug mir bis zum Halse.
*to **pay for** [peɪ]	If you want to buy sth, you have to *pay for* it.	bezahlen
thief, *pl.* **thieves** [θi:f; θi:vz]	A person who has stolen sth.	Dieb(in)
• to **protest** [prəʊˈtest]	! Achte auf die Betonung: [-ˈ-]	protestieren
to **interrupt** [ˌɪntəˈrʌpt]	To speak in the middle of what sb else is saying.	unterbrechen
It's nothing to do with me. [ɪts ˌnʌθɪŋ tə ˌdu: wɪð ˈmi:]	I haven't got anything to do with this.	Ich habe damit nichts zu tun.
bloody [ˈblʌdi]	! *Bloody* is a very rude word.	verdammt
to **order** [ˈɔ:də]	The Sheriff *ordered* his men to hunt the outlaws.	befehlen
• **dance** [dɑ:nts]	to dance → a *dance*	Tanz
• to **pause** [pɔ:z]	To stop for a moment.	Pause machen; anhalten; verharren
key [ki:]		Schlüssel
mistake [mɪˈsteɪk]		Fehler
I don't get it. [aɪ ˌdəʊnt ˈget‿ɪt]	I don't understand.	Das kapiere ich nicht.
Lucky you did. [ˌlʌki jə ˈdɪd]		Zum Glück hast du das getan.
to **reply** [rɪˈplaɪ]	Another word for 'to answer'.	antworten, erwidern, entgegnen
*to **be out of one's mind** [bi:‿ˌaʊt‿əv wʌnz ˈmaɪnd]	mind → *to be out of one's mind* ! *"You're out of your mind!"* is a very rude way of saying that you don't agree.	verrückt sein
for [fɔ:; fə]	All that trouble just *for* a game!	wegen
*to **feel sorry for** [fi:l ˈsɒri]	I *felt sorry* for him. = Er hat mir Leid getan.	Mitleid haben mit; bedauern
1 • **creative** [kriˈeɪtɪv]	In *creative* writing exercises you can use your own ideas.	kreativ

Skills

skill [skɪl]	When you learn new *skills*, you learn how to do special kinds of work really well.	Fertigkeit; Geschick
*to **give a talk** [ˌgɪv‿ə ˈtɔ:k]	to talk → *to give a talk*	einen Vortrag halten
• **talk** [tɔ:k]		Vortrag; Rede
2 **source** [sɔ:s]	What was your *source* of information? = Where did your information come from?	Quelle
audience [ˈɔ:diənts]	The people who have come together to see or listen to sth (a play, a talk or a concert). ! Achte auf die Betonung: [ˈ--] *audience* ≠ Audienz!	Publikum
3 **complete** [kəmˈpli:t]	Whole.	vollständig
key word [ˈki: wɜ:d]	key → *key word*	Stichwort; Schlüsselbegriff
conclusion [kənˈklu:ʒn]	introduction ↔ *conclusion*	Schluss; Schlussfolgerung

Let's check

4 **cheap** [tʃi:p]	expensive ↔ *cheap*	billig
• **grass** [grɑ:s]		Gras

focus 1 Focus on British history

BC (= before Christ) [bi:'si:]	Before the first millennium started.	vor Christus
AD (= Anno Domini) [eɪ'di:]	After the first millennium started.	nach Christus
1 Roman ['rəʊmən]		Römer; römisch
to invade [ɪn'veɪd]	If you *invade* a country, you move to it with an *army* and try to conquer it.	einmarschieren
army ['ɑ:mi]		Armee
to defeat [dɪ'fi:t]	To beat.	besiegen
battle ['bætl]	Armies fight in *battles*.	Schlacht
• to **control** [kən'trəʊl]	It can be easier to invade a country than to *control* it.	kontrollieren; beherrschen
Anglo-Saxon [ˌæŋgləʊ'sæksn]	The people that lived in England when the Normans invaded can be called the *Anglo-Saxons*.	Angelsachse; angelsächsisch
Angles *(pl.)* ['æŋglz]		Angeln *(Volksstamm)*
gradual ['grædʒuəl]	A *gradual* change is a slow change.	allmählich
Celt [kelt]		Kelte, Keltin
Briton ['brɪtn]	! Britain = Großbritannien a *Briton* = ein Brite, eine Britin	Brite, Britin
*to **be known as** [bi: 'nəʊn‿əz]	To be called.	bekannt sein als
• **separate** ['seprət]	When things are *separate* from each other, they aren't together. ! Achte auf die Betonung: ['--]	separat; getrennt; verschieden
• **kingdom** ['kɪŋdəm]	king → *kingdom*	Königreich
queen [kwi:n]	A kingdom can be controlled by a king or a *queen*.	Königin
• **rebellion** [rɪ'beliən]		Rebellion
• *to **set fire to** [set 'faɪə tə]	fire → *to set fire to*	in Brand stecken
• *to **take one's own life** [ˌteɪk wʌnz‿əʊn 'laɪf]	life → *to take one's own life*	sich das Leben nehmen
prisoner ['prɪznə]		Gefangene(r)
*to take sb prisoner [teɪk 'prɪznə]	The Sheriff caught one of the outlaws and *took* him *prisoner*. Soon the outlaw was a *prisoner* in Nottingham Castle.	gefangen nehmen
origin ['ɒrɪdʒɪn]	A name that comes from Latin is a name of Latin *origin*.	Ursprung
• **native** ['neɪtɪv]	People who were born in a country are its *native* people.	eingeboren
empire ['empaɪə]	A number of different parts of the world that are all controlled by one country.	Reich; Kaiserreich
to **found** [faʊnd]	! to find, found, found (finden) to *found*, founded, founded (gründen)	gründen

after ['ɑ:ftə]	! Look at the difference: – after the show – after the show finished	nachdem
trading centre ['treɪdɪŋ ˌsentə]	city centre – shopping centre – *trading centre*	Handelszentrum
• **time line** ['taɪm laɪn]	time → *time line*	Zeitstrahl
2 **soldier** ['səʊldʒə]	Sb whose job is to fight, usually for his or her country.	Soldat(in)
Asia ['eɪʃə]	*Asia* → Asian	Asien
Egypt ['i:dʒɪpt]		Ägypten
Greece [gri:s]		Griechenland
Rome [rəʊm]		Rom
medal ['medl]		Medaille
prehistory [ˌpri:'hɪstri]		Vorgeschichte
3 tapestry ['tæpɪstri]	The Bayeux *Tapestry* tells the story (in pictures) of the Normans who invaded England.	Wandteppich
• **original** [ə'rɪdʒnl]	origin → *original*	original; ursprünglich

unit 2 Welcome to Wales

Tipps zur Lernorganisation

Zur rechten Zeit
Überlege dir, wann du gut lernen kannst. Bist du zu bestimmten Zeiten eher müde (z. B. nach dem Mittagessen)? Dann suche dir eine günstigere Zeit aus, in der du körperlich und geistig „fit" bist.
Nutze diese „Spitzenzeiten", so gut du kannst.
Das bedeutet nicht, dass du unbedingt mehrere Stunden lang lernen musst. Vielleicht lernst du nicht gern zu lange auf einmal, weil es sehr anstrengend und ermüdend ist. Du kannst z. B. am Nachmittag eine Zeit lang lernen und dann wieder am Abend.

Nicht immer alleine
Wenn es euch nicht so gut gefällt, alle Vokabeln allein der Reihe nach von vorn bis hinten zu wiederholen, dann könnt ihr euch auch interessantere Methoden ausdenken, z. B. durch gegenseitiges Abfragen. Das macht mehr Spaß und bringt Abwechslung. Wie wäre es z. B., wenn eine(r) für die/den andere(n) einen kleinen „Test" entwirft? Dazu kann euch die Mittelspalte eine große Hilfe sein. Ihr könnt eine Erklärung aus der Mittelspalte aufschreiben, zu der die/der andere dann die entsprechende Vokabel finden soll.
Lasst euch auch selbst etwas einfallen, z. B. eigene Zeichnungen o. Ä., zu denen die/der andere das entsprechende Wort oder den gesuchten Ausdruck finden soll.

Häufige Fehler im Blick
Wenn ihr feststellt, dass ihr bei einigen Wörtern immer wieder Schwierigkeiten habt, könnt ihr gemeinsam die schwierigsten Wörter auf große Blätter schreiben und mit Zeichnungen o. Ä. illustrieren. Wenn ihr immer denselben Fehler bei der Rechtschreibung macht, könnt ihr diese Stelle mit roter Farbe oder durch besonders große oder unterstrichene Buchstaben hervorheben. Ihr könnt auch Eselsbrücken und Merkverse ergänzen, die euch dazu einfallen. Wenn ihr diese Bilder in eurem Klassenzimmer oder auch in eurem Zimmer zu Hause eine Zeit lang aufhängt, habt ihr sie immer gut im Blick!

Intro

1 **greeting** ['gri:tɪŋ]	If sb gives you a friendly *greeting*, they say hello in a friendly way.	Gruß
guide [gaɪd]	A person or a book that gives you information (for example about a city or a museum).	Führer(in)
hardly ['hɑ:dli]	! You're working hard. = Du arbeitest hart. I can *hardly* believe it. = Ich kann es kaum glauben.	kaum
*to **be pleased** [bi: 'pli:zd]	If *you're pleased*, you're happy about sth.	erfreut sein
to **manage** to (do sth.) ['mænɪdʒ]	manager → *to manage* It wasn't an easy job – but I've *managed* it!	schaffen (etw. zu tun)
• to **arrange** [ə'reɪndʒ]	If you *arrange* an event, you make plans so that it will happen.	ausmachen; arrangieren
scenery ['si:nri]	What you see around you when you're out in the country.	Landschaft
magnificent [məg'nɪfɪsnt]	Very very good or beautiful.	großartig, prachtvoll
choir ['kwaɪə]	A *choir* is a group of people who sing together.	Chor
to **rent** [rent]	To pay money for sth you use, for example an apartment or a car.	mieten

Language A The Welsh Morgans

Welsh [welʃ]	*Welsh* people are from Wales.	walisisch; Walisisch; Waliser(in)
Don't mention it. [ˌdəʊnt 'mentʃn‿ɪt]	"Thank you so much!" – *"Don't mention it!"*	Bitte schön!; Gern geschehen.
to **mention** ['mentʃn]	If you *mention* sth, you say sth about it or talk about it for a moment.	erwähnen
to **switch on** [swɪtʃ‿'ɒn]	When you *switch* the TV *on*, the picture and the sound come on.	einschalten
King Arthur [ˌkɪŋ‿'ɑ:θə]		König Artus
for [fɔ:; fə]	We've been learning English *for* two years. = We started to learn English two years ago.	seit
to **move** [mu:v]	To leave your old home and go to live in a different house or town.	umziehen
post office ['pəʊst‿ɒfɪs]	post – postcard – *post office*	Postamt
factory ['fæktri]	A large building or group of buildings where things are made.	Fabrik; Werk
You bet! [ju: 'bet]	You can be sure of that!	Das kannst du mir aber glauben!
*to **bet** [bet]	I *bet* you £10 that our team will win!	wetten
pub [pʌb]	A place where people can go and have drinks (especially beer, wine, whisky etc.) and talk to their friends.	Kneipe; Gasthaus
2 • **period** ['pɪəriəd]	An hour is a short *period* of time. ! Achtung Aussprache!	Periode; Zeitspanne

3 dragon ['drægn]		Drache
• **DVD player** [ˌdi:vi:di: 'pleɪə]		DVD-Player
• *to **begin** [bɪ'gɪn]		beginnen; anfangen
4 *to **get to know** [ˌget tə 'nəʊ]	When you *get to know* sb, you find out more about them.	kennen lernen
• **industry** ['ɪndəstri]	! Achte auf die Betonung: ['---]	Industrie

Language B An e-mail from Ceri

• **element** ['elɪmənt]	! Achte auf die Betonung: ['---]	Element
medieval [ˌmedi'i:vl]	From the Middle Ages.	mittelalterlich
• **camp** [kæmp]	A group of buildings or tents.	Camp; Lager
to **admit** [əd'mɪt]	If you have done sth wrong or silly, it isn't always easy to *admit* it.	zugeben
• **highlight** ['haɪlaɪt]	light → *highlight*	Highlight
grave [greɪv]	The place where a dead person's body is put.	Grab
• **disaster** [dɪ'zɑ:stə]	A terrible event, especially when a lot of people are hurt or killed.	Desaster; Katastrophe
2 **progressive form** [prəʊ'gresɪv]		Verlaufsform
3 **out of work** [ˌaʊt‿əv 'wɜ:k]	work → *out of work* Sb who isn't able to find a job is *out of work*.	arbeitslos
4 to die out [daɪ‿'aʊt]	to die → *to die out*	aussterben
• **programme** *(BE)* ['prəʊgræm]	There's an interesting *programme* about the Celts on TV tonight.	Programm; Sendung
5 to **prove** [pru:v]	To show definitely that sth is true.	beweisen

Skills

skimming ['skɪmɪŋ]	Looking at a text very quickly, just to get the main ideas.	Überfliegen
scanning ['skænɪŋ]	Looking at sth (a text etc.) very carefully because you are looking for special details.	Durchsuchen nach Details; Abtasten
to **save** [seɪv]	! to *save* time or money = sparen to *save* a person's life = retten	sparen
1 *to **get the gist** [ˌget ðə 'dʒɪst]	To understand the main ideas or general meaning.	das Wesentliche erfassen
to **cover (up)** ['kʌvə]	If you put a piece of paper over a page in your book, you *cover* it *up*.	zudecken
• to fear [fɪə]	fear → *to fear*	fürchten
to rumble ['rʌmbl]		donnern
• alarm [ə'lɑ:m]		Alarm
• mass [mæs]		Masse
dreadful ['dredfl]		furchtbar
silence ['saɪlənts]		Stille
• rescuer ['reskju:ə]	to rescue → *rescuer*	Retter(in)
blood [blʌd]		Blut
• to close [kləʊz]	closed → *to close*	schließen
• bulldozer ['bʊlˌdəʊzə]		Bulldozer

nur die Fettgedruckten

muck [mʌk]		Dreck
lorry ['lɒri]		Lastwagen
• interval ['ɪntəvl]		Intervall
• cry [kraɪ]	to cry → a *cry*	Schrei
• movement ['mu:vmənt]	to move → *movement*	Bewegung
• hope [həʊp]	to hope → *hope*	Hoffnung
• official [ə'fɪʃl]		offiziell
bereavement [bɪ'ri:vmənt]		schmerzlicher Verlust
• to identify [aɪ'dentɪfaɪ]		identifizieren
chapel ['tʃæpl]		Kapelle
body ['bɒdi]		Leiche
to wrap [ræp]		einwickeln
bereaved [bɪ'ri:vd]		von einem schmerzlichen Verlust betroffen
• respect [rɪ'spekt]		Respekt
• thankful ['θæŋkfl]	to thank → thanks → *thankful*	dankbar
2 • to **ignore** [ɪg'nɔ:]	If you don't look at sth and don't listen to it, even if you know it's there, you *ignore* it.	ignorieren
knight [naɪt]	! Achtung Aussprache! Das 'k' wird nicht gesprochen.	Ritter
• to exist [ɪg'zɪst]		existieren
• inland ['ɪnlænd]	land → *inland*	landeinwärts
to settle ['setl]		siedeln; sich niederlassen
Arthurian [ɑ:'θjʊəriən]	Arthur → *Arthurian*	Artus-
the Round Table [ˌraʊnd 'teɪbl]		die Tafelrunde
• courage ['kʌrɪdʒ]	! Achtung Aussprache!	Mut
honour ['ɒnə]	! Achtung Aussprache! Das 'h' wird nicht gesprochen.	Ehre
noble ['nəʊbl]		edel; adlig
• ideal [aɪ'dɪəl]	! Achtung Aussprache!	Ideal
in return [ɪn rɪ'tɜ:n]		als Gegenleistung
• page [peɪdʒ]		Page
• household ['haʊshəʊld]	house → *household*	Haushalt
weapon ['wepən]		Waffe
squire [skwaɪə]		Junker
• servant ['sɜ:vnt]	to serve → *servant*	Diener(in)
master ['mɑ:stə]		Herr
• symbol ['sɪmbl]		Symbol
to destroy [dɪ'strɔɪ]		zerstören
• symbolic [sɪm'bɒlɪk]	symbol → *symbolic*	symbolisch
• importance [ɪm'pɔ:tnts]	important → *importance*	Bedeutung, Wichtigkeit
ruler ['ru:lə]		Herrscher(in)
• baron ['bærn]		Baron
• bishop ['bɪʃəp]		Bischof
• to dominate ['dɒmɪneɪt]		dominieren
• owner ['əʊnə]	to own → *owner*	Besitzer(in)

Tipps zum Lesen
Den Inhalt eines unbekannten Textes in einer fremden Sprache kann man erst nach mehrmaligem Lesen voll erschließen.
Dazu einige Tipps:

1 Vor dem Lesen
- Versuche herauszufinden, worum es in dem Text gehen könnte. Hilfen dazu geben dir Einleitungen, Bilder und oft schon die Überschrift.

2 Das erste Lesen des Textes
- Lies den Text ganz durch. Dass unbekannte Wörter vorkommen, ist ganz normal. Bleibe beim Lesen nicht an diesen hängen.
- Beantworte danach die folgenden Fragen: *Who? What? Where? When?*

3 Das zweite Lesen des Textes
- Lies den Text nochmals ganz durch und teile ihn in verschiedene Abschnitte auf. Oft hat der Text diese Einteilung schon durch Absätze.
- Finde nun eine Überschrift für jeden Absatz oder Textteil. Aus den Überschriften kannst du eine *mind map* für jeden Abschnitt entwickeln.

4 Unbekannte Wörter und Grammatik
- Einige unbekannte Wörter lassen sich erschließen, weil sie so ähnlich wie die deutschen Entsprechungen aussehen, z. B. *industry* oder *symbolic.*
- Allerdings können *false friends* dich auf eine falsche Fährte locken. Deshalb: *False friends,* z. B. *hardly,* immer besonders einprägen!
- Oft lassen sich neue Wörter in ihrer Bedeutung erschließen, weil du ein anderes Wort aus der gleichen Wortfamilie kennst, z. B. *to use* → *useful*
- Der Kontext, in dem ein unbekanntes Wort auftaucht, kann auch bei der Erschließung der Bedeutung helfen.
- Über unbekannte Grammatikformen solltest du dir nicht zu viele Gedanken machen. Meistens verstehst du den Sinn des Satzes trotzdem.

Text How Percival became a Knight of the Round Table

armour ['ɑ:mə]	Knights wore *armour* to protect them in battle.	Rüstung
Sir [sɜ:]	When a man becomes a knight, he can put *'Sir'* in front of his name.	Sir *(Anrede für einen Ritter)*
knee [ni:]	Part of the leg: →	Knie
angel ['eɪndʒl]	Some people believe that *angels* help us in times of trouble.	Engel
amazement [ə'meɪzmənt]	amazed → *amazement* Great surprise.	Erstaunen
perhaps [pə'hæps]	Another word for 'maybe'.	vielleicht
eager ['i:gə]	If you want to do sth very much, you are *eager* to do it.	eifrig
as soon as [əz 'su:n‿əz]	soon → *as soon as*	sobald
to **wonder** ['wʌndə]	If you *wonder* about sth, you aren't sure about it, but would like to know.	sich Gedanken machen, sich fragen
• **useless** ['ju:sləs]	! Achtung Aussprache: to use [z] → useful [s] → *useless* [s]	nutzlos
armed [ɑ:md]	A soldier can only fight in battle if he is *armed.*	bewaffnet

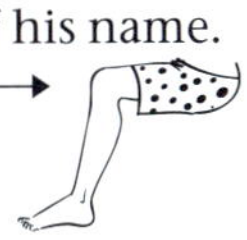

• **hunting** ['hʌntɪŋ]	to hunt → *hunting* 	Jagd; Jagd-
• **spear** [spɪə]		Speer
deep [di:p]	You mustn't go into *deep* water if you can't swim.	tief
• **gold** [gəʊld]	gold → *gold(en)*	golden
to **appear** [ə'pɪə]	To come in sight; to be there suddenly.	erscheinen
cup [kʌp]		Pokal; Kelch
horrified ['hɒrɪfaɪd]	horror → *horrified* With a feeling of shock and surprise (because sth terrible has happened).	entsetzt
*to **take off** [teɪk‿'ɒf]	to put on ↔ *to take off* 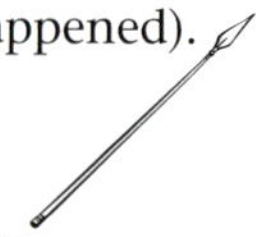	ausziehen
• **lance** [lɑ:nts]		Lanze
• **fall** [fɔ:l]	to fall → a *fall*	Sturz
blow [bləʊ]	If sth hits you, it gives you a *blow*.	Hieb, Schlag
blood [blʌd]	I've cut my finger on the bread knife. Look at all the *blood!*	Blut
ground [graʊnd]	When you go camping, you usually sleep on the *ground*.	Boden; Grund
quiet [kwaɪət]	If you sit there *quietly*, you don't speak or move.	still

Let's check

1 **instead of** [ɪn'sted‿əv]	We're going to have a holiday in the winter *instead of* the summer.	anstatt

unit 3 Living history

Wörter lernen – am besten durch Vernetzen

Wörter nur als Wortgleichung zu lernen ist nicht die wirkungsvollste Art, neue Vokabeln zu behalten. Wenn du dir beim Lernen für ein Wort möglichst mehrere dazugehörige Wörter einprägst, machst du damit dieses Wort für dein Gedächtnis besser „merkwürdig". Das Gedächtnis baut dann ein Netzwerk von Erinnerungswegen zu diesem Wort. Die Mittelspalte des Vokabulars gibt dir oft Anregungen dazu.
Hier sind einige Beispiele:

Neues Wort	Erinnerungsweg für das Gedächtnis
to compete	Welches Wort kenne ich noch aus dieser Wortfamilie? → *competition*
perhaps	Welches Wort hat die gleiche Bedeutung? → *maybe*
useless	Welches Wort bedeutet das Gegenteil? ↔ *useful*
busy	Wie unterscheiden sich die beiden Bedeutungen dieses Wortes im Deutschen?
bone	Auch Reime helfen beim Merken: *bone – stone*
each other	Ein Wortbild oder eine Zeichnung kann die Bedeutung festigen.
grape	In welches Thema lässt sich das Wort einordnen? → *fruit*
gym(nasium)	Mit welchem deutschen Wort darf ich dieses Wort nicht verwechseln?

Intro

	•**workshop** ['wɜ:kʃɒp]	to work → *workshop*	Workshop, Werkstatt
	weapon ['wepən]	Guns, spears, knives and arrows are different kinds of *weapons*.	Waffe
	sword [sɔ:d]	! Das 'w' wird nicht gesprochen.	Schwert
	shield [ʃi:ld]	The thing that soldiers carried centuries ago to protect their bodies while they were fighting.	Schild
	arts and crafts [ˌɑ:ts‿nd 'krɑ:fts]	art → *arts and crafts* In *arts and crafts* you learn how to make things with your hands.	Kunsthandwerk
	pottery ['pɒtri]	If you learn *pottery*, you learn how to make cups, plates, bowls etc.	Töpferei
	leather ['leðə]	The skin of animals that is specially treated and then used to make shoes, bags etc.	Leder
	wood [wʊd]	The hard material from trees that can be used to make tables, chairs etc. – or to make a fire.	Holz
1	•**historical** [hɪ'stɒrɪkl]	history → *historical*	geschichtlich, historisch
	re-enactment [ˌri:ɪ'næktmənt]		Nachspielen/Nachvollzug eines Ereignisses
	most of the time ['məʊst‿əv ðə ˌtaɪm]		meistens
2	**exchange** [ɪks'tʃeɪndʒ]	to change → *exchange* In an *exchange* between schools in different countries, pupils and teachers visit each other's schools for a few days or weeks.	Austausch

Language A An e-mail to Ms Deneuve

•**meeting** ['mi:tɪŋ]	to meet → *meeting*	Meeting, Treffen
since [sɪnts]	! *'Since'* has two meanings: – *since* I was little = seit … – *since* it's too late = da …	da
•**instruction** [ɪn'strʌkʃn]	If you give people *instructions*, you tell them what to do.	Instruktion, Anweisung
by mistake [ˌbaɪ mɪ'steɪk]	We made a silly mistake – we got on the wrong train *by mistake*.	versehentlich
up (to) [ʌp]	After the tennis match we went *up to* the players and asked for their autographs.	*(hier:)* herbei (zu); auf … zu
close (to) [kləʊs]	! Achtung: *close* to [s] – closed [z] 	nahe (bei)
tear [tɪə]	! Achtung Aussprache: *tear* reimt sich nicht mit 'bear' oder 'wear'.	Träne
to **remove** [rɪ'mu:v]	to move → *to remove* To take away (sth that you don't want).	entfernen
*to **stick** [stɪk]	You can *stick* pictures and newspaper articles in a scrapbook.	kleben; stecken

myself [maɪ'self]	I did it *myself*. = Nobody else did it for me.	(ich) selbst; mich (selbst)
headache ['hedeɪk]	head → a *headache*	Kopfweh
cleaning staff ['kli:nɪŋ ˌstɑ:f]	The people whose job is to clean the buildings.	Reinigungspersonal
staff [stɑ:f]	The people who work for a company, school etc.	Personal; Kollegium
to **lock** [lɒk]	lock → *to lock* To shut with a key.	abschließen
staff room ['stɑ:f rʊm]	room → *staff room* At a school, the room which is especially for teachers only.	Lehrerzimmer
caretaker *(BE)* ['keəˌteɪkə]	The person who looks after a large building (for example a school) and checks it.	Hausmeister(in)
to **score** [skɔ:]	Just before the end of the match our team *scored* a *goal* and we won 1-0.	punkten; ein Tor schießen
goal [gəʊl]		Tor; Ziel
2 **past perfect** [ˌpɑ:st 'pɜ:fɪkt]		Plusquamperfekt
•to **form** [fɔ:m]	form → *to form*	formen; bilden
•**active** ['æktɪv]	action → to act → *active*	aktiv; Aktiv
•**conjunction** [kən'dʒʌŋkʃn]		Konjunktion
3 **gym(nasium)** [dʒɪm; dʒɪm'neɪziəm]	The room in a school where PE lessons often take place.	Turnhalle
changing room ['tʃeɪndʒɪŋ ˌrʊm]	The place where you change your clothes (for example at a swimming pool or a gym).	Umkleideraum
note [nəʊt]	A small piece of paper with a message on it.	Notiz; Zettel
4 **bone** [bəʊn]		Knochen

Language B On the way

coach [kəʊtʃ]	A big bus (for holidays or long trips).	Reisebus
by [baɪ]	Not later than.	bis
to **cause** [kɔ:z]	because → *to cause* If you *cause* sth, you make it happen.	verursachen
*to shut up [ʃʌt‿'ʌp]	! *"Shut up!"* can sound very rude. It's safer to say "Be quiet!"	die Klappe halten
not until [nɒt‿ən'tɪl]	! until = bis *not ... until* = erst (wenn/als)	nicht (be)vor; erst (wenn/als)
lion [laɪən]		Löwe
pot [pɒt]	pottery → *pot* A *pot* of *paint*:	Topf
•**paint** [peɪnt]	to paint → *paint* 	Farbe
to **fancy** ['fænsi]	She *fancies* him. = She likes him and would like him as a boyfriend. ! Use this word only with your friends.	angetan sein von
*to **bend over** [ˌbend‿'əʊvə]	To move the top part of the body towards the ground.	sich vorbeugen

*to **spill** [spɪl]	If you put too much water in a glass, you'll easily *spill* it.	verschütten
1 **frequency** ['fri:kwəntsi]	How often sth happens.	Frequenz; Häufigkeit
• **position** [pə'zɪʃn]		Position
4 to **march** [mɑ:tʃ]	When soldiers walk together as a group, they march.	marschieren

Besonderheiten bei *by* und *until*

Englisch	Umschreibung	Deutsch	Bedeutung
Be there **by** 8 pm.	**before or at** 8 pm	**bis** 20 Uhr	irgendwann zwischen jetzt und spätestens diesem Zeitpunkt
Wait **until** 8 pm.	**before and at** 8 pm	**bis** 20 Uhr	die ganze Zeit ab jetzt bis zu diesem Zeitpunkt
Don't ring **until** 8 pm.	**not earlier than** 8 pm	**erst** um 20 Uhr/ **nicht vor** 20 Uhr	nicht vor diesem Zeitpunkt

Text Memories of the battle

memory ['memri]	If you can remember things easily, you have a good *memory*. Your *memories* are what you remember about sth.	Erinnerung; Gedächtnis
to **groan** [grəʊn]	To make a 'slow' sound that shows you are hurt, unhappy or disappointed.	stöhnen
curtain ['kɜ:tn]	A piece of material you can pull across a window, for example when it gets dark outside.	Vorhang
plaster ['plɑ:stə]	If you break your leg or arm, it has to be put in *plaster*.	Gips
• **still** [stɪl]	Keep your arm *still*. = Don't move your arm.	still
• **pill** [pɪl]		Pille, Tablette
two at a time [ˌtu:‿ət‿ə 'taɪm]	Two together at the same time.	zwei auf einmal
to **injure** ['ɪndʒə]	To hurt (in an accident, battle etc.)	verletzen
dizzy ['dɪzi]	Some people feel *dizzy* if they look down from a height.	schwindlig
• **local** ['ləʊkl]	The schools in your area are your *local* schools.	lokal, örtlich
muddy ['mʌdi]	If you walk in the country in wet weather, your shoes usually get *muddy*.	schlammig
• **clean** [kli:n]	If you clean sth, it becomes *clean*.	sauber
mud-fight ['mʌdfaɪt]	A *fight* in the *mud*.	Schlammschlacht
mud [mʌd]	muddy → *mud* When you walk in the *mud*, it makes your shoes muddy.	Schlamm
• **cold** [kəʊld]	to get cold → to catch a *cold* People often sneeze when they have a *cold*.	Erkältung; Kälte

• **snack** [snæk]		Snack, Imbiss
• **free** [fri:]	It's *free!* You needn't pay for it.	kostenlos
to **knock out** [nɒk‿'aʊt]	knock → *to knock out* If sth hits your head hard enough, it will *knock* you *out*. ! Achtung Aussprache! Das 'k' wird nicht gesprochen.	k.o. schlagen; umhauen
grape [greɪp]	Wine is made from *grapes*: 	Traube
• to **roll** [rəʊl]	! Achte auf die Aussprache: [əʊ]	rollen
crown [kraʊn]		Krone
himself [hɪm'self]	He did it *himself.* = Nobody else did it for him.	(er) selbst; sich (selbst)
strange [streɪndʒ]	*strange* → stranger	fremd; seltsam; merkwürdig
embarrassing [ɪm'bærəsɪŋ]	! *embarrassing* = peinlich embarrassed = verlegen Achtung Schreibung!	peinlich
by the way [ˌbaɪ ðə 'weɪ]		übrigens
Get well soon! [get ˌwel 'su:n]	I hope you'll soon feel better.	Gute Besserung!
well [wel]		gesund
royal ['rɔɪəl]	Buckingham Palace is a *royal* palace.	königlich
ambulance ['æmbjələnts]	! Achte auf die Betonung: ['---] If people are suddenly very ill or have had an accident, they are usually taken to hospital in an *ambulance.*	Krankenwagen
• **banana** [bə'nɑ:nə]	Apples, oranges, strawberries, grapes and *bananas* are all fruit.	Banane
pillow ['pɪləʊ]	When you go to sleep in bed, you usually lie with your head on a *pillow.*	Kopfkissen
to **slip** [slɪp]	slippery → *to slip*	(aus)rutschen
2 • **graffiti** [grə'fi:ti]		Graffiti

Skills

1 **direction** [dɪ'rekʃn]	direct → *direction* In all *directions*: 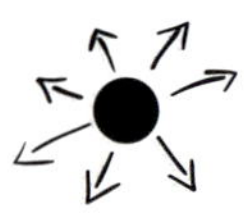	Richtung
2 **mistranslation** [ˌmɪstrænz'leɪʃn]	translation → *mistranslation* A wrong translation.	falsche Übersetzung; Übersetzungsfehler
to **translate** [trænz'leɪt]	*to translate* → translation	übersetzen
3 • **expression** [ɪk'spreʃn]	to express → *expression*	Ausdruck
4 **pronunciation** [prəˌnʌntsi'eɪʃn]	The way you speak or the way you say a word.	Aussprache

Let's check

6 **head teacher** *(BE)* [ˌhed 'ti:tʃə]	! *AE:* principal *BE: head teacher*	Schulleiter(in)

Unbekannte Wörter umschreiben

Beim Englischsprechen kann es vorkommen, dass du ein bestimmtes Wort nicht kennst.
Oder dass du ein Wort benutzt, das dein Gesprächspartner nicht versteht. Solche Wörter musst du entsprechend umschreiben oder erklären können. Wenn du einmal die Mittelspalte des Begleitvokabulars in diesem Buch studierst, findest du Beispiele dafür, wie man das macht.
Hier sind einige Grundmuster vorgestellt:

Beschreibung für …	Grundmuster
● eine Person	X is a person/man/woman/someone **who** …
● einen Ort	X is a place/town/city/country **where** …
● eine Sache	X is something **which/that** …
● eine Eigenschaft	**When/if** you can …, you are X.
● eine Tätigkeit	X is an activity **where/in which** …
● ein Geschehen	X is an event **which/that** …

focus 2 Focus on the United Tastes of America

taste [teɪst]	to taste → *taste*	Geschmack
•**pancake** ['pænkeɪk]	cake → *pancake*	Pfannkuchen
rich [rɪtʃ]	Food that is *rich* is often made with a lot of cream or butter.	reichhaltig
raspberry ['rɑ:zbri]	A red summer fruit, smaller than a strawberry. 	Himbeere
•**sauce** [sɔ:s]	I love ice cream with chocolate *sauce*.	Sauce
•to **serve** [sɜ:v]	service → *to serve* Steak is often *served* with chips.	servieren
to **whip** [wɪp]	If you want to put *cream* in the centre of a cake or on top, you have to *whip* it first.	schlagen
•**shake** [ʃeɪk]	to shake → a *shake*	Shake, Milchshake
flavor *(AE)* ['fleɪvə]	"Two ice creams, please." – "Which *flavor*?" – "One chocolate and one strawberry."	Geschmack, Aroma
low [ləʊ]	high ↔ *low*	niedrig
fat [fæt]	Butter is a kind of *fat*.	Fett
sugar ['ʃʊgə]	You can put it in foods and drinks to make them sweet.	Zucker
Tex-Mex [ˌteks'meks]	An 'American' kind of Mexican food.	texanisch-mexikanisch
crispy ['krɪspi]	crisp → *crispy* If you open a new packet of crisps, they should taste nice and *crispy*.	knusprig, kross
•**taco** ['tɑ:kəʊ]	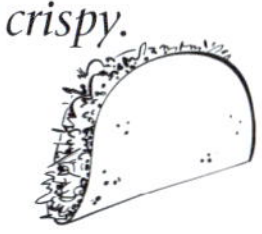	Taco *(mexikanische gefüllte Teigtasche)*
tasty ['teɪsti]	to taste → taste → *tasty*	schmackhaft
•to **grill** [grɪl]		grillen

Themen-Wortketten

1 Mit den Wörtern aus einem Themenbereich (z. B. *food*) könnt ihr gut eine Wortkette bilden, in der die Wörter durch ihre Anfangs- und Endbuchstaben verbunden sind, z. B.

CEREALUNCHONEY

oder

RESTAURANTACOSALADESSERTASTEATAKEAWAYUMMY

Ihr könnt euch diese Ketten entweder einzeln oder in Gruppen ausdenken und aufschreiben. Anschließend tauscht ihr eure Wortkettenrätsel aus und versucht alle Wörter herauszuschreiben, die ihr entdecken könnt. Dabei ist es natürlich am besten, wenn die Kette so lang wie möglich ist, damit die andere Gruppe lange zu tun hat. Denn: Wer zuerst fertig ist, hat gewonnen!

2 Diese Ketten könnt ihr auch reihum gehen lassen. Das geht dann so: Eine(r) fängt mit einem Wort an, das er/sie auf einen Zettel schreibt und weitergibt. Der/die Nächste muss ein Wort finden, das mit dem letzten Buchstaben des vorigen Wortes beginnt. Besonders schwierig wird es, wenn das Wort nur aus dem vorgegebenen Themenbereich (z. B. *food and eating, house and living etc.*) stammen darf. Deshalb könnt ihr überlegen, ob ihr das *Dictionary* aus eurem Buch als Hilfe zulassen wollt, in dem ihr nachschlagen dürft, wenn es besonders kritisch wird. Wenn ihr die Kette in zwei Gruppen gleichzeitig fortsetzt, hat die Gruppe gewonnen, die in der gleichen Zeit die längere Kette gebildet hat.

3 Und zuletzt noch eine Möglichkeit, das Ganze noch interessanter zu gestalten: Jede Gruppe kann in ihre Kette noch kleine Fallen einbauen, indem sie zwischen die Wörter aus einem Themenbereich auch Wörter setzt, die zwar von den Buchstaben her passen, aber thematisch nicht dazugehören. Wenn die andere Gruppe diese Kette „auseinander nimmt", sollte sie diese Wörter aussortieren. Für jedes gefundene Wort, das nicht passt, gibt es einen Punkt, für jedes unentdeckte Wort, das nicht dazugehört, werden zwei Punkte abgezogen.

beef [biːf]	Meat that comes from cattle.	Rindfleisch
pepper [ˈpepə]		Pfeffer; Paprikaschote
sweetcorn [ˈswiːtkɔːn]	sweet → *sweetcorn* A yellow vegetable that tastes sweet.	Mais
hot [hɒt]	Curry can taste very *hot* and *spicy.*	scharf
spicy [ˈspaɪsi]		würzig; pikant
to **microwave** [ˈmaɪkrəʊweɪv]	wave → *to microwave*	in der Mikrowelle zubereiten
lettuce [ˈletɪs]	You can make a lot of different salads with *lettuce* leaves.	Kopfsalat
sour [saʊə]	Without sugar, yoghurt can taste quite *sour.*	sauer
• **dip** [dɪp]		Dip *(cremige Sauce zum Einstippen)*
TV dinner [ˌtiːviː ˈdɪnə]	A quick dish that you can buy at a supermarket and that you can serve in 5 minutes or so.	Fernsehmahlzeit
crunchy [ˈkrʌntʃi]	Biscuits taste best if they're really *crunchy.*	knusprig; knackig
key ring [ˈkiː ˌrɪŋ]	key → *key ring*	Schlüsselbund; Schlüsselanhänger
pack [pæk]	to pack → a *pack*	Packung

	cereal ['sɪəriəl]	You buy *cereals* in a *pack*.	Zerealie; Getreideprodukt *(z. B. Cornflakes oder Müsli)*
	healthy ['helθi]	health → *healthy*	gesund
	wholewheat ['həʊlwi:t]	whole + wheat = *wholewheat*	Vollkornweizen
	topping ['tɒpɪŋ]	top → *topping*	Belag
	suitable ['su:təbl]	Food without fish or meat in it is *suitable* for vegetarians.	geeignet; passend
1	**mouth** [maʊθ]	Before you can speak, you have to open your *mouth*.	Mund
	• **product** ['prɒdʌkt]	! Achte auf die Betonung: ['--]	Produkt
2	taco shell [ˌtɑ:kəʊ 'ʃel]	taco → *taco shell*	Taco-Tasche *(mexikanische Teigtasche)*
	bun [bʌn]		Brötchen
	to **mince** [mɪnts]	To make hamburgers, the meat (usually beef) has to be *minced*.	hacken
	pork [pɔ:k]	The meat you get from pigs.	Schweinefleisch
	salt [sɔ:lt]		Salz
	• **lemonade** [ˌlemə'neɪd]		Limonade
3	• **teenager** ['ti:nˌeɪdʒə]	Sb between the age of thir*teen* and nine*teen*.	Teenager; Jugendliche(r)
	fast food restaurant [ˌfɑ:st fu:d 'restrənt]	A good place to go if you want sth quick to eat.	Schnellrestaurant
	an average of [ən‿'ævrɪdʒ‿əv]	The *average* of 5 and 7 is 6.	durchschnittlich; im Durchschnitt
	• **dollar** ['dɒlə]	"How much did you pay for the food?" – "Six *dollars per* person."	Dollar *(Währung)*
	per [pɜ:; pə]		pro
	fifth [fɪfθ]	One *fifth* of 25 is 5.	Fünftel
	third [θɜ:d]	A *third* of 9 is 3.	Drittel
	packed lunch [ˌpækt 'lʌntʃ]	to pack → *packed lunch*	Lunchpaket; Vesper
	average ['ævrɪdʒ]	the *average* teenager = a typical teenager	durchschnittlich
	meal [mi:l]	The three *meals* are breakfast, lunch and dinner (or tea).	Mahlzeit

unit 4 Living together

disability [ˌdɪsə'bɪləti]	to be able → *disabled* → *disability*	Behinderung; Unfähigkeit
disabled [dɪ'seɪbld]		behindert
• **as a result of** [əz‿ə rɪ'zʌlt‿əv]	result → *as a result of*	infolge (von)
illness ['ɪlnəs]	ill → *illness*	Krankheit
*to **overcome** [ˌəʊvə'kʌm]	to come → *to overcome* Disabled people's problems can be very difficult to *overcome*.	überwinden
able-bodied [ˌeɪbl'bɒdɪd]	disabled ↔ *able-bodied*	körperlich gesund; nicht-behindert
to **sail** [seɪl]	surfing – windsurfing – rowing – *sailing*	segeln
equal ['i:kwəl]	Sb who is your *equal* is not more or less important than you.	Gleichgestellte(r); Gleich-wertige(r); Ebenbürtige(r)
• **professor** [prə'fesə]		Professor(in)
brief [bri:f]	Another word for 'short'.	kurz

Englisch – so oft wie möglich

Sprich Englisch so oft wie möglich.
Vielleicht ist in deiner Nachbarschaft jemand, mit dem du dich nur auf Englisch unterhalten kannst. Oder hast du vielleicht im Urlaub Gelegenheit, Englisch zu sprechen? Nimm an einem Schüleraustausch teil, wenn du kannst. Und hab keine Angst vor Fehlern. Wer dich nicht versteht, wird nachfragen. Versuche es dann mit anderen Wörtern und Wendungen.

Höre Englisch so oft wie möglich.
Englische Musik, englisches Radio und Fernsehen bieten dazu gute Möglichkeiten. Versuche einzelne Wörter herauszuhören und ihre Bedeutung zu erschließen oder ungefähr zu erraten. Wenn möglich, sieh dir Filme, die du schon kennst, noch einmal auf Englisch an. Manchmal haben z. B. auch Bibliotheken englische Videos. Du wirst staunen, was du alles verstehst.

Lies Englisch so oft wie möglich.
Bibliotheken haben auch oft englische Bücher, Zeitungen und Zeitschriften. Vielleicht findest du auch etwas über deine Hobbys. Beginne aber mit kürzeren Texten – Comics sind z. B. gut geeignet – und gib nicht bei den ersten unbekannten Wörtern auf.

Schreibe Englisch so oft wie möglich.
Wie wäre es mit einer Brieffreundschaft? Frage doch mal deinen Lehrer oder deine Lehrerin in der Schule. Oft haben auch deutsche Vereine englischsprachige Partnervereine, die dir dabei weiterhelfen könnten. Auch über das Internet kannst du Kontakte auf Englisch knüpfen. Vielleicht kannst du deine Brieffreundin oder deinen Brieffreund auch einmal besuchen. Vergiss nicht, dass du dich oft mit Jugendlichen aus der ganzen Welt auf Englisch verständigen kannst.

• **universe** ['ju:nɪvɜ:s]		Universum
• to **communicate** [kə'mju:nɪkeɪt]	The easiest way to *communicate* with people is to speak to them.	kommunizieren, sich verständigen
speech [spi:tʃ]	to speak → *speech*	Sprache; Rede
	! *Speech* can mean – spoken language – the way you speak – a talk	
• synthesizer ['sɪntθəˌsaɪzə]		Synthesizer
mental ['mentl]	physical ↔ *mental*	geistig
• therapy ['θerəpi]		Therapie
dolphin ['dɒlfɪn]		Delphin
relationship [rɪ'leɪʃnʃɪp]	relative → *relationship* The first *relationship* in life is usually between mother and child.	Beziehung
the Paralympics [ˌpærə'lɪmpɪks]	An international sports event for disabled people.	Paralympics *(Behindertenolympiade)*
• **athlete** ['æθli:t]	! Achte auf die Betonung: ['--]	(Leicht-)Athlet(in)
• **judo** ['dʒu:dəʊ]		Judo
wheelchair ['wi:ltʃeə]	chair → *wheelchair*	Rollstuhl
• **swimmer** ['swɪmə]	to swim → *swimmer*	Schwimmer(in)
• the **Olympics** *(Olympic Games)* [əʊ'lɪmpɪks; əʊˌlɪmpɪk 'geɪmz]		Olympiade, Olympische Spiele
• **blind** [blaɪnd]	! Achtung Aussprache!	blind
• **sculpture** ['skʌlptʃə]	! Achtung Aussprache!	Skulptur
work of art [ˌwɜ:k‿əv‿'ɑ:t]	art → *work of art*	Kunstwerk
caption ['kæpʃn]	A short text, under a picture or cartoon, for example.	Untertitel; Bildunterschrift

	• decoder [ˌdiːˈkəʊdə]		Decoder *(Gerät, das ein verschlüsseltes Signal entschlüsseln kann)*
	deaf [def]	Some people are so *deaf* that they can't hear anything at all.	gehörlos; schwerhörig
3	**according to** [əˈkɔːdɪŋ tə]	*According to* the weather forecast, it'll be warm and sunny tomorrow. = The weather forecast says that it'll be warm and sunny tomorrow.	laut, gemäß

Language A Online

	to **advise (sb to do sth)** [ədˈvaɪz]	If you *advise* sb to do sth, you tell them it would be a good idea.	(jmdm) raten
	• **forum** [ˈfɔːrəm]		Forum
	• **author** [ˈɔːθə]		Autor(in)
	to **post** [pəʊst]	To send (for example a letter).	aufgeben *(einen Brief)*; abschicken
	device [dɪˈvaɪs]	Sth that has been made or built to help in a special way.	Gerät, Vorrichtung
	• **alarm** [əˈlɑːm]	An *alarm* (or *alarm* clock) wakes you up in the morning.	Wecker
	• to **vibrate** [vaɪˈbreɪt]		vibrieren
	• to **repair** [rɪˈpeə]	To mend.	reparieren
	• **girlfriend** [ˈgɜːlfrend]	boyfriend ↔ *girlfriend*	Freundin *(in einer Paarbeziehung)*
	*to lip-read [ˈlɪpriːd]	to read → *to lip-read*	von den Lippen ablesen
	• **experiment** [ɪkˈsperɪmənt]	! Achte auf die Betonung: [-ˈ---]	Experiment, Versuch
	• to **switch off** [swɪtʃ‿ˈɒf]	to switch on ↔ *to switch off*	ausschalten
1	**similar** [ˈsɪmɪlə]	Becky looks like her mother. They look very *similar.*	ähnlich
2	**conditional** [kənˈdɪʃnl]		Konditional
	• **type** [taɪp]		Typ
3	hearing aid [ˈhɪərɪŋ‿eɪd]	to hear → *hearing aid* A device that can help people to hear more clearly.	Hörgerät
6	• **advice** [ədˈvaɪs]	! ein Ratschlag = some advice Let me give you some *advice.* Achtung Aussprache: to advise [z] → some *advice* [s]	Rat
7	to **cure** [kjʊə]		heilen; kurieren

Skills

2	announcement [əˈnaʊntsmənt]	A statement (often through a loudspeaker) that gives people information about what has happened or will happen.	Ankündigung; Durchsage
	passenger [ˈpæsndʒə]	Sb who is travelling by plane, train, bus, car etc. (but who is not the driver).	Passagier(in); Beifahrer(in)
3	to **pronounce** [prəˈnaʊnts]	! Achtung unterschiedliche Schreibung: *to pronounce* → pronunciation	aussprechen

commercial [kəˈmɜːʃl]	*Commercials* on radio or TV sometimes persuade people to buy products they don't really need.	Werbespot
to **record** [rɪˈkɔːd]	To 'copy' (films, music etc.) on tape.	aufnehmen; aufzeichnen

Language B Party clothes

pants *(AE) (pl.)* [pænts]	pants *(AE)* = trousers *(BE)* ! Achtung Plural: These *pants* **are** *comfortable.*	Hose
• **comfortable** [ˈkʌmpftəbl]	If your shoes are *comfortable,* they don't hurt your feet when you walk. ! Achtung Aussprache!	komfortabel; bequem
might [maɪt]	Maybe he'll play well in the match. He *might* even win it!	könnte(n)
the next size down [ðə ˌnekst saɪz ˈdaʊn]	One size smaller.	eine Größe kleiner
• **glitter** [ˈglɪtə]		etwas Glitzerndes
• **top** [tɒp]		Top
• *to **cost** [kɒst]	If sth is cheap, it doesn't *cost* much.	kosten

Wichtige Unterschiede zwischen amerikanischem und britischem Englisch

Unterschiedliche Wörter
Einige Wörter im amerikanischen Englisch sind unterschiedlich zum britischen Englisch.

BE	AE	BE	AE
autumn	fall	holiday	vacation
biscuit	cookie	mobile (phone)	cellphone
chips	fries	pupil	student
flat	apartment	rubbish	trash
football	soccer	sweets	candy
head teacher	principal	trousers	pants

Unterschiedliche Schreibung
Die Teile dieses Buchs, die in Amerika spielen, sind in amerikanischem Englisch gehalten, daher sind manche Wörter, die ihr aus dem britischen Englisch kennt, an diesen Stellen anders geschrieben.

BE	AE	BE	AE
centre	center	flavour	flavor
metre	meter	favourite	favorite
travelled	traveled	to practise	to practice
colour	color	programme	program
neighbour	neighbor	Mum	Mom

Unterschiedliche Aussprache
Amerikanische Sprecher sprechen einige Laute anders aus, als du es von britischen Sprechern gewöhnt bist.

	BE	AE
after, answer, ask, half	[ɑː]	[æː]
car, other, sure, work	[-]	[r]
beautiful, better, notice, water	[t]	[d]

may [meɪ]	! Two meanings: 1. *May* I come in? = Darf ich hereinkommen? 2. I *may* be late. = Ich komme vielleicht zu spät.	könnte(n) vielleicht; mögen; dürfen
to **suit** [su:t]	*to suit* → suitable You look good in red. Red *suits* you. = Rot steht dir.	passen (zu); (jmdm) stehen
to **borrow** ['bɒrəʊ]	"Can I *borrow* this book?" – "OK, but please remember to give it back."	(sich) ausleihen
5 • **formal** ['fɔ:ml]		formal; formell; förmlich
• **informal** [ɪn'fɔ:ml]	*formal* ↔ *informal*	informell; zwanglos
polite [pə'laɪt]	rude ↔ *polite*	höflich
6 **possibility** [ˌpɒsə'bɪləti]	If sth is a *possibility*, it might happen.	Möglichkeit
permission [pə'mɪʃn]		Erlaubnis
ability [ə'bɪləti]	able → *ability* → disability	Fähigkeit
obligation [ˌɒblɪ'geɪʃn]		Verpflichtung

Text Helpless

Moscow ['mɒskəʊ]		Moskau
• **arrival** [ə'raɪvl]	to arrive → *arrival*	Ankunft
suitcase ['su:tkeɪs]	Have you packed your *suitcase*?	Koffer
tug [tʌg]	The movement of pulling at sth quickly.	Ziehen; Zupfen
zipper ['zɪpə]		Reißverschluss
none [nʌn]	no → nobody → nothing → nowhere → *none*	keine(r)
basement ['beɪsmənt]	The lowest floor of a building, below street level.	Kellergeschoss, Untergeschoss
solution [sə'lu:ʃn]	If you have a problem, you want to find a *solution* to it.	Lösung
independent [ˌɪndɪ'pendənt]	People who are *independent* can manage their life without others' help.	unabhängig
• to **unpack** [ʌn'pæk]	to pack ↔ *to unpack*	auspacken
cellphone *(AE)* ['selfəʊn]	phone → *cellphone* *cellphone (AE)* = mobile *(BE)*	Handy, Mobiltelefon
to **search** [sɜ:tʃ]	Although the store detectives *searched* Gareth's pockets, they didn't find the computer game.	durchsuchen
to **search for** ['sɜ:tʃ fə]	If you *search for* sth, you look for sth that is difficult to find.	suchen (nach)
• **package** ['pækɪdʒ]	to pack → a pack → a *package*	Paket
familiar [fə'mɪliə]	Things that you know well are *familiar* to you. ! *familiar* ≠ familiär	vertraut
to **seem familiar** [ˌsi:m fə'mɪliə]	It *seems familiar*. = Es kommt mir bekannt vor.	bekannt vorkommen
stairs *(pl.)* [steəz]	! The *stairs* **are** steep. = Die Treppe **ist** steil.	Treppe
footstep ['fʊtstep]	foot → *footstep*	Schritt
• **aftershave** ['ɑ:ftəʃeɪv]	to shave → *aftershave*	Aftershave, Rasierwasser

	corner ['kɔ:nə]	Most rooms have four *corners*.	Ecke
	fuse box ['fju:z bɒks]	If you know where the *fuse box* is, you can switch off all the lights in the house at once.	Sicherungskasten
	• **shout** [ʃaʊt]	to shout → a *shout*	Schrei, Ruf
	to **curse** [kɜ:s]	To say "damn!" (or sth worse) when you feel annoyed.	fluchen
	advantage [əd'vɑ:ntɪdʒ]	In basketball, it's an *advantage* to be tall.	Vorteil
	*to **creep** [kri:p]	To move very quietly (so that nobody will notice you).	schleichen; kriechen
	• **as if** [əz‿'ɪf]		als ob
	icon ['aɪkɒn]		Ikone
	valuable ['væljuəbl]	Sth that is *valuable* could be sold for a lot of money.	wertvoll
	officer ['ɒfɪsə]	A police *officer* is a man or woman in the police.	Beamter, Beamtin
2	**turning point** ['tɜ:nɪŋ ˌpɔɪnt]	to turn → *turning point* A point (usually in a story) when sth suddenly changes so that things start to happen differently.	Wendepunkt

Let's check

3	• **everyday** ['evrideɪ]	An *everyday* situation is the kind of thing that happens every day.	alltäglich

unit 5 In and around Seattle

O Schreck! Ein langes Wort! – Wie spricht man das nur aus?

Bei längeren Wörtern ist die Betonung besonders wichtig. Mit der Lautschrift kann man auch die richtige Betonung herausfinden und lernen.

Beispiel:

- Schau dir das lange Wort *elementary school* [ˌelɪ'mentri ˌsku:l] an. Bei der Lautschrift steht vor der Silbe mit der Hauptbetonung dieses Zeichen ['].
- Beginne die Aussprache mit dieser Silbe und der nachfolgenden unbetonten Silbe ['mentri]. Sprich diesen Wortteil mehrmals laut und klopfe bei der betonten Silbe auf den Tisch.
- Füge dann die davor stehende Silbe dazu. Das Zeichen [ˌ] soll zeigen, dass die folgende Silbe die Nebenbetonung trägt. Sprich beide Teile zusammen aus.
- Sprich das ganze Wort anfangs mit überdeutlicher Unterscheidung zwischen betonten und unbetonten Silben aus.
- Markiere auf deinen Wörterkarten für Wörter mit schwieriger Aussprache die Betonung mit einem Markierstift: *elementary school*
- Bei englischen Wörtern, die deutschen ähnlich sind, ist die Betonung manchmal tückisch: *photographer* [fə'tɒgrəfə]
- Vorsicht auch bei Substantiven, Adjektiven und Verben, die sich ähneln! Die Betonung liegt nicht immer auf der gleichen Silbe: *decorated* → *decoration*

Intro

• **nature** ['neɪtʃə]	*nature* → natural All the animals, plants and other things in the world that are not made by people, and also all the events (like the weather) that we cannot control.	Natur
such as ['sʌtʃ‿əz]	Another expression for 'like', when you want to give examples of sth.	(solche) wie
• **drive** [draɪv]	to drive → a *drive* (in the car)	Autofahrt
to **hike** [haɪk]	To go for a long walk in the country.	wandern
• wilderness ['wɪldənəs]	! Be careful with the pronunciation: wild [aɪ] → *wilderness* [ɪ].	Wildnis
trail [treɪl]	A path in the open country or through a forest.	Wanderweg
• **possible** ['pɒsəbl]	possibility → *possible*	möglich
• **grunge** [grʌndʒ]		Grunge *(Musikrichtung)*
• **coffee bar** ['kɒfi: ˌbɑ:]	A small café where you can buy drinks and snacks.	Café
• **lifestyle** ['laɪfstaɪl]	life → *lifestyle*	Lebensart
needle [ni:dl]	If you want to mend your clothes, you'll need a *needle*.	Nadel
second ['seknd]	*second* – minute – hour	Sekunde
elevator *(AE)* ['elɪveɪtə]	Going up in an *elevator* is usually much quicker than walking up the stairs.	Aufzug, Lift
square [skweə]	Areas are often given in *square* miles.	Quadrat
population [ˌpɒpjə'leɪʃn]	The number of people that live in a town, a country etc.	Bevölkerung
• **zone** [zəʊn]		Zone
• **standard** ['stændəd]		Standard
cool [ku:l]	The weather can be cold, *cool*, *mild*, warm or hot.	kühl
• **mild** [maɪld]	! Achtung Aussprache!	mild
• **carton** ['kɑ:tn]	! Achtung Aussprache!	Karton *(Verbundverpackung)*
• **derby** ['dɜ:bi]	*BE* pronunciation: ['dɑ:bi]	Derby
few [fju:]	! He's got a few friends. = … ein paar Freunde. He's got *few* friends. = … wenige Freunde.	wenige
fishmonger ['fɪʃˌmʌŋgə]	fish → *fishmonger*	Fischhändler(in)
salmon, *pl.* **salmon** ['sæmən]	A tasty kind of fish which looks pink when you cut it open.	Lachs
whale [weɪl]	A huge animal that lives in the sea (although it is not a fish).	Wal
sound [saʊnd]		Sund, Meerenge
root [ru:t]	The *roots* of a tree are under the ground. *Roots* can also mean the place where sb first came from – or where sth started.	Wurzel
soul [səʊl]		Seele
• **gospel** ['gɒspl]		Gospel
• **country** ['kʌntri]		Countrymusik
• **blues** [blu:z]		Blues

influence ['ɪnfluənts]	How people behave has a big *influence* on whether you like them or not.	Einfluss
to **discover** [dɪ'skʌvə]	to cover → *to discover* If you *discover* a feeling, you experience it for the first time.	entdecken
• **distance** ['dɪstnts]	Things that are in the *distance* are things that you can see that are far away (such as mountains).	Distanz, Entfernung
• **volcano**, *pl.* **volcanoes** [vɒl'keɪnəʊ]		Vulkan

Language A Preparing for a trip

handout ['hændaʊt]	hand → *handout* A piece of paper that gives important information (e. g. from a talk).	Informationsblatt
safety ['seɪfti]	safe → *safety* 	Sicherheit
whistle ['wɪsl]		Trillerpfeife
• **fit** [fɪt]	If you are *fit*, you are healthy and physical activities don't make you tired.	fit
• **hike** [haɪk]	to hike → a *hike*	Wanderung
to **dry** [draɪ]	*Dried* fruit makes a healthy snack.	trocknen
• **fruit** [fru:t]	! *fruit (sg.)* = Obst *fruits (pl.)* = Früchte	Frucht
mushroom ['mʌʃrʊm]		Pilz
sleeping bag ['sli:pɪŋ ˌbæg]	to sleep → *sleeping bag*	Schlafsack
change of clothing [ˌtʃeɪndʒ_əv 'kləʊðɪŋ]		Satz/Garnitur Kleidung zum Wechseln
clothing ['kləʊðɪŋ]	clothes → *clothing*	Kleidung
necessary ['nesəsri]	It won't be *necessary* to book in advance. = You won't need to book in advance.	notwendig, nötig
• **unnecessary** [ʌn'nesəsri]	necessary → *unnecessary*	unnötig
waterproof ['wɔ:təpru:f]	water → *waterproof* You won't get wet if you wear *waterproof* clothing	wasserdicht
• to **camp** [kæmp]	camp → *to camp* If you *camp* somewhere, you stay or live there for a time (usually in a tent).	campen, zelten, kampieren
to **reach** [ri:tʃ]	When you *reach* a place, you arrive there.	erreichen
campsite ['kæmpsaɪt]	camp → camping → *campsite* → *campfire*	Campingplatz, Zeltplatz
flat [flæt]	Country where there are no hills is *flat*.	flach, platt
• **dry** [draɪ]	to dry → *dry*	trocken
*to **put up** [pʊt_'ʌp]	to put in → to put on → *to put up*	aufstellen; errichten
• **campfire** ['kæmpfaɪə]		Lagerfeuer
aluminum foil *(AE)* [əˌlu:mɪnəm 'fɔɪl]		Alufolie
stream [stri:m]	A small river.	Bach
to **boil** [bɔɪl]	If you *boil* eggs or potatoes, you cook them in water.	kochen
branch [brɑ:ntʃ]	A tree has *branches*. 	Zweig, Ast

	to **pick** [pɪk]	to pick up → *to pick* Raspberries taste best when they are freshly *picked*.	pflücken
	*to **leave sb alone** [ˌliːv‿əˈləʊn]		jemanden in Ruhe lassen
	waste [weɪst]	Food, material etc. that is no longer wanted and can be thrown away.	Abfall; Verschwendung
1	**in order to** [ɪn‿ˈɔːdə tə]		um … zu
	backpack [ˈbækpæk]	back + pack = *backpack* A bag that you carry on your back.	Rucksack
2	**purpose** [ˈpɜːpəs]	If you have a *purpose*, you have a reason to do sth.	Zweck
5	• **disco** [ˈdɪskəʊ]		Disco, Diskothek

Language B Chatroom messages

	• **chatroom** [ˈtʃætrʊm]		Chatroom *(Internetforum, wo man sich online unterhalten kann)*
	to erupt [ɪˈrʌpt]		ausbrechen *(Vulkan)*
	herself [hɜːˈself]		(sie) selbst; sich (selbst)
	Valentine's card [ˈvæləntaɪnz ˌkɑːd]	For Valentine's Day (February 14th) it's a custom to send a card to sb you love.	Valentinskarte
	• **fat** [fæt]	! A thick book:  A *fat* cat: 	fett, dick
	• **insect** [ˈɪnsekt]		Insekt
	RUOK? [ˌɑː juː‿əʊˈkeɪ]	Are you OK?	Alles in Ordnung bei dir?
	to **enjoy oneself** [ɪnˈdʒɔɪ]	To have a good time.	Spaß haben; sich amüsieren
	to **type** [taɪp]	It's easier to read a text that has been *typed* than one that has been written by hand.	tippen
	to **bake** [beɪk]	You *bake* bread, cakes and biscuits.	backen
	by oneself [ˌbaɪ‿wʌnˈself]	Alone, or without help.	allein
	Never mind! [ˌnevə ˈmaɪnd]	to mind → *Never mind!* You can say this to sb to make them feel better when sth has gone wrong – or to explain that sth isn't important.	Mach dir nichts draus!; Macht nichts.
	• to **amuse oneself** [əˈmjuːz]	To do sth interesting so that time goes more quickly.	sich amüsieren; sich die Zeit vertreiben
1	• **object** [ˈɒbdʒɪkt]		Objekt; Gegenstand
2	**reflexive** [rɪˈfleksɪv]		reflexiv
	to **prepare (for)** [prɪˈpeə]	Have you *prepared for* the test?	sich vorbereiten (auf)

Text A day to remember

	• **photographer** [fəˈtɒgrəfə]	! a photograph [ˈ---] = ein Foto a photographer [-ˈ---] = ein Fotograf	Fotograf(in)
	ridge [rɪdʒ]		Bergrücken, Hügelkette
	• **call** [kɔːl]	to call → a *call* The *call* of a bird is the sound it makes when it sings.	Ruf

raccoon [rə'ku:n]		Waschbär
to **whisper** ['wɪspə]	To speak to sb very quietly so that nobody else will hear.	flüstern
spooky ['spu:ki]		gespenstisch
earthquake ['ɜ:θkweɪk]	earth → *earthquake*	Erdbeben
mirror ['mɪrə]	If you look at yourself in a *mirror*, you see a true 'picture' of yourself.	Spiegel
• **explosion** [ɪk'spləʊʒn]		Explosion
avalanche ['ævlɑ:ntʃ]		Lawine
smoke [sməʊk]	When sth burns, *smoke* goes up into the air.	Rauch
steam [sti:m]	When water boils, you get *steam*.	Dampf
to **turn (into)** ['tɜ:n‿ɪntə]	If the weather *turns* cold, it changes and becomes cold.	werden; (sich) verwandeln in
• **unable** [ʌn'eɪbl]	able ↔ *unable*	unfähig
to **disappear** [ˌdɪsə'pɪə]	to appear ↔ *to disappear*	verschwinden
• **ash** [æʃ]	What is left after sth is burned.	Asche
• *to **be trapped** [bi: 'træpt]	a trap → *to be trapped*	in der Falle sitzen
• **panic** ['pænɪk]		Panik
eruption [ɪ'rʌpʃn]		Ausbruch *(Vulkan)*
lung [lʌŋ]		Lunge
• to **explode** [ɪk'spləʊd]	explosion → *to explode*	explodieren
thirsty ['θɜ:sti]	If your body needs water, you begin to feel *thirsty*.	durstig
to **breathe** [bri:ð]	To take air into your lungs, then let it out again.	atmen
throat [θrəʊt]		Kehle; Hals
• lava ['lɑ:və]		Lava
• to **concentrate** ['kɒntsntreɪt]	If you don't *concentrate* on the traffic while you're driving, you might have an accident.	(sich) konzentrieren
1 • **foot**, *pl.* **feet** [fʊt; fi:t]	In British and American English, heights are often given in *feet*.	Fuß *(Längenmaß: 30,48 cm)*
crater ['kreɪtə]		Krater
damage ['dæmɪdʒ]	Disasters such as earthquakes can cause a lot of *damage*.	Schaden
death [deθ]	dead → *death* life ↔ *death*	Tod
3 sweetie ['swi:ti]	sweet → *sweetie*	Süße(r)

Skills

1 • to **react** [ri'ækt]	reaction → *to react*	reagieren
clerk [*BE:* klɑ:k; *AE:* klɜ:rk]	Sb who works in an office or at an information desk.	Angestellte(r)
instead [ɪn'sted]	If the weather is too cold for swimming, we could go for a walk *instead*. ! 'Instead of' is a preposition. *'Instead'* is an adverb.	stattdessen
You're welcome. [jɔ: 'welkəm]	If sb says 'thank you', it's polite to answer: "That's OK", "Don't mention it" or *"You're welcome"*.	Bitte schön./Gern geschehen.

arboretum, *pl.* arboreta [ˌɑ:br'i:təm]		Baumschule

Wichtige Vor- und Nachsilben
Einige Vor- und Nachsilben tauchen im Englischen immer wieder auf und helfen dir, die Bedeutung vieler Wörter zu erschließen.

dis-	un-	-less	-ful
disabled **dis**agree **dis**appear **dis**appointed **dis**cover **dis**like	**un**happy **un**necessary **un**pack **un**usual	end**less** help**less** home**less** use**less**	beauti**ful** care**ful** thank**ful** use**ful** wonder**ful**

focus 3 Focus on regions of the USA

• **region** ['ri:dʒn]		Region; Gegend
Midwesterner [ˌmɪd'westənə]	A person from the Midwest.	Person aus dem Mittleren Westen
• **climate** ['klaɪmət]	The kind of weather that is typical of a country or area.	Klima
buffalo, *pl.* buffalo ['bʌfləʊ]		Büffel
range [reɪndʒ]	An area of open country, where there are cattle.	Freiland, Weideland *(AE)*
location [ləʊ'keɪʃn]	to be located → *location*	Lage; Standort
economy [ɪ'kɒnəmi]	The *economy* of a country or area is the way money and industry etc. are organized.	Wirtschaft
lobster ['lɒbstə]		Hummer
moose, *pl.* moose [mu:s]	A kind of deer that is found in North America.	Elch
nickname ['nɪkneɪm]	name → *nickname* An informal name, usually for a person that you know well.	Spitzname
pine (tree) [paɪn]	A forest tree.	Kiefer
• **cactus** ['kæktəs]	A plant that doesn't need much water, so it can even grow in the desert.	Kaktus
redwood (tree) ['redwʊd]	wood → *redwood* A huge tree that grows in California.	Mammutbaum
up to ['ʌp tə]	They live *up to* 100 years. = They can reach the age of 100.	bis zu
• to **exist** [ɪg'zɪst]	To live or to be there.	existieren
• **dinosaur** ['daɪnəsɔ:]	About 65 million years ago the *dinosaurs* died out.	Dinosaurier

unit 6 Sports in the US

True friends and false friends

True friends

Du hast bereits eine Menge von Wörtern kennen gelernt, die im Englischen und Deutschen sehr ähnlich aussehen und auch eine ähnliche oder die gleiche Bedeutung haben.
Diese Wörter helfen dir beim Sprechen, Lesen und Schreiben. Sie sind „wahre Freunde", auf die du dich verlassen kannst, z. B. *explosion, begin, lemonade, standard, perspective, zone* etc., nur die Aussprache ist häufig anders als im Deutschen, z. B. [ɪk'spləʊʒn]. Kennst du noch mehr?
Du kannst auch deine eigene Vokabelkartei durchgehen und dabei entscheiden, bei welchen Wörtern es sich um *true friends* handelt.
Wenn es dir hilft, diese Wörter besser zu behalten, kannst du dir ein Zeichen für *true friends* ausdenken.

False friends

Es gibt aber auch „falsche Freunde", die nur ähnlich oder gleich aussehen, aber etwas anderes im Englischen bedeuten als im Deutschen. In der Mittelspalte des Begleitvokabulars von *Green Line New Bayern* steht bei ihnen ein Ausrufezeichen und ein entsprechender Hinweis.
To become heißt nicht „bekommen", sondern „werden". Mehr Beispiele: *actually, to take place, …*
Findest du noch mehr?

Intro

basketball court ['bɑ:skɪtbɔ:l ˌkɔ:t]	Basketball and tennis are played on a *court.*	Basketballplatz
baseball field ['beɪsbɔ:l ˌfi:ld]	Baseball is played on a *field.*	Baseballplatz
helmet ['helmət]	You wear a *helmet* to protect your head.	Helm
• **golf** [gɒlf]	You play tennis with a racket, baseball or table tennis with a bat and *golf* with a *club.*	Golf
• **golf ball** ['gɒlf ˌbɔ:l]		Golfball
bowling ball ['bəʊlɪŋ ˌbɔ:l]		Bowlingkugel
baseball bat ['beɪsbɔ:l ˌbæt]		Baseballschläger
bowling alley ['bəʊlɪŋ‿ˌæli]	Lots of people go to the *bowling alley* regularly with friends.	Bowlingbahn
golf course ['gɒlf ˌkɔ:s]	A *golf course* usually has 18 holes.	Golfplatz
glove [glʌv]	You wear shoes on your feet and *gloves* on your hands.	Handschuh
golf club ['gɒlf ˌklʌb]	! Schläger = racket or bat or *club*: 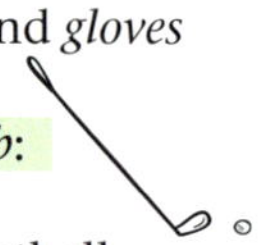	Golfschläger
football field ['fʊtbɔ:l ˌfi:ld]	baseball field – *football field*	Footballplatz
4 **referee** [ˌrefr'i:]	The person who controls a football game.	Schiedsrichter(in)

Language A A top athlete

track and field [ˌtræk‿ənd 'fi:ld]	Running races are *track* events, and high jump, long jump etc. are *field* events.	Leichtathletik

	•**marathon** ['mærəθn]		Marathon
	awful ['ɔ:fl]	Another word for 'terrible'.	schrecklich, furchtbar
	to **recover** [rɪ'kʌvə]	To get better (from an illness or a shock).	sich erholen
	to **force** [fɔ:s]	If you *force* sb to do sth, you make them do it.	zwingen
	in spite of [ɪn 'spaɪt‿əv]	*In spite of* the rain = although it was raining.	trotz
	•**muscle** ['mʌsl]	If you didn't have *muscles* in your body, you wouldn't be able to move.	Muskel
	•to **study** ['stʌdi]	If you *study* a subject, you learn a lot about it (sometimes at a college).	studieren; lernen
	to **retire** [rɪ'taɪə]	My grandpa *retired* from work when he was 65.	sich zurückziehen; sich zur Ruhe setzen
2	•**direct speech** [dɪˌrekt 'spi:tʃ]		direkte Rede
	•**indirect speech** [ˌɪndɪrekt 'spi:tʃ]	Reported speech.	indirekte Rede
3	to **point out** [pɔɪnt‿'aʊt]	If you *point out* a fact, you tell sb about it.	hinweisen auf
	sportsman, *pl.* **sportsmen** ['spɔ:tsmən]	sport → *sportsman* A man who does sports.	Sportler
	sportswoman, *(pl.)* **sports-women** ['spɔ:tsˌwʊmən]	sport → *sportswoman* A woman who does sports.	Sportlerin
5	**glad** [glæd]	happy – pleased – *glad* ☺	froh

Language B Cheerleaders

	•**cheerleader** ['tʃɪəˌli:də]	leader → *cheerleader*	Cheerleader *(Mädchen, das in einer Gruppe eine Sportmannschaft anfeuert)*
	•**cheerleading** ['tʃɪəli:dɪŋ]	to cheer → *cheerleading*	Cheerleading *(Aktivitäten der Cheerleader)*
	coach [kəʊtʃ]	! Two different meanings: 1. A bus for long journeys 2. Sb who gives special help in a subject or sport	Trainer(in)
	*to **get one's act together** [ˌget wʌnz‿'ækt təgeðə]	To control oneself (and behave better).	sich am Riemen reißen
	dumb [dʌm]	Another word for 'stupid' (especially in *AE*).	dumm, doof
	•**half-time** [ˌhɑ:f'taɪm]	The break in the middle of a (football) game.	Halbzeit
	•**cheer** [tʃɪə]	to cheer → a *cheer*	Jubel
	whether ['weðə]	*whether* = if (in indirect speech)	ob
	to **kick sb off a team** [kɪk‿'ɒf]	If the coach *kicks* you *off* the team, you're no longer part of it.	jmdn aus dem Team werfen
	*to **be on a team** [ˌbi:‿ɒn‿ə 'ti:m]	To be one of the team.	Mitglied eines Teams sein
	captain ['kæptɪn]	The leader of a sports team.	Kapitän; Mannschaftsführer(in)
1	•**expectation** [ˌekspek'teɪʃn]	to expect → *expectation*	Erwartung
	high school ['haɪ ˌsku:l]	school → elementary school → middle school → *high school* A school in the USA for people between the ages of 15 and 18.	High School *(weiterführende Schule in den USA, Oberstufe)*

command [kəˈmɑːnd]	"Come here at once!" is an example of a *command*.	Befehl
pompom [ˈpɒmpɒm]		Pompon *(bunte Quaste der Cheerleader)*
5 **victory** [ˈvɪktri]	When you have beaten another team, you can celebrate your *victory*.	Sieg

Text The big game

season [ˈsiːzn]	! Summer is the warmest *season*. The football *season* is the period of time when matches are played.	Saison; Jahreszeit
• **rival** [ˈraɪvl]	! Achtung Aussprache!	Rivale, Rivalin; Konkurrent(in)
revenge [rɪˈvendʒ]	If you are eager for *revenge*, you want to beat (or hurt) sb who has beaten (or hurt) you.	Rache, Revanche
• **scorer** [ˈskɔːrə]	to score → *scorer*	Torjäger(in); Korbjäger(in)
as well [əz ˈwel]	Another word for 'too' or 'also'.	auch
scout [skaʊt]	A person who is searching for new 'stars' (for sports etc.).	Talentsucher(in)
• **cleaner** [ˈkliːnə]	to clean → a *cleaner*	Raumpfleger(in), Putzkraft
to **live on sth** [ˈlɪv‿ɒn]	If you have enough money to *live on*, you have just enough money to buy the necessary things.	von etw leben
scholarship [ˈskɒləʃɪp]	If you can win a *scholarship* to a school or college, your parents don't have to pay.	Stipendium
pep talk [ˈpep ˌtɔːk]	talk → *pep talk*	aufmunternde Worte
• to **motivate** [ˈməʊtɪveɪt]	When you feel *motivated*, you are eager to do sth.	motivieren
hoop [huːp]	When you throw the ball through the basketball *hoop*, you score a basket.	Reifen *(z. B. am Basketballkorb)*
behind [bɪˈhaɪnd]	in front ↔ *behind*	hinten; im Rückstand
• **score** [skɔː]	! What's the *score*? = Wie steht es?	Punktestand
• throw [ˌθrəʊ]	to throw → a *throw*	Wurf
team-mate [ˈtiːmmeɪt]	Your *team-mates* are the people who play with you in your team.	Mannschaftskamerad(in)
mate [meɪt]	Boys and men often call their friends their *mates*.	Kamerad(in)
wherever [weəˈrevə]	where → *wherever*	wo(hin) auch immer
spiky [ˈspaɪki]		stachlig
on purpose [ɒn ˈpɜːpəs]	purpose → *on purpose* It wasn't an accident – he hit me *on purpose!*	absichtlich
No way! [ˌnəʊ ˈweɪ]	If you don't want to do sth that sb suggests, you can say: *"No way!"*	Auf keinen Fall!
• **bandage** [ˈbændɪdʒ]		Bandage; Verband
*to **blow** [bləʊ]	The wind *blows* – or you can *blow* a candle out.	blasen
*to **blow a whistle** [ˌbləʊ‿əˈwɪsl]	The referee *blows* his *whistle* to stop the game.	auf einer Trillerpfeife pfeifen

*to **shake** [ʃeɪk]	! Two meanings: 1. *shake* + object = schütteln 2. *shake* (without object) = zittern	zittern
• **breath** [breθ]	! Achtung unterschiedliche Aussprache: to breathe [iː] – *breath* [e]	Atem; Atemzug
plop [plɒp]	The noise you hear when sth drops into water.	Plumps; Plopp
• to **pass** [pɑːs]	To throw the ball to another player in the same team.	zupassen, zuspielen; reichen
tie [taɪ]	The game ended in a *tie*: 58-58.	Unentschieden
*to **feel sick** [fiːl 'sɪk]	! I *feel sick*. = Mir ist schlecht.	Übelkeit verspüren
certain ['sɜːtn]	! Nicht verwechseln: curtain – *certain* If you say you have *certain* things to do, you mean definite things, but you don't say what they are.	bestimmt; sicher
2 **decision** [dɪ'sɪʒn]	! Achtung Aussprache: to decide [aɪ] – *decision* [ɪ]	Entscheidung

Lerntipps zum Schreiben englischer Texte

Wenn du einen kurzen Text zu einem bestimmten Thema verfassen sollst, solltest du so vorgehen:

- Notiere dir zuerst deine Ideen zum Thema, so wie sie dir einfallen. Du kannst sie auch schon in Form einer *mind map* aufschreiben.
- Bringe dann deine Gedanken in eine nachvollziehbare und logische Reihenfolge. Mit Hilfe dieses roten Fadens kannst du deinen Text nun schreiben.
- Plane den Rest der Zeit nicht völlig fürs Schreiben ein, sondern überprüfe in den letzten Minuten der Schreibzeit jeden einzelnen Satz anhand der folgenden Checkliste:

Checkliste für englische Texte

✓ Stimmt die Grundregel für den Satzbau bei meinen Sätzen? S – V – O oder auf Deutsch Subjekt – Prädikat – Objekt?
✓ Stehen die Orts- und Zeitangaben an den jeweils richtigen Stellen? (Z. B. am Satzende die Ortsangabe vor der Zeitangabe?)
✓ Habe ich die Fragen und Verneinungen richtig gebildet?
✓ Habe ich die richtige Zeitform gewählt?
✓ Habe ich die richtigen Präpositionen verwendet?
✓ Habe ich die richtigen Formen der unregelmäßigen Verben verwendet?
✓ Muss ein verwendetes Adjektiv nicht eher ein Adverb sein? Oder umgekehrt?
✓ Habe ich auch das richtige Wort verwendet? Ist z. B. in dem Satz *bring* oder *take* das richtige Wort?

Skills

• **perfect** ['pɜːfɪkt]		perfekt, vollkommen
topic ['tɒpɪk]	Another word for 'subject'.	Thema
• **comment** ['kɒment]	! Achte auf die Betonung: ['--] A *comment* gives your opinion on sth.	Kommentar
• **perspective** [pə'spektɪv]	! Achte auf die Betonung: [-'--]	Perspektive, Blickwinkel

Stadt – Land – Fluss

Warum spielt ihr nicht einmal dieses Spiel auf Englisch?
So könnt ihr gut eure Vokabelkenntnisse spielerisch festigen.

Überlegt euch zunächst mehrere Kategorien,
z. B. *city, name, animal, object.*
Macht dann eine Tabelle mit den entsprechenden Spalten in euer Heft:

Letter	**City**	**Name**	**Animal**	**Object**
L	London	Lenny	lamb	lunchbox
S	Seattle	Sarah	snake	spoon
C	Cardiff	Chuck	...	...
...	...	...	...	...

Ein Buchstabe wird vorgegeben, und dann muss jeder versuchen, so schnell wie möglich einen englischen Eintrag mit diesem Anfangsbuchstaben für jede Spalte zu finden.
Bei der Bewertung der Ergebnisse könnt ihr mehr Punkte vergeben für Wörter, die niemandem sonst eingefallen sind. Natürlich muss alles richtig geschrieben sein! Nehmt ein Wörterbuch zur Kontrolle, falls nötig. Die Tabelle könnt ihr natürlich nach Belieben erweitern oder verändern.

focus 4 The small screen

screen [skri:n]	'The small *screen*' is another name for television.	Leinwand
1 • **medium**, *pl.* **media** ['mi:diəm; 'mi:diə]	Television, radio and newspapers are sometimes called 'the *media*'.	Medium
• **satellite** ['sætlaɪt]	! Achtung Aussprache!	Satellit
• **cable** ['keɪbl]		Kabel
channel ['tʃænl]	! a TV program = eine Fernsehsendung a TV *channel* = ein Fernsehprogramm	Kanal; Programm
every ['evri]	! *every* 15 minutes = alle 15 Minuten	alle
particular [pə'tɪkjələ]	a *particular* day = a certain day	bestimmt
particularly [pə'tɪkjələli]	*particularly* good = especially good	besonders
2 • **to aim at** ['eɪm‿ət]	an aim → *to aim at*	zielen auf, sich richten an
• **video clip** ['vɪdiəʊ klɪp]	video → *video clip*	Videoclip
prize [praɪz]	Sth valuable (often money, a cup or a book) that you get if you win a competition or do very good work.	Preis
viewer ['vju:ə]	view → *viewer* Sb who watches TV. 	Zuschauer(in)
• **sitcom** ['sɪtkɒm]		Situationskomödie
• **comedy** ['kɒmədi]	! Achte auf die Betonung: ['---] A play or film that is written to make the audience laugh.	Komödie

entertainment [ˌentə'teɪnmənt]	Programs, shows or other activities that aim to give the audience fun.	Unterhaltung
• **episode** ['epɪsəʊd]	! Achte auf die Betonung: ['---]	Episode; Folge
• to **film** [fɪlm]	a film → *to film*	filmen; drehen
• **series**, *pl.* **series** ['sɪəriːz]	A TV *series* is a number of programs with the same title, all about a particular subject, family etc.	Serie
*to **make fun of** [ˌmeɪk 'fʌn‿əv]	fun → *to make fun of* If you *make fun of* sb, you tease them or make jokes about them.	sich lustig machen über
• **attractive** [ə'træktɪv]	*to attract* → attraction → *attractive* ! Achte auf die Betonung: [-'--]	attraktiv
• to **attract** [ə'trækt]		anziehen
• to **produce** [prə'djuːs]	*to produce* → product	herstellen, produzieren
prime-time ['praɪmtaɪm]	At the best time (usually between about 7.30 and 10 pm, when there are most viewers).	zur besten Sendezeit ausgestrahlt
• **millionaire** [ˌmɪljə'neə]		Millionär(in)
contestant [kən'testnt]	A person who takes part in a competition, quiz show etc.	Kandidat(in)
step [step]	*step* → footstep	Stufe; Schritt
*to **take a risk** [ˌteɪk‿ə 'rɪsk]	If you *take a risk*, you do sth that might be dangerous or might have negative results.	ein Risiko eingehen
risk [rɪsk]		Risiko
*to **run** [rʌn]	To organize (a company, business etc.).	führen, leiten
fashion ['fæʃn]	If you are interested in *fashion*, you want to know about the latest styles of clothes etc.	Mode
• **cost** [kɒst]	to cost → the *cost* If you think of the *cost* of sth, you think how much it costs.	Preis; Kosten
3 • **reality** [ri'æləti]	real → realistic → *reality*	Realität; Wirklichkeit
to **survive** [sə'vaɪv]	To go on living although you are in a difficult situation that brings you close to death.	überleben
4 nope [nəʊp]	! Use this word only with your friends.	nö
survey ['sɜːveɪ]	With the help of a *questionnaire*, you can do a *survey* to find out about people's opinions or how they behave etc.	Umfrage; Studie
questionnaire [ˌkwestʃə'neə]	! Achte auf die Schreibung: million → millionaire question → *questionnaire*	Fragebogen
• **game show** ['geɪm ˌʃəʊ]	game → *game show*	Spielshow
• **documentary** [ˌdɒkjə'mentri]	A television or radio program (or a film) that gives information about a particular subject.	Dokumentarfilm

extra line

A Jimmy's travel diary

campervan ['kæmpə͵væn]	Wohnmobil
comfortable ['kʌmpftəbl]	komfortabel, bequem
suitcase ['su:tkeɪs]	Koffer
motorway *(BE)* ['məʊtəweɪ]	Autobahn
campsite ['kæmpsaɪt]	Campingplatz, Zeltplatz
It's raining cats and dogs. [ɪts ͵reɪnɪŋ ͵kæts‿ənd 'dɒgz]	Es schüttet wie aus Eimern.
toilet ['tɔɪlɪt]	Toilette
wood [wʊd]	Wäldchen
hole [həʊl]	Loch
match [mætʃ]	Streichholz
to rub [rʌb]	reiben
stick [stɪk]	Stock
pioneer [͵paɪə'nɪə]	Pionier
sleeping bag ['sli:pɪŋ ͵bæg]	Schlafsack
hot dog ['hɒt ͵dɒg]	Hot Dog *(Würstchen im Brötchen)*
cycling ['saɪklɪŋ]	Radfahren
flat [flæt]	platt
tyre *(BE)* [taɪə]	Reifen
healthy ['helθi]	gesund
heart attack ['hɑ:t‿ə͵tæk]	Herzinfarkt
*to break down [͵breɪk 'daʊn]	liegen bleiben
rest [rest]	Rast
* to lend [lend]	leihen
perfect ['pɜ:fɪkt]	perfekt, vollkommen
3 fantasy ['fæntəsi]	Fantasie

B Acrostic poems

1 acrostic [ə'krɒstɪk]	Akrostichon *(Form, bei der die Anfangsbuchstaben hintereinander gelesen einen Sinn ergeben)*
to contain [kən'teɪn]	enthalten
Never mind … [͵nevə 'maɪnd]	Mach dir keine Sorgen um …

C Communication

communication [kə͵mju:nɪ'keɪʃn]	Kommunikation
to share [ʃeə]	teilen
gesture ['dʒestʃə]	Geste, Gebärde
to represent [͵reprɪ'zent]	repräsentieren, stehen für
combination [͵kɒmbɪ'neɪʃn]	Kombination
to develop [dɪ'veləp]	(sich) entwickeln
to exist [ɪg'zɪst]	existieren
morse code [͵mɔ:s 'kəʊd]	Morsealphabet
code [kəʊd]	Code, Verschlüsselung
basis, *pl.* bases ['beɪsɪs; 'beɪsi:z]	Basis, Grundlage
possible ['pɒsəbl]	möglich
bee [bi:]	Biene
3 torch [tɔ:tʃ]	Fackel; Taschenlampe
telegraph ['telɪgrɑ:f]	Telegraf
Greek [gri:k]	Grieche; griechisch
distance ['dɪstnts]	Distanz, Entfernung
column ['kɒləm]	Spalte

D A sketch: George's first computer

Pentium ['pentiəm]	*Name eines Mikroprozessors*	in time [ɪn 'taɪm]	mit der Zeit
Gigahertz ['gɪgəhɜ:ts]	*Frequenzangabe, drückt Rechengeschwindigkeit eines Prozessors aus*	expert ['ekspɜ:t]	Experte
Meg = megabyte [meg; 'megəbaɪt]	*Einheit der Arbeitsspeicherkapazität*	Yessir-ee! [ˌjessə'ri:]	Jawoll!
RAM [ræm]	*Arbeitsspeicher*	Uh huh. [ʌ'hʌ]	Mhm.
Gig = gigabyte [gɪg; 'gɪgəbaɪt]	*Einheit der Arbeitsspeicherkapazität*	button ['bʌtn]	Knopf
hard drive [ˌhɑ:d 'draɪv]	Festplattenlaufwerk	to click [klɪk]	klicken
8X = 8-speed ['eɪt spi:d]	achtfach	*to shut off/down [ʃʌt‿'ɒf]	herunterfahren
DVD writer [ˌdi:vi:di: 'raɪtə]	DVD-Brenner	*to be willing to do sth [bi: 'wɪlɪŋ]	gewillt sein, etwas zu tun
terrific [tə'rɪfɪk]	ausgezeichnet, hervorragend	to cease [si:s]	aufhören, beenden
		to desist [dɪ'sɪst]	von etwas absehen
		*to be in one's right mind [ɪn wʌnz ˌraɪt 'maɪnd]	ganz richtig im Kopf sein
		ridiculous [rɪ'dɪkjələs]	lächerlich
		it's about time [ˌɪts‿əbaʊt 'taɪm]	es ist höchste Zeit

E Nathan and Lara

comprehensive school [ˌkɒmprɪ'hentsɪv ˌsku:l]	Gesamtschule	car park ['kɑ: ˌpɑ:k]	Parkplatz
worksheet ['wɜ:kʃi:t]	Arbeitsblatt	pretty ['prɪti]	hübsch
to care for sb [keə]	für jemanden etwas empfinden	excuse [ɪk'skju:s]	Ausrede
		lie [laɪ]	Lüge

dictionary

In dieser alphabetischen Liste ist das gesamte Vokabular von Green Line NEW Bayern I, II und III enthalten, mit Ausnahme der nicht zum Lernwortschatz gehörenden Wörter aus Band I und II. Namen werden in gesonderten Listen nach dem Vokabular aufgeführt.
Die mit * gekennzeichneten Verben sind unregelmäßig (siehe S. 198). Die Wörter, deren Fundstellen in Spitzklammern stehen, gehören nicht zum aktiv zu beherrschenden Lernwortschatz.
Die Fundstellen verweisen auf das erstmalige Vorkommen der Wörter, z. B.
advantage [əd'vɑːntɪdʒ] Vorteil **III U4**, 61 kommt zum ersten Mal vor in Band III, Unit 4, Seite 61
a(n) [ə; ən] ein(e) **I** kommt zum ersten Mal vor in Band I
address [ə'dres] Adresse **II** kommt zum ersten Mal vor in Band II
lobster ['lɒbstə] Hummer ⟨**III F3**, 80⟩ kommt zum ersten Mal vor in Band III, Focus 3, Seite 80
motorway *(BE)* ['məʊtəweɪ] Autobahn ⟨**III EL**, 100⟩ kommt zum ersten Mal vor in Band III, Extra Line, Seite 100
F = Focus, U = Unit, EL = Extra Line

A

a(n) [ə; ən] ein(e) **I**
a bit [ə 'bɪt] ein bisschen **I**
a few [ə 'fjuː] einige, ein paar **II**
a hundred [ə'hʌndrəd] hundert **I**
a lot of [ə 'lɒt‿əv] viele, eine Menge **I**
a pair of [ə 'peər‿əv] ein Paar **I**
a week [ə 'wiːk] pro Woche, in der Woche **II**
ability [ə'bɪləti] Fähigkeit ⟨**III U4**, 59⟩
able ['eɪbl] fähig, begabt **II**
to be able to (do sth) [biː‿'eɪbl] fähig sein (zu); können; dürfen **II**
able-bodied [ˌeɪbl'bɒdɪd] körperlich gesund; nichtbehindert ⟨**III U4**, 52⟩
Aboriginal [ˌæbə'rɪdʒnl] Ureinwohner(in) Australiens **I**
about [ə'baʊt] ungefähr, circa, etwa **II**
about [ə'baʊt] über; wegen **I**
above [ə'bʌv] oben, über, oberhalb **I**
accent ['æksnt] Akzent **II**
accident ['æksɪdnt] Unfall **II**
according to [ə'kɔːdɪŋ tə] laut, gemäß **III U4**, 53
acrobat ['ækrəbæt] Akrobat(in) **II**
across [ə'krɒs] über, hinüber, quer durch/darüber **II**
acrostic [ə'krɒstɪk] Akrostichon *(Form, bei der die Anfangsbuchstaben hintereinander gelesen einen Sinn ergeben)* ⟨**III EL**, 102⟩
*to get one's **act** together [ˌget wʌnz‿'ækt təgeðə] sich am Riemen reißen **III U6**, 86
to **act something out** [ˌækt sʌmθɪŋ‿'aʊt] etwas durchspielen **I**
action ['ækʃn] Aktion, Handlung **I**
active ['æktɪv] aktiv; Aktiv **III U3**, 41
activity [æk'tɪvəti] Aktivität **II**
activity centre [æk'tɪvəti ˌsentə] Jugendzentrum **II**
actor ['æktə] Schauspieler(in) **II**
actually ['æktʃuəli] eigentlich; tatsächlich **I**
AD (= Anno Domini) [eɪ'diː] nach Christus **III F1**, 20
to **add** [æd] hinzufügen, addieren **II**
address [ə'dres] Adresse **II**
adjective ['ædʒəktɪv] Adjektiv **II**
to **admit** [əd'mɪt] zugeben **III U2**, 26
adult ['ædʌlt] Erwachsene(r) **II**
in **advance** [ɪn‿əd'vɑːnts] im Voraus **III U1**, 10
advantage [əd'vɑːntɪdʒ] Vorteil **III U4**, 61
adventure [əd'ventʃə] Abenteuer **II**
adverb ['ædvɜːb] Adverb **II**
adverb of manner [ˌædvɜːb‿əv 'mænə] Adverb der Art und Weise **II**
advice [əd'vaɪs] Rat **III U4**, 55
to **advise (sb to do sth)** [əd'vaɪz] (jmdm) raten **III U4**, 54
*to be **afraid** (of) [biː‿ə'freɪd] (sich) fürchten, Angst haben (vor) **II**
African ['æfrɪkən] afrikanisch; Afrikaner(in) **I**
after ['ɑːftə] nach **I**
after ['ɑːftə] nachdem **III F1**, 21
afternoon [ˌɑːftə'nuːn] Nachmittag **I**
aftershave ['ɑːftəʃeɪv] Aftershave, Rasierwasser **III U4**, 61
again [ə'gen] wieder **I**
again and again [ə'gen‿ənd‿ə'gen] immer wieder **I**
against [ə'gentst] gegen **II**
age [eɪdʒ] Alter; Zeitalter **II**
for ages [fr‿'eɪdʒɪz] ewig lange **III U1**, 14
Middle Ages [ˌmɪdl‿'eɪdʒɪz] Mittelalter **II**
agent ['eɪdʒnt] Agent(in), Vertreter(in) **II**
travel agent's ['trævl ˌeɪdʒnts] Reisebüro **II**
ago [ə'gəʊ] vor *(zeitlich)* **I**
to **agree** (with) [ə'griː] zustimmen, (mit jmdm) einer Meinung sein **II**
to agree (on) [ə'griː] sich einigen (auf) **II**
hearing **aid** ['hɪərɪŋ‿eɪd] Hörgerät ⟨**III U4**, 55⟩
aim [eɪm] Ziel **II**
to **aim at** ['eɪm‿ət] zielen auf, sich richten an **III F4**, 98
air [eə] Luft **I**
airport ['eəpɔːt] Flughafen **I**
alarm [ə'lɑːm] Wecker **III U4**, 54
alarm [ə'lɑːm] Alarm ⟨**III U2**, 28⟩
*to be **alive** [biː‿ə'laɪv] lebendig sein; leben **I**
all [ɔːl] alle(s); ganz **I**
all the time [ˌɔːl ðə 'taɪm] die ganze Zeit **I**
all right [ɔːl 'raɪt] in Ordnung; alles klar **II**
at all [ət‿'ɔːl] überhaupt **II**
most of **all** ['məʊst‿əv‿ɔːl] am meisten **II**
allergic [æ'lɜːdʒɪk] allergisch **II**
bowling **alley** ['bəʊlɪŋ‿æli] Bowlingbahn **III U6**, 83
to **allow** [ə'laʊ] erlauben, gestatten **II**
to be allowed to (do sth) [biː‿ə'laʊd] dürfen **II**
almost ['ɔːlməʊst] fast, beinahe **I**
alone [ə'ləʊn] alleine **I**
to leave sb alone [ˌliːv‿ə'ləʊn] jemanden in Ruhe lassen **III U5**, 70
alphabet ['ælfəbet] Alphabet **I**
already [ɔːl'redi] schon **I**
also ['ɔːlsəʊ] auch **I**
although [ɔːl'ðəʊ] obwohl **II**
aluminum foil *(AE)* [əˌluːmɪnəm 'fɔɪl] Alufolie ⟨**III U5**, 70⟩
always ['ɔːlweɪz] immer, ständig **I**
am [ˌeɪ'em] vormittags *(Uhrzeit)* **I**
amazed [ə'meɪzd] erstaunt, verblüfft **II**
amazement [ə'meɪzmənt] Erstaunen **III U2**, 30
ambulance ['æmbjələnts] Krankenwagen **III U3**, 45
American [ə'merɪkən] amerikanisch; Amerikaner(in) **I**
Native American [ˌneɪtɪv‿ə'merɪkən] Ureinwohner(in) Amerikas, Indianer(in); indianisch **II**
to **amuse** oneself [ə'mjuːz] sich amüsieren; sich die Zeit vertreiben **III U5**, 72
and [ænd; ən(d)] und **I**
angel ['eɪndʒl] Engel **III U2**, 30
Angles *(pl.)* ['æŋglz] Angeln *(Volksstamm)* ⟨**III F1**, 21⟩
Anglo-Saxon [ˌæŋgləʊ'sæksn] Angelsachse; angelsächsisch ⟨**III F1**, 21⟩
angry ['æŋgri] verärgert, böse **I**
animal ['ænɪml] Tier **I**
announcement [ə'naʊntsmənt] Ankündigung; Durchsage ⟨**III U4**, 57⟩
annoyed [ə'nɔɪd] verärgert **II**
annoying [ə'nɔɪɪŋ] ärgerlich, lästig **II**
anorak ['ænəræk] Anorak **I**
another [ə'nʌðə] noch ein(e); ein(e) andere(-r/-s) **I**
answer ['ɑːntsə] Antwort **I**
to **answer** ['ɑːntsə] (be)antworten **I**
any ['eni] irgendein(-e/-er); irgendwelche **I**
not any better [ˌnɒt‿eni 'betə] (überhaupt) nicht besser **II**

not any more [ˌnɒt‿eni 'mɔː] nicht mehr II
anybody ['eniˌbɒdi] irgendjemand; jeder (beliebige) II
anyone ['eniwʌn] irgendjemand; jeder (beliebige) II
anything ['eniθɪŋ] irgendetwas II
anyway ['eniweɪ] jedenfalls, sowieso II
anywhere ['eniweə] irgendwo; überall (egal, wo) II
apart from [ə'pɑːt frəm] außer, abgesehen von I
apartment *(AE)* [ə'pɑːtmənt] Apartment, Wohnung I
to **appear** [ə'pɪə] erscheinen III U2, 30
appetite ['æpɪtaɪt] Appetit II
apple ['æpl] Apfel I
April ['eɪprl] April I
arboretum, *pl.* **arboreta** [ˌɑːbr'iːtəm] Baumschule ⟨III U5, 77⟩
archaeology [ˌɑːki'ɒlədʒi] Archäologie II
archery ['ɑːtʃri] Bogenschießen II
area ['eəriə] Areal; Fläche; Gebiet III U1, 12
argument ['ɑːgjəmənt] Argument; Streit II
arm [ɑːm] Arm I
armed [ɑːmd] bewaffnet ⟨III U2, 30⟩
armour ['ɑːmə] Rüstung ⟨III U2, 30⟩
army ['ɑːmi] Armee ⟨III F1, 21⟩
around [ə'raʊnd] herum, umher I
to hang around [ˌhæŋ‿ə'raʊnd] herumhängen II
to **arrange** [ə'reɪndʒ] ausmachen; arrangieren III U2, 23
arrival [ə'raɪvl] Ankunft III U4, 60
to **arrive** (at) [ə'raɪv] ankommen I
arrow ['ærəʊ] Pfeil II
art [ɑːt] Kunst II
arts and crafts [ˌɑːts‿nd 'krɑːfts] Kunsthandwerk III U3, 38
work of art [ˌwɜːk‿əv‿'ɑːt] Kunstwerk ⟨III U4, 53⟩
Arthurian [ɑː'θjʊəriən] Artus- ⟨III U2, 29⟩
article ['ɑːtɪkl] Artikel *(in der Zeitung, etc.)* I
as [æz; əz] als II
as … as [æz; əz] so … wie … II
as a result of [əz‿ə rɪ'zʌlt‿əv] infolge (von) III U4, 52
as far as [əz 'fɑːr‿əz] bis III U1, 9
as soon as [əz 'suːn‿əz] sobald III U2, 30
as well [əz 'wel] auch III U6, 88
ash [æʃ] Asche III U5, 75
Asian ['eɪʃn] asiatisch; Asiat(in) II
as if [əz‿'ɪf] als ob III U4, 61
to **ask** [ɑːsk] fragen I
to ask (for) [ɑːsk] bitten (um) II
aspect ['æspekt] Aspekt II
Assembly [ə'sembli] Versammlung; Morgenappell I
assignment *(AE)* [ə'saɪnmənt] Aufgabe II
assistant [ə'sɪstnt] Assistent(in) I
shop assistant ['ʃɒp‿əˌsɪstnt] Verkäufer(in) I
at [æt; ət] in, auf, bei, an I
at all [ət‿'ɔːl] überhaupt II
at first [ət 'fɜːst] zuerst; zunächst II
at home [ət 'həʊm] zu Hause I
at last [ət 'lɑːst] endlich I
at least [ət 'liːst] mindestens, wenigstens II
at once [ət 'wʌnts] sofort, plötzlich I
at the Burtons' [ət ðə 'bɜːtnz] bei den Burtons II
at the seaside [ət ðə 'siːsaɪd] am Meer I
athlete ['æθliːt] (Leicht-)Athlet(in) III U4, 53
athletic [æθ'letɪk] athletisch II
Atishoo! [ə'tɪʃuː] Hatschi! II
to **attack** [ə'tæk] angreifen I
heart attack ['hɑːt‿əˌtæk] Herzinfarkt ⟨III EL, 101⟩
to **attract** [ə'trækt] anziehen III F4, 99
attraction [ə'trækʃn] Attraktion, Sehenswürdigkeit I
attractive [ə'træktɪv] attraktiv III F4, 99
audience ['ɔːdiənts] Publikum III U1, 18
August ['ɔːgəst] August I
aunt [ɑːnt] Tante I
Australian ['ɒstreɪliən] australisch; Australier(in) I
author ['ɔːθə] Autor(in) III U4, 54
autograph ['ɔːtəgrɑːf] Autogramm II
autumn ['ɔːtəm] Herbst II
avalanche ['ævlɑːntʃ] Lawine ⟨III U5, 74⟩
an **average** of [ən‿'ævrɪdʒ‿əv] durchschnittlich; im Durchschnitt III F2, 51
average ['ævrɪdʒ] durchschnittlich III F2, 51
away [ə'weɪ] weg (von) I
right away [raɪt‿ə'weɪ] sofort, gleich I
awful ['ɔːfl] schrecklich, furchtbar III U6, 84

B

baby ['beɪbi] Baby, Säugling II
back [bæk] Rücken I
back [bæk] Hinter-, rückwärtig II
back [bæk] zurück I
background ['bækgraʊnd] Hintergrund II
backpack ['bækpæk] Rucksack III U5, 70
backstage [bæk'steɪdʒ] backstage, hinter der Bühne II
bacon ['beɪkn] Schinkenspeck II
bad [bæd] schlecht I
to be in a bad way [ɪn‿ə 'bæd ˌweɪ] in schlechter Verfassung sein I
bag [bæg] Tasche I; Sack II
mixed bag [ˌmɪkst 'bæg] buntes Allerlei I
school bag ['skuːl bæg] Schultasche I
sleeping bag ['sliːpɪŋ ˌbæg] Schlafsack III U5, 70; ⟨III EL, 100⟩
bagpipes *pl.* ['bægpaɪps] Dudelsack I
to **bake** [beɪk] backen III U5, 72
ball [bɔːl] Ball I
bowling ball ['bəʊlɪŋ ˌbɔːl] Bowlingkugel III U6, 82
golf ball ['gɒlf ˌbɔːl] Golfball III U6, 82
banana [bə'nɑːnə] Banane III U3, 45
band [bænd] Band, Kapelle II
bandage ['bændɪdʒ] Bandage; Verband III U6, 89
bank [bæŋk] Bank II
bar [bɑː] Tafel; Riegel; Stück; Stange I
to **bark** (at) [bɑːk] (an)bellen I
baron ['bærn] Baron ⟨III U2, 29⟩
barrel ['bærl] Fass, Tonne II
barrier ['bæriə] Barriere, Sperre III U1, 11
baseball ['beɪsbɔːl] Baseball I
baseball bat ['beɪsbɔːl ˌbæt] Baseballschläger III U6, 82
baseball field ['beɪsbɔːl ˌfiːld] Baseballplatz III U6, 82
basement ['beɪsmənt] Kellergeschoss, Untergeschoss ⟨III U4, 60⟩
basic ['beɪsɪk] grundlegend, Grund-, einfach II
basis, *pl.* **bases** ['beɪsɪs; 'beɪsiːz] Basis, Grundlage ⟨III EL, 103⟩
basket ['bɑːskɪt] Korb, Körbchen I
basketball court ['bɑːskɪtbɔːl ˌkɔːt] Basketballplatz III U6, 82
basketball ['bɑːskɪtbɔːl] Basketball II
bass [beɪs] Bass II
bat [bæt] Schläger (Tischtennis-, Baseball-); Fledermaus II
baseball bat ['beɪsbɔːl ˌbæt] Baseballschläger III U6, 82
bath [bɑːθ] Bad I
bathroom ['bɑːθrʊm] Badezimmer I
battery ['bætri] Batterie, Akku II
battle ['bætl] Schlacht III F1, 21
bazaar [bə'zɑː] Bazar II
the **BBC** [ˌbiːbiː'siː] *britische Rundfunkanstalt* ⟨III U1, 10⟩
BC (= before Christ) [biː'siː] vor Christus III F1, 20
*to **be** [biː] sein I
to be able to (do sth) [biː‿'eɪbl] fähig sein (zu); können; dürfen II
to be afraid (of) [biː‿ə'freɪd] (sich) fürchten, Angst haben (vor) II
to be alive [biː‿ə'laɪv] lebendig sein; leben I
to be allowed to (do sth) [biː‿ə'laʊd] dürfen II
to be as hungry as a horse [əz ˌhʌŋgri‿əz‿ə 'hɔːs] einen Bärenhunger haben II
to be born [biː 'bɔːn] geboren werden II
to be called [biː 'kɔːld] heißen, genannt werden II
to be fast [biː 'fɑːst] vorgehen III U1, 13
to be frightened (of) [biː 'fraɪtnd] Angst haben (vor) I
to be going on [biː ˌgəʊɪŋ‿'ɒn] los sein II
to be gone [biː 'gɒn] verschwunden sein II
to be good at [biː 'gʊd‿ət] gut sein in I
to be hurt [biː 'hɜːt] verletzt sein/werden I
to be in a bad way [ɪn‿ə 'bæd ˌweɪ] in schlechter Verfassung sein I
to be in love (with) [ˌbiː‿ɪn 'lʌv] verliebt sein (in) II
to be in one's right mind [biː‿ɪn wʌnz ˌraɪt 'maɪnd] ganz richtig im Kopf sein ⟨III EL, 105⟩
to be interested in [biː‿'ɪntrəstɪd‿ɪn] interessiert sein an, sich interessieren für I
to be keen on [biː 'kiːn‿ɒn] scharf sein auf, begeistert sein von II

to be known as [bi: 'nəʊn‿əz] bekannt sein als III F1,21
to be late [bi: 'leɪt] zu spät dran sein, zu spät kommen I
to be located [bi: ləʊ'keɪtɪd] gelegen sein II
to be lucky [bi: 'lʌki] Glück haben I
to be made of [bi: 'meɪd‿əv] hergestellt sein aus II
to be married to [bi: 'mærid tə] verheiratet sein mit I
to be on [bi:‿'ɒn] im Gange sein, laufen I
to be on a team [ˌbi:‿ɒn‿ə 'ti:m] Mitglied eines Teams sein III U6,86
to be out of one's mind [bi:‿aʊt‿əv wʌnz 'maɪnd] verrückt sein III U1,15
to be pleased [bi: 'pli:zd] erfreut sein III U2,23
to be scared [bi: 'skeəd] Angst haben, erschrocken sein I
to be stuck [bi: 'stʌk] stecken bleiben, festklemmen II
to be surprised [bi: sə'praɪzd] überrascht sein I
to be trapped [bi: 'træpt] in der Falle sitzen III U5,75
to be willing to do sth [bi: 'wɪlɪŋ] ⟨III EL,105⟩
to be worried [bi: 'wʌrid] besorgt, beunruhigt sein I
to be wrong [bi: 'rɒŋ] Unrecht haben II
beach [bi:tʃ] Strand I
black **bear** [ˌblæk 'beə] Schwarzbär II
teddy bear ['tedi ˌbeə] Teddybär III U1,14
*to **beat** [bi:t] besiegen; schlagen I
beautiful ['bju:tɪfl] wunderschön, hübsch I
because [bɪ'kɒz] weil I
*to **become** [bɪ'kʌm] werden II
bed [bed] Bett I
bed and breakfast [ˌbed‿n 'brekfəst] Zimmer mit Frühstück I
bedroom ['bedrʊm] Schlafzimmer I
bee [bi:] Biene ⟨III EL,103⟩
beef [bi:f] Rindfleisch III F2,50
Beefeater ['bi:fˌi:tə] Beefeater, königlicher Leibgardist ⟨III U1,14⟩
beer [bɪə] Bier II
before [bɪ'fɔ:] vorher; zuvor; schon einmal II
before [bɪ'fɔ:] vor I
before [bɪ'fɔ:] bevor I
*to **begin** [bɪ'gɪn] beginnen; anfangen III U2,25
beginning [bɪ'gɪnɪŋ] Anfang, Beginn I
to **behave** [bɪ'heɪv] sich verhalten, sich benehmen II
behind [bɪ'haɪnd] hinten; im Rückstand III U6,88
behind [bɪ'haɪnd] hinter II
to **believe** [bɪ'li:v] glauben II
bell [bel] Glocke II
below [bɪ'ləʊ] unterhalb, unten I
*to **bend** over [ˌbend‿'əʊvə] sich vorbeugen III U3,42
bereaved [bɪ'ri:vd] von einem schmerzlichen Verlust betroffen ⟨III U2,28⟩
bereavement [bɪ'ri:vmənt] schmerzlicher Verlust ⟨III U2,28⟩
best [best] beste(-r/-s) I
*to **bet** [bet] wetten III U2,24
You bet! [ju: 'bet] Das kannst du mir aber glauben! ⟨III U2,24⟩
better ['betə] besser I
between [bɪ'twi:n] zwischen II
in between [ˌɪn bɪ'twi:n] dazwischen II
big [bɪg] groß; dick I
bike [baɪk] Fahrrad I
biking ['baɪkɪŋ] Radfahren II
mountain biking ['maʊntɪn ˌbaɪkɪŋ] Mountainbikefahren II
biology [baɪ'ɒlədʒi] Biologie II
bird [bɜ:d] Vogel I
biro ['baɪrəʊ] Kugelschreiber, Kuli I
birthday ['bɜ:θdeɪ] Geburtstag I
biscuit ['bɪskɪt] Keks II
bishop ['bɪʃəp] Bischof ⟨III U2,29⟩
a **bit** [ə 'bɪt] ein bisschen I
bitter ['bɪtə] bitter II
black [blæk] schwarz I
black bear [ˌblæk 'beə] Schwarzbär II
blackboard, board ['blækbɔ:d; bɔ:d] Tafel I
blanket ['blæŋkɪt] (Woll-)Decke II
bless you ['bles ju:] Gesundheit! II
blind [blaɪnd] blind III U4,53
blonde [blɒnd] blond I
blood [blʌd] Blut ⟨III U2,28⟩; III U2,31
bloody ['blʌdi] verdammt ⟨III U1,15⟩
blow [bləʊ] Hieb, Schlag III U2,31
*to **blow** [bləʊ] blasen III U6,89
to blow a whistle [ˌbləʊ‿ə'wɪsl] auf einer Trillerpfeife pfeifen III U6,89
blue [blu:] blau I
blues [blu:z] Blues III U5,69
board, blackboard ['blækbɔ:d; bɔ:d] Tafel I
to **board** [bɔ:d] an Bord gehen, besteigen II
boarding pass ['bɔ:dɪŋ ˌpɑ:s] Bordkarte II
boat [bəʊt] Boot, Schiff I
body ['bɒdi] Körper I; Leiche ⟨III U2,28⟩
to **boil** [bɔɪl] kochen III U5,70
bone [bəʊn] Knochen III U3,41
book [bʊk] Buch; Heft I
exercise book ['eksəsaɪz ˌbʊk] Übungsheft I
to **book** [bʊk] buchen, reservieren II
bookshop ['bʊkʃɒp] Buchhandlung I
boot [bu:t] Stiefel II
bored [bɔ:d] gelangweilt II
boring ['bɔ:rɪŋ] langweilig I
*to be **born** [bi: 'bɔ:n] geboren werden II
to **borrow** ['bɒrəʊ] (sich) ausleihen III U4,58
boss [bɒs] Boss, Chef II
both [bəʊθ] beide I
bottle ['bɒtl] Flasche I
bow [bəʊ] Bogen II
bowl [bəʊl] Schale, Schälchen I; Bowlingkugel III U6,82
bowling alley ['bəʊlɪŋ‿æli] Bowlingbahn III U6,83
bowling ball ['bəʊlɪŋ ˌbɔ:l] Bowlingkugel III U6,82
box [bɒks] Kiste, Schachtel; Kasten I
fuse box ['fju:z bɒks] Sicherungskasten ⟨III U4,61⟩
boy [bɔɪ] Junge I
boyfriend ['bɔɪfrend] Freund I
branch [brɑ:ntʃ] Zweig, Ast III U5,70
brave [breɪv] tapfer, mutig I
bread [bred] Brot II
break [breɪk] Pause; Bruch II
to take a break [ˌteɪk‿ə 'breɪk] Pause machen II
*to **break** [breɪk] (zer)brechen; kaputtmachen II
to break down [ˌbreɪk‿'daʊn] liegen bleiben ⟨III EL,101⟩
to break in [breɪk‿'ɪn] einlaufen; einreiten II
breakfast ['brekfəst] Frühstück I
bed and breakfast [ˌbed‿n 'brekfəst] Zimmer mit Frühstück I
breath [breθ] Atem; Atemzug III U6,89
to **breathe** [bri:ð] atmen III U5,75
bridge [brɪdʒ] Brücke I
brief [bri:f] kurz III U4,52
bright [braɪt] leuchtend, strahlend II
brilliant ['brɪljənt] toll, prima; leuchtend I
*to **bring** [brɪŋ] bringen I
Made in **Britain** [ˌmeɪd‿ɪn 'brɪtn] Hergestellt in Großbritannien I
British ['brɪtɪʃ] britisch I
Briton ['brɪtn] Brite, Britin III F1,21
broad [brɔ:d] breit II
brochure ['brəʊʃə] Broschüre, Prospekt II
brother ['brʌðə] Bruder I
brown [braʊn] braun I
budgie ['bʌdʒi] Wellensittich I
buffalo, *pl.* **buffalo** ['bʌfləʊ] Büffel ⟨III F3,80⟩
*to **build** [bɪld] bauen III U1,10
building ['bɪldɪŋ] Gebäude I
bulldozer ['bʊlˌdəʊzə] Bulldozer ⟨III U2,28⟩
bull's-eye ['bʊlsˌaɪ] Mittelpunkt der Zielscheibe II
bully ['bʊli] Rabauke, Rüpel, Tyrann II
*to give somebody the **bumps** [ˌgɪv ðə 'bʌmps] jemanden hochwerfen und wieder auffangen I
to **bump** [bʌmp] (an)stoßen, stoßen I
bumpy ['bʌmpi] holprig II
bun [bʌn] Brötchen III F2,50
burger ['bɜ:gə] Hamburger I
*to **burn** [bɜ:n] (ver)brennen II
at the **Burtons'** [ət ðə 'bɜ:tnz] bei den Burtons II
bus [bʌs] Bus I
by (bus) [baɪ] mit (dem Bus), per I
bush [bʊʃ] Busch, Strauch I
business ['bɪznɪs] Geschäft; Branche I
on business [ɒn 'bɪznɪs] geschäftlich I
busker ['bʌskə] Straßenmusikant(in) ⟨III U1,13⟩
busy ['bɪzi] beschäftigt; belebt; voller Menschen I
but [bʌt; bət] aber I
butter ['bʌtə] Butter II
button ['bʌtn] Knopf ⟨III EL,105⟩
*to **buy** [baɪ] kaufen I

by [baɪ] von **I**; bei; an **I**; bis *(siehe Box auf S. 147)* **III U3**,42
by (bus) [baɪ] mit (dem Bus), per **I**
by mistake [ˌbaɪ mɪˈsteɪk] versehentlich **III U3**,40
by oneself [ˌbaɪ‿wʌnˈself] allein **III U5**,72
by the way [ˌbaɪ ðə ˈweɪ] übrigens **III U3**,45
Bye! [baɪ] Tschüss! **I**

C

cable [ˈkeɪbl] Kabel **III F4**,98
cactus [ˈkæktəs] Kaktus **III F3**,81
café [ˈkæfeɪ] Café **I**
cake [keɪk] Kuchen **I**
calendar [ˈkæləndə] Kalender **I**
calf, *pl.* **calves** [kɑːf; kɑːvz] Kalb **II**
call [kɔːl] Anruf **I**; Ruf **III U5**,74
to **call** [kɔːl] (an)rufen; Bescheid geben **I**; nennen **II**
to be called [biː ˈkɔːld] heißen, genannt werden **II**
caller [ˈkɔːlə] Anrufer(in) **II**
camera [ˈkæmrə] Kamera, Fotoapparat **I**
camp [kæmp] Camp; Lager **III U2**,26
to **camp** [kæmp] campen, zelten, kampieren **III U5**,70
campervan [ˈkæmpəˌvæn] Wohnmobil ⟨**III EL**,100⟩
campfire [ˈkæmpfaɪə] Lagerfeuer **III U5**,70
camping [ˈkæmpɪŋ] Camping, Zelten **II**
campsite [ˈkæmpsaɪt] Campingplatz, Zeltplatz **III U5**,70; ⟨**III EL**,100⟩
can [kæn; kən] kann, können **I**
can't [kɑːnt] nicht können **I**
candle [ˈkændl] Kerze **I**
candy *(AE)* [ˈkændi] Süßigkeiten **II**
canoeing [kəˈnuːɪŋ] Kanufahren **II**
canyon [ˈkænjən] Canyon **II**
cap [kæp] Kappe, Mütze **II**
capital [ˈkæpɪtl] Hauptstadt **I**
captain [ˈkæptɪn] Kapitän; Mannschaftsführer(in) **III U6**,86
caption [ˈkæpʃn] Untertitel; Bildunterschrift **III U4**,53
car [kɑː] Auto **I**
car park [ˈkɑː ˌpɑːk] Parkplatz ⟨**III EL**,106⟩
card [kɑːd] Karte **I**
Valentine's card [ˈvæləntaɪnz ˌkɑːd] Valentinskarte **III U5**,72
to **care** for sb [keə] für jemanden etwas empfinden ⟨**III EL**,106⟩
careful [ˈkeəfl] vorsichtig; sorgfältig **II**
caretaker *(BE)* [ˈkeəˌteɪkə] Hausmeister(in) **III U3**,40
Caribbean [ˌkærɪˈbiːən; kəˈrɪbiən] karibisch **III U1**,13
carnival [ˈkɑːnɪvl] Karneval **III U1**,9
to **carry** [ˈkæri] tragen **I**
carton [ˈkɑːtn] Karton *(Verbundverpackung)* **III U5**,69
cartoon [kɑːˈtuːn] Cartoon; Zeichentrickfilm **I**
in **case** [ɪn ˈkeɪs] falls; für den Fall, dass … **II**
pencil case [ˈpentsl ˌkeɪs] Federmäppchen **I**
castle [ˈkɑːsl] Schloss; Burg **I**
cat [kæt] Katze **I**
It's raining cats and dogs. [ɪts ˌreɪnɪŋ ˌkæts‿ənd ˈdɒgz] Es schüttet wie aus Eimern. ⟨**III EL**,100⟩
*to **catch** [kætʃ] fangen **II**
cattle *(pl. only)* [ˈkætl] (Rind-)Vieh **II**
cattle drive [ˈkætl ˌdraɪv] Viehtrieb **II**
to **cause** [kɔːz] verursachen **III U3**,42
CCTV (closed-circuit TV) [ˌsiːsiːtiːˈviː] Fernsehüberwachungsanlage ⟨**III U1**,14⟩
CD [siːˈdiː] CD **I**
CD player [ˌsiːˈdiː ˌpleɪə] CD-Spieler **I**
CD-ROM [ˌsiːdiːˈrɒm] CD-ROM **III U1**,14
to **cease** [siːs] aufhören, beenden ⟨**III EL**,105⟩
ceiling [ˈsiːlɪŋ] (Zimmer-)Decke **I**
to **celebrate** [ˈseləbreɪt] feiern **II**
celebration [ˌseləˈbreɪʃn] Feier **II**
cellphone *(AE)* [ˈselfəʊn] Handy, Mobiltelefon **III U4**,60
Celt [kelt] Kelte, Keltin ⟨**III F1**,21⟩
Celtic [ˈkeltɪk; ˈseltɪk] keltisch **II**
centre [ˈsentə] Zentrum **I**
activity centre [ækˈtɪvəti ˌsentə] Jugendzentrum **II**
city centre [ˌsɪti ˈsentə] Stadtzentrum, Stadtmitte **I**
shopping centre [ˈʃɒpɪŋ ˌsentə] Einkaufszentrum **I**
trading centre [ˈtreɪdɪŋ ˌsentə] Handelszentrum ⟨**III F1**,21⟩
century [ˈsentʃri] Jahrhundert **III U1**,10
cereal [ˈsɪəriəl] Zerealie; Getreideprodukt *(z. B. Cornflakes oder Müsli)* **III F2**,51
certain [ˈsɜːtn] bestimmt; sicher **III U6**,89
chair [tʃeə] Stuhl **I**
champion [ˈtʃæmpiən] Gewinner; Champion **I**
chance [tʃɑːnts] Chance, Möglichkeit, Gelegenheit **II**
change [tʃeɪndʒ] Wechsel, Änderung **II**
change of clothing [ˌtʃeɪndʒ‿əv ˈkləʊðɪŋ] Satz/Garnitur Kleidung zum Wechseln ⟨**III U5**,70⟩
to **change** [tʃeɪndʒ] tauschen, wechseln; (sich) ändern **I**; umsteigen **III U1**,9
to change sth into sth [tʃeɪndʒ] in … verwandeln **II**
changing room [ˈtʃeɪndʒɪŋ ˌrʊm] Umkleideraum **III U3**,41
to change one's mind [tʃeɪndʒ] seine Meinung ändern **II**
channel [ˈtʃænl] Kanal; Programm **III F4**,98
chaos [ˈkeɪɒs] Chaos; Durcheinander **II**
chapel [ˈtʃæpl] Kapelle ⟨**III U2**,28⟩
character [ˈkærəktə] Charakter, Figur **II**
charity [ˈtʃærɪti] Wohltätigkeitsverein; tätige Nächstenliebe **II**
to **chase** [tʃeɪs] verfolgen, jagen **I**
chatroom [ˈtʃætrʊm] Chatroom *(Internetforum, wo man sich online unterhalten kann)* **III U5**,72
cheap [tʃiːp] billig **III U1**,19
to **check** [tʃek] (über)prüfen; kontrollieren **I**
Let's check! [lets ˈtʃek] Lass(t) uns überprüfen! **I**
check-in [ˈtʃekɪn] Gepäckaufgabe **II**
cheer [tʃɪə] Jubel **III U6**,86
to **cheer** [tʃɪə] (zu)jubeln, anfeuern **II**
cheerleader [ˈtʃɪəˌliːdə] Cheerleader *(Mädchen, das in einer Gruppe eine Sportmannschaft anfeuert)* **III U6**,86
cheerleading [ˈtʃɪəliːdɪŋ] Cheerleading *(Aktivitäten der Cheerleader)* **III U6**,86
cheese [tʃiːz] Käse **I**
chick [tʃɪk] Küken **I**
chicken [ˈtʃɪkɪn] Huhn, Hähnchen **I**
chief [tʃiːf] Häuptling **II**
child, *pl.* **children** [ˈtʃaɪld; ˈtʃɪldrn] Kind **I**
chime [tʃaɪm] Glockenspiel, Glockengeläut ⟨**III U1**,10⟩
Chinese [tʃaɪˈniːz] chinesisch; Chinese, Chinesin **II**
chip *(AE)* [tʃɪp] Kartoffelchip **I**
chips pl. (BE) [tʃɪps] Pommes frites **I**
fish and chips [ˌfɪʃ‿n ˈtʃɪps] Fisch und Pommes frites **I**
chocolate [ˈtʃɒklət] Schokolade **I**
choir [ˈkwaɪə] Chor ⟨**III U2**,23⟩
*to **choose** [tʃuːz; tʃəʊz] (aus)wählen **I**
Christian [ˈkrɪstʃən] Christ(in) **II**
church [tʃɜːtʃ] Kirche **I**
cinema [ˈsɪnəmə] Kino **I**
circle [ˈsɜːkl] Kreis **I**
city [ˈsɪti] Stadt; Großstadt **I**
city centre [ˌsɪti ˈsentə] Stadtzentrum, Stadtmitte **I**
to **clap** [klæp] klatschen **I**
class [klɑːs] Schulklasse, Klasse **I**; Kurs, Unterricht **II**
in class [ɪn ˈklɑːs] in/vor der Klasse **I**
classroom [ˈklɑːsrʊm] Klassenzimmer **I**
clause [klɔːz] Satz *(Teil eines Satzgefüges)* **II**
contact clause [ˈkɒntækt ˌklɔːz] *Relativsatz ohne Relativpronomen* **II**
relative clause [ˌrelətɪv ˈklɔːz] Relativsatz **II**
to **clean** [kliːn] säubern, reinigen **I**
cleaning staff [ˈkliːnɪŋ ˌstɑːf] Reinigungspersonal ⟨**III U3**,40⟩
clean [kliːn] sauber **III U3**,44
cleaner [ˈkliːnə] Raumpfleger(in), Putzkraft **III U6**,88
clear [klɪə] klar **II**
clerk [klɑːk; klɜːrk] Angestellte(r) **III U5**,77
clever [ˈklevə] schlau, klug, intelligent **II**
to **click** [klɪk] klicken ⟨**III EL**,105⟩
climate [ˈklaɪmət] Klima **III F3**,80
to **climb** [ˈklaɪm] klettern, (be)steigen **II**
*to **cling** (to) [ˈklɪŋ] sich festhalten (an), sich festklammern (an) **I**
video **clip** [ˈvɪdiəʊ klɪp] Videoclip **III F4**,98
clock [klɒk] Uhr **III U1**,10
clock tower [ˈklɒk taʊə] Uhrenturm ⟨**III U1**,10⟩
o'clock [əˈklɒk] Uhr *(Zeitangabe bei vollen Stunden)* **I**
to **close** [kləʊz] schließen ⟨**III U2**,28⟩
close [kləʊs] eng, knapp **II**

close (to) [kləʊs] nahe (bei) **III U3,40**
closed [kləʊzd] geschlossen **I**
clothes *pl.* [kləʊðz] Kleider, Kleidung **I**
clothing ['kləʊðɪŋ] Kleidung **III U5,70**
change of clothing [ˌtʃeɪndʒ_əv 'kləʊðɪŋ] Satz/Garnitur Kleidung zum Wechseln ⟨**III U5,70**⟩
cloud [klaʊd] Wolke **I**
club [klʌb] Club, Verein **II**
golf club ['gɒlf ˌklʌb] Golfschläger **III U6,83**
health club ['helθ klʌb] Fitnessklub **III U1,12**
clue [klu:] Hinweis, Spur, Schlüssel **II**
CO [ˌkɒlr'ɑ:dəʊ] Colorado *(Abkürzung)* **II**
coach [kəʊtʃ] Reisebus **III U3,42**; Trainer(in) **III U6,86**
coal [kəʊl] Kohle **II**
coast [kəʊst] Küste **I**
coat [kəʊt] Mantel **II**
code [kəʊd] Code; Verschlüsselung ⟨**III EL,103**⟩
morse code [ˌmɔ:s 'kəʊd] Morsealphabet ⟨**III EL,103**⟩
coffee ['kɒfi:] Kaffee **II**
coffee bar ['kɒfi: ˌbɑ:] Café **III U5,68**
cold [kəʊld] Erkältung; Kälte **III U3,44**
cold [kəʊld] kalt **I**
collage [kɒ'lɑ:ʒ] Collage **I**
to **collect** [kə'lekt] sammeln **I**
college ['kɒlɪdʒ] College; Institut **II**
colonist ['kɒlənɪst] Kolonist(in), Siedler(in) **II**
colored *(AE)* ['kʌləd] bunt, farbig **II**
colour ['kʌlə] Farbe **I**
What colour is/are ... ? [ˌwɒt 'kʌlər_ɪz/ɑ:] Welche Farbe hat/haben ... ? **I**
column ['kɒləm] Spalte ⟨**III EL,104**⟩
combination [ˌkɒmbɪ'neɪʃn] Kombination ⟨**III EL,103**⟩
*to **come** [kʌm] kommen **I**
Come on! [kʌm_'ɒn] Komm(t)! **I**
to come in [kʌm_'ɪn] hereinkommen **I**
comedy ['kɒmədi] Komödie **III F4,99**
comfortable ['kʌmpftəbl] komfortabel; bequem **III U4,58**; ⟨**III EL,100**⟩
comic ['kɒmɪk] Comic(heft) **I**
comma ['kɒmə] Komma **II**
command [kə'mɑ:nd] Befehl **III U6,87**
comment ['kɒment] Kommentar **III U6,92**
commercial [kə'mɜ:ʃl] Werbespot **III U4,57**
to **communicate** [kə'mju:nɪkeɪt] kommunizieren, sich verständigen **III U4,52**
communication [kəˌmju:nɪ'keɪʃn] Kommunikation ⟨**III EL,103**⟩
community [kə'mju:nəti] Gemeinde; Gemeinschaft **I**
commuter [kə'mju:tə] Pendler(in) ⟨**III U1,10**⟩
company ['kʌmpəni] Gesellschaft; Firma; Kompanie **II**
comparative [kəm'pærətɪv] Komparativ **II**
to **compare** (with/to) [kəm'peə] vergleichen (mit) **II**
competition [ˌkɒmpə'tɪʃn] Wettbewerb, Turnier **II**
competitor [kəm'petɪtə] Teilnehmer(in); Mitbewerber(in) **II**
to **complain** [kəm'pleɪn] sich beschweren, sich beklagen **II**
to **complete** [kəm'pli:t] vervollständigen **II**
complete [kəm'pli:t] vollständig **III U1,18**
compound ['kɒmpaʊnd] Kompositum *(zusammengesetztes Wort)* **II**
comprehensive school [kɒmprɪ'hentsɪv ˌsku:l] Gesamtschule ⟨**III EL,106**⟩
computer [ˌkəm'pju:tə] Computer **I**
to **concentrate** ['kɒntsntreɪt] (sich) konzentrieren **III U5,75**
concert ['kɒnsət] Konzert **II**
conclusion [kən'klu:ʒn] Schluss; Schlussfolgerung ⟨**III U1,18**⟩
conditional [kən'dɪʃnl] Konditional **III U4,54**
conjunction [kən'dʒʌŋkʃn] Konjunktion **III U3,41**
to **connect (to)** [kə'nekt] verbinden (mit) **I**
to **conquer** ['kɒŋkə] erobern **II**
contact ['kɒntækt] Kontakt **II**
contact clause ['kɒntækt ˌklɔ:z] *Relativsatz ohne Relativpronomen* **II**
to **contain** [kən'teɪn] enthalten ⟨**III EL,102**⟩
contestant [kən'testnt] Kandidat(in) ⟨**III F4,99**⟩
context ['kɒntekst] Kontext, Zusammenhang **II**
to **control** [kən'trəʊl] kontrollieren; beherrschen **III F1,21**
conversation [ˌkɒnvə'seɪʃn] Konversation, Gespräch **II**
to **cook** [kʊk] kochen **II**
cookie *(AE)* ['kʊki] Keks **II**
cool [ku:l] cool, prima **II**; kühl **III U5,68**
copy ['kɒpi] Kopie **II**
to **copy** ['kɒpi] abschreiben, kopieren **I**
corner ['kɔ:nə] Ecke **III U4,61**
to **correct** [kə'rekt] korrigieren, verbessern **I**
correct [kə'rekt] richtig, korrekt **I**
cost [kɒst] Preis; Kosten **III F4,98**
*to **cost** [kɒst] kosten **III U4,58**
costume ['kɒstju:m] Kostüm **II**
cougar ['ku:gə] Puma, Berglöwe **II**
could [kʊd] konnte(n) **II**; könnte(n) **II**
country ['kʌntri] Land; ländliche Gegend, Landschaft **I**; Countrymusik **III U5,69**
courage ['kʌrɪdʒ] Mut ⟨**III U2,29**⟩
course [kɔ:s] Gang **II**
golf course ['gɒlf ˌkɔ:s] Golfplatz **III U6,83**
of course [əv 'kɔ:s] natürlich, selbstverständlich **I**
basketball **court** ['bɑ:skɪtbɔ:l ˌkɔ:t] Basketballplatz **III U6,82**
cousin ['kʌzn] Cousin, Cousine **I**
to **cover (up)** ['kʌvə] zudecken **III U2,28**
cow [kaʊ] Kuh **I**
cowboy ['kaʊbɔɪ] Cowboy, Rinderhirte **II**
arts and **crafts** [ˌɑ:ts_nd 'krɑ:fts] Kunsthandwerk **III U3,38**
to **crash** [kræʃ] aufschlagen, gegen etwas krachen **I**
crash! [kræʃ] Krach! Bumm!; Zusammenstoß **I**
crater ['kreɪtə] Krater ⟨**III U5,76**⟩
crazy ['kreɪzi] verrückt **II**
cream [kri:m] Creme; Sahne **I**
ice cream [aɪs 'kri:m] Eis, Eiscreme **I**
creative [kri'eɪtɪv] kreativ **III U1,16**
*to **creep** [kri:p] schleichen; kriechen **III U4,61**
crime [kraɪm] Verbrechen, Kriminalität **II**
crisp *(BE)* [krɪsp] Kartoffelchip **I**
crispy ['krɪspi] knusprig, kross **III F2,50**
crossword (puzzle) ['krɒswɜ:d] Kreuzworträtsel **II**
crowd [kraʊd] Menschenmenge **II**
crown [kraʊn] Krone ⟨**III U3,45**⟩
cruel ['kru:əl] grausam **II**
crunchy ['krʌntʃi] knusprig; knackig **III F2,51**
cry [kraɪ] Schrei ⟨**III U2,28**⟩
to **cry** [kraɪ] schreien, rufen; weinen **I**
cultural ['kʌltʃrl] kulturell **II**
culture ['kʌltʃə] Kultur **II**
cup [kʌp] Tasse **I**; Pokal; Kelch **III U2,30**
cupboard ['kʌbəd] Küchenschrank, Schrank **I**
to **cure** [kjʊə] heilen; kurieren **III U4,56**
curry ['kʌri] Curry *(Gewürz oder Gericht)* **II**
to **curse** [kɜ:s] fluchen **III U4,61**
curtain ['kɜ:tn] Vorhang **III U3,44**
custom ['kʌstəm] Brauch, Sitte **II**
customer ['kʌstəmə] Kunde, Kundin **I**
short **cut** ['ʃɔ:t kʌt] Abkürzung **II**
*to **cut** (off) [kʌt_'ɒf] (ab)schneiden **II**
cycling ['saɪklɪŋ] Radfahren ⟨**III EL,101**⟩

D

dad [dæd] Papa **I**
daily ['deɪli] täglich **II**
damage ['dæmɪdʒ] Schaden **III U5,76**
damn [dæm] verdammt **II**
dance [dɑ:nts] Tanz **III U1,15**
square dance ['skweə ˌdɑ:nts] Square Dance **II**
to **dance** [dɑ:nts] tanzen **II**
dangerous ['deɪndʒrəs] gefährlich **I**
Danish ['deɪnɪʃ] dänisch **II**
dark [dɑ:k] dunkel **I**
darkness ['dɑ:knəs] Dunkelheit **II**
date [deɪt] Datum **I**
to **date** from ['deɪt frəm] zurückgehen auf **III U1,10**
daughter ['dɔ:tə] Tochter **II**
day [deɪ] Tag **I**
every day [ˌevri 'deɪ] jeden Tag **I**
the day before yesterday [ðə ˌdeɪ bɪfɔ: 'jestədeɪ] vorgestern **I**
these days ['ði:z ˌdeɪz] heutzutage **II**
dead [ded] tot **I**
deaf [def] gehörlos; schwerhörig **III U4,53**
*to **deal** with ['di:l wɪð] sich befassen/umgehen mit **II**
Oh **dear**! ['əʊ ˌdɪə] Oje! **I**
dear [dɪə] lieb **I**
death [deθ] Tod **III U5,76**
December [dɪ'sembə] Dezember **I**
to **decide** [dɪ'saɪd] entscheiden **II**

decision [dɪ'sɪʒn] Entscheidung **III U6,90**
decoder [ˌdi:'kəʊdə] Decoder *(Gerät, das ein verschlüsseltes Signal entschlüsseln kann)* ⟨**III U4,53**⟩
decorated ['dekreɪtɪd] dekoriert, geschmückt **II**
decoration [ˌdek'reɪʃn] Dekoration **II**
deep [di:p] tief **III U2,30**
deer, *pl.* **deer** [dɪə] Hirsch, Reh; Rotwild **II**
to **defeat** [dɪ'fi:t] besiegen ⟨**III F1,21**⟩
definite ['defɪnət] definitiv, bestimmt, eindeutig **II**
definition [ˌdefɪ'nɪʃn] Definition; Festlegung **II**
delayed [dɪ'leɪd] verspätet, verzögert **II**
delicious [dɪ'lɪʃəs] köstlich **II**
department [dɪ'pɑ:tmənt] Abteilung **III U1,14**
departure [dɪ'pɑ:tʃə] Abflug, Abreise **II**
derby ['dɜ:bi] Derby **III U5,69**
to **describe** [dɪ'skraɪb] beschreiben **II**
description [dɪ'skrɪpʃn] Beschreibung **II**
to **design** [dɪ'zaɪn] entwerfen **II**
to **desist** [dɪ'sɪst] von etwas absehen ⟨**III EL,105**⟩
desk [desk] Schreibtisch **I**
dessert [dɪ'zɜ:t] Dessert, Nachspeise **II**
to **destroy** [dɪ'strɔɪ] zerstören ⟨**III U2,29**⟩
detail ['di:teɪl] Detail, Einzelheit **II**
detective [dɪ'tektɪv] Detektiv(in) **III U1,14**
devastated ['devəsteɪtɪd] niedergeschmettert ⟨**III U1,12**⟩
to **develop** [dɪ'veləp] (sich) entwickeln ⟨**III EL,103**⟩
device [dɪ'vaɪs] Gerät, Vorrichtung **III U4,54**
diagram ['daɪəgræm] Diagramm **II**
dialect ['daɪəlekt] Dialekt **I**
dialogue ['daɪəlɒg] Dialog, Gespräch **I**
diary ['daɪəri] Tagebuch; Terminkalender **II**
dictionary ['dɪkʃnri] Wörterbuch **I**
to **die** [daɪ] sterben **I**
  to die out [daɪ‿'aʊt] aussterben ⟨**III U2,27**⟩
difference ['dɪfrnts] Unterschied **II**
different ['dɪfrnt] anders, verschieden **I**
difficult ['dɪfɪklt] schwierig **II**
dinner ['dɪnə] Abendessen **I**
  to have dinner [hæv 'dɪnə] zu Abend essen **I**
  TV dinner [ˌti:vi: 'dɪnə] Fernsehmahlzeit ⟨**III F2,50**⟩
dinosaur ['daɪnəsɔ:] Dinosaurier **III F3,81**
dip [dɪp] Dip *(cremige Sauce zum Einstippen)* **III F2,50**
direct [dɪ'rekt] direkt **II**
  direct speech [dɪˌrekt 'spi:tʃ] direkte Rede **III U6,84**
direction [dɪ'rekʃn] Richtung **III U3,47**
disability [ˌdɪsə'bɪləti] Behinderung; Unfähigkeit **III U4,52**
disabled [dɪ'seɪbld] behindert **III U4,52**
to **disagree** [ˌdɪsə'gri:] anderer Meinung sein; nicht einverstanden sein **II**
to **disappear** [ˌdɪsə'pɪə] verschwinden **III U5,75**
disappointed [ˌdɪsə'pɔɪntɪd] enttäuscht **II**
disaster [dɪ'zɑ:stə] Desaster; Katastrophe **III U2,26**
disco ['dɪskəʊ] Disco, Diskothek **III U5,71**
to **discover** [dɪ'skʌvə] entdecken **III U5,69**
to **discuss** [dɪ'skʌs] diskutieren **II**
discussion [dɪ'skʌʃn] Diskussion **II**
disguise [dɪs'gaɪz] Verkleidung **II**
  in disguise [ɪn dɪs'gaɪz] verkleidet **II**
dish [dɪʃ] Gericht, Speise **II**
dislike [dɪ'slaɪk] Abneigung **II**
distance ['dɪstnts] Distanz, Entfernung **III U5,69**; ⟨**III EL,104**⟩
to **divide** [dɪ'vaɪd] teilen **II**
dizzy ['dɪzi] schwindlig **III U3,44**
*to **do** [du:] tun, machen **I**
  It's nothing to do with me. [ɪts ˌnʌθɪŋ tə ˌdu: wɪð 'mi:] Ich habe damit nichts zu tun. **III U1,15**
doctor ['dɒktə] Arzt, Ärztin **II**
documentary [ˌdɒkjə'mentri] Dokumentarfilm **III F4,99**
dog [dɒg] Hund **I**
  hot dog ['hɒt ˌdɒg] Hot Dog *(Würstchen im Brötchen)* ⟨**III EL,100**⟩
  It's raining cats and dogs. [ɪts ˌreɪnɪŋ ˌkæts‿ənd 'dɒgz] Es schüttet wie aus Eimern. ⟨**III EL,100**⟩
dollar ['dɒlə] Dollar *(Währung)* **III F2,51**
dolphin ['dɒlfɪn] Delphin ⟨**III U4,52**⟩
to **dominate** ['dɒmɪneɪt] dominieren ⟨**III U2,29**⟩
door [dɔ:] Tür **I**
double ['dʌbl] Doppel-, zweimal **I**
down [daʊn] entlang; herunter, hinunter, nach unten **I**
  the next size down [ðə ˌnekst saɪz 'daʊn] eine Größe kleiner **III U4,58**
downstairs [daʊn'steəz] (nach) unten; im Untergeschoss **II**
downtown *(AE)* [ˌdaʊn'taʊn] im Stadtzentrum **I**
dragon ['drægn] Drache ⟨**III U2,25**⟩
drama ['drɑ:mə] Theater; Drama **II**
*to **draw** [drɔ:] zeichnen **I**
drawer [drɔ:] Schublade **I**
dreadful ['dredfl] furchtbar ⟨**III U2,28**⟩
*to **dream** [dri:m] träumen **I**
dress [dres] Kleid **I**
drill [drɪl] Bohrer, Bohrmaschine **I**
  electric drill [ɪˌlektrɪk 'drɪl] elektrische Bohrmaschine **I**
drink [drɪŋk] Getränk **I**
*to **drink** [drɪŋk] trinken **I**
drive [draɪv] Autofahrt **III U5,68**
  cattle drive ['kætl ˌdraɪv] Viehtrieb **II**
  hard drive [ˌhɑ:d 'draɪv] Festplattenlaufwerk ⟨**III EL,105**⟩
*to **drive** [draɪv] fahren **I**
driver ['draɪvə] Fahrer(in) **I**
to **drop** [drɒp] fallen (lassen) **II**
drum [drʌm] Trommel, *pl.:* Schlagzeug **II**
drummer ['drʌmə] Schlagzeuger(in) **II**
to **dry** [draɪ] trocknen **III U5,70**
dry [draɪ] trocken **III U5,70**
duck [dʌk] Ente **I**
dumb [dʌm] dumm, doof **III U6,86**
dungeon ['dʌndʒn] Verlies ⟨**III U1,8**⟩
during *(+ noun)* ['djʊərɪŋ] während *(+ Nomen)* **III U1,10**
DVD player [ˌdi:vi:di: 'pleɪə] DVD-Player **III U2,25**
  DVD writer [ˌdi:vi:di: 'raɪtə] DVD-Brenner ⟨**III EL,105**⟩

E

each [i:tʃ] jede(-r/-s) **I**
each [i:tʃ] pro Person, pro Stück **II**
  each other [ˌi:tʃ‿'ʌðə] sich gegenseitig **II**
eager ['i:gə] eifrig **III U2,30**
ear [ɪə] Ohr **II**
early ['ɜ:li] früh **I**
to **earn** [ɜ:n] verdienen **I**
earring ['ɪərɪŋ] Ohrring **II**
earth [ɜ:θ] Erde **II**
earthquake ['ɜ:θkweɪk] Erdbeben ⟨**III U5,74**⟩
east [i:st] Osten **I**
easy ['i:zi] einfach, leicht **I**
*to **eat** [i:t] essen **I**
economy [ɪ'kɒnəmi] Wirtschaft **III F3,80**
education [edʒʊ'keɪʃn] Erziehung, Bildung **II**
  Physical Education [ˌfɪzɪkl‿edʒʊ'keɪʃn] Sport *(Schulfach)* **II**
  Religious Education [rɪˌlɪdʒəs‿edʒʊ'keɪʃn] Religionsunterricht **II**
egg [eg] Ei **I**
  fried egg [fraɪd‿'eg] Spiegelei **II**
eight [eɪt] acht **I**
  8X = 8-speed ['eɪtspi:d] achtfach ⟨**III EL,105**⟩
eighteen [eɪ'ti:n] achtzehn **I**
eighteenth [eɪ'ti:nθ] achtzehnte(-r/-s) **I**
eighth [eɪtθ] achte(-r/-s) **I**
eight-hundred-year-old [ˌeɪt hʌndrəd ˌjɪər‿əʊld] achthundert Jahre alt **I**
eighty ['eɪti] achtzig **I**
electric [ɪ'lektrɪk] elektrisch **I**
  electric drill [ɪˌlektrɪk 'drɪl] elektrische Bohrmaschine **I**
element ['elɪmənt] Element **III U2,26**
elementary [elɪ'mentri] elementar, grundlegend **II**
  elementary school *(AE)* [elɪ'mentri ˌsku:l] Grundschule **II**
elevator *(AE)* ['elɪveɪtə] Aufzug, Lift **III U5,68**
eleven [ɪ'levn] elf **I**
eleventh [ɪ'levnθ] elfte(-r/-s) **I**
else [els] andere(-r/-s) **I**
  what else [ˌwɒt‿'els] was sonst/noch **II**
e-mail ['i:meɪl] E-mail **I**
embarrassed [ɪm'bærəst] verlegen **III U1,14**
embarrassing [ɪm'bærəsɪŋ] peinlich **III U3,45**
emergency [ɪ'mɜ:dʒntsi] Notfall, Notlage **I**
empire ['empaɪə] Reich; Kaiserreich **III F1,21**
empty ['empti] leer **I**
end [end] Ende, Schluss **I**
  in the end [ˌɪn ði:‿'end] schließlich, zum Schluss **II**

to **end** [end] enden **II**
ending ['endɪŋ] Ende, Schluss *(einer Geschichte)* **I**
enemy ['enəmi] Feind(in) **II**
engaged [ɪŋ'geɪdʒd] besetzt, belegt **I**
engine ['endʒɪn] Motor **I**
English ['ɪŋglɪʃ] englisch; Englisch **I**
What's ... in English? [ˌwɒts ... ɪn‿'ɪŋglɪʃ] Was heißt ... auf Englisch? **I**
to **enjoy** [ɪn'dʒɔɪ] genießen **II**
to enjoy oneself [ɪn'dʒɔɪ] Spaß haben; sich amüsieren **III U5,72**
enough [ɪ'nʌf] genug, genügend **I**
entertainment [ˌentə'teɪnmənt] Unterhaltung **III F4,99**
episode ['epɪsəʊd] Episode; Folge **III F4,99**
equal ['i:kwəl] Gleichgestellte(r); Gleichwertige(r); Ebenbürtige(r) **III U4,52**
er [3:] äh **I**
to **erupt** [ɪ'rʌpt] ausbrechen *(Vulkan)* ⟨**III U5,72**⟩
eruption [ɪ'rʌpʃn] Ausbruch *(Vulkan)* ⟨**III U5,75**⟩
to **escape** [ɪ'skeɪp] flüchten, entkommen **II**
especially [ɪ'speʃli] besonders, vor allem **I**
etc. [ɪt'setrə] usw., et cetera **II**
even ['i:vn] sogar **II**
even (+ comparative) ['i:vn] noch *(+ Komparativ)* **II**
not even [nɒt‿'i:vn] nicht einmal **II**
even if [ˌi:vn‿'ɪf] auch wenn **III U1,12**
evening ['i:vnɪŋ] Abend **I**
event [ɪ'vent] Ereignis **I**
ever ['evə] jemals **II**
every ['evri] jede(-r/-s) **I**
every day [ˌevri 'deɪ] jeden Tag **I**
every ['evri] alle **III F4,98**
everybody ['evribɒdi] jeder; alle **I**
everyday ['evrideɪ] alltäglich **III U5,77**
everyone ['evriwʌn] jeder **II**
everything ['evriθɪŋ] alles **I**
everywhere ['evriweə] überall **II**
evil ['i:vl] böse, schlecht **II**
exactly [ɪg'zæktli] genau **II**
to **examine** [ɪg'zæmɪn] untersuchen, kontrollieren **I**
example [ɪg'zɑ:mpl] Beispiel **I**
for example [fər‿ɪg'zɑ:mpl] zum Beispiel **I**
except [ɪk'sept] außer **I**
exchange [ɪks'tʃeɪndʒ] Austausch **III U3,39**
excited [ɪk'saɪtɪd] aufgeregt **I**
exciting [ɪk'saɪtɪŋ] spannend, aufregend **I**
excuse [ɪk'skju:s] Ausrede ⟨**III EL,107**⟩
Excuse me! [ɪk'skju:z mi] Entschuldigung! Entschuldigen Sie! **I**
exercise ['eksəsaɪz] Übung **I**
exercise book ['eksəsaɪz ˌbʊk] Übungsheft **I**
exhibition [ˌeksɪ'bɪʃn] Ausstellung; Vorführung **II**
to **exist** [ɪg'zɪst] existieren ⟨**III U2,29**⟩; **III F3,81**; ⟨**III EL,103**⟩
to **expect** [ɪk'spekt] erwarten **II**
expectation [ˌekspek'teɪʃn] Erwartung **III U6,86**
expensive [ɪk'spentsɪv] teuer **II**
experience [ɪk'spɪəriənts] Erfahrung; Erlebnis **II**
to **experience** [ɪk'spɪəriənts] erfahren, erleben **II**
experiment [ɪk'sperɪmənt] Experiment, Versuch **III U4,54**
expert ['ekspɜ:t] Experte, Expertin ⟨**III EL,105**⟩
to **explain** [ɪk'spleɪn] erklären, erläutern **I**
to **explode** [ɪk'spləʊd] explodieren **III U5,75**
explosion [ɪk'spləʊʒn] Explosion **III U5,74**
to **express** [ɪk'spres] ausdrücken **II**
expression [ɪk'spreʃn] Ausdruck **III U3,47**
extra ['ekstrə] extra, besonders **II**
eye [aɪ] Auge **I**

F

face [feɪs] Gesicht **I**
fact [fækt] Fakt, Tatsache **II**
in fact [ɪn 'fækt] tatsächlich; eigentlich **III U1,10**
factory ['fæktri] Fabrik; Werk **III U2,24**
to **faint** [feɪnt] ohnmächtig werden **I**
fair [feə] Messe, Jahrmarkt **II**
fair [feə] gerecht, fair **I**
fairy ['feəri] Fee **II**
fairy tale ['feəri ˌteɪl] Märchen **II**
fall [fɔ:l] Sturz **III U2,31**
falls *(pl.)* [fɔ:lz] Wasserfall **I**
fall *(AE)* [fɔ:l] Herbst **II**
*to **fall** (over) [fɔ:l‿'əʊvə] (hin)fallen; umfallen **I**
to fall in love (with) [ˌfɔ:l‿ɪn 'lʌv] sich verlieben (in) **II**
false [fɔ:ls] falsch **I**
familiar [fə'mɪliə] vertraut **III U4,60**
to seem familiar [ˌsi:m fə'mɪliə] bekannt vorkommen **III U4,60**
family ['fæmli] Familie **I**
famous ['feɪməs] berühmt **II**
fan [fæn] Fan, Anhänger(in) **II**
to **fancy** ['fæntsi] angetan sein von **III U3,42**
fantastic [fæn'tæstɪk] fantastisch, großartig **I**
fantasy ['fæntəsi] Fantasie ⟨**III EL,101**⟩
far [fɑ:] weit **I**
so far ['səʊ fɑ:] bis jetzt **II**
far more interesting [ˌfɑ: mɔ:r‿'ɪntrəstɪŋ] weitaus interessanter **I**
farm [fɑ:m] Farm, Bauernhof **I**
farmer ['fɑ:mə] Farmer, Landwirt(in) **I**
farmyard ['fɑ:mjɑ:d] Hof *(auf einem Bauernhof)* **I**
fashion ['fæʃn] Mode **III F4,98**
fast [fɑ:st] schnell **I**
fast food restaurant [ˌfɑ:st fu:d 'restrənt] Schnellrestaurant **III F2,51**
to be fast [bi: 'fɑ:st] vorgehen **III U1,13**
fat [fæt] Fett **III F2,50**
fat [fæt] fett, dick **III U5,72**
father ['fɑ:ðə] Vater **I**
(my) fault ['maɪ ˌfɔ:lt] (meine) Schuld **III U1,13**
favourite ['feɪvrɪt] Lieblings- **I**
fax [fæks] Fax **II**
fear [fɪə] Angst, Furcht **II**
to **fear** [fɪə] fürchten ⟨**III U2,28**⟩
February ['februri] Februar **I**
*to **feed** [fi:d] füttern **I**
feedback ['fi:dbæk] Feedback, Rückmeldung **II**
*to **feel** [fi:l] (sich) fühlen **I**
to feel sick [fi:l 'sɪk] Übelkeit verspüren **III U6,89**
to feel sorry for [fi:l 'sɒri] Mitleid haben mit; bedauern **III U1,15**
feeling ['fi:lɪŋ] Gefühl **II**
fence [fents] Zaun **II**
festival ['festɪvl] Festival, Fest **II**
to **fetch** [fetʃ] (ab)holen **I**
few [fju:] wenige **III U5,69**
a few [ə 'fju:] einige, ein paar **II**
fiddle ['fɪdl] Geige **II**
field [fi:ld] Feld; Acker **I**
baseball field ['beɪsbɔ:l ˌfi:ld] Baseballplatz **III U6,82**
football field ['fʊtbɔ:l ˌfi:ld] Footballplatz **III U6,83**
track and field [ˌtræk‿ənd 'fi:ld] Leichtathletik **III U6,84**
fifteen [fɪf'ti:n] fünfzehn **I**
fifteenth [fɪf'ti:nθ] fünfzehnte(-r/-s) **I**
fifth [fɪfθ] Fünftel **III F2,51**
fifth [fɪfθ] fünfte(-r/-s) **I**
fifty ['fɪfti] fünfzig **I**
*to **fight** [faɪt] streiten, kämpfen **I**
figure ['fɪgə] Figur, Gestalt; Ziffer **II**
to **fill in** [fɪl‿'ɪn] ausfüllen **II**
film [fɪlm] Film **II**
to **film** [fɪlm] filmen; drehen **III F4,99**
final ['faɪnl] Finale **II**
finally ['faɪnli] schließlich, endlich **II**
*to **find** [faɪnd] finden **I**
Find the odd word out! [ˌɒd wɜ:d‿'aʊt] Finde das Wort, das nicht in die Gruppe passt! *(Wortschatzübung)* **I**
fine [faɪn] gut, in Ordnung; schön **I**
I'm fine. [aɪm 'faɪn] Mir geht es gut. **I**
finger ['fɪŋgə] Finger **I**
fingertip ['fɪŋgətɪp] Fingerspitze **II**
to **finish** ['fɪnɪʃ] fertig machen; aufhören **I**
fire [faɪə] Feuer; Kamin; Ofen **II**
to set fire to [set 'faɪə tə] in Brand stecken **III F1,21**
first [fɜ:st] erste(-r/-s); zuerst **I**
at first [ət 'fɜ:st] zuerst; zunächst **II**
fish and chips [ˌfɪʃ‿n‿'tʃɪps] Fisch und Pommes frites **I**
fishing ['fɪʃɪŋ] Angeln, Fischen **II**
fishmonger ['fɪʃˌmʌŋgə] Fischhändler(in) ⟨**III U5,69**⟩
fit [fɪt] fit **III U5,70**
five [faɪv] fünf **I**
flag [flæg] Flagge **I**
flat [flæt] Wohnung **I**
flat [flæt] flach, platt **III U5,70**; ⟨**III EL,101**⟩
flavor *(AE)* ['fleɪvə] Geschmack, Aroma **III F2,50**
flight [flaɪt] Flug **I**
floor [flɔ:] Fußboden; Stockwerk **I**

flower ['flaʊə] Blume II
fly [flaɪ] Fliege II
*to **fly** [flaɪ] fliegen I
to fly on [flaɪ‿'ɒn] weiterfliegen I
focus ['fəʊkəs] Blickpunkt I
fog [fɒg] Nebel II
foggy ['fɒgi] neblig II
aluminum **foil** *(AE)* [ə‚lu:mɪnəm 'fɔɪl] Alufolie ⟨III U5,70⟩
folder ['fəʊldə] Ordner, Mappe I
to **follow** ['fɒləʊ] hinterhergehen; (be)folgen I
food [fu:d] Essen, Nahrung; Lebensmittel I
fool [fu:l] Narr, Dummkopf II
foot, *pl.* **feet** [fʊt; fi:t] Fuß I; Fuß *(Längenmaß: 30,48 cm)* III U5,75
football ['fʊtbɔ:l] Fußball I
football field ['fʊtbɔ:l ‚fi:ld] Footballplatz III U6,83
football magazine ['fʊtbɔ:l mægə‚zi:n] Fußballzeitschrift I
footstep ['fʊtstep] Schritt III U4,60
for [fɔ:; fə] für I; wegen III U1,15; seit III U2,24
for example [fər‿ɪg'zɑ:mpl] zum Beispiel I
for many years [fə ‚mæni 'jɪəz] viele Jahre lang III U1,10
to **force** [fɔ:s] zwingen III U6,84
forecast ['fɔ:kɑ:st] Vorhersage II
weather forecast ['weðə ‚fɔ:kɑ:st] Wettervorhersage II
forest ['fɒrɪst] Wald I
*to **forget** [fə'get] vergessen I
fork [fɔ:k] Gabel I; Gabelung II
form [fɔ:m] Form I
progressive form [prəʊ'gresɪv] Verlaufsform III U2,26
to **form** [fɔ:m] formen; bilden III U3,41
formal ['fɔ:ml] formal; formell; förmlich III U4,59
forty ['fɔ:ti] vierzig I
forum ['fɔ:rəm] Forum III U4,54
to **found** [faʊnd] gründen III F1,21
four [fɔ:] vier I
fourteen [fɔ:'ti:n] vierzehn I
fourteenth [fɔ:'ti:nθ] vierzehnte(-r/-s) I
fourth [fɔ:θ] vierte(-r/-s) I
free [fri:] frei I; kostenlos III U3,44
French [frentʃ] französisch; Französisch I
frequency ['fri:kwəntsi] Frequenz; Häufigkeit ⟨III U3,42⟩
fresh [freʃ] frisch I
Friday ['fraɪdeɪ] Freitag I
fried [fraɪd] in der Pfanne gebraten II
fried egg [fraɪd‿'eg] Spiegelei II
friend [frend] Freund(in) I
to make friends (with) [‚meɪk 'frendz] Freundschaft schließen (mit) III U1,13
friendly ['frendli] freundlich, nett II
fries *pl. (AE)* [fraɪz] Pommes frites I
to **frighten** ['fraɪtn] erschrecken, Angst machen II
*to be **frightened** (of) [bi: 'fraɪtnd] Angst haben (vor) I
frog [frɒg] Frosch I
from [frɒm; frəm] aus, von I
Where are you from? [‚weər‿ə jə 'frɒm] Woher kommst du/kommt ihr/kommen Sie? I
Where … from? [‚weə … 'frɒm] Woher … ? I
front [frʌnt] Vorderseite II
in front of [ɪn 'frʌnt‿əv] vor, davor I
fruit [fru:t] Frucht III U5,70
fruit *(pl.)* [fru:t] Obst II
full [fʊl] voll I
fun [fʌn] Freude, Spaß I
to make fun of [‚meɪk 'fʌn‿əv] sich lustig machen über III F4,99
funky ['fʌŋki] irre ⟨III U1,13⟩
funny ['fʌni] komisch, lustig I
fuse box ['fju:z bɒks] Sicherungskasten ⟨III U4,61⟩
future ['fju:tʃə] Zukunft II

G

gallery ['gæləri] Galerie III U1,8
game [geɪm] Spiel I
game show ['geɪm ‚ʃəʊ] Spielshow III F4,99
gang [gæŋ] Gang, Bande II
gangster ['gæŋkstə] Gangster, Verbrecher I
garage ['gærɑ:ʒ] Garage I
garden ['gɑ:dn] Garten I
gate [geɪt] Tor, Pforte I; Gate, Flugsteig, Ausgang II
gear [gɪə] Ausrüstung, Zeug II
general ['dʒenrl] allgemein II
gentle ['dʒentl] sanft, liebenswürdig II
gentleman, *pl.* **gentlemen** ['dʒentlmən] Gentleman, (feiner) Herr II
ladies and gentlemen [‚leɪdiz‿n 'dʒentlmən] meine Damen und Herren II
geography [dʒi'ɒgrəfi] Geographie, Erdkunde I
German ['dʒɜ:mən] deutsch; Deutsche(r); Deutsch I
gerund ['dʒernd] Gerundium I
gesture ['dʒestʃə] Geste, Gebärde ⟨III EL,103⟩
*to **get** [get] (be)kommen; kriegen I; werden II
Get well soon! [get ‚wel 'su:n] Gute Besserung! III U3,45
I don't get it. [aɪ ‚dəʊnt 'get‿ɪt] Das kapiere ich nicht. III U1,15
to get into [get‿'ɪntə] in etwas hineingelangen I
to get lost [get 'lɒst] verloren gehen, sich verirren I
to get married [get 'mærid] heiraten II
to get off (the bus) [get‿'ɒf] aussteigen (aus dem Bus) I
to get on (the bus) [get‿'ɒn] einsteigen (in den Bus) I
to get one's act together [‚get wʌnz‿'ækt təgeðə] sich am Riemen reißen III U6,86
to get rid of [get 'rɪd‿əv] loswerden II
to get the gist [‚get ðə 'dʒɪst] das Wesentliche erfassen III U2,28
to get to know [‚get tə 'nəʊ] kennen lernen III U2,25
to get up [get‿'ʌp] aufstehen I
to get wet [get 'wet] nass werden I
ghost [gəʊst] Geist II
Gig = gigabyte [gɪg; 'gɪgəbaɪt] *Einheit der Arbeitsspeicherkapazität* ⟨III EL,105⟩
Gigahertz ['gɪgəhɜ:ts] *Frequenzangabe, drückt Rechengeschwindigkeit eines Prozessors aus* ⟨III EL,105⟩
girl [gɜ:l] Mädchen I
girlfriend ['gɜ:lfrend] Freundin *(in einer Paarbeziehung)* III U4,54
*to get the **gist** [‚get ðə 'dʒɪst] das Wesentliche erfassen III U2,28
*to **give** [gɪv] geben; schenken I
to give a talk [‚gɪv‿ə 'tɔ:k] einen Vortrag halten III U1,18
to give somebody the bumps [‚gɪv ðə 'bʌmps] jemanden hochwerfen und wieder auffangen I
to give up [gɪv‿'ʌp] aufgeben I
glad [glæd] froh III U6,85
glass [glɑ:s] Glas I
glasses *pl.* ['glɑ:sɪz] Brille I
glitter ['glɪtə] etwas Glitzerndes ⟨III U4,58⟩
glove [glʌv] Handschuh III U6,83
gm (= gram) [græm] Gramm I
*to **go** [gəʊ] gehen I
to go (+ adjective) [gəʊ] werden II
Let's go! [lets 'gəʊ] Lass(t) uns gehen! I
to be going on [bi: ‚gəʊɪŋ‿'ɒn] los sein II
to be gone [bi: 'gɒn] verschwunden sein II
to go down [gəʊ 'daʊn] untergehen *(Sonne)* II
to go for a walk [‚gəʊ fər‿ə 'wɔ:k] spazieren gehen I
to go on [gəʊ‿'ɒn] weitermachen, weiterführen I
to go on (+ doing) [gəʊ‿'ɒn] etwas weiter/immer wieder tun II
to go shopping [‚gəʊ 'ʃɒpɪŋ] einkaufen gehen I
to go to sleep [gəʊ tə 'sli:p] einschlafen I
to go wrong [gəʊ 'rɒŋ] schief gehen II
goal [gəʊl] Tor; Ziel III U3,40
God [gɒd] Gott II
thank God [‚θæŋk 'gɒd] Gott sei Dank II
gold [gəʊld] Gold II
gold [gəʊld] golden III U2,30
golf [gɒlf] Golf III U6,83
golf ball ['gɒlf ‚bɔ:l] Golfball III U6,82
golf club ['gɒlf ‚klʌb] Golfschläger III U6,83
golf course ['gɒlf ‚kɔ:s] Golfplatz III U6,83
good [gʊd] gut I
no good [nəʊ 'gʊd] nutzlos, wertlos II
not any better [‚nɒt‿eni 'betə] (überhaupt) nicht besser II
to be good at [bi: 'gʊd‿ət] gut sein in I
Goodbye! [gʊd'baɪ] Auf Wiedersehen! I
gospel ['gɒspl] Gospel III U5,69
*to have **(got)** [hæv 'gɒt] besitzen, haben I

government ['gʌvnmənt] Regierung III U1,10
to **grab** [græb] greifen; schnappen I
grade *(AE)* [greɪd] Klasse *(AE)*; Note *(AE)* II
grader *(AE)* ['greɪdə] -Klässler(in) II
gradual ['grædʒuəl] allmählich III F1,21
graffiti [grə'fi:ti] Graffiti III U3,46
grammar ['græmə] Grammatik I
grandma ['grændmɑ:] Oma I
grandpa ['grændpɑ:] Opa I
grape [greɪp] Traube III U3,44
grass [grɑ:s] Gras III U1,19
grave [greɪv] Grab III U2,26
great [greɪt] großartig, toll I; groß II
Greek [gri:k] Grieche; griechisch; Griechisch ⟨III EL,104⟩
green [gri:n] grün I
greeting ['gri:tɪŋ] Gruß III U2,22
grey [greɪ] grau I
grid [grɪd] Gitter, Tabelle II
to **grill** [grɪl] grillen III F2,50
to **grin** [grɪn] grinsen III U1,14
to **groan** [grəʊn] stöhnen III U3,44
ground [graʊnd] Boden; Grund III U2,31
group [gru:p] Klasse; Gruppe I
tutor group ['tju:tə ˌgru:p] Klasse *(in einer englischen Schule)* I
*to **grow** [grəʊ] anbauen; wachsen I
to grow up [grəʊ‿'ʌp] aufwachsen, erwachsen werden II
grunge [grʌndʒ] Grunge *(Musikrichtung)* III U5,68
guard [gɑ:d] Wache; Wächter(in) ⟨III U1,14⟩
to **guess** [ges] raten, vermuten I
guest [gest] Gast II
guide [gaɪd] Führer(in) III U2,22
guitar [gɪ'tɑ:] Gitarre I
guitarist [gɪ'tɑ:rɪst] Gitarrist(in) II
gun [gʌn] Schusswaffe I
guy [gaɪ] Typ, Kerl; *pl.:* Leute II
gym(nasium) [dʒɪm; dʒɪm'neɪziəm] Turnhalle III U3,41

H

hair [heə] Haar(e) II
hairstyle ['heəstaɪl] Frisur III U1,13
half past (two) ['hɑ:f pɑ:st] halb (drei) I
half-time [ˌhɑ:f'taɪm] Halbzeit III U6,86
hall [hɔ:l] Flur, Diele, Korridor I; Halle, Saal II
ham [hæm] Schinken II
hamster ['hæmstə] Hamster I
hand [hænd] Hand I
handout ['hændaʊt] Informationsblatt III U5,70
*to **hang** around [ˌhæŋ‿ə'raʊnd] herumhängen II
to hang out (with) [hæŋ‿'aʊt] sich herumtreiben (mit) II
to **happen** ['hæpn] geschehen, passieren I
happy ['hæpi] glücklich, froh I
harbour ['hɑ:bə] Hafen I
hard [hɑ:d] hart; schwer II
hard drive [ˌhɑ:d 'draɪv] Festplattenlaufwerk ⟨III EL,105⟩
hardly ['hɑ:dli] kaum III U2,23
hat [hæt] Hut II
to **hate** [heɪt] hassen, nicht mögen I
*to **have** [hæv] haben II; essen; trinken II
to have (got) [hæv 'gɒt] besitzen, haben I
to have a look (at) [ˌhæv‿ə 'lʊk] anschauen III U1,14
to have a race [ˌhæv‿ə 'reɪs] ein Rennen veranstalten I
to have dinner [hæv 'dɪnə] zu Abend essen I
to have on [hæv‿'ɒn] anhaben II
to have to (do sth) [hæv] etwas tun müssen II
he [hi:] er I
head [hed] Kopf I
head teacher *(BE)* [ˌhed 'ti:tʃə] Schulleiter(in) III U3,49
to **head (for)** [hed] zusteuern auf III U1,14
headache ['hedeɪk] Kopfweh III U3,40
heading ['hedɪŋ] Überschrift I
health club ['helθ klʌb] Fitnessklub III U1,12
health [helθ] Gesundheit; Gesundheitslehre II
healthy ['helθi] gesund III F2,51; ⟨III EL,101⟩
*to **hear** [hɪə] hören I
hearing aid ['hɪərɪŋ‿eɪd] Hörgerät ⟨III U4,55⟩
heart [hɑ:t] Herz I
heart attack ['hɑ:t‿əˌtæk] Herzinfarkt ⟨III EL,101⟩
My heart jumped into my mouth. [maɪ ˌhɑ:t dʒʌmpt‿ɪntə maɪ 'maʊθ] Das Herz schlug mir bis zum Halse. ⟨III U1,14⟩
heavy ['hevi] schwer II
height [haɪt] Höhe III U1,10
helicopter ['helɪˌkɒptə] Helikopter, Hubschrauber I
Hello! [hə'ləʊ] Hallo! I
to say hello [seɪ hə'ləʊ] Hallo sagen, sich begrüßen I
helmet ['helmət] Helm III U6,82
help [help] Hilfe, Rettung I
to **help** [help] helfen I
help yourself [ˌhelp jɔ:'self] bediene dich!/bedienen Sie sich! II
helpless ['helpləs] hilflos I
her [hɜ:] ihr(e); sie; ihr I
here [hɪə] hier I
Here you are! [ˌhɪə ju:‿'ɑ:] Hier bitte! Bitteschön! I
hero, *pl.* **heroes** ['hɪərəʊ] Held II
heroine ['herəʊɪn] Heldin II
herself [hɜ:'self] (sie) selbst; sich (selbst) III U5,72
Hey! [heɪ] He! I
Hi! [haɪ] Hi! Hallo! I
*to **hide** [haɪd] (sich) verstecken II
high [haɪ] hoch; groß I
high school ['haɪ ˌsku:l] High School *(weiterführende Schule in den USA, Oberstufe)* III U6,86
highlight ['haɪlaɪt] Highlight III U2,26
hike [haɪk] Wanderung III U5,70
to **hike** [haɪk] wandern III U5,68
hill [hɪl] Berg; Hügel I
him [hɪm] ihm; ihn I
himself [hɪm'self] (er) selbst; sich (selbst) III U3,45
hip-hop ['hɪp hɒp] Hip-Hop II
his [hɪz] sein(e) I
historical [hɪ'stɒrɪkl] geschichtlich, historisch III U3,38
history ['hɪstri] Geschichte II
natural history [ˌnætʃrl 'hɪstri] Naturgeschichte ⟨III U1,8⟩
hit [hɪt] Hit II
*to **hit** [hɪt] schlagen; treffen; *hier:* gegen etwas fahren I
hobby ['hɒbi] Hobby II
*to **hold** [həʊld] halten II
hole [həʊl] Loch ⟨III EL,100⟩
holiday ['hɒlədeɪ] Urlaub, Feiertag I
hollow ['hɒləʊ] hohl II
home [həʊm] Heim; nach Hause I
at home [ət 'həʊm] zu Hause I
old people's home [ˌəʊld pi:plz 'həʊm] Altersheim II
homeless ['həʊmləs] obdachlos III U1,9
homepage ['həʊmpeɪdʒ] Homepage II
homework ['həʊmwɜ:k] Hausaufgaben I
honey ['hʌni] Honig; Schätzchen *(AE)* III U1,13
honour ['ɒnə] Ehre ⟨III U2,29⟩
hoop [hu:p] Reifen *(z. B. am Basketballkorb)* ⟨III U6,88⟩
hope [həʊp] Hoffnung ⟨III U2,28⟩
to **hope** [həʊp] hoffen I
horrified ['hɒrɪfaɪd] entsetzt III U2,30
horror ['hɒrə] Horror, Schrecken II
horse [hɔ:s] Pferd I
to be as hungry as a horse [əz ˌhʌŋgri‿əz‿ə 'hɔ:s] einen Bärenhunger haben II
horseback riding [ˌhɔ:sbæk 'raɪdɪŋ] Reiten II
hospital ['hɒspɪtl] Hospital, Krankenhaus II
hot [hɒt] heiß I; scharf III F2,50
hot dog ['hɒt ˌdɒg] Hot Dog *(Würstchen im Brötchen)* ⟨III EL,100⟩
hotel [həʊ'tel] Hotel II
hour ['aʊə] Stunde II
opening hours ['əʊpnɪŋ‿aʊəz] Öffnungszeiten I
house [haʊs] Haus I
household ['haʊshəʊld] Haushalt ⟨III U2,29⟩
how [haʊ] wie I
How about …? ['haʊ‿əˌbaʊt] Wie ist es mit …? I
How are you? [ˌhaʊ‿'ɑ: ju:] Wie geht es dir/euch/Ihnen? I
how many [haʊ 'meni] wie viele I
How much is/are … ? [ˌhaʊ 'mʌtʃ ɪz/ɑ:] Wie viel kostet/kosten … ? I
How old are you? [haʊ‿'əʊld‿ə ju:] Wie alt bist du/sind Sie? I
how to do sth ['haʊ tə] wie man etwas macht II

however [haʊ'evə] jedoch **II**
huge [hju:dʒ] riesig, gewaltig **I**
Huh? [hʌ; hə] Was? Hä? **I**
a **hundred** [ə'hʌndrəd] hundert **I**
Hungarian [hʌŋ'geəriən] ungarisch; Ungar(in) **II**
hungry ['hʌŋgri] hungrig **I**
to be as hungry as a horse [əz ˌhʌŋgri‿əz‿ə 'hɔ:s] einen Bärenhunger haben **II**
to **hunt** [hʌnt] jagen **II**
hunting ['hʌntɪŋ] Jagd; Jagd- ⟨**III U2**, 30⟩
to **hurry (up)** [ˌhʌri‿'ʌp] (sich) (be)eilen **II**
*to **hurt** [hɜ:t] verletzen, weh tun **II**
*to be **hurt** [bi: 'hɜ:t] verletzt sein/werden **I**
husband ['hʌzbənd] Ehemann **II**
husky ['hʌski] Husky *(Schlittenhunderasse)* **II**

I

I [aɪ] ich **I**
I'd [aɪd] Ich würde **II**
I don't get it. [aɪ ˌdəʊnt 'get‿ɪt] Das kapiere ich nicht. **III U1**, 15
I'm fine. [aɪm 'faɪn] Mir geht es gut. **I**
I see. [aɪ 'si:] aha; ach so **II**
ice [aɪs] Eis **I**
ice cream [aɪs 'kri:m] Eis, Eiscreme **I**
icon ['aɪkɒn] Ikone ⟨**III U4**, 61⟩
idea [aɪ'dɪə] Einfall, Idee; Ahnung **I**
No idea! [ˌnəʊ‿aɪ'dɪə] Keine Ahnung! **I**
ideal [aɪ'dɪəl] Ideal ⟨**III U2**, 29⟩
to **identify** [aɪ'dentɪfaɪ] identifizieren ⟨**III U2**, 28⟩
identity [aɪ'dentəti] Identität **II**
idiot ['ɪdiət] Idiot(in) **III U1**, 14
if [ɪf] wenn, falls; ob **I**
to **ignore** [ɪg'nɔ:] ignorieren **III U2**, 29
ill [ɪl] krank **II**
illness ['ɪlnəs] Krankheit **III U4**, 52
imaginative [ɪ'mædʒɪnətɪv] einfallsreich, fantasievoll **II**
to **imagine** [ɪ'mædʒɪn] sich (etwas) vorstellen **II**
immediately [ɪ'mi:diətli] sofort, gleich **I**
importance [ɪm'pɔ:tnts] Bedeutung, Wichtigkeit ⟨**III U2**, 29⟩
important [ɪm'pɔ:tnt] wichtig; einflussreich **I**
to **improve** [ɪm'pru:v] (sich) verbessern **II**
in [ɪn] in; rein, herein **I**
in advance [ɪn‿əd'vɑ:nts] im Voraus **III U1**, 10
in between [ˌɪn bɪ'twi:n] dazwischen **II**
in case [ɪn 'keɪs] falls; für den Fall, dass … **II**
in class [ɪn 'klɑ:s] in/vor der Klasse **I**
in disguise [ɪn dɪs'gaɪz] verkleidet **II**
in fact [ɪn 'fækt] tatsächlich; eigentlich **III U1**, 10
in front of [ɪn 'frʌnt‿əv] vor, davor **I**
in order to [ɪn‿'ɔ:də tə] um … zu **III U5**, 70
in return [ɪn rɪ'tɜ:n] als Gegenleistung ⟨**III U2**, 29⟩
in spite of [ɪn 'spaɪt‿əv] trotz **III U6**, 84
in the end [ˌɪn ði:‿'end] schließlich, zum Schluss **II**
in the late 1100s [leɪt] im späten 12. Jahrhundert **II**
in time [ɪn 'taɪm] mit der Zeit ⟨**III EL**, 105⟩
in time for [ɪn 'taɪm fə] rechtzeitig zu **III U1**, 10
independent [ˌɪndɪ'pendənt] unabhängig **III U4**, 60
Indian ['ɪndiən] indisch; Inder(in); indianisch; Indianer(in) **I**
indirect speech [ˌɪndɪrekt 'spi:tʃ] indirekte Rede **III U6**, 84
industry ['ɪndəstri] Industrie **III U2**, 25
infinitive [ɪn'fɪnətɪv] Infinitiv **III U1**, 12
influence ['ɪnfluənts] Einfluss **III U5**, 69
informal [ɪn'fɔ:ml] informell; zwanglos **III U4**, 59
information [ˌɪnfə'meɪʃn] Information(en) **I**
to **injure** ['ɪndʒə] verletzen **III U3**, 44
inland ['ɪnlænd] landeinwärts ⟨**III U2**, 29⟩
insect ['ɪnsekt] Insekt **III U5**, 72
inside [ɪn'saɪd] innen, drin; nach drinnen **I**
instead [ɪn'sted] stattdessen **III U5**, 77
instead of [ɪn'sted‿əv] anstatt **III U2**, 33
instruction [ɪn'strʌkʃn] Instruktion, Anweisung **III U3**, 40
instrument ['ɪntstrəmənt] Instrument **I**
intention [ɪn'tentʃn] Absicht, Intention **II**
interactive [ˌɪntər'æktɪv] interaktiv **II**
*to be **interested** in [bi:‿'ɪntrəstɪd‿ɪn] interessiert sein an, sich interessieren für **I**
interesting ['ɪntrəstɪŋ] interessant **I**
far more interesting [ˌfɑ: mɔ:r‿'ɪntrəstɪŋ] weitaus interessanter **I**
international [ˌɪntə'næʃnl] international **I**
Internet ['ɪntənet] Internet **I**
to **interrupt** [ˌɪntə'rʌpt] unterbrechen **III U1**, 15
interval ['ɪntəvl] Intervall ⟨**III U2**, 28⟩
interview ['ɪntəvju:] Interview; Befragung **I**
to **interview** ['ɪntəvju:] interviewen **II**
into ['ɪntu; 'ɪntə] in, hinein **I**
to **introduce** [ˌɪntrə'dju:s] vorstellen, einführen **II**
introduction [ˌɪntrə'dʌkʃn] Einführung; Vorstellung **II**
to **invade** [ɪn'veɪd] einmarschieren ⟨**III F1**, 21⟩
to **invent** [ɪn'vent] erfinden **II**
invisible [ɪn'vɪzəbl] unsichtbar **II**
invitation [ˌɪnvɪ'teɪʃn] Einladung **I**
to **invite** [ɪn'vaɪt] einladen **I**
Irish ['aɪrɪʃ] irisch; Irisch **I**
irregular [ɪ'regjələ] unregelmäßig **I**
island ['aɪlənd] Insel **I**
it [ɪt] es **I**
it's about time [ˌɪts‿əbaʊt 'taɪm] es ist höchste Zeit ⟨**III EL**, 105⟩
It's nothing to do with me. [ɪts ˌnʌθɪŋ tə ˌdu: wɪð 'mi:] Ich habe damit nichts zu tun. **III U1**, 15
It's raining cats and dogs. [ɪts ˌreɪnɪŋ ˌkæts‿ənd 'dɒgz] Es schüttet wie aus Eimern. ⟨**III EL**, 100⟩
It's your turn. ['jɔ: tɜ:n] Du bist/Sie sind dran. **I**
Italian [ɪ'tæliən] italienisch; Italiener(in); Italienisch **I**
its [ɪts] sein(e); ihr(e) **I**

J

jacket ['dʒækɪt] Jacke **II**
jam [dʒæm] Marmelade **II**; Gedränge; Klemme **II**
traffic jam ['træfɪk ˌdʒæm] Stau **II**
January ['dʒænjuri] Januar **I**
jazz [dʒæz] Jazz **II**
jealous (of) ['dʒeləs] eifersüchtig, neidisch **II**
jeans *pl.* [dʒi:nz] Jeans **I**
jelly ['dʒeli] Wackelpudding, Gelee **I**
jerk [dʒɜ:k] Trottel **II**
job [dʒɒb] Arbeitsstelle, Job **I**
jogging ['dʒɒgɪŋ] Jogging **I**
to **join** [dʒɔɪn] beitreten, sich anschließen; verbinden **II**
joke [dʒəʊk] Witz **II**
to **joke** [dʒəʊk] scherzen **II**
journalist ['dʒɜ:nlɪst] Journalist(in) **I**
journey ['dʒɜ:ni] Reise, Fahrt **II**
judo ['dʒu:dəʊ] Judo **III U4**, 53
to **juggle** ['dʒʌgl] jonglieren **II**
juice [dʒu:s] Saft **II**
July [dʒʊ'laɪ] Juli **I**
to **jump** [dʒʌmp] springen **I**
My heart jumped into my mouth. [maɪ ˌhɑ:t dʒʌmpt‿ɪntə maɪ 'maʊθ] Das Herz schlug mir bis zum Halse. ⟨**III U1**, 14⟩
June [dʒu:n] Juni **I**
just [dʒʌst] gerade; nur **I**

K

kayaking ['kaɪækɪŋ] Kajakfahren **II**
*to be **keen** on [bi: 'ki:n‿ɒn] scharf sein auf, begeistert sein von **II**
*to **keep** [ki:p] (be)halten **II**
to keep (+ doing) [ki:p] etwas weiter/immer wieder tun **II**
to keep up [ki:p‿'ʌp] aufrecht erhalten **II**
keeper ['ki:pə] Wärter(in), Aufseher(in) **I**; Wächter(in), Aufpasser(in), Hüter(in) **II**
key [ki:] Schlüssel **III U1**, 15
key ring ['ki: ˌrɪŋ] Schlüsselbund; Schlüsselanhänger **III F2**, 51
key word ['ki: wɜ:d] Stichwort; Schlüsselbegriff **III U1**, 18
to **kick** [kɪk] kicken, treten **II**
to kick sb off a team [kɪk‿'ɒf] jmdn aus dem Team werfen **III U6**, 86
kid [kɪd] Kind; Kitz **I**
to **kill** [kɪl] töten **II**
kilometre ['kɪləʊˌmi:tə; kɪ'lɒmɪtə] Kilometer **II**
kind [kaɪnd] Art, Sorte **II**
kind [kaɪnd] freundlich, nett **II**
kindergarten ['kɪndəgɑ:tn] Kindergarten **I**

king [kɪŋ] König **I**
kingdom ['kɪŋdəm] Königreich **III F1,21**
kitchen ['kɪtʃɪn] Küche **I**
knee [ni:] Knie **III U2,30**
knife, *pl.* **knives** [naɪf; naɪvz] Messer **I**
knight [naɪt] Ritter **III U2,29**
knock [nɒk] Klopfen, Schlag **II**
to **knock out** [nɒk‿'aʊt] k.o. schlagen; umhauen **III U3,44**
to knock over [ˌnɒk‿'əʊvə] umstoßen **II**
*to **know** [nəʊ] wissen; kennen **I**
*to be **known** as [bi: 'nəʊn‿əz] bekannt sein als **III F1,21**

L

lady ['leɪdi] Dame, Frau **I**
ladies and gentlemen [ˌleɪdiz‿n 'dʒentlmən] meine Damen und Herren **II**
lake [leɪk] See **II**
lamb [læm] Lamm, Lämmchen **I**
lance [lɑ:nts] Lanze **III U2,31**
land [lænd] Land **II**
to **land** [lænd] landen **I**
landscape ['lændskeɪp] Landschaft **I**
lane [leɪn] Gasse; Fahrspur **I**
language ['læŋgwɪdʒ] Sprache **I**
lantern ['læntən] Laterne **II**
laptop ['læptɒp] Laptop **II**
largest ['lɑ:dʒɪst] (der, die, das) größte **I**
to **last** [lɑ:st] dauern, anhalten **II**
last [lɑ:st] letzte(-r/-s) **I**
at last [ət 'lɑ:st] endlich **I**
last night [lɑ:st 'naɪt] gestern Abend/Nacht **II**
late [leɪt] spät **I**
in the late 1100s [leɪt] im späten 12. Jahrhundert **II**
to be late [bi: 'leɪt] zu spät dran sein, zu spät kommen **I**
later ['leɪtə] später **I**
latest ['leɪtɪst] neueste(-r/-s) **II**
Latin ['lætɪn] Latein **II**
to **laugh** [lɑ:f] lachen **I**
lava ['lɑ:və] Lava ⟨**III U5,75**⟩
layout ['leɪaʊt] Layout, Anordnung **II**
lazy ['leɪzi] faul **I**
leader ['li:də] Führer(in), Anführer(in) **II**
leaf, *pl.* **leaves** [li:f; li:vz] Blatt **II**
*to **learn** [lɜ:n; lɜ:nt] lernen **I**
at **least** [ət 'li:st] mindestens, wenigstens **II**
leather ['leðə] Leder **III U3,38**
*to **leave** [li:v] (ver)lassen; abfahren **II**
to leave out [li:v‿'aʊt] auslassen **II**
to leave sb alone [ˌli:v‿ə'ləʊn] jemanden in Ruhe lassen **III U5,70**
left [left] links; linke(-r/-s) **I**
on somebody's right/left [ɒn ˌsʌmbədiz 'raɪt/'left] zur Rechten/zur Linken von jemandem **I**
left [left] übrig **II**
leg [leg] Bein **I**
legend ['ledʒənd] Legende, Sage **II**
lemonade [ˌlemə'neɪd] Limonade **III F2,50**
*to **lend** [lend] leihen ⟨**III EL,101**⟩
less [les] weniger **II**
lesson ['lesn] Unterrichtsstunde, Schulstunde **I**
*to **let** [let] lassen **I**
Let's check! [lets 'tʃek] Lass(t) uns überprüfen! **I**
Let's go! [lets 'gəʊ] Lass(t) uns gehen! **I**
Let's start! [lets 'stɑ:t] Lass(t) uns anfangen **I**
letter ['letə] Buchstabe; Brief **I**
thank you letter ['θæŋk ju: ˌletə] Dankschreiben **I**
lettuce ['letɪs] Kopfsalat **III F2,50**
level ['levl] Level, Höhe, Niveau **II**
library ['laɪbri] Bibliothek **II**
lie [laɪ] Lüge ⟨**III EL,107**⟩
to **lie** [laɪ] lügen **II**
*to **lie** [laɪ] liegen **I**
life, *pl.* **lives** [laɪf] Leben **I**
to take one's own life [ˌteɪk wʌnz‿əʊn 'laɪf] sich das Leben nehmen **III F1,21**
lifestyle ['laɪfstaɪl] Lebensart **III U5,68**
light [laɪt] Licht **II**
lighthouse ['laɪthaʊs] Leuchtturm **I**
like [laɪk] Vorliebe **II**
to **like** [laɪk] mögen, gern haben **I**
Would you like ...? [ˌwʊd jə 'laɪk] Möchtest du/möchten Sie/möchtet ihr ...? **II**
What's it **like?** [ˌwɒts‿ɪt 'laɪk] Wie ist es? **II**
like (this/that) [laɪk 'ðɪs/ðæt] so wie (hier/dort) **I**
line [laɪn] Zeile; Linie **I**
time line ['taɪm laɪn] Zeitstrahl **III F1,20**
link [lɪŋk] Link; Verbindung **II**
lion [laɪən] Löwe ⟨**III U3,42**⟩
*to **lip-read** ['lɪpri:d] von den Lippen ablesen ⟨**III U4,54**⟩
list [lɪst] Liste **I**
to **listen** (to) ['lɪsn] zuhören, (an)hören **I**
listening ['lɪsnɪŋ] Hören, *hier:* Hörübung **I**
little [lɪtl] klein **I**
to **live** [lɪv] wohnen, leben **I**
to live on sth ['lɪv‿ɒn] von etw leben **III U6,88**
living room ['lɪvɪŋ rʊm] Wohnzimmer **I**
lobster ['lɒbstə] Hummer ⟨**III F3,80**⟩
local ['ləʊkl] lokal, örtlich **III U3,44**
*to be **located** [bi: ləʊ'keɪtɪd] gelegen sein **II**
location [ləʊ'keɪʃn] Lage; Standort ⟨**III F3,80**⟩
lock [lɒk] (Fahrrad-)Schloss **I**
to **lock** [lɒk] abschließen **III U3,40**
Londoner ['lʌndənə] Londoner(in) **III U1,10**
long [lɒŋ] lang; weit **I**
no longer [nəʊ 'lɒŋgə] nicht mehr, nicht länger **I**
*to have a **look** (at) [ˌhæv‿ə 'lʊk] anschauen **III U1,14**
to **look** [lʊk] (aus)sehen; schauen **I**
to look after [lʊk‿'ɑ:ftə] aufpassen auf; hüten **I**
to look at ['lʊk‿ət] anschauen **I**
to look for ['lʊk fɔ:] suchen **II**
to look forward to [ˌlʊk 'fɔ:wəd] sich freuen auf **II**
to look like ['lʊk laɪk] aussehen wie **I**
to look out for [ˌlʊk‿'aʊt fə] Ausschau halten nach; sich in Acht nehmen vor **II**
to look up [lʊk‿'ʌp] nachschlagen, nachschauen **II**
lord [lɔ:d] Lord, Herr **II**
lorry ['lɒri] Lastwagen ⟨**III U2,28**⟩
*to **lose** [lu:z] verlieren **I**
to get lost [get 'lɒst] verloren gehen, sich verirren **I**
a **lot** of [ə 'lɒt‿əv] viele, eine Menge **I**
lots of ['lɒts‿əv] viel(e) **I**
you lot ['ju: ˌlɒt] ihr alle **I**
loud [laʊd] laut **I**
loudspeaker [ˌlaʊd'spi:kə] Lautsprecher ⟨**III U1,10**⟩
love [lʌv] Liebe; Herzliche Grüße *(am Briefende)* **I**
to be in love (with) [ˌbi:‿ɪn 'lʌv] verliebt sein (in) **II**
*to fall in **love** (with) [ˌfɔ:l‿ɪn 'lʌv] sich verlieben (in) **II**
to **love** [lʌv] lieben, gern mögen **I**
lovely ['lʌvli] schön, hübsch; herrlich **I**
low [ləʊ] niedrig **III F2,50**
luck [lʌk] Glück **I**
Lucky you did. [ˌlʌki jə 'dɪd] Zum Glück hast du das getan. ⟨**III U1,15**⟩
to be lucky [bi: 'lʌki] Glück haben **I**
lunch [lʌntʃ] Mittagessen **I**
packed lunch [ˌpækt 'lʌntʃ] Lunchpaket; Vesper **III F2,51**
lunchbox ['lʌntʃbɒks] Pausenbrotbehälter **I**
lunchroom *(AE)* ['lʌntʃrʊm] Speisesaal **II**
lung [lʌŋ] Lunge ⟨**III U5,75**⟩

M

MA [ˌmæsə'tʃu:sɪts] Massachusetts **II**
mad [mæd] verrückt; wütend **II**
madam ['mædəm] Gnädige Frau *(Anrede)* **I**
magazine [mægə'zi:n] Zeitschrift, Magazin **I**
football magazine ['fʊtbɔ:l mægəˌzi:n] Fußballzeitschrift **I**
magic ['mædʒɪk] Magie, Zauberei **II**
magnificent [məg'nɪfɪsnt] großartig, prachtvoll **III U2,23**
to **mail** [meɪl] mailen, per E-Mail schicken **II**
main [meɪn] Haupt- **II**
*to **make** [meɪk] machen, tun **I**
Made in Britain [ˌmeɪd‿ɪn 'brɪtn] Hergestellt in Großbritannien **I**
to be made of [bi: 'meɪd‿əv] hergestellt sein aus **II**
to make friends (with) [ˌmeɪk 'frendz] Freundschaft schließen (mit) **III U1,13**
to make fun of [ˌmeɪk 'fʌn‿əv] sich lustig machen über **III F4,99**
to make sb do sth [meɪk] jmdn veranlassen, etw. zu tun **II**
to make the most of [ˌmeɪk ðə 'məʊst‿əv] ausnutzen **II**
man, *pl.* **men** [mæn; men] Mann **I**
to **manage** to (do sth.) ['mænɪdʒ] schaffen (etw. zu tun) **III U2,23**

manager ['mænɪdʒə] Manager(in), Geschäftsführer(in) II
adverb of **manner** [ˌædvɜ:b‿əv 'mænə] Adverb der Art und Weise II
many ['meni] viele I
how **many** [haʊ 'meni] wie viele I
map [mæp] Stadtplan, Landkarte I
mind map ['maɪnd mæp] Wörternetz (*eine Art Schaubild*) I
marathon ['mærəθn] Marathon III U6,84
to **march** [mɑ:tʃ] marschieren III U3,43
March [mɑ:tʃ] März I
to **mark** [mɑ:k] markieren I
marked [mɑ:kt] markiert II
market ['mɑ:kɪt] Markt I
marmalade ['mɑ:məleɪd] Marmelade von Zitrusfrüchten II
*to be **married** to [bi: 'mærid tə] verheiratet sein mit I
to get married [get 'mærid] heiraten II
to **marry** ['mæri] heiraten II
mask [mɑ:sk] Maske II
mass [mæs] Masse ⟨III U2,28⟩
master ['mɑ:stə] Herr ⟨III U2,29⟩
mouse **mat** ['maʊs mæt] Mauspad I
match [mætʃ] Wettkampf; Spiel; Match I; Streichholz ⟨III EL,100⟩
to **match** [mætʃ] zusammenbringen, zusammenfügen I
mate [meɪt] Kamerad(in) III U6,89
material [mə'tɪəriəl] Material II
Math *(AE)* [mæθ] Mathematik II
Maths [mæθs] Mathematik I
What's the **matter**? [ˌwɒts ðə 'mætə] Was ist los? Was hast du? I
may [meɪ] könnte(n) vielleicht; mögen; dürfen III U4,58
May [meɪ] Mai I
maybe ['meɪbi] vielleicht I
me [mi:] mich; mir I
Me, too. [ˌmi: 'tu:] Ich auch. II
meal [mi:l] Mahlzeit III F2,51
*to **mean** [mi:n] bedeuten; meinen I
mean [mi:n] gemein II
meaning ['mi:nɪŋ] Bedeutung, Sinn II
means, *pl.* **means** [mi:nz] Mittel II
means of transport *(sg. and pl.)* [ˌmi:nz‿əv 'træntspɔ:t] Transportmittel, Verkehrsmittel II
meat [mi:t] Fleisch II
medal ['medl] Medaille ⟨III F1,20⟩
media *pl.* ['mi:diə] Medien I
medieval [ˌmedi'i:vl] mittelalterlich ⟨III U2,26⟩
medium, *pl.* **media** ['mi:diəm; 'mi:diə] Medium III F4,98
*to **meet** [mi:t] (sich) treffen I
Nice to meet you. [ˌnaɪs tə 'mi:t ju:] Nett, dich/Sie/euch kennen zu lernen. II
meeting ['mi:tɪŋ] Meeting, Treffen III U3,40
Meg = **megabyte** [meg; 'megəbaɪt] *Einheit der Arbeitsspeicherkapazität* ⟨III EL,105⟩
memory ['memri] Erinnerung; Gedächtnis III U3,44
to **mend** [mend] flicken, reparieren II
mental ['mentl] geistig ⟨III U4,52⟩
to **mention** ['mentʃn] erwähnen III U2,24
Don't mention it. [ˌdəʊnt 'mentʃn‿ɪt] Bitte schön!; Gern geschehen. III U2,24
menu ['menju:] Speisekarte; Menü II
merry ['meri] fröhlich II
mess [mes] Durcheinander; Schweinerei II
message ['mesɪdʒ] Nachricht I
metre ['mi:tə] Meter I
Mexican ['meksɪkən] mexikanisch; Mexikaner(in) II
microphone ['maɪkrəfəʊn] Mikrofon II
to **microwave** ['maɪkrəʊweɪv] in der Mikrowelle zubereiten III F2,50
middle ['mɪdl] Mitte; Mittel- I
Middle Ages [ˌmɪdl‿'eɪdʒɪz] Mittelalter II
middle school ['mɪdl ˌsku:l] Mittelschule *(weiterführende Schule in den USA, Mittelstufe)* II
Midwesterner [ˌmɪd'westənə] Person aus dem Mittleren Westen ⟨III F3,80⟩
might [maɪt] könnte(n) III U4,58
mild [maɪld] mild III U5,68
mile [maɪl] Meile *(brit. Längenmaß)* I
milk [mɪlk] Milch I
to **milk** [mɪlk] melken I
milkman, *pl.* **milkmen** ['mɪlkmən] Milchmann II
Milky Way [ˌmɪlki 'weɪ] Milchstraße II
millennium, *pl.* **millennia** [mɪ'leniəm] Jahrtausend III U1,8
million ['mɪljən] Million III F3,81
millionaire [ˌmɪljə'neə] Millionär(in) III F4,99
to **mince** [mɪnts] hacken III F2,50
mind [maɪnd] Geist, Verstand II
mind map ['maɪnd mæp] Wörternetz (*eine Art Schaubild*) I
to be in one's right mind [bi:‿ɪn wʌnz ˌraɪt 'maɪnd] ganz richtig im Kopf sein ⟨III EL,105⟩
to be out of one's mind [bi:‿aʊt‿əv wʌnz 'maɪnd] verrückt sein III U1,15
to change one's mind [tʃeɪndʒ] seine Meinung ändern II
to **mind** [maɪnd] etwas dagegen haben; nichts ausmachen I
Never mind! [ˌnevə 'maɪnd] Mach dir nichts draus!; Macht nichts. III U5,72
Never mind ... [ˌnevə 'maɪnd] Mach dir keine Sorgen um ... ⟨III EL,102⟩
mine [maɪn] Mine II
minus ['maɪnəs] minus; weniger I
minute ['mɪnɪt] Minute I
mirror ['mɪrə] Spiegel III U5,74
mischievous ['mɪstʃɪvəs] schelmisch, zu Streichen aufgelegt II
to **miss** [mɪs] vermissen; verpassen, verfehlen II
What's missing? [ˌwɒts 'mɪsɪŋ] Was fehlt? I
mission ['mɪʃn] Mission, Auftrag II
mistake [mɪ'steɪk] Fehler III U1,15
by mistake [ˌbaɪ mɪ'steɪk] versehentlich III U3,40
mistranslation [ˌmɪstrænz'leɪʃn] falsche Übersetzung; Übersetzungsfehler ⟨III U3,47⟩
mixed [mɪkst] gemischt II
mixed bag [ˌmɪkst 'bæg] buntes Allerlei I
ml (= millilitre) ['mɪlɪˌli:tə] Milliliter I
mobile ['məʊbaɪl] Handy, Mobiltelefon I
modern ['mɒdn] modern II
Mom *(AE)* [mɒm] Mama II
moment ['məʊmənt] Moment, Augenblick I
Monday ['mʌndeɪ] Montag I
money ['mʌni] Geld I
pocket money ['pɒkɪt ˌmʌni] Taschengeld I
monitor ['mɒnɪtə] Monitor III U1,14
monster ['mɒnstə] Monster I
month [mʌnθ] Monat I
moose, *pl.* **moose** [mu:s] Elch ⟨III F3,80⟩
more [mɔ:] mehr I
not any more [ˌnɒt‿eni 'mɔ:] nicht mehr II
morning ['mɔ:nɪŋ] Morgen; Vormittag I
morse code [ˌmɔ:s 'kəʊd] Morsealphabet ⟨III EL,103⟩
most [məʊst] das meiste; die meisten II
most of the time ['məʊst‿əv ðə ˌtaɪm] meistens III U3,38
most of all ['məʊst‿əv‿ˌɔ:l] am meisten II
*to make the **most** of [ˌmeɪk ðə 'məʊst‿əv] ausnutzen II
mother ['mʌðə] Mutter I
to **motivate** ['məʊtɪveɪt] motivieren III U6,88
motorway *(BE)* ['məʊtəweɪ] Autobahn ⟨III EL,100⟩
mountain ['maʊntɪn] Berg I
mountain biking ['maʊntɪn ˌbaɪkɪŋ] Mountainbikefahren II
Mountain Rescue [ˌmaʊntɪn 'reskju:] Bergwacht II
mouse, *pl.* **mice** [maʊs; maɪs] Maus I
mouse mat ['maʊs mæt] Mauspad I
mouth [maʊθ] Mund III F2,50
My heart jumped into my mouth. [maɪ ˌhɑ:t dʒʌmpt‿ɪntə maɪ 'maʊθ] Das Herz schlug mir bis zum Halse. ⟨III U1,14⟩
to **move** [mu:v] (sich) bewegen I; umziehen III U2,24
movement ['mu:vmənt] Bewegung ⟨III U2,28⟩
movie ['mu:vi] Film II
Mr ['mɪstə] Herr *(Anrede)* I
Mrs ['mɪsɪz] Frau *(Anrede)* I
Ms [mɪz] Frau *(Anrede)* II
MT [mɒn'tænə] Montana II
much [mʌtʃ] viel I
How much is/are ... ? [ˌhaʊ 'mʌtʃ‿ɪz/ɑ:] Wie viel kostet/kosten ... ? I
muck [mʌk] Dreck ⟨III U2,28⟩
mud [mʌd] Schlamm III U3,44
muddy ['mʌdi] schlammig III U3,44
mud-fight ['mʌdfaɪt] Schlammschlacht ⟨III U3,44⟩
muesli ['mju:zli] Müsli I
mug [mʌg] Becher; Krug I
Mum [mʌm] Mama I
muscle ['mʌsl] Muskel III U6,84
museum [mju:'zi:əm] Museum I
mushroom ['mʌʃrʊm] Pilz III U5,70
music ['mju:zɪk] Musik I

musical ['mju:zɪkl] Musical **II**
musical ['mju:zɪkl] musikalisch, Musik- **III U1,11**
***must** [mʌst; məst] müssen **I**
mustang ['mʌstæŋ] Mustang **II**
my [maɪ] mein(e) **I**
(my) own [əʊn] (mein) eigen(-e/-r/-s) **I**
My name is ... [maɪ 'neɪm‿ɪz] Ich heiße ... **I**
myself [maɪ'self] (ich) selbst; mich (selbst) **III U3,40**
mystery ['mɪstri] Mysterium, Rätsel, Geheimnis **III U1,12**

N

name [neɪm] Name **I**
My name is ... [maɪ 'neɪm‿ɪz] Ich heiße ... **I**
What's your name? [ˌwɒts jə 'neɪm] Wie heißt du/heißen Sie? **I**
narrow ['nærəʊ] eng, schmal **II**
nasty ['nɑ:sti] garstig, gemein; scheußlich **II**
national ['næʃnl] national, landesweit **I**
national park [ˌnæʃnl 'pɑ:k] Nationalpark, Naturpark **I**
nationality [ˌnæʃn'æləti] Nationalität, Staatsangehörigkeit **II**
native ['neɪtɪv] eingeboren **III F1,21**
Native American [ˌneɪtɪv‿ə'merɪkən] Ureinwohner(in) Amerikas, Indianer(in); indianisch **II**
natural ['nætʃrl] natürlich, Natur- **III U1,8**
natural history [ˌnætʃrl 'hɪstri] Naturgeschichte ⟨**III U1,8**⟩
nature ['neɪtʃə] Natur **III U5,68**
near [nɪə] nahe, in der Nähe von **I**
nearly ['nɪəli] fast, annähernd **II**
necessary ['nesəsri] notwendig, nötig **III U5,70**
to **need** [ni:d] brauchen, benötigen **I**
needle [ni:dl] Nadel **III U5,68**
negative ['negətɪv] negativ, verneint **I**
neighborhood *(AE)* ['neɪbəhʊd] Nachbarschaft **II**
neighbour ['neɪbə] Nachbar(in) **I**
nervous ['nɜ:vəs] nervös, aufgeregt **I**
never ['nevə] nie, niemals **I**
Never mind! [ˌnevə 'maɪnd] Mach dir nichts draus!; Macht nichts. **III U5,72**
Never mind ... [ˌnevə 'maɪnd] Mach dir keine Sorgen um ... ⟨**III EL,102**⟩
new [nju:] neu **I**
news *(sg.)* [nju:z] Nachricht(en), Neuigkeit(en) **II**
newspaper ['nju:sˌpeɪpə] Zeitung **I**
next [nekst] nächste(-r/-s) **I**
the next size down [ðə ˌnekst saɪz 'daʊn] eine Größe kleiner **III U4,58**
next [nekst] als nächstes **II**
next to ['nekst tə] neben **I**
nice [naɪs] nett **I**
Nice to meet you. [ˌnaɪs tə 'mi:t ju:] Nett, dich/Sie/euch kennen zu lernen. **II**
nickname ['nɪkneɪm] Spitzname ⟨**III F3,80**⟩
night [naɪt] Nacht **I**
last night [lɑ:st 'naɪt] gestern Abend/Nacht **II**
nil [nɪl] null **II**
nine [naɪn] neun **I**
nineteen [naɪn'ti:n] neunzehn **I**
nineteenth [naɪn'ti:nθ] neunzehnte(-r/-s) **I**
ninety ['naɪnti] neunzig **I**
ninth [naɪnθ] neunte(-r/-s) **I**
no [nəʊ] kein(e) **I**
no good [nəʊ 'gʊd] nutzlos, wertlos **II**
No idea! [ˌnəʊ‿aɪ'dɪə] Keine Ahnung! **I**
no longer [nəʊ 'lɒŋgə] nicht mehr, nicht länger **I**
No way! [ˌnəʊ 'weɪ] Auf keinen Fall! **III U6,89**
no [nəʊ] nein **I**
noble ['nəʊbl] edel; adlig ⟨**III U2,29**⟩
nobody ['nəʊbədi] niemand **II**
noise [nɔɪz] Geräusch, Lärm **I**
noisy ['nɔɪzi] laut **I**
none [nʌn] keine(r) **III U4,60**
nope [nəʊp] nö ⟨**III F4,99**⟩
Norman ['nɔ:mən] Normanne, Normannin; normannisch **II**
north [nɔ:θ] **I**
nose [nəʊz] Nase **I**
not [nɒt] nicht **I**
not any better [ˌnɒt‿eni 'betə] (überhaupt) nicht besser **II**
not any more [ˌnɒt‿eni 'mɔ:] nicht mehr **II**
not even [nɒt‿'i:vn] nicht einmal **II**
not until [nɒt‿ən'tɪl] nicht (be)vor; erst (wenn/als) *(siehe Box auf S. 147)* **III U3,42**
note [nəʊt] Notiz; Zettel **III U3,41**
notes *pl.* [nəʊts] Notizen, Anmerkungen **I**
nothing ['nʌθɪŋ] nichts **II**
It's nothing to do with me. [ɪts ˌnʌθɪŋ tə ˌdu: wɪð 'mi:] Ich habe damit nichts zu tun. **III U1,15**
notice ['nəʊtɪs] Anschlag, Notiz **III U1,12**
to **notice** ['nəʊtɪs] bemerken **II**
noun [naʊn] Nomen **II**
November [nəʊ'vembə] November **I**
now [naʊ] jetzt, nun **I**
right now [ˌraɪt 'naʊ] jetzt gleich **II**
nowhere ['nəʊweə] nirgendwo; nirgendwohin **II**
number ['nʌmbə] Zahl, Nummer **I**
nurse [nɜ:s] Krankenschwester, Krankenpfleger **II**

O

o'clock [ə'klɒk] Uhr *(Zeitangabe bei vollen Stunden)* **I**
oak [əʊk] Eiche **II**
object ['ɒbdʒɪkt] Objekt; Gegenstand **III U5,72**
obligation [ˌɒblɪ'geɪʃn] Verpflichtung ⟨**III U4,59**⟩
October [ɒk'təʊbə] Oktober **I**
odd [ɒd] seltsam, nicht passend **I**
Find the odd word out! [ˌɒd wɜ:d‿'aʊt] Finde das Wort, das nicht in die Gruppe passt! *(Wortschatzübung)* **I**
of [ɒv; əv] von **I**
of course [əv 'kɔ:s] natürlich, selbstverständlich **I**
off [ɒf] von ... weg/ab/herunter **I**
off to ['ɒf tə] auf nach **I**
Off to the USA! [ˌɒf tə ðə ju:es‿'eɪ] Auf in die USA! **I**
offer ['ɒfə] Angebot **I**
special offer [ˌspeʃl‿'ɒfə] Sonderangebot **I**
to **offer** ['ɒfə] anbieten **II**
office ['ɒfɪs] Büro **I**
post office ['pəʊst‿ɒfɪs] Postamt **III U2,24**
officer ['ɒfɪsə] Beamter, Beamtin **III U4,61**
official [ə'fɪʃl] offiziell ⟨**III U2,28**⟩
often ['ɒfn] oft **I**
oh [əʊ] oh; null **I**
Oh dear! ['əʊ ˌdɪə] Oje! **I**
OK [əʊ'keɪ] OK **I**
old [əʊld] alt **I**
How old are you? [haʊ‿'əʊld‿ə ju:] Wie alt bist du/sind Sie? **I**
old people's home [ˌəʊld pi:plz 'həʊm] Altersheim **II**
omelette ['ɒmlət] Omelett **I**
*to be **on** [bi:‿'ɒn] im Gange sein, laufen **I**
on [ɒn] auf **I**
on business [ɒn 'bɪznɪs] geschäftlich **I**
on purpose [ɒn 'pɜ:pəs] absichtlich **III U6,89**
on somebody's right/left [ɒn ˌsʌmbədiz 'raɪt/'left] zur Rechten/zur Linken von jemandem **I**
on time [ɒn 'taɪm] pünktlich **II**
on top (of) [ɒn 'tɒp] obendrauf **II**
to be on a team [ˌbi:‿ɒn‿ə 'ti:m] Mitglied eines Teams sein **III U6,86**
to live on sth ['lɪv‿ɒn] von etw leben **III U6,88**
once [wʌnts] einmal; einst **I**
at once [ət 'wʌnts] sofort, plötzlich **I**
one [wʌn] eins; ein(e) **I**
onion ['ʌnjən] Zwiebel **I**
online [ˌɒn'laɪn] online **II**
only ['əʊnli] einzige(-r/-s) **II**
only ['əʊnli] nur; erst; bloß **I**
onto ['ɒntə] auf ... hinauf **II**
Oops! [u:ps] Hoppla! Huch! **I**
to **open** ['əʊpn] öffnen, aufmachen **I**
open ['əʊpn] offen; geöffnet **I**
opening hours ['əʊpnɪŋ‿aʊəz] Öffnungszeiten **I**
opinion [ə'pɪnjən] Meinung **II**
opposite ['ɒpəzɪt] Gegenteil **II**
or [ɔ:] oder **I**
orange ['ɒrɪndʒ] Orange **II**
orange ['ɒrɪndʒ] orange **I**
order ['ɔ:də] Reihenfolge, Ordnung **II**
in **order** to [ɪn‿'ɔ:də tə] um ... zu **III U5,70**
to **order** ['ɔ:də] bestellen **II**; befehlen **III U1,15**
to **organize** ['ɔ:gənaɪz] organisieren **II**
origin ['ɒrɪdʒɪn] Ursprung **III F1,21**
original [ə'rɪdʒnl] original; ursprünglich **III F1,21**
other ['ʌðə] anders; andere(-r/-s) **I**
each other [ˌi:tʃ‿'ʌðə] sich gegenseitig **II**
otherwise ['ʌðəwaɪz] sonst **I**

our ['aʊə] unser(e) I
out [aʊt] außerhalb, (nach) draußen, raus I
out of ['aʊt‿əv] aus ... heraus I
out of work [ˌaʊt‿əv 'wɜ:k] arbeitslos III U2, 27
outlaw ['aʊtlɔ:] Geächtete(r), Vogelfreie(r) II
outside [aʊt'saɪd] (nach) (dr)außen; außerhalb I
over ['əʊvə] (hin)über I; vorüber II
over there [ˌəʊvə 'ðeə] da drüben I
*to **overcome** [ˌəʊvə'kʌm] überwinden III U4, 52
*to **oversleep** [ˌəʊvə'sli:p] verschlafen II
overweight [ˌəʊvə'weɪt] übergewichtig II
Ow! [aʊ] Autsch! I
to **own** [əʊn] besitzen II
(my) own [əʊn] (mein) eigen(-e/-r/-s) I
owner ['əʊnə] Besitzer(in) ⟨III U2, 29⟩

P

pack [pæk] Packung III F2, 51
to **pack** [pæk] packen II
packed lunch [ˌpækt 'lʌntʃ] Lunchpaket; Vesper III F2, 51
package ['pækɪdʒ] Paket III U4, 60
page [peɪdʒ] Seite I; Page ⟨III U2, 29⟩
pain [peɪn] Schmerz II
paint [peɪnt] Farbe III U3, 42
to **paint** [peɪnt] (an)malen, streichen II
pair [peə] Paar I
a pair of [ə 'peər‿əv] ein Paar I
palace ['pælɪs] Palast ⟨III U1, 9⟩
pancake ['pænkeɪk] Pfannkuchen III F2, 50
panic ['pænɪk] Panik III U5, 75
pants *(AE) (pl.)* [pænts] Hose III U4, 58
parade [pə'reɪd] Parade, Umzug II
paragraph ['pærəgrɑ:f] Paragraph, Absatz II
parents *pl.* ['peərənts] Eltern I
park [pɑ:k] Park I
car park ['kɑ: ˌpɑ:k] Parkplatz ⟨III EL, 106⟩
national park [ˌnæʃnl 'pɑ:k] Nationalpark, Naturpark I
parliament ['pɑ:ləmənt] Parlament III U1, 10
part [pɑ:t] Teil I; Rolle II
to take part (in) [teɪk 'pɑ:t] teilnehmen (an) II
particular [pə'tɪkjələ] bestimmt III F4, 98
particularly [pə'tɪkjələli] besonders III F4, 98
partner ['pɑ:tnə] Partner(in) I
party ['pɑ:ti] Party, Feier I
pass [pɑ:s] Ausweis, Pass II
boarding pass ['bɔ:dɪŋ ˌpɑ:s] Bordkarte II
to **pass** [pɑ:s] zupassen, zuspielen; reichen III U6, 89
passenger ['pæsndʒə] Passagier(in); Beifahrer(in) III U4, 57
passive ['pæsɪv] Passiv III U1, 10
past [pɑ:st] Vergangenheit I
past perfect [ˌpɑ:st 'pɜ:fɪkt] Plusquamperfekt III U3, 41
past [pɑ:st] vorbei, vorüber I
half **past** (two) ['hɑ:f pɑ:st] halb (drei) I
pasta ['pæstə] Pasta, Nudeln II
path [pɑ:θ] Pfad, Weg II
to **pause** [pɔ:z] Pause machen; anhalten; verharren III U1, 15
*to **pay for** [peɪ] bezahlen III U1, 15
PE [pi:‿'i:] Sportunterricht II
peasant ['peznt] Kleinbauer II
pen [pen] Füller I
pencil ['pentsl] Bleistift; Buntstift I
pencil case ['pentsl ˌkeɪs] Federmäppchen I
penny, *pl.* **pence** [peni; pents] Penny, Pence *(brit. Währungseinheit)* I
people ['pi:pl] Leute, Menschen I
old people's home [ˌəʊld pi:plz 'həʊm] Altersheim II
pep talk ['pep ˌtɔ:k] aufmunternde Worte ⟨III U6, 88⟩
pepper ['pepə] Pfeffer; Paprikaschote III F2, 50
per [pɜ:; pə] pro III F2, 51
percent, *pl.* **percent** [pə'sent] Prozent II
past **perfect** [ˌpɑ:st 'pɜ:fɪkt] Plusquamperfekt III U3, 41
perfect ['pɜ:fɪkt] perfekt, vollkommen III U6, 91; ⟨III EL, 101⟩
to **perform** [pə'fɔ:m] aufführen, auftreten III U1, 11
perhaps [pə'hæps] vielleicht III U2, 30
period ['pɪəriəd] Periode; Zeitspanne III U2, 25
permission [pə'mɪʃn] Erlaubnis ⟨III U4, 59⟩
person ['pɜ:sn] Person I
perspective [pə'spektɪv] Perspektive, Blickwinkel III U6, 92
to **persuade** [pə'sweɪd] überreden III U1, 10
pet [pet] Haustier; Liebling I
phone [fəʊn] Telefon II
to **phone** [fəʊn] telefonieren I
photo ['fəʊtəʊ] Foto, Fotografie I
to take photos [teɪk 'fəʊtəʊz] fotografieren, Fotos machen I
photographer [fə'tɒgrəfə] Fotograf(in) III U5, 74
phrase [freɪz] Redewendung, Ausdruck I
physical ['fɪzɪkl] physisch, körperlich II
Physical Education [ˌfɪzɪkl‿edʒʊ'keɪʃn] Sport *(Schulfach)* II
piano [pi'ænəʊ] Klavier, Piano II
to **pick** [pɪk] pflücken III U5, 70
to pick up [pɪk‿'ʌp] aufheben; abholen I
pickup ['pɪkʌp] Pickup II
picnic ['pɪknɪk] Picknick I
picture ['pɪktʃə] Bild I
piece [pi:s] Stück II
pig [pɪg] Schwein I
pigsty ['pɪgstaɪ] Schweinestall I
pill [pɪl] Pille, Tablette III U3, 44
pillow ['pɪləʊ] Kopfkissen III U3, 45
pilot ['paɪlət] Pilot(in) I
pine (tree) [paɪn] Kiefer III F3, 80
pink [pɪŋk] pink, rosa I
pint [paɪnt] Pinte *(engl. Hohlmaß: 0,57 l)* II
pioneer [ˌpaɪə'nɪə] Pionier ⟨III EL, 100⟩
What a **pity**! [ˌwɒt‿ə 'pɪti] Wie schade! II
place [pleɪs] Platz, Stelle, Ort I
plain [pleɪn] Ebene II
plan [plæn] Plan I
to **plan** [plæn] planen II
plane [pleɪn] Flugzeug I
to **plant** [plɑ:nt] pflanzen II
plaster ['plɑ:stə] Gips III U3, 44
plate [pleɪt] Teller I
platform ['plætfɔ:m] Plattform, Tribüne; Bahnsteig II
play [pleɪ] Spiel, Theaterstück I
role play ['rəʊl pleɪ] Rollenspiel I
to **play** [pleɪ] spielen I
player ['pleɪə] Spieler, Mitspieler I
CD player [ˌsi:'di: ˌpleɪə] CD-Spieler I
DVD player [ˌdi:vi:di: 'pleɪə] DVD-Player III U2, 25
playground ['pleɪgraʊnd] Schulhof, Pausenhof I
please [pli:z] bitte I
*to be **pleased** [bi: 'pli:zd] erfreut sein III U2, 23
plop [plɒp] Plumps; Plopp ⟨III U6, 89⟩
plural ['plʊərl] Plural, Mehrzahl I
plus [plʌs] plus I
pm [ˌpi:'em] nachmittags *(Uhrzeit)* I
pocket ['pɒkɪt] Hosen- oder Jackentasche I
pocket money ['pɒkɪt ˌmʌni] Taschengeld I
poem ['pəʊɪm] Gedicht I
point [pɔɪnt] Punkt I
turning point ['tɜ:nɪŋ ˌpɔɪnt] Wendepunkt III U4, 62
2.45 (point) ['tu: pɔɪnt ˌfɔ: 'faɪv] Komma *(bei Zahlenangaben)* I
to **point** out [pɔɪnt‿'aʊt] hinweisen auf III U6, 85
police [pə'li:s] Polizei I
polite [pə'laɪt] höflich III U4, 59
pompom ['pɒmpɒm] Pompon *(bunte Quaste der Cheerleader)* ⟨III U6, 87⟩
pony ['pəʊni] Pony I
pony trekking ['pəʊni ˌtrekɪŋ] Ponyreiten im Gelände II
Pooh! [pu:] Pfui! Bäh! I
swimming **pool** ['swɪmɪŋ ˌpu:l] Schwimmbecken; Schwimmbad I
poor [pɔ:; pʊə] arm I
pop [pɒp] Pop II
pop star ['pɒp stɑ:] Popstar I
popcorn ['pɒpkɔ:n] Popcorn II
popular ['pɒpjələ] populär, beliebt II
population [ˌpɒpjə'leɪʃn] Bevölkerung III U5, 68
pork [pɔ:k] Schweinefleisch III F2, 50
port [pɔ:t] Hafen I
position [pə'zɪʃn] Position III U3, 42
positive ['pɒzətɪv] positiv II
possibility [ˌpɒsə'bɪləti] Möglichkeit III U4, 59
possible ['pɒsəbl] möglich III U5, 68; ⟨III EL, 103⟩
post [pəʊst] Post I; Pfosten, Mast II
post office ['pəʊst‿ɒfɪs] Postamt III U2, 24
to **post** [pəʊst] aufgeben *(einen Brief)*; abschicken III U4, 54

postcard ['pəʊstkɑ:d] Postkarte I
poster ['pəʊstə] Poster I
pot [pɒt] Topf III U3, 42
potato, *pl.* **potatoes** [pə'teɪtəʊ] Kartoffel II
pottery ['pɒtri] Töpferei III U3, 38
pound [paʊnd] Pfund *(brit. Währungseinheit)* I
power ['paʊə] Kraft, Stärke, Macht I
Word power ['wɜ:d ˌpaʊə] *Besondere Wortschatzübung* I
practice ['præktɪs] Übung I
sound practice ['saʊnd ˌpræktɪs] *Hör-/Ausspracheübung* I
to **practice** *(AE)* ['præktɪs] üben, praktizieren II
to **pray** [preɪ] beten II
prayer [preə] Gebet II
prediction [prɪ'dɪkʃn] Voraussage II
to **prefer** [prɪ'fɜ:] vorziehen II
prehistory [ˌpri:'hɪstri] Vorgeschichte ⟨III F1, 20⟩
Premiership ['premiəʃɪp] *erste Division, vgl. Deutsche Bundesliga* II
to **prepare** [prɪ'peə] vorbereiten; zubereiten II
to prepare (for) [prɪ'peə] sich vorbereiten (auf) III U5, 73
preposition [ˌprepə'zɪʃn] Präposition II
present ['preznt] Gegenwart, Präsens I; Geschenk I
to **present** [prɪ'zent] präsentieren II
pretty ['prɪti] hübsch ⟨III EL, 106⟩
prime-time ['praɪmtaɪm] zur besten Sendezeit ausgestrahlt ⟨III F4, 99⟩
prince [prɪnts] Prinz II
principal *(AE)* ['prɪntsɪpl] Schulleiter(in) II
printer ['prɪntə] Drucker(in) II
prisoner ['prɪznə] Gefangene(r) III F1, 21
to take sb prisoner [teɪk 'prɪznə] gefangen nehmen ⟨III F1, 21⟩
prize [praɪz] Preis III F4, 98
probably ['prɒbəbli] wahrscheinlich II
problem ['prɒbləm] Problem, Schwierigkeit I
to **produce** [prə'dju:s] herstellen, produzieren III F4, 99
product ['prɒdʌkt] Produkt III F2, 50
professor [prə'fesə] Professor(in) III U4, 52
profile ['prəʊfaɪl] Profil; Porträt; Steckbrief II
program *(AE)* ['prəʊgræm] Programm II
programme *(BE)* ['prəʊgræm] Programm; Sendung III U2, 27
progressive form [prəʊ'gresɪv] Verlaufsform III U2, 26
project ['prɒdʒekt] Projekt II
promise ['prɒmɪs] Versprechen I
to **promise** ['prɒmɪs] versprechen II
pronoun ['prəʊnaʊn] Pronomen II
relative pronoun [ˌrelətɪv 'prəʊnaʊn] Relativpronomen II
to **pronounce** [prə'naʊnts] aussprechen III U4, 57
pronunciation [prəˌnʌntsi'eɪʃn] Aussprache III U3, 47
to **protect sb** (from) [prə'tekt] jmdn (be)schützen (vor) II
to **protest** [prəʊ'test] protestieren III U1, 15
to **prove** [pru:v] beweisen III U2, 27
pub [pʌb] Kneipe; Gasthaus III U2, 24
to **pull** [pʊl] ziehen II
pump [pʌmp] Pumpe, Luftpumpe I
pumpkin ['pʌmpkɪn] Kürbis II
to **punish** ['pʌnɪʃ] bestrafen II
punk [pʌŋk] Punk III U1, 8
pupil ['pju:pl] Schüler(in) I
purple ['pɜ:pl] lila, violett I
purpose ['pɜ:pəs] Zweck III U5, 71
on purpose [ɒn 'pɜ:pəs] absichtlich III U6, 89
to **push** [pʊʃ] stoßen, schieben, drücken II
*to **put** [pʊt] setzen, stellen, legen I
to put in [pʊt‿'ɪn] einsetzen I
to put on [pʊt‿'ɒn] anziehen II
to put up [pʊt‿'ʌp] aufstellen; errichten III U5, 70
puzzle ['pʌzl] Rätsel; Puzzle I
crossword (puzzle) ['krɒswɜ:d] Kreuzworträtsel II

Q

quarter past/to ['kwɔ:tə pɑ:st/tə] Viertel nach/vor I
queen [kwi:n] Königin III F1, 21
question ['kwestʃn] Frage I
question tag ['kwestʃən ˌtæg] Frageanhängsel, Bestätigungsfrage II
questionnaire [ˌkwestʃə'neə] Fragebogen III F4, 99
quick [kwɪk] schnell II
quiet [kwaɪət] leise I; still III U2, 31
quite [kwaɪt] ziemlich; ganz, völlig I
quiz [kwɪz] Quiz, Rätsel I

R

rabbit ['ræbɪt] Kaninchen I
raccoon [rə'ku:n] Waschbär ⟨III U5, 74⟩
race [reɪs] Wettlauf, Rennen I
to have a race [ˌhæv‿ə 'reɪs] ein Rennen veranstalten I
racket ['rækɪt] Schläger I
radio ['reɪdiəʊ] Radio I
rag [ræg] Lumpen, Fetzen II
rain [reɪn] Regen I
to **rain** [reɪn] regnen I
It's raining cats and dogs. [ɪts ˌreɪnɪŋ ˌkæts‿ənd 'dɒgz] Es schüttet wie aus Eimern. ⟨III EL, 100⟩
rainbow ['reɪnbəʊ] Regenbogen II
to **raise** [reɪz] anheben, erhöhen, (Kinder) großziehen, (Geld) aufbringen II
RAM [ræm] Arbeitsspeicher ⟨III EL, 105⟩
ranch [rɑ:ntʃ; ræntʃ] Ranch II
range [reɪndʒ] Freiland, Weideland *(AE)* ⟨III F3, 80⟩
rap [ræp] Rap I
raspberry ['rɑ:zbri] Himbeere III F2, 50
RE [ɑ:r‿'i:] Religion *(Schulfach)* II
to **reach** [ri:tʃ] erreichen III U5, 70
to **react** [ri'ækt] reagieren III U5, 77
reaction [ri'ækʃn] Reaktion II
*to **read** [ri:d] lesen I
ready ['redi] fertig, bereit I
real [rɪəl] echt, richtig, wirklich II
realistic [ˌrɪə'lɪstɪk] realistisch II
reality [ri'æləti] Realität; Wirklichkeit III F4, 98
to **realize** ['rɪəlaɪz] erkennen, realisieren II
really ['rɪəli] wirklich I
reason ['ri:zn] Grund II
rebellion [rɪ'beliən] Rebellion III F1, 21
recipe ['resɪpi:] Rezept II
to **recognize** ['rekəgnaɪz] erkennen II
to **record** [rɪ'kɔ:d] aufnehmen; aufzeichnen III U4, 57
to **recover** [rɪ'kʌvə] sich erholen III U6, 84
red [red] rot I
redwood (tree) ['redwʊd] Mammutbaum ⟨III F3, 81⟩
re-enactment [ˌri:ɪ'næktmənt] Nachspielen/Nachvollzug eines Ereignisses ⟨III U3, 38⟩
referee [ˌrefr'i:] Schiedsrichter(in) III U6, 83
reflexive [rɪ'fleksɪv] reflexiv III U5, 73
region ['ri:dʒn] Region; Gegend III F3, 80
regular ['regjələ] regelmäßig; gleichmäßig I
relationship [rɪ'leɪʃnʃɪp] Beziehung III U4, 52
relative ['relətɪv] Verwandte(r) I
relative ['relətɪv] relativ II
relative clause [ˌrelətɪv 'klɔ:z] Relativsatz II
relative pronoun [ˌrelətɪv 'prəʊnaʊn] Relativpronomen II
to **relax** [rɪ'læks] sich entspannen, sich ausruhen I
religious [rɪ'lɪdʒəs] religiös II
Religious Education [rɪˌlɪdʒəs‿edʒʊ'keɪʃn] Religionsunterricht II
to **remember** [rɪ'membə] sich erinnern (an); sich merken I
to **remove** [rɪ'mu:v] entfernen III U3, 40
to **rent** [rent] mieten III U2, 23
to **repair** [rɪ'peə] reparieren III U4, 54
to **repeat** [rɪ'pi:t] wiederholen II
to **reply** [rɪ'plaɪ] antworten, erwidern, entgegnen III U1, 15
to **report** [rɪ'pɔ:t] berichten; (sich) melden III U1, 12
to **represent** [ˌreprɪ'zent] repräsentieren; stehen für ⟨III EL, 103⟩
rescue ['reskju:] Rettung II
Mountain Rescue [ˌmaʊntɪn 'reskju:] Bergwacht II
to **rescue** ['reskju:] retten II
rescuer ['reskju:ə] Retter(in) ⟨III U2, 28⟩
respect [rɪ'spekt] Respekt ⟨III U2, 28⟩
rest [rest] Rest I; Rast ⟨III EL, 101⟩
restaurant ['restrɒnt] Restaurant, Gaststätte I
fast food restaurant [ˌfɑ:st fu:d 'restrɒnt] Schnellrestaurant III F2, 51
result [rɪ'zʌlt] Ergebnis, Resultat II
as a result of [əz‿ə rɪ'zʌlt‿əv] infolge (von) III U4, 52
to **retire** [rɪ'taɪə] sich zurückziehen; sich zur Ruhe setzen III U6, 84

in **return** [ɪn rɪ'tɜ:n] als Gegenleistung ⟨**III U2**, 29⟩
to **return** [rɪ'tɜ:n] zurückgeben, zurückschlagen; zurückkehren **II**
revenge [rɪ'vendʒ] Rache, Revanche **III U6**, 88
review [rɪ'vju:] Kritik **II**
rice [raɪs] Reis **II**
rich [rɪtʃ] reich **I**; reichhaltig **III F2**, 50
*to get **rid** of [get 'rɪd‿əv] loswerden **II**
ride [raɪd] Fahrt, Ritt **II**
*to **ride** [raɪd] fahren; reiten **I**
rider ['raɪdə] Reiter(in) **II**
ridge [rɪdʒ] Bergrücken, Hügelkette ⟨**III U5**, 74⟩
ridiculous [rɪ'dɪkjələs] lächerlich ⟨**III EL**, 105⟩
horseback **riding** [ˌhɔ:sbæk 'raɪdɪŋ] Reiten **II**
right [raɪt] richtig, korrekt **I**; rechts; rechte(-r/-s) **I**
all right [ɔ:l 'raɪt] in Ordnung; alles klar **II**
on somebody's right/left [ɒn ˌsʌmbədiz 'raɪt/'left] zur Rechten/zur Linken von jemandem **I**
to be in one's right mind [bi:‿ɪn wʌnz ˌraɪt 'maɪnd] ganz richtig im Kopf sein ⟨**III EL**, 105⟩
right away [raɪt‿ə'weɪ] sofort, gleich **I**
right now [ˌraɪt 'naʊ] jetzt gleich **II**
key **ring** ['ki: ˌrɪŋ] Schlüsselbund; Schlüsselanhänger **III F2**, 51
*to **ring** [rɪŋ] klingeln; anrufen **II**
risk [rɪsk] Risiko **III F4**, 99
to take a risk [ˌteɪk‿ə 'rɪsk] ein Risiko eingehen **III F4**, 99
rival ['raɪvl] Rivale, Rivalin; Konkurrent(in) **III U6**, 88
river ['rɪvə] Fluss **I**
road [rəʊd] Straße **I**
rock [rɒk] Fels, Stein **I**
rock [rɒk] Rock *(Musik)* **II**
rodeo [rəʊ'deɪəʊ; 'rəʊdiəʊ] Rodeo **I**
role [rəʊl] Rolle **I**
role play ['rəʊl pleɪ] Rollenspiel **I**
roll [rəʊl] Brötchen **II**
to **roll** [rəʊl] rollen **III U3**, 45
Roman ['rəʊmən] Römer; römisch ⟨**III F1**, 20⟩
roof [ru:f] Dach **I**
room [ru:m] Zimmer; Platz **I**
changing room ['tʃeɪndʒɪŋ ˌrʊm] Umkleideraum **III U3**, 41
living room ['lɪvɪŋ rʊm] Wohnzimmer **I**
staff room ['stɑ:f rʊm] Lehrerzimmer **III U3**, 40
root [ru:t] Wurzel **III U5**, 69
rope [rəʊp] Seil **II**
round [raʊnd] Runde **II**
the **Round** Table [ˌraʊnd 'teɪbl] die Tafelrunde ⟨**III U2**, 29⟩
round [raʊnd] um … herum **I**
route [ru:t; *AE:* raʊt] Route **II**
row [rəʊ] Sträßchen; Reihe **I**
to **row** [rəʊ] rudern **I**
royal ['rɔɪəl] königlich **III U3**, 45
to **rub** [rʌb] reiben ⟨**III EL**, 100⟩
rubber ['rʌbə] Radiergummi **I**
rubbish ['rʌbɪʃ] Müll; Quatsch **II**
rude [ru:d] unhöflich; unverschämt **II**
rugby ['rʌgbi] Rugby **I**
to **ruin** ['ru:ɪn] ruinieren, zerstören **II**
rule [ru:l] Regel **I**
ruler ['ru:lə] Lineal **I**; Herrscher(in) ⟨**III U2**, 29⟩
to **rumble** ['rʌmbl] donnern ⟨**III U2**, 28⟩
*to **run** [rʌn] rennen, laufen **I**; führen, leiten **III F4**, 99
to run down [rʌn 'daʊn] leer werden **II**
RUOK? [ˌɑ: ju:‿əʊ'keɪ] Alles in Ordnung bei dir? ⟨**III U5**, 72⟩
to **rush** [rʌʃ] sich beeilen **I**

S

sack [sæk] Sack **II**
sad [sæd] traurig, schmerzlich **I**
saddle ['sædl] Sattel **II**
safe [seɪf] sicher **I**
safety ['seɪfti] Sicherheit **III U5**, 70
to **sail** [seɪl] segeln **III U4**, 52
salad ['sæləd] Salat **II**
salmon, *pl.* **salmon** ['sæmən] Lachs **III U5**, 69
salt [sɔ:lt] Salz **III F2**, 50
the **same** [seɪm] derselbe (die-/das-) **I**
sand [sænd] Sand **I**
sandwich ['sændwɪdʒ] Sandwich, belegtes Brot **I**
satellite ['sætlaɪt] Satellit **III F4**, 98
Saturday ['sætədeɪ] Samstag **I**
sauce [sɔ:s] Sauce **III F2**, 50
saucer ['sɔ:sə] Untertasse **I**
sausage ['sɒsɪdʒ] Wurst **II**
to **save** [seɪv] retten, bergen **I**; sparen **III U2**, 28
Saxon ['sæksn] Sachse, Sächsin; sächsisch **II**
*to **say** [seɪ] sagen, sprechen **I**
to say hello [seɪ hə'ləʊ] Hallo sagen, sich begrüßen **I**
scanning ['skænɪŋ] Durchsuchen nach Details; Abtasten ⟨**III U2**, 28⟩
scar [skɑ:] Narbe **II**
*to be **scared** [bi: 'skeəd] Angst haben, erschrocken sein **I**
scary ['skeəri] unheimlich, gruselig; schreckhaft **II**
scene [si:n] Szene; Schauplatz **I**
scenery ['si:nri] Landschaft **III U2**, 23
schedule ['ʃedju:l; 'skedʒu:l] Stundenplan; Fahrplan **II**
scholarship ['skɒləʃɪp] Stipendium ⟨**III U6**, 88⟩
school [sku:l] Schule **I**
comprehensive school [kɒmprɪ'hentsɪv ˌsku:l] Gesamtschule ⟨**III EL**, 106⟩
elementary school *(AE)* [elɪ'mentri ˌsku:l] Grundschule **II**
high school ['haɪ ˌsku:l] High School *(weiterführende Schule in den USA, Oberstufe)* **III U6**, 86
middle school ['mɪdl ˌsku:l] Mittelschule *(weiterführende Schule in den USA, Mittelstufe)* **II**
school bag ['sku:l bæg] Schultasche **I**
science [saɪənts] (Natur-)Wissenschaft **II**
scooter ['sku:tə] Roller **I**
score [skɔ:] Punktestand **III U6**, 88
to **score** [skɔ:] punkten; ein Tor schießen **III U3**, 40
scorer ['skɔ:rə] Torjäger(in); Korbjäger(in) **III U6**, 88
scout [skaʊt] Talentsucher(in) ⟨**III U6**, 88⟩
scrapbook ['skræpbʊk] Sammelalbum **II**
to **scream** [skri:m] schreien, kreischen **I**
screen [skri:n] Bildschirm **I**; Leinwand **III F4**, 98
sculpture ['skʌlptʃə] Skulptur **III U4**, 53
sea [si:] Meer **I**
seal [si:l] Seehund **I**
to **search** [sɜ:tʃ] durchsuchen **III U4**, 60
to **search for** ['sɜ:tʃ fə] suchen (nach) **III U4**, 60
seaside ['si:saɪd] Küste, Meeresküste **I**
at the seaside [ət ðə 'si:saɪd] am Meer **I**
season ['si:zn] Saison; Jahreszeit **III U6**, 88
seat [si:t] Sitz, Sitzplatz **II**
second ['seknd] Sekunde **III U5**, 68
second ['seknd] zweite(-r/-s) **I**
second-hand [ˌseknd 'hænd] gebraucht **II**
second-hand shop [ˌseknd hænd 'ʃɒp] Gebrauchtwarenladen **II**
secret ['si:krət] Geheimnis **I**
*to **see** [si:] sehen **I**
I see. [aɪ 'si:] aha; ach so **II**
See you! ['si: ju:] Bis dann!, Bis … **I**
to **seem** [si:m] scheinen **II**
to seem familiar [ˌsi:m fə'mɪliə] bekannt vorkommen **III U4**, 60
*to **sell** [sel] verkaufen **II**
*to **send** [send] schicken **I**
sentence ['sentənts] Satz **I**
separate ['seprət] separat; getrennt; verschieden **III F1**, 21
September [sep'tembə] September **I**
series, *pl.* **series** ['sɪəri:z] Serie **III F4**, 99
serious ['sɪəriəs] ernst **II**
servant ['sɜ:vnt] Diener(in) ⟨**III U2**, 29⟩; ⟨**III U2**, 31⟩
to **serve** [sɜ:v] (be)dienen; aufschlagen *(Sport)* **II**; servieren **III F2**, 50
service ['sɜ:vɪs] Service, Dienst **III U1**, 10
*to **set** fire to [set 'faɪə tə] in Brand stecken **III F1**, 21
to set off [set‿'ɒf] aufbrechen **II**
to set the table [ˌset ðə 'teɪbl] den Tisch decken **I**
to **settle** ['setl] siedeln; sich niederlassen ⟨**III U2**, 29⟩
seven [sevn] sieben **I**
seventeen [ˌsevn'ti:n] siebzehn **I**
seventeenth [ˌsevn'ti:nθ] siebzehnte(-r/-s) **I**
seventh ['sevntθ] siebte(-r/-s) **I**
seventy ['sevnti] siebzig **I**
shake [ʃeɪk] Shake, Milchshake **III F2**, 50
*to **shake** [ʃeɪk] schütteln **I**; zittern **III U6**, 89
to **share** [ʃeə] teilen **III EL**, 103
to **shave** [ʃeɪv] (sich) rasieren **II**

she [ʃi:] sie I
shed [ʃed] Schuppen, Stall I
sheep, *pl.* **sheep** [ʃi:p] Schaf I
sheepdog ['ʃi:pdɒg] Hütehund; Schäferhund I
shelf, *pl.* **shelves** [ʃelf; ʃelvz] Regal, Regalbrett I
taco **shell** [ˌtɑ:kəʊ 'ʃel] Taco-Tasche *(mexikanische Teigtasche)* ⟨III F2,50⟩
sheriff ['ʃerɪf] Sheriff II
shield [ʃi:ld] Schild ⟨III U3,38⟩
*to **shine** [ʃaɪn] scheinen; glänzen I
shiny ['ʃaɪni] glänzend II
ship [ʃɪp] Schiff I
shirt [ʃɜ:t] Hemd; Shirt I
shock [ʃɒk] Schock II
shoe [ʃu:] Schuh I
*to **shoot** (at) [ʃu:t] schießen (auf) II
shop [ʃɒp] Geschäft, Laden I
 second-hand shop [ˌseknd hænd 'ʃɒp] Gebrauchtwarenladen II
 shop assistant ['ʃɒp‿əˌsɪstnt] Verkäufer(in) I
shopping ['ʃɒpɪŋ] Einkaufen; Einkäufe I
 shopping centre ['ʃɒpɪŋ ˌsentə] Einkaufszentrum I
 to go shopping [ˌgəʊ 'ʃɒpɪŋ] einkaufen gehen I
short [ʃɔ:t] kurz I
 short cut ['ʃɔ:t kʌt] Abkürzung II
shot [ʃɒt] Schuss, Schlag II
should [ʃʊd] sollte(n) II
shoulder ['ʃəʊldə] Schulter I
shout [ʃaʊt] Schrei, Ruf III U4,61
to **shout** [ʃaʊt] schreien, rufen I
show [ʃəʊ] Show, Schau, Aufführung II
 game show ['geɪm ˌʃəʊ] Spielshow III F4,99
*to **show** [ʃəʊ] zeigen I
 to show sb around (a place) [ʃəʊ] jmdn (an einem Ort) herumführen III U1,11
show-off ['ʃəʊ‿ɒf] Angeber(in) II
Shsh! [ʃ] Pssst! I
*to **shut** [ʃʌt] zumachen, schließen I
 to shut off/down [ʃʌt‿'ɒf; ʃʌt daʊn] herunterfahren ⟨III EL,105⟩
 to shut up [ʃʌt‿'ʌp] die Klappe halten ⟨III U3,42⟩
*to feel **sick** [fi:l 'sɪk] Übelkeit verspüren III U6,89
side [saɪd] Seite II
to **sigh** [saɪ] seufzen III U1,14
sight [saɪt] Sehenswürdigkeit; Sicht, Anblick II
sightseeing ['saɪtsi:ɪŋ] Besichtigungstour I
sign [saɪn] Zeichen; Schild III U1,12
signal ['sɪgnl] Signal, Zeichen II
silence ['saɪlənts] Stille ⟨III U2,28⟩
silly ['sɪli] Dummkopf I
silly ['sɪli] dumm, doof, albern I
silver ['sɪlvə] Silber II
similar ['sɪmɪlə] ähnlich III U4,54
simple ['sɪmpl] einfach, simpel II
since [sɪnts] seit, seitdem II; da III U3,40
*to **sing** [sɪŋ] singen I
 to sing along [ˌsɪŋ‿ə'lɒŋ] mitsingen I
singer ['sɪŋə] Sänger(in) II
sir [sɜ:] mein Herr *(Anrede)* I
Sir [sɜ:] Sir *(Anrede für einen Ritter)* III U2,30
sister ['sɪstə] Schwester I
*to **sit** [sɪt] sitzen I
 to sit (down) [sɪt 'daʊn] sich (hin)setzen I
sitcom ['sɪtkɒm] Situationskomödie III F4,99
situation [ˌsɪtju'eɪʃn] Situation II
six [sɪks] sechs I
sixteen [ˌsɪk'sti:n] sechzehn I
sixteenth [ˌsɪk'sti:nθ] sechzehnte(-r/-s) I
sixth [sɪksθ] sechste(-r/-s) I
sixty ['sɪksti] sechzig I
size [saɪz] Größe, Kleidergröße I
 the next size down [ðə ˌnekst saɪz 'daʊn] eine Größe kleiner III U4,58
skateboard ['skeɪtbɔ:d] Skateboard I
skates *pl.* [skeɪts] Inlineskates, Rollschuhe, Schlittschuhe I
skating ['skeɪtɪŋ] Inlineskate/Schlittschuh fahren I
skiing ['ski:ɪŋ] Skifahren I
skill [skɪl] Fertigkeit; Geschick III U1,18
skimming ['skɪmɪŋ] Überfliegen ⟨III U2,28⟩
skin [skɪn] Haut, Fell I
skirt [skɜ:t] Rock I
sky [skaɪ] Himmel I
skyscraper ['skaɪskreɪpə] Wolkenkratzer I
slate [sleɪt] Schiefer II
sled [sled] Schlitten II
*to go to **sleep** [gəʊ tə 'sli:p] einschlafen I
*to **sleep** [sli:p] schlafen I
 sleeping bag ['sli:pɪŋ ˌbæg] Schlafsack III U5,70; ⟨III EL,100⟩
to **slip** [slɪp] (aus)rutschen III U3,45
slippery ['slɪpri] rutschig, glitschig II
slow [sləʊ] langsam I
slowly ['sləʊli] langsam I
small [smɔ:l] klein I
smell [smel] Geruch, Gestank I
*to **smell** [smel] riechen (an) II
smile [smaɪl] Lächeln I
to **smile** [smaɪl] lächeln I
smoke [sməʊk] Rauch III U5,74
to **smuggle** ['smʌgl] schmuggeln II
smuggler ['smʌglə] Schmuggler(in) II
snack [snæk] Snack, Imbiss III U3,44
snake [sneɪk] Schlange I
to **sneer** [snɪə] spotten, spöttisch grinsen II
to **sneeze** [sni:z] niesen II
snow [snəʊ] Schnee II
so [səʊ] so I
 so far ['səʊ fɑ:] bis jetzt II
so [səʊ] also, deshalb I
 so (that) ['səʊ ðət] damit; so dass I
soap [səʊp] Seife I
soccer *(AE)* ['sɒkə] Fußball I
social ['səʊʃl] sozial, gesellschaftlich II
society [sə'saɪəti] Gesellschaft II
sock [sɒk] Socke I
soldier ['səʊldʒə] Soldat(in) III F1,20
solution [sə'lu:ʃn] Lösung III U4,60
some [sʌm] einige; etwas I
somebody ['sʌmbədi] jemand I
someone ['sʌmwʌn] jemand II
something ['sʌmθɪŋ] etwas I
sometime ['sʌmtaɪm] irgendwann II
sometimes ['sʌmtaɪmz] manchmal I
somewhere ['sʌmweə] irgendwo II
son [sʌn] Sohn II
song [sɒŋ] Lied, Song I
soon [su:n] bald I
sorry ['sɒri] Tut mir Leid, Entschuldigung I
 to feel sorry for [fi:l 'sɒri] Mitleid haben mit; bedauern III U1,15
soul [səʊl] Seele III U5,69
sound [saʊnd] Ton, Geräusch I; Sund, Meerenge ⟨III U5,69⟩
 sound practice ['saʊnd ˌpræktɪs] *Hör-/Ausspracheübung* I
to **sound** [saʊnd] klingen II
soup [su:p] Suppe II
sour [saʊə] sauer III F2,50
source [sɔ:s] Quelle III U1,18
south [saʊθ] Süden I
southern ['sʌðən] südlich II
souvenir [ˌsu:və'nɪə] Souvenir, Andenken I
space [speɪs] Raum; Weltraum I
Spanish ['spænɪʃ] spanisch; Spanisch I
*to **speak** [spi:k] sprechen I
speaker ['spi:kə] Lautsprecher II
spear [spɪə] Speer III U2,30
special ['speʃl] besonders, speziell I
 special offer [ˌspeʃl‿'ɒfə] Sonderangebot I
speech [spi:tʃ] Sprache; Rede III U4,52
direct **speech** [dɪˌrekt 'spi:tʃ] direkte Rede III U6,84
 indirect speech [ˌɪndɪrekt 'spi:tʃ] indirekte Rede III U6,84
*to **spell** [spel] buchstabieren I
spelling ['spelɪŋ] Orthographie, Rechtschreibung II
*to **spend** [spend] ausgeben; verbringen I
spicy ['spaɪsi] würzig; pikant III F2,50
spider ['spaɪdə] Spinne II
spiky ['spaɪki] stachlig ⟨III U6,89⟩
*to **spill** [spɪl] verschütten III U3,42
in **spite** of [ɪn 'spaɪt‿əv] trotz III U6,84
splash [splæʃ] Spritzer, Planscher I
spooky ['spu:ki] gespenstisch ⟨III U5,74⟩
spoon [spu:n] Löffel I
sport [spɔ:t] Sport I
sportsman, *pl.* **sportsmen** ['spɔ:tsmən] Sportler III U6,85
sportswoman, *(pl.)* **sportswomen** ['spɔ:tsˌwʊmən] Sportlerin III U6,85
spring [sprɪŋ] Frühling II
spur [spɜ:] Sporn II
square [skweə] Platz I; Quadrat III U5,68
 square dance ['skweə ˌdɑ:nts] Square Dance II
squire [skwaɪə] Junker ⟨III U2,29⟩
stable ['steɪbl] Stall I
staff [stɑ:f] Personal; Kollegium III U3,40
 cleaning staff ['kli:nɪŋ ˌstɑ:f] Reinigungspersonal ⟨III U3,40⟩
 staff room ['stɑ:f rʊm] Lehrerzimmer III U3,40
stage [steɪdʒ] Bühne II

to **stagger (about)** ['stægə] (herum)torkeln II
stairs *(pl.)* [steəz] Treppe III U4,60
stall [stɔ:l] Stand, Bude III U1,13
*to **stand** [stænd] ertragen, ausstehen II
to stand (up) [stænd‿'ʌp] (auf)stehen I
standard ['stændəd] Standard III U5,68
star [stɑ:] Star; Stern I
pop star ['pɒp stɑ:] Popstar I
to **start** [stɑ:t] anfangen, starten I
Let's start! [lets 'stɑ:t] Lass(t) uns anfangen I
starter ['stɑ:tə] Vorspeise II
state [steɪt] Staat, Land I
statement ['steɪtmənt] Aussage, Behauptung II
station ['steɪʃn] Haltestelle, Bahnhof I
statue ['stætʃu:] Statue, Standbild I
status ['steɪtəs] Status II
to **stay** [steɪ] bleiben I; übernachten II
steak [steɪk] Steak II
*to **steal** [sti:l] stehlen II
steam [sti:m] Dampf III U5,74
steep [sti:p] steil II
step [step] Stufe; Schritt III F4,99
stepmother ['stepmʌðə] Stiefmutter II
stepsister ['stepsɪstə] Stiefschwester II
stereo ['steriəʊ] Stereoanlage I
stick [stɪk] Stock ⟨III EL,100⟩
*to **stick** [stɪk] kleben; stecken III U3,40
to be stuck [bi: 'stʌk] stecken bleiben, festklemmen II
still [stɪl] still III U3,44
still [stɪl] noch, immer noch I
stone [stəʊn] Stein I
stop [stɒp] Haltestelle III U1,9
to **stop** [stɒp] aufhören; anhalten I
store [stɔ:] Laden, Geschäft III U1,14
storm [stɔ:m] Sturm I
story ['stɔ:ri] Geschichte, Erzählung I
straight [streɪt] gerade, geradewegs, direkt I
strange [streɪndʒ] fremd; seltsam; merkwürdig III U3,45
stranger ['streɪndʒə] Fremde(r) II
strawberry ['strɔ:bri] Erdbeere II
stream [stri:m] Bach III U5,70
street [stri:t] Straße I
stress [stres] Stress II
to **stress** [stres] betonen III U1,13
string [strɪŋ] Schnur III U1,14
strong [strɒŋ] stark I
student ['stju:dnt] Student(in); Schüler(in) II
to **study** ['stʌdi] studieren; lernen III U6,84
stuff [stʌf] Zeug II
stupid ['stju:pɪd] dumm, blöd I
style [staɪl] Stil II
subject ['sʌbdʒɪkt] Schulfach; Thema I
success [sək'ses] Erfolg II
such as ['sʌtʃ‿əz] (solche) wie III U5,68
suddenly ['sʌdnli] plötzlich, auf einmal I
sugar ['ʃʊgə] Zucker III F2,50
to **suggest** [sə'dʒest] vorschlagen II
suggestion [sə'dʒestʃn] Vorschlag, Anregung I
to **suit** [su:t] passen (zu); (jmdm) stehen III U4,58
suitable ['su:təbl] geeignet; passend III F2,51
suitcase ['su:tkeɪs] Koffer III U4,60; ⟨III EL,100⟩
summer ['sʌmə] Sommer I
sun [sʌn] Sonne I
Sunday ['sʌndeɪ] Sonntag I
sunny ['sʌni] sonnig I
sunscreen ['sʌnskri:n] Sonnencreme I
sunshine ['sʌnʃaɪn] Sonnenschein II
super ['su:pə] super II
superlative [su:'pɜ:lətɪv] Superlativ II
supermarket ['su:pəˌmɑ:kɪt] Supermarkt I
sure [ʃʊə; ʃɔ:] sicher I
surfing ['sɜ:fɪŋ] Wellenreiten, Surfen I
surprise [sə'praɪz] Überraschung I
*to be **surprised** [bi: sə'praɪzd] überrascht sein I
survey ['sɜ:veɪ] Umfrage; Studie III F4,99
to **survive** [sə'vaɪv] überleben III F4,98
sweatshirt ['swetʃɜ:t] Sweatshirt I
sweets *pl.* [swi:ts] Süßigkeiten, Bonbons I
sweet [swi:t] süß I
sweetcorn ['swi:tkɔ:n] Mais III F2,50
sweetie ['swi:ti] Süße(r) ⟨III U5,76⟩
*to **swim** [swɪm] schwimmen I
swimmer ['swɪmə] Schwimmer(in) III U4,53
swimming ['swɪmɪŋ] Schwimmen I
swimming pool ['swɪmɪŋ ˌpu:l] Schwimmbecken; Schwimmbad I
to **switch** off [swɪtʃ‿'ɒf] ausschalten III U4,54
to switch on [swɪtʃ‿'ɒn] einschalten III U2,24
sword [sɔ:d] Schwert ⟨III U3,38⟩
symbol ['sɪmbl] Symbol ⟨III U2,29⟩
symbolic [sɪm'bɒlɪk] symbolisch ⟨III U2,29⟩
synthesizer ['sɪntθəˌsaɪzə] Synthesizer ⟨III U4,52⟩
system ['sɪstəm] System II

T

table ['teɪbl] Tisch I; Tabelle II
table tennis ['teɪbl ˌtenɪs] Tischtennis II
the Round Table [ˌraʊnd 'teɪbl] die Tafelrunde ⟨III U2,29⟩
to set the table [ˌset ðə 'teɪbl] den Tisch decken I
taco ['tɑ:kəʊ] Taco *(mexikanische gefüllte Teigtasche)* III F2,50
taco shell [ˌtɑ:kəʊ 'ʃel] Taco-Tasche *(mexikanische Teigtasche)* ⟨III F2,50⟩
question **tag** ['kwestʃən ˌtæg] Frageanhängsel, Bestätigungsfrage II
*to **take** [teɪk] (mit)nehmen; bringen I; dauern, (Zeit) brauchen II
to take a break [ˌteɪk‿ə 'breɪk] Pause machen II
to take off [teɪk‿'ɒf] abheben I; ausziehen III U2,31
to take one's own life [ˌteɪk wʌnz‿əʊn 'laɪf] sich das Leben nehmen III F1,21
to take part (in) [teɪk 'pɑ:t] teilnehmen (an) II
to take photos [teɪk 'fəʊtəʊz] fotografieren, Fotos machen I
to take sb prisoner [teɪk 'prɪznə] gefangen nehmen ⟨III F1,21⟩
to take sb (time) to do sth [teɪk] jmdn (Zeit) kosten II
*to **take** a risk [ˌteɪk‿ə 'rɪsk] ein Risiko eingehen III F4,99
takeaway ['teɪkəweɪ] *(Restaurant, das Speisen zum Mitnehmen verkauft)* II
*to **take place** [teɪk 'pleɪs] stattfinden III U1,12
tale [teɪl] Geschichte, Erzählung II
fairy tale ['feəri ˌteɪl] Märchen II
talk [tɔ:k] Vortrag; Rede III U1,18
to give a talk [ˌgɪv‿ə 'tɔ:k] einen Vortrag halten III U1,18
pep **talk** ['pep ˌtɔ:k] aufmunternde Worte ⟨III U6,88⟩
to **talk** [tɔ:k] sprechen, reden I
tall [tɔ:l] groß; hoch I
tape [teɪp] (Ton-)Band II
tapestry ['tæpɪstri] Wandteppich ⟨III F1,21⟩
target ['tɑ:gɪt] Ziel(scheibe) II
taste [teɪst] Geschmack III F2,50
to **taste** [teɪst] schmecken II
tasty ['teɪsti] schmackhaft III F2,50
taxi ['tæksi] Taxi I
tea [ti:] Tee; Abendessen I
*to **teach** [ti:tʃ] unterrichten, lehren I
teacher ['ti:tʃə] Lehrer(in) I
head teacher *(BE)* [ˌhed 'ti:tʃə] Schulleiter(in) III U3,49
team [ti:m] Gruppe, Team I
to be on a team [ˌbi:‿ɒn‿ə 'ti:m] Mitglied eines Teams sein III U6,86
team-mate ['ti:mmeɪt] Mannschaftskamerad(in) ⟨III U6,89⟩
tear [tɪə] Träne III U3,40
teatime ['ti:taɪm] Zeit für Nachmittagstee; Abendessen I
techno ['teknəʊ] Techno II
technology [tek'nɒlədʒi] Technologie, Computerunterricht II
teddy bear ['tedi ˌbeə] Teddybär III U1,14
teenager ['ti:nˌeɪdʒə] Teenager; Jugendliche(r) III F2,51
telegraph ['telɪgrɑ:f] Telegraf ⟨III EL,104⟩
telephone ['telɪfəʊn] Telefon I
telescope ['telɪskəʊp] Teleskop; Fernrohr I
television ['telɪvɪʒn] Fernsehen; Fernseher I
*to **tell** (somebody) [tel] (jemandem) sagen, mitteilen I
ten [ten] zehn I
tennis ['tenɪs] Tennis I
table tennis ['teɪbl ˌtenɪs] Tischtennis II
tense [tens] Zeit, Zeitform *(grammatisch)* I
tent [tent] Zelt II
tenth [tenθ] zehnte(-r/-s) I
terrible ['terəbl] schrecklich, furchtbar I
terrific [tə'rɪfɪk] ausgezeichnet, hervorragend ⟨III EL,105⟩
terrified ['terəfaɪd] außer sich vor Schrecken II

test [test] Test; Klassenarbeit; Schulaufgabe **II**
Tex-Mex [ˌteks'meks] texanisch-mexikanisch ⟨**III F2**,50⟩
text [tekst] Text; Textnachricht (SMS) **I**
than [ðæn; ðən] als *(bei Vergleichen)* **I**
to **thank** [θæŋk] danken **II**
thank God [ˌθæŋk 'gɒd] Gott sei Dank **II**
thank you letter ['θæŋk ju: ˌletə] Dankschreiben **I**
Thank you very much! [ˌθæŋk ju: veri 'mʌtʃ] Vielen Dank! Herzlichen Dank! **I**
thankful ['θæŋkfl] dankbar ⟨**III U2**,28⟩
thanks [θæŋks] danke **I**
that [ðæt; thət] dass **I**
that [ðæt] das; jenes **I**
that [ðæt] der, dem, den, die, das *(Relativpronomen)* **II**
the [ðə; ði] der, die (*auch pl.*), das **I**
the same [seɪm] derselbe (die-/das-) **I**
theatre ['θɪətə] Theater **I**
their [ðeə] ihr, ihre *(Plural)* **I**
them [ðem; ðəm] sie; ihnen **I**
then [ðen] dann **I**
therapy ['θerəpi] Therapie ⟨**III U4**,52⟩
there [ðeə] dort **I**
over there [ˌəʊvə 'ðeə] da drüben **I**
there are [ðeər‿'ɑ:] da sind; es gibt **I**
there's [ðeəz] (= there is) da ist, es gibt **I**
these [ði:z] diese (hier) **I**
these days ['ði:z ˌdeɪz] heutzutage **II**
they [ðeɪ] sie (*Plural*) **I**; *(hier:)*man **III U1**,12
they're (= they are) ['ðeə] sie sind **I**
thick [θɪk] dick *(nicht für Personen)*; dumm *(für Personen)* **II**
thief, *pl.* **thieves** [θi:f; θi:vz] Dieb(in) **III U1**,15
thin [θɪn] dünn **II**
thing [θɪŋ] Sache, Ding **I**
*to **think** (of) ['θɪŋk‿əv] denken (an) **I**
to think of ['θɪŋk‿əv] halten von **II**
third [θɜ:d] Drittel **III F2**,51
third [θɜ:d] dritte(-r/-s) **I**
thirsty ['θɜ:sti] durstig **III U5**,75
thirteen [θɜ:'ti:n] dreizehn **I**
thirteenth [θɜ:'ti:nθ] dreizehnte(-r/-s) **I**
thirty ['θɜ:ti] dreißig **I**
this [ðɪs] diese(-r/-s) **I**
those [ðəʊz] diese dort, jene **I**
two **thousand** [ˌtu: 'θaʊznd] zweitausend **III U1**,8
three [θri:] drei **I**
throat [θrəʊt] Kehle; Hals ⟨**III U5**,75⟩
through [θru:] durch **I**
throw [ˌθrəʊ] Wurf ⟨**III U6**,88⟩
*to **throw** [θrəʊ] werfen **I**
Thursday ['θɜ:zdeɪ] Donnerstag **I**
ticket ['tɪkɪt] Ticket, Fahrschein, Eintrittskarte **I**
to **tidy (up)** ['taɪdi] aufräumen, in Ordnung bringen **II**
tidy ['taɪdi] sauber, ordentlich **I**
tie [taɪ] Unentschieden ⟨**III U6**,89⟩
to **tie** [taɪ] binden, fesseln **II**
time [taɪm] Zeit **I**; Mal **I**
all the time [ˌɔ:l ðə 'taɪm] die ganze Zeit **I**
in time [ɪn 'taɪm] mit der Zeit ⟨**III EL**,105⟩
in time for [ɪn 'taɪm fə] rechtzeitig zu **III U1**,10
it's about time [ˌɪts‿əbaʊt 'taɪm] es ist höchste Zeit ⟨**III EL**,105⟩
most of the time ['məʊst‿əv ðə ˌtaɪm] meistens **III U3**,38
on time [ɒn 'taɪm] pünktlich **II**
time line ['taɪm laɪn] Zeitstrahl **III F1**,20
What time ... ? [wɒt 'taɪm] (Um) wie viel Uhr ... ? **I**
timetable ['taɪmteɪbl] Stundenplan; Fahrplan **II**
tin [tɪn] Dose, Büchse **I**
tip [tɪp] Tipp **I**
tired ['taɪəd] müde **I**
title ['taɪtl] Titel, Überschrift **I**
to [tʊ; tə] *Hier*: in; nach; zu **I**; bis **I**
toast [təʊst] Toast **II**
today [tə'deɪ] heute **I**
together [tə'geðə] zusammen, miteinander **I**
toilet ['tɔɪlɪt] Toilette ⟨**III EL**,100⟩
tomato, *pl.* **tomatoes** [tə'mɑ:təʊ] Tomate **II**
tomorrow [tə'mɒrəʊ] morgen **I**
ton [tʌn] Tonne (*Gewicht*) **I**
tonight [tə'naɪt] heute Abend/Nacht **II**
too [tu:] auch **I**; zu **I**
Me, too. [ˌmi: 'tu:] Ich auch. **II**
tool [tu:l] Werkzeug, Gerät **II**
tooth, *pl.* **teeth** [tu:θ; ti:θ] Zahn **I**
top [tɒp] Spitze, oberer Teil **II**; Top **III U4**,58
on top (of) [ɒn 'tɒp] obendrauf **II**
topic ['tɒpɪk] Thema **III U6**,91
topping ['tɒpɪŋ] Belag **III F2**,51
torch [tɔ:tʃ] Fackel; Taschenlampe ⟨**III EL**,104⟩
to **touch** [tʌtʃ] berühren; antippen **I**
tour [tʊə] Tour, Fahrt, Reise **I**
tourist ['tʊərɪst] Tourist **I**
towards [tə'wɔ:dz] in Richtung; auf ... zu, darauf zu **I**
towel ['taʊəl] Handtuch **I**
tower ['taʊə] Turm **II**
clock tower ['klɒk taʊə] Uhrenturm ⟨**III U1**,10⟩
town [taʊn] Stadt **I**
toy [tɔɪ] Spielzeug **II**
track and field [ˌtræk‿ənd 'fi:ld] Leichtathletik **III U6**,84
trading centre ['treɪdɪŋ ˌsentə] Handelszentrum ⟨**III F1**,21⟩
tradition [trə'dɪʃn] Tradition **I**
traditional [trə'dɪʃnl] traditionell **II**
traffic ['træfɪk] Verkehr **II**
traffic jam ['træfɪk ˌdʒæm] Stau **II**
trail [treɪl] Wanderweg **III U5**,68
train [treɪn] Zug **I**
to **train** [treɪn] trainieren, ausbilden **II**
training ['treɪnɪŋ] Training, Ausbildung **II**
to **translate** [trænz'leɪt] übersetzen **III U3**,47
translation [trænz'leɪʃn] Übersetzung **II**
transport ['træntspɔ:t] Transport **II**
means of transport *(sg. and pl.)* [ˌmi:nz‿əv 'træntspɔ:t] Transportmittel, Verkehrsmittel **II**
to **transport** [træn'spɔ:t] transportieren **II**
trap [træp] Falle **II**
*to be **trapped** [bi: 'træpt] in der Falle sitzen **III U5**,75
trash *(AE)* [træʃ] Abfall, Müll **II**
travel ['trævl] (das) Reisen **II**
travel agent's ['trævl ˌeɪdʒnts] Reisebüro **II**
to **travel** ['trævl] reisen **II**
treat [tri:t] besondere Freude; Belohnung **II**
to **treat** [tri:t] behandeln **II**
tree [tri:] Baum **I**
to **trek** [trek] wandern, marschieren **II**
pony **trekking** ['pəʊni ˌtrekɪŋ] Ponyreiten im Gelände **II**
to **tremble** ['trembl] zittern **II**
tribe [traɪb] Stamm **I**
trick [trɪk] Trick; Streich **I**
to **trick** [trɪk] austricksen, täuschen **I**
trifle ['traɪfl] *englischer Nachtisch* **I**
trip [trɪp] Trip, Reise, Ausflug **I**
to **trip** (over) [trɪp] stolpern (über) **II**
trouble [trʌbl] Ärger, Probleme **II**
trousers *pl.* ['traʊzəz] Hose **I**
trout, *pl.* **trout** [traʊt] Forelle **II**
truck [trʌk] Truck, Lastwagen **II**
true [tru:] wahr **I**
trumpet ['trʌmpɪt] Trompete **II**
to **trust** [trʌst] vertrauen **II**
truth [tru:θ] Wahrheit **II**
to **try** (on) [traɪ‿'ɒn] (an)probieren; versuchen **I**
T-shirt ['ti:ʃɜ:t] T-Shirt **II**
Tuesday ['tju:zdeɪ] Dienstag **I**
tug [tʌg] Ziehen; Zupfen ⟨**III U4**,60⟩
tune [tju:n] Melodie **II**
turkey ['tɜ:ki] Truthahn, Pute **I**
It's your **turn.** ['jɔ: tɜ:n] Du bist/Sie sind dran. **I**
to **turn** [tɜ:n] einbiegen, abbiegen; drehen, wenden **I**
to turn (into) ['tɜ:n‿ɪntə] werden; (sich) verwandeln in **III U5**,74
turning point ['tɜ:nɪŋ ˌpɔɪnt] Wendepunkt **III U4**,62
tutor ['tju:tə] Klassenlehrer(in) **I**
tutor group ['tju:tə ˌgru:p] Klasse (*in einer englischen Schule*) **I**
TV [ti:'vi:] Fernsehen; Fernseher **I**
to watch TV [ˌwɒtʃ ti:'vi:] fernsehen **I**
TV dinner [ˌti:vi: 'dɪnə] Fernsehmahlzeit ⟨**III F2**,50⟩
twelfth [twelfθ] zwölfte(-r/-s) **I**
twelve [twelv] zwölf **I**
twentieth ['twentiɪθ] zwanzigste(-r/-s) **I**
twenty ['twenti] zwanzig **I**
twenty-one [ˌtwenti'wʌn] einundzwanzig **I**
twice [twaɪs] zweimal **II**
two [tu:] zwei **I**
2-1 [ˌtu: 'wʌn] zwei zu eins **II**
a two-minute walk away from ... [ˌtu:mɪnɪt 'wɔ:k] zwei Minuten zu Fuß von ... entfernt **II**

two thousand [ˌtu: 'θaʊznd] zweitausend III U1,8
2.45 (point) ['tu: pɔɪnt ˌfɔ: 'faɪv] Komma *(bei Zahlenangaben)* I
two at a time [ˌtu:‿ət‿ə 'taɪm] zwei auf einmal ⟨III U3,44⟩
to **type** [taɪp] tippen III U5,72
type [taɪp] Typ III U4,54
typical (of) ['tɪpɪkl] typisch (für) I
tyre *(BE)* [taɪə] Reifen ⟨III EL,101⟩

U

Ugh! [ɜ:] Igitt! *(Ausruf des Ekels)* I
Uh huh. [ʌ'hʌ] Mhm. ⟨III EL,105⟩
unable [ʌn'eɪbl] unfähig III U5,74
uncle ['ʌŋkl] Onkel I
under ['ʌndə] unter I
*to **understand** [ˌʌndə'stænd] verstehen I
unhappy [ʌn'hæpi] unglücklich II
uniform ['ju:nɪfɔ:m] Uniform I
unit ['ju:nɪt] Kapitel; Einheit I
universe ['ju:nɪvɜ:s] Universum III U4,52
unnecessary [ʌn'nesəsri] unnötig III U5,70
to **unpack** [ʌn'pæk] auspacken III U4,60
until [ʌn'tɪl; n'tɪl] bis I
not until [nɒt‿ən'tɪl] nicht (be)vor; erst (wenn/als) *(s. Box auf S. 147)* III U3,42
up (to) [ʌp] *(hier:)* herbei (zu); auf … zu III U3,40
up to ['ʌp tə] bis zu III F3,81
up [ʌp] (hin)auf, hoch I
upstairs [ʌp'steəz] (nach) oben, im Obergeschoss I
us [ʌs] wir; uns I
US [ju:'es] Vereinigte Staaten; US-amerikanisch I
to **use** [ju:z] benutzen, verwenden I
useful ['ju:sfl] nützlich II
useless ['ju:sləs] nutzlos III U2,30
usual ['ju:ʒl] üblich II
usually ['ju:ʒli] normalerweise, gewöhnlich I

V

vacation *(AE)* [və'keɪʃn] Ferien, Urlaub II
Valentine's card ['væləntaɪnz ˌkɑ:d] Valentinskarte III U5,72
valley ['væli] Tal II
valuable ['væljuəbl] wertvoll III U4,61
vegetable ['vedʒtəbl] Gemüse I
vegetarian [ˌvedʒɪ'teəriən] Vegetarier(in) II
version ['vɜ:ʃn] Version II
very ['veri] sehr I
vet [vet] Tierarzt, Tierärztin I
to **vibrate** [vaɪ'breɪt] vibrieren III U4,54
victory ['vɪktri] Sieg III U6,87
video ['vɪdiəʊ] Video I
video clip ['vɪdiəʊ klɪp] Videoclip III F4,98
view [vju:] Aussicht, Sicht I
viewer ['vju:ə] Zuschauer(in) ⟨III F4,98⟩
village ['vɪlɪdʒ] Dorf I
visit ['vɪzɪt] Besuch II
to **visit** ['vɪzɪt] besuchen; besichtigen I
visitor ['vɪzɪtə] Besucher I

voice [vɔɪs] Stimme I
volcano, *pl.* **volcanoes** [vɒl'keɪnəʊ] Vulkan III U5,69

W

to **wait (for)** [weɪt] warten (auf) I
waiter ['weɪtə] Kellner, Bedienung II
*to **wake** (somebody) **up** [weɪk‿'ʌp] (jemanden) aufwecken; aufwachen I
walk [wɔ:k] Spaziergang I
a two-minute walk away from … [ˌtu:mɪnɪt 'wɔ:k] zwei Minuten zu Fuß von … entfernt II
to go for a walk [ˌgəʊ fər‿ə 'wɔ:k] spazieren gehen I
to **walk** [wɔ:k] gehen, laufen I
wall [wɔ:l] Wand; Mauer I
to **want (to)** ['wɒnt tə] wollen, mögen I
to want sb to do sth [wɒnt] wollen, dass jmd etw. tut II
warm [wɔ:m] warm I
to **warn** [wɔ:n] warnen II
to **wash** [wɒʃ] (sich) waschen; spülen I
to wash up [wɒʃ‿'ʌp] abwaschen, abspülen II
waste [weɪst] Abfall; Verschwendung III U5,70
watch [wɒtʃ] Armbanduhr III U1,13
to **watch** [wɒtʃ] beobachten, (sich) ansehen I
to watch TV [ˌwɒtʃ ti:'vi:] fernsehen I
Watch out! [wɒtʃ‿'aʊt] Achtung! Pass(t) auf! I
water ['wɔ:tə] Wasser I
waterproof ['wɔ:təpru:f] wasserdicht III U5,70
wave [weɪv] Welle I
to **wave** [weɪv] winken; schwenken I
way [weɪ] Weg; Art und Weise I
by the way [ˌbaɪ ðə 'weɪ] übrigens III U3,45
Milky Way [ˌmɪlki 'weɪ] Milchstraße II
No way! [ˌnəʊ 'weɪ] Auf keinen Fall! III U6,89
to be in a bad way [ɪn‿ə 'bæd ˌweɪ] in schlechter Verfassung sein I
we [wi:] wir I
we're [wɪə] (= we are) wir sind I
weak [wi:k] schwach I
weapon ['wepən] Waffe III U3,38
*to **wear** [weə] anhaben, tragen I
weather ['weðə] Wetter I
weather forecast ['weðə ˌfɔ:kɑ:st] Wettervorhersage II
website ['websaɪt] Website, Internetauftritt II
Wednesday ['wenzdeɪ] Mittwoch I
week [wi:k] Woche I
a week [ə 'wi:k] pro Woche, in der Woche II
What a week! [ˌwɒt‿ə 'wi:k] Was für eine Woche! II
weekend ['wi:kend] Wochenende I
to **weigh** [weɪ] wiegen I
to **welcome** ['welkəm] willkommen heißen II

You're **welcome.** [jɔ: 'welkəm] Bitte schön./Gern geschehen. III U5,77
Welcome! ['welkəm] Willkommen! I
well [wel] gesund III U3,45
Get well soon! [get ˌwel 'su:n] Gute Besserung! III U3,45
well [wel] gut I
as well [əz 'wel] auch III U6,88
well [wel] also; na ja; nun gut II
welly ['weli] Gummistiefel I
Welsh [welʃ] walisisch; Walisisch; Waliser(in) III U2,24
west [west] I
western ['westən] Western-; westlich II
wet [wet] nass I
to get wet [get 'wet] nass werden I
wetter and wetter [ˌwetər‿ənd 'wetə] immer nasser, immer verregneter II
whale [weɪl] Wal ⟨III U5,69⟩
what [wɒt] was I
What about you? [ˌwɒt‿əbaʊt 'ju:] Und dir/euch/Ihnen? Und du/ihr/Sie? I
What a pity! [ˌwɒt‿ə 'pɪti] Wie schade! II
What a week! [ˌwɒt‿ə 'wi:k] Was für eine Woche! II
What colour is/are … ? [ˌwɒt 'kʌlər‿ɪz/ɑ:] Welche Farbe hat/haben … ? I
what else [ˌwɒt‿'els] was sonst/noch II
What's … in English? [ˌwɒts … ɪn‿'ɪŋglɪʃ] Was heißt … auf Englisch? I
What's it like? [ˌwɒts‿ɪt 'laɪk] Wie ist es? II
What's missing? [ˌwɒts 'mɪsɪŋ] Was fehlt? I
What's the matter? [ˌwɒts ðə 'mætə] Was ist los? Was hast du? I
What's your name? [ˌwɒts jə 'neɪm] Wie heißt du/heißen Sie? I
What time … ? [wɒt 'taɪm] (Um) wie viel Uhr … ? I
wheat [wi:t] Weizen I
wheel [wi:l] Rad I
wheelchair ['wi:ltʃeə] Rollstuhl III U4,53
when [wen] wann; als; wenn I
where [weə] wo; wohin I
Where are you from? [ˌweər‿ə jə 'frɒm] Woher kommst du/kommt ihr/kommen Sie? I
Where … from? [ˌweə … 'frɒm] Woher …? I
wherever [weə'revə] wo(hin) auch immer III U6,89
whether ['weðə] ob III U6,86
which [wɪtʃ] welche(-r/-s) I
which [wɪtʃ] der, dem, den, die, das *(Relativpronomen)* II
while [waɪl] während I
to **whip** [wɪp] schlagen III F2,50
whisky ['wɪski] Whisky I
to **whisper** ['wɪspə] flüstern III U5,74
whistle ['wɪsl] Trillerpfeife III U5,70
to blow a whistle [ˌbləʊ‿ə'wɪsl] auf einer Trillerpfeife pfeifen III U6,89
white [waɪt] weiß I
white horses [waɪt 'hɔ:sɪz] Schaumkronen I
who [hu:] wer I; wem, wen I
who [hu:] der, dem, den, die *(Relativpronomen)* II

whole [həʊl] ganz II
wholewheat ['həʊlwi:t] Vollkornweizen ⟨III F2,51⟩
whose [hu:z] wessen I
whose [hu:z] dessen, deren *(Relativpronomen)* II
why [waɪ] warum I
wide [waɪd] groß; breit; weit I
wife, *pl.* **wives** [waɪf; waɪvz] Ehefrau II
wild [waɪld] wild II
wilderness ['wɪldənəs] Wildnis III U5,68
wildlife ['waɪldlaɪf] Tierwelt (in freier Wildbahn) II
***will** [wɪl] werden *(futurisch)* II
*to be **willing** to do sth [bi: 'wɪlɪŋ] ⟨III EL,105⟩
*to **win** [wɪn] gewinnen, siegen I
wind [wɪnd] Wind I
window ['wɪndəʊ] Fenster I
windsurfing ['wɪndsɜ:fɪŋ] Windsurfen II
wine [waɪn] Wein II
winner ['wɪnə] Gewinner(in), Sieger(in) II
winter ['wɪntə] Winter II
with [wɪð] mit I
without [wɪ'ðaʊt] ohne I
wizard ['wɪzəd] Zauberer II
woman, *pl.* **women** ['wʊmən; 'wɪmɪn] Frau I
to **wonder** ['wʌndə] sich Gedanken machen, sich fragen III U2,30
wonderful ['wʌndəfl] wunderbar II
***won't** [wəʊnt] nicht werden *(futurisch)* II
wood [wʊd] Wäldchen ⟨III EL,100⟩
wood [wʊd] Holz III U3,38
Woof! [wʊf] Wau! I
word [wɜ:d] Wort I
  words *(pl.)* [] *hier:* Text(e) II
  Find the odd word out! [ˌɒd wɜ:d‿'aʊt] Finde das Wort, das nicht in die Gruppe passt! *(Wortschatzübung)* I
  key word ['ki: wɜ:d] Stichwort; Schlüsselbegriff III U1,18
  Word power ['wɜ:d ˌpaʊə] *Besondere Wortschatzübung* I
work [wɜ:k] Arbeit I
  out of work [ˌaʊt‿əv 'wɜ:k] arbeitslos III U2,27
  work of art [ˌwɜ:k‿əv‿'ɑ:t] Kunstwerk ⟨III U4,53⟩
to **work** [wɜ:k] arbeiten I; funktionieren II
workman, *pl.* **workmen** ['wɜ:kmən] Handwerker I
to **work out** [ˌwɜ:k‿'aʊt] herausbringen, herausfinden; ausarbeiten III U1,9
worksheet ['wɜ:kʃi:t] Arbeitsblatt ⟨III EL,106⟩
workshop ['wɜ:kʃɒp] Workshop, Werkstatt III U3,38
world [wɜ:ld] Erde, Welt I
*to be **worried** [bi: 'wʌrid] besorgt, beunruhigt sein I
to **worry** ['wʌri] (sich) Sorgen machen I
***would** [wʊd] würde(n) II
  I'd [aɪd] Ich würde II
  Would you like ...? [ˌwʊd jə 'laɪk] Möchtest du/möchten Sie/möchtet ihr ...? II
wow! [waʊ] Wow! Toll! I
to **wrap** [ræp] einwickeln ⟨III U2,28⟩
wreck [rek] Wrack I
*to **write** [raɪt] schreiben I
DVD **writer** [ˌdi:vi:di: 'raɪtə] DVD-Brenner ⟨III EL,105⟩
wrong [rɒŋ] falsch I
  to be wrong [bi: 'rɒŋ] Unrecht haben II
  to go wrong [gəʊ 'rɒŋ] schief gehen II

Y

yard [jɑ:d] Hof I
yeah [jeə] *umgangsspr.*: ja I
year [jɪə] Jahr; Jahrgang I
  for many years [fə ˌmæni 'jɪəz] viele Jahre lang III U1,10
yearbook ['jɪəbʊk] Jahrbuch II
yellow ['jeləʊ] gelb I
yes [jes] ja I
Yessir-ee! [ˌjessə'ri:] Jawoll! ⟨III EL,105⟩
yesterday ['jestədeɪ] gestern I
  the day before yesterday [ðə ˌdeɪ bɪfɔ: 'jestədeɪ] vorgestern I
yet [jet] schon; noch II
yoghurt ['jɒgət] Joghurt II
you [ju:; jə] du, ihr, Sie I; man I
  bless you ['bles ju:] Gesundheit! II
  You bet! [ju: 'bet] Das kannst du mir aber glauben! ⟨III U2,24⟩
  you lot ['ju: ˌlɒt] ihr alle I
  You're welcome. [jɔ: 'welkəm] Bitte schön./Gern geschehen. III U5,77
young [jʌŋ] jung I
your [jɔ:; jə] dein(e); euer/eure; Ihr(e) I
  It's your turn. ['jɔ: tɜ:n] Du bist/Sie sind dran. I
help **yourself** [ˌhelp jɔ:'self] bediene dich!/bedienen Sie sich! II
Yuk! [jʌk] Igitt! I
yummy ['jʌmi] lecker I

Z

zipper ['zɪpə] Reißverschluss III U4,60
zone [zəʊn] Zone III U5,68
zoo [zu:] Zoo, Tierpark I

Boys' names

Alan ['ælən] I
Alex ['ælɪks] III U3,40
Anil [æ'ni:l] I
Arthur ['ɑ:θə] I
Balujee ['bɑ:luˌdʒi:] I
Barry ['bæri] II
Bart [bɑ:t] III F4,99
Ben [ben] III U5,72
Bill [bɪl] II
Bobby ['bɒbi] III U6,86
Brooklyn ['brʊklɪn] I
Bruce [bru:s] II
Chad [tʃæd] II
Chuck [tʃʌk] II
Colin ['kɒlɪn] I
Daniel ['dænjəl] I
Darren ['dærn] III U1,13
Dave [deɪv] II
David ['deɪvɪd] I
Ed [ed] II
Eddy ['edi] I
Evan ['evn] III U1,8
Frank [fræŋk] I
Gareth ['gærəθ] III U1,8
George [dʒɔ:dʒ] ⟨III EL,105⟩
Hanif [hæ'ni:f] I
Harold ['hærəld] III F1,21
Henry ['henri] II
Homer ['həʊmə] III F4,99
Jack [dʒæk] I
Jason ['dʒeɪsn] II
Jerome [dʒə'rəʊm] III U4,54
Jerry ['dʒeri] III F3,80
Jim [dʒɪm] III U6,85
John [dʒɒn] II
José [heʊ'zeɪ] I
Joshua ['dʒɒʃuə] I
Kevin ['kevɪn] II
Lenny ['leni] I
Liam ['li:əm] ⟨III EL,101⟩
Lou [lu:] II
Mark [mɑ:k] I
Martin ['mɑ:tɪn] III U3,40
Marty ['mɑ:ti] III U5,74
Marvin ['mɑ:vɪn] III U6,88
Nathan ['neɪθn] ⟨III EL,106⟩
Nick [nɪk] III U5,77
Ollie ['ɒli] II
Owen ['əʊɪn] III U2,23
Paul [pɔ:l] I
Percival ['pɜ:sɪvl] III U2,30
Pete [pi:t] III U4,58
Philip ['fɪlɪp] II
Rajiv [rə'dʒi:v] I
Rob [rɒb] III U5,74
Robert ['rɒbət] I
Romeo ['rəʊmiəʊ] I
Ryan [raɪən] Ryan I
Sam [sæm] I
Scott [skɒt] II
Slim [slɪm] II
Steve [sti:v] III U1,14
Tejinder [tə'dʒɪndə] I
Tim [tɪm] III U3,43
Tom [tɒm] I
Tommy ['tɒmi] I
Wayne [weɪn] II
William ['wɪljəm] III F1,21
Willy ['wɪli] II

Girls' names

Angela ['ændʒlə] III U1,15
Anna ['ænə] II
Annie ['æni] II
Anuja [æ'nu:dʒə] I
Barbara ['bɑ:brə] III U4,53
Becky ['beki] I
Bessy ['besi] III U6,87
Bronwen ['brɒnwen] III U2,23
Caitlin ['keɪtlɪn] II
Carina [kə'ri:nə] II
Caroline ['kærlaɪn] III U3,39
Cathy ['kæθi] III U6,85
Ceri ['keri] III U1,8

Cheryl ['tʃerl] II
Donna ['dɒnə] II
Emily ['emɪli] I
Emma ['emə] II
Fiona [fi'əʊnə] I
Gemma ['dʒemə] I
Glenda ['glendə] III U2, 33
Grace [greɪs] I
Gwen [gwen] III U2, 27
Hazel ['heɪzl] II
Helen ['helɪn] I
Jamila [dʒə'mi:lə] I
Janet ['dʒænɪt] I
Jeanie ['dʒi:ni] II
Jenny ['dʒeni] I
Jill [dʒɪl] III U2, 33
Joan [dʒəʊn] II
Joanne [dʒəʊ'æn] II
Judy ['dʒu:di] II
Kim [kɪm] I
Kristi ['krɪsti] II
Laura ['lɔ:rə] II
Lisa ['li:sə] III F4, 99
Liz [lɪz] II
Lizzy ['lɪzi] I
Lucy ['lu:si] III U5, 77
Maggie ['mægi] III F4, 99
Margaret ['mɑ:grət] I
Marge [mɑ:dʒ] III F4, 99
Mari ['mɑ:ri] III U2, 23
Martha ['mɑ:θə] II
Mary ['meəri] I
Mary-Beth [ˌmeəri 'beθ] I
Meg [meg] I
Milly ['mɪli] II
Naomi ['neɪəmi:; neɪ'əʊmi] III U4, 58
Natasha [nə'tæʃə] II
Noreen [nɒ'ri:n] I
Pam [pæm] III U1, 8
Pat [pæt] I
Peggy ['pegi] I
Polly ['pɒli] II
Rita ['ri:tə] I
Rosa ['rəʊzə] I
Sally ['sæli] II
Sarah ['seərə] Sarah I
Sharon ['ʃærən] II
Sue [su:] I
Susan ['su:zn] ⟨III EL, 106⟩
Susie ['su:zi] III U4, 60
Tina ['ti:nə] II
Tricia ['trɪʃə] III U2, 26
Vanessa [və'nesə] I
Vicky ['vɪki] III F3, 80
Victoria [vɪk'tɔ:riə] I

Surnames

Batty ['bæti] III U3, 49
Baxter ['bækstə] III U5, 70
Braden ['breɪdn] ⟨III EL, 101⟩
Bryan [braɪən] II
Burton ['bɜ:tn] I
Chung [tʃʌŋ] II
Clifton ['klɪftn] ⟨III EL, 100⟩
Cooper ['ku:pə] I
Croft [krɒft] Croft I
Csonka ['tʃɒŋkə] II
Dane [deɪn] Dane I
Dixon ['dɪksən] I
Eden ['i:dn] III U3, 39
Eglamore ['egləmɔ:] II
Fernandez [fɜ:'nændez] II
Fleetwood ['fli:twʊd] II
Fox [fɒks] ⟨III EL, 106⟩
Franklin ['fræŋklɪn] III U6, 88
Gerlernter [ˌgə'lɜ:ntə] II
Gooch [gu:tʃ] II
Gray [greɪ] II
Griffiths ['grɪfɪθs] III U3, 40
Grimson ['grɪmsn] III U6, 88
Hamilton ['hæmltən] II
Holden ['həʊldən] II
Hudson ['hʌdsn] III U4, 53
Jergensen ['dʒɜ:gənsn] II
Johnson ['dʒɒntsn] II
Jones [dʒəʊnz] I
Kellerman ['keləmən] II
Kershaw ['kɜ:ʃɔ:] III U6, 85
Lepage [lə'peɪdʒ] II
Lewinsky [lu:'ɪnzki] III U6, 85
Lo [ləʊ] III U6, 85
Logan ['ləʊgən] II
MacDonald [mək'dɒnld] I
Morgan ['mɔ:gn] III U1, 8
Nelson ['nelsn] ⟨III EL, 106⟩
O'Brien [əʊ'braɪən] III U4, 60
Penrose ['penrəʊz] I
Pilewski [pɪ'levski] I
Pledger ['pledʒə] II
Potter ['pɒtə] I
Preston ['prestən] II
Robinson ['rɒbɪnsn] II
Rollins ['rɒlɪnz] II
Rudd [rʌd] I
Simpson ['sɪmpsən] III F4, 99
Singh [sɪŋ] I
Smith [smɪθ] I
Snyder ['snaɪdə] III U6, 86
Spencer ['spentsə] III U1, 15
Taylor ['teɪlə] III U3, 49
Wallace ['wɒlɪs] I
Walters ['wɒltəz] II
Wray [reɪ] I

Place names

Aberfan [ˌæbə'væn] III U2, 22
Aberystwyth [ˌæbə'rɪstwɪθ] III U2, 22
Alaska [ə'læskə] I
Alps [ælps] Alpen II
America [ə'merɪkə] I
Arndale Road [ˌɑ:ndeɪl 'rəʊd] I
Arnot Hill Park [ˌɑ:nət hɪl 'pɑ:k] I
Asia ['eɪʃə] Asien III F1, 20
Atlantic [ət'læntɪk] II
Australia ['ɒstreɪliə] I
Baker Street ['beɪkə ˌstri:t] III U1, 9
Bamburgh ['bæmbrə] I
Beastmarket Hill [ˌbi:stmɑ:kɪt 'hɪl] I
Belfast [bel'fɑ:st] I
Belsize Road [ˌbelsaɪz 'rəʊd] III U2, 2
Bermuda [bə'mju:də] III U6, 85
Berwick-upon-Tweed [ˌberɪk‿əpɒn 'twi:d] I
Big Harcar Rock [bɪg ˌhɑ:kə 'rɒk] I
Billings ['bɪlɪŋz] II
Birmingham ['bɜ:mɪŋəm] I
Blackpool ['blækpu:l] I
Boston ['bɒstn] I
Broadway ['brɔ:dweɪ] I
Caerleon [kɑ:'li:ən] III U2, 22
Caernarfon [kə'nɑ:vn] III U2, 25
California [ˌkælɪ'fɔ:niə] I
Camden ['kæmdən] III U1, 8
Camden Town ['kæmdən ˌtaʊn] III U1, 9
Camelot ['kæməlɒt] III U2, 30
Cardiff ['kɑ:dɪf] I
Cascade Mountains [ˌkæskeɪd 'maʊntɪnz] III U5, 68
Castle Road [ˌkɑ: sl 'rəʊd] I
Central Park [ˌsentrl 'pɑ:k] I
Chapel Bar [ˌtʃæpl 'bɑ:] I
Chicago [ʃɪ'kɑ:gəʊ] II
China ['tʃaɪnə] China II
Chinatown ['tʃaɪnətaʊn] I
Colorado [ˌkɒlr'ɑ:dəʊ] II
Conwy ['kɒnwi] III U2, 22
Cornwall ['kɔ:nwɔ:l] I
Cumberland ['kʌmblənd] II
Delhi ['deli] I
Denmark ['denmɑ:k] Dänemark II
Denver ['denvə] I
Derwentwater ['dɜ:wəntˌwɔ:tə] II
Devon ['devn] I
Dinosaur Ridge [ˌdaɪnəsɔ: 'rɪdʒ] II
the **Docklands** ['dɒklændz] Docklands *(Hafengebiet in London)* ⟨III U1, 12⟩
Dockray ['dɒkri] II
Dundee [dʌn'di:] I
Edinburgh ['edɪnbrə] I
Edwards Lane [ˌedwədz 'leɪn] I
Egypt ['i:dʒɪpt] Ägypten ⟨III F1, 20⟩
England ['ɪŋglənd] I
Europe ['jʊərəp] Europa II
Euston Station [ˌju:stn 'steɪʃn] ⟨III U1, 17⟩
Everglades National Park [ˌevəgleɪdz ˌnæʃnl 'pɑ:k] I
Exchange Walk [ɪksˌtʃeɪndʒ 'wɔ:k] I
Farne Islands [fɑ:n‿'aɪləndz] I
Florida ['flɒrɪdə] I
France [frɑ:nts] I
Friar Lane [ˌfraɪə 'leɪn] I
Germany ['dʒɜ:məni] I
Glamorgan [glə'mɔ:gən] III U2, 23
Gotham City [ˌgɒθəm 'sɪti] II
Grand Canyon [ˌgrænd 'kænjən] I
Great Gable [ˌgreɪt 'geɪbl] II
Greece [gri:s] Griechenland ⟨III F1, 20⟩
Happyville ['hæpivɪl] II
Hastings ['heɪstɪŋz] III F1, 21
Haywood ['heɪwʊd] I
Heathrow [ˌhi:θ'rəʊ] I
Highbury ['haɪbri] II
Holyhead [ˌhɒli'hed] III U2, 22
Honister ['hɒnɪstə] II
Hudson River [ˌhʌdsn 'rɪvə] I
Hull [hʌl] I
Hungary ['hʌŋgri] Ungarn II
India ['ɪndiə] I
Ireland ['aɪələnd] I
Johannesburg [dʒəʊ'hænɪsbɜ:g] I

Kansas ['kænzəs] III F3, 80
Kensington ['kenzɪŋtən] III U1, 9
Keswick ['kezɪk] II
Kingston ['kɪŋstən] ⟨III U1, 17⟩
King Street ['kɪŋ ˌstri:t] I
Lake District ['leɪk ˌdɪstrɪkt] II
Lakewood ['leɪkwʊd] II
Larwood Grove [ˌlɑ:wʊd 'grəʊv] I
Leicester Square [ˌlestə 'skweə] III U1, 9
Lexington ['leksɪŋtən] II
Leytonstone ['leɪtnstəʊn] I
Liverpool ['lɪvəpu:l] I
Llandudno [læn'dɪdnəʊ] III U2, 22
London ['lʌndən] I
Long Row [ˌlɒŋ 'rəʊ] I
Los Angeles [lɒs‿'ændʒɪli:z] I
Madison Square Garden [ˌmædɪsn ˌskweə 'gɑ:dn] I
Maid Marian Way [ˌmeɪd ˌmæriən 'weɪ] I
Manchester ['mæntʃɪstə] I
Manhattan [mæn'hætn] I
Mansfield Road [ˌmænsfi:ld 'rəʊd] I
Market Square [ˌmɑ:kɪt 'skweə] I
Market Street ['mɑ:kɪt ˌstri:t] I
Massachusetts [ˌmæsə'tʃu:sɪts] II
Mexico ['meksɪkəʊ] I
Miami [maɪ'æmi] II
the **Midwest** [ˌmɪd'west] Mittlerer Westen III F3, 80
Mississippi River [ˌmɪsɪsɪpi 'rɪvə] I
Montana [mɒn'tænə] II
Moscow ['mɒskəʊ] Moskau ⟨III U4, 60⟩
Mount Rainier [ˌmaʊnt 'reɪniə] III U5, 69
Mount St. Helens [ˌmaʊnt snt 'helənz] III U5, 72
Mount Street ['maʊnt ˌstri:t] I
Munich ['mju:nɪk] I
Naples ['neɪplz] Neapel II
Nethercott ['neðəkət] I
Newcastle-upon-Tyne [ˌnju:kɑ:sl‿əpɒn 'taɪn] I
New England [ˌnju:‿'ɪŋglənd] Neuengland III F3, 80
Newport ['nju:pɔ:t] III U2, 22
New York [ˌnju: 'jɔ:k] I
New York City [ˌnju: jɔ:k 'sɪti] I
New Zealand [ˌnju: 'zi:lənd] III U2, 24
Niagara Falls [naɪˌægrə 'fɔ:lz] I
Normandy ['nɔ:məndi] III F1, 21
Northern Ireland [ˌnɔ:ðn‿'aɪələnd] I
North Sea [ˌnɔ:θ 'si:] I
Northumbria [nɔ:'θʌmbriə] I
Nottingham ['nɒtɪŋəm] I
Nottingham Road [ˌnɒtɪŋəm 'rəʊd] I
Notting Hill [ˌnɒtɪŋ 'hɪl] III U1, 9
Old Kent Road [ˌəʊld ˌkent 'rəʊd] ⟨III U1, 17⟩
Old Market Square [ˌəʊld ˌmɑ:kɪt 'skweə] I
Omaha ['əʊmahɑ:] II
Oxclose Lane [ˌɒkskləʊs 'leɪn] I
Oxford Circus [ˌɒksfəd 'sɜ:kəs] III U1, 9
Parliament Street ['pɑ:ləmənt ˌstri:t] I
Penryn [pen'rɪn] ⟨III EL, 101⟩
Philadelphia [ˌfɪlə'delfiə] I
Piccadilly [ˌpɪkə'dɪli] III U1, 9
Pontypridd [ˌpɒntɪ'pri:ð] III U2, 22
Puget Sound [ˌpju:dʒət 'saʊnd] III U5, 69
Republic of Ireland [rɪˌpʌblɪk‿əv‿'aɪələnd] I
Richmond ['rɪtʃmənd] ⟨III U1, 17⟩
Rocky Mountains [ˌrɒki 'maʊntɪnz] I
Rome [rəʊm] Rom ⟨III F1, 20⟩
San Diego [ˌsæn di'eɪgəʊ] I
San Francisco [ˌsæn frən'sɪskəʊ] II
Scotland ['skɒtlənd] I
Seahouses ['si:haʊzɪz] I
Seattle [si'ætl] II
Sherwood ['ʃɜ:wʊd] I
Sherwood Forest [ˌʃɜ:wʊd 'fɒrɪst] I
Silvertop ['sɪlvəˌtɒp] II
Smithy Row [ˌsmɪði 'rəʊ] I
Snowdon ['snəʊdn] III U2, 22
Snowdonia [snəʊ'dəʊniə] III U2, 22
South Africa [ˌsaʊθ‿'æfrɪkə] I
South Parade [ˌsaʊθ pə'reɪd] I
South Street Seaport [ˌsaʊθ stri:t 'si:pɔ:t] I
Southwark ['sʌðək] ⟨III U1, 17⟩
St Peter's Gate [snt 'pi:təz ˌgeɪt] I
Stratford-upon-Avon [ˌstrætfəd‿əpɒn‿'eɪvn] ⟨III EL, 106⟩
Swansea ['swɒnzi] III U2, 22
Swiss Cottage [ˌswɪs 'kɒtɪdʒ] III U1, 9
Texas ['teksəs] I
the **Thames** [temz] I
Thoresby Park [ˌθɔ:zbi 'pɑ:k] I
Tower Hill [ˌtaʊə 'hɪl] III U1, 9
UK [ju:'keɪ] Vereinigtes Königreich von Großbritannien und Nordirland I
Ullswater ['ʌlzˌwɔ:tə] II
United Kingdom [ju:ˌnaɪtɪd 'kɪŋdəm] Vereinigtes Königreich von Großbritannien und Nordirland I
United States of America [ju:ˌnaɪtɪd 'steɪts‿əv‿ə'merɪkə] Vereinigte Staaten von Amerika I
the **USA** [ju:es'eɪ] USA I
Wales [weɪlz] I
Washington ['wɒʃɪŋtən] I
Washington, D.C. [ˌwɒʃɪŋtən ˌdi:'si:] I
Watford ['wɒtfəd] ⟨III EL, 106⟩
the **West End** [ˌwest 'end] III U1, 8
Westminster [west'mɪntstə] III U1, 10
Wheeler Gate ['wi:lə ˌgeɪt] I
Yellowstone National Park [ˌjeləʊstəʊn ˌnæʃnl 'pɑ:k] II
Yorkshire ['jɔ:kʃə] I
Yorkshire Dales [ˌjɔ:kʃə 'deɪlz] ⟨III EL, 101⟩

Other names

Archway Tavern [ˌɑ:tʃweɪ 'tævn] ⟨III U1, 17⟩
Arena [ə'ri:nə] II
Ballard ['bæləd] III U6, 88
Bamburgh Castle [ˌbæmbrə 'kɑ:sl] I
Barker ['bɑ:kə] I
Big Apple [ˌbɪg‿'æpl] I
Big Ben [ˌbɪg 'ben] III U1, 10
Bluebell ['blu:bel] I
Bronco Bill ['brɒŋkəʊ 'bɪl] II
Buckingham Palace [ˌbʌkɪŋəm 'pælɪs] III U1, 9
Burtons' Bike Shop [ˌbɜ:tnz 'baɪk ʃɒp] I
City Ground [ˌsɪti 'graʊnd] II
City Information Centre [ˌsɪti‿ɪnfə'meɪʃn ˌsentə] I
Cooper Courier [ˌku:pə 'kʊriə] II
Crow [krəʊ] *Name eines Indianerstammes* II
Day Rider Ticket [ˌdeɪ 'raɪdə ˌtɪkɪt] I
Disney World ['dɪzni ˌwɜ:ld] I
Earth Keepers ['ɜ:θ ˌki:pəz] *Umweltschutzorganisation* II
Easter ['i:stə] Ostern II
Empire State Building [ˌempaɪə 'steɪt ˌbɪldɪŋ] I
Evening Post [ˌi:vnɪŋ 'pəʊst] Abendpost *(Name einer Zeitung)* II
FA Cup [ˌef‿eɪ 'kʌp] *Pokal des englischen Fußballverbands, vgl. DFB-Pokal* II
Forfarshire ['fɔ:fəʃə] I
Giants ['dʒaɪənts] I
the **Globe Theatre** ['gləʊb ˌθɪətə] III U1, 11
Golden Gate Bridge [ˌgəʊldn ˌgeɪt 'brɪdʒ] I
Grace Darling Museum [ˌgreɪs ˌdɑ:lɪŋ mju:'zi:əm] I
Greenfield Farm [ˌgri:nfi:ld 'fɑ:m] I
Halloween [ˌhæləʊ'i:n] Halloween *(Tag vor Allerheiligen)* II
Haywood School [ˌheɪwʊd 'sku:l] I
Hillside Farm [ˌhɪlsaɪd 'fɑ:m] I
Hogwarts ['hɒgwəts] II
Hokey Cokey [ˌhəʊki 'kəʊki] *Name eines Tanzes* I
the **Houses of Parliament** [ðə ˌhaʊzɪz‿əv 'pɑ:ləmənt] III U1, 10
Information Centre [ɪnfə'meɪʃn ˌsentə] I
Jubilee Line ['dʒu:bɪli: ˌlaɪn] III U1, 9
Kennedy Space Center [ˌkenədi 'speɪs ˌsentə] I
King Ethelred [kɪŋ‿'eθlred] *brit. Spiel* I
Koolkats ['ku:lkæts] II
Lazy G [ˌleɪzi 'dʒi:] II
London Eye [ˌlʌndən‿'aɪ] I
Longstone Lighthouse [ˌlɒŋstəʊn 'laɪthaʊs] I
Major Oak [ˌmeɪdʒər‿'əʊk] II
Martins Media [ˌmɑ:tɪnz 'mi:diə] I
Monny ['mɒni] I
National Museum of the American Indian [ˌnæʃnl mju:'zi:əm‿əv ði‿əˌmerɪkn‿'ɪndiən] I
Nuclear Puppy [ˌnju:kliə 'pʌpi] II
the **Olympics** *(Olympic Games)* [əʊ'lɪmpɪks; əʊˌlɪmpɪk 'geɪmz] Olympiade, Olympische Spiele III U4, 53
Oxford Street ['ɒksfəd ˌstri:t] III U1, 8
Pantglas Junior School [ˌpæntgləs 'dʒu:niə sku:l] ⟨III U2, 28⟩
the **Paralympics** [ˌpærə'lɪmpɪks] Paralympics *(Behindertenolympiade)* ⟨III U4, 53⟩
Pentium ['pentiəm] *Name eines Mikroprozessors* ⟨III EL, 105⟩
Pike Place Market [ˌpaɪk pleɪs 'mɑ:kɪt] III U5, 69
Rock City [ˌrɒk 'sɪti] II
Rockefeller Center [ˌrɒkəfelə 'sentə] I
Romeo and Juliet [ˌrəʊmiəʊ‿ənd 'dʒu:liət] III U1, 11
Rusty ['rʌsti] II
Seafair ['si:feə] III U5, 69
Simon says [ˌsaɪmən 'sez] *Brit. Spiel* I
Space Needle ['speɪs ˌni:dl] III U5, 68
Springfield Farm [ˌsprɪŋfi:ld 'fɑ:m] I
Statue of Liberty [ˌstætʃu:‿əv 'lɪbəti] I

St Peter's Church [snt ˌpiːtəz ˈtʃɜːtʃ] I
Strong Wind [ˌstrɒŋ ˈwɪnd] II
Tabby [ˈtæbi] I
Tate Modern [ˌteɪt ˈmɒdn] III U1, 8
Thanksgiving [ˌθæŋksˈɡɪvɪŋ] II
The Bell Inn [ðə ˌbel‿ˈɪn] I
The Tales of Robin Hood [ˌteɪlz‿əv rɒbɪn ˈhʊd] II
The Underdogs [ðɪ ˈʌndədɒɡz] I
Tower Bridge [ˌtaʊə ˈbrɪdʒ] III U1, 8
the**Tower of London** [ðə ˌtaʊər‿əv ˈlʌndən] III U1, 8
Underground [ˈʌndəɡraʊnd] Londoner U-Bahn III U1, 9
Victoria Shopping Centre [vɪkˌtɔːriə ˈʃɒpɪŋ ˌsentə] I

Famous names

Alan a Dale [ˌælən‿ə ˈdeɪl] II
Amelia Earhart [əˌmiːliə ˈeəhɑːt] III F3, 80
Arsenal [ˈɑːsnl] II
Atomic Kitten [əˌtɒmɪk ˈkɪtn] II
Batman [ˈbætmæn] II
Blondie [ˈblɒndi] II
Boudicca [ˈbuːdɪkə] III F1, 21
Bruce Springsteen [ˌbruːs ˈsprɪŋstiːn] III F3, 81
Cinderella [ˌsɪndrˈelə] Aschenputtel II
Daniel Boone [ˌdænjəl ˈbuːn] ⟨III EL, 100⟩
David Beckham [ˌdeɪvɪd ˈbekəm] I
Donald Duck [ˌdɒnld ˈdʌk] II
Friar Tuck [ˌfraɪə ˈtʌk] II
Grace Darling [ˌɡreɪs ˈdɑːlɪŋ] Grace Darling I
Hadrian [ˈheɪdriən] III F1, 20
Harry Potter [ˌhæri ˈpɒtə] II
Hermione Granger [hɜːˌmaɪəni ˈɡreɪndʒə] II
Huckleberry Finn [ˌhʌklberi ˈfɪn] II
the **Hulk** [hʌlk] II
John Rolfe [ˌdʒɒn ˈrɒlf] II
the **Joker** [ˈdʒəʊkə] II
Jon Bon Jovi [ˌdʒɒn bɒn ˈdʒeʊvi] I
King Arthur [ˌkɪŋ‿ˈɑːθə] König Artus ⟨III U2, 24⟩
Lara Croft [ˌlɑːrə ˈkrɒft] II
Lenny Kravitz [ˌleni ˈkrævɪts] I
Letters to Cleo [ˌletəz tə ˈkliːəʊ] ⟨III U5, 71⟩
The Levellers [ðə ˈlevləz] ⟨III U1, 17⟩
Little John [ˌlɪtl ˈdʒɒn] II
Lou Reed [ˌluː ˈriːd] ⟨III U6, 91⟩
Madonna [məˈdɒnə] I
Maid Marian [ˌmeɪd ˈmæriən] II
Manchester United [ˌmæntʃɪstə juːˈnaɪtɪd] I
Marla Runyan [ˌmɑːlə ˈrʌnjən] III U6, 84
Michael Jackson [ˌmaɪkl ˈdʒæksn] II
Mickey Mouse [ˌmɪki ˈmaʊs] II
MTV [ˌemtiːˈviː] II
Old Moses [ˌəʊld ˈməʊzɪz] II
Paragons [ˈpærəɡənz] II
Pocahontas [ˌpɒkəˈhɒntəs] II
The Rasmus [ðə ˈræːzməs] ⟨III U4, 62⟩
REM [ˌɑːriːˈem] ⟨III U2, 27⟩
Rick Mansfield [ˌrɪk ˈmænsfiːld] I
Robbie Williams [ˌrɒbi ˈwɪljəmz] I
Robin Hood [ˌrɒbɪn ˈhʊd] I
Robin Hood and his Merry Men [ˌrɒbɪn ˈhʊd‿ənd hɪz ˌmeri ˈmen] II
Ron Weasley [ˌrɒn ˈwiːzli] II
Sherlock Holmes [ˌʃɜːlɒk ˈhəʊmz] III U1, 14
Sir Guy of Gisborne [sɜː ˌɡaɪ‿əv ˈɡɪzbɔːn] II
Sir Kay [ˌsɜː ˈkeɪ] III U2, 31
Sir Lancelot [ˌsɜː ˈlɑːntsəlɒt] III U2, 30
Stephen Hawking [ˌstiːvn ˈhɔːkɪŋ] III U4, 52
Superman [ˈsuːpəmæn] II
Tom Sawyer [ˌtɒm ˈsɔːjə] II
U2 [juːˈtuː] II
Voldemort [ˈvɒldəmɔːt] II

Bildquellen: US1: (1) Corbis/Bohemian Nomad Picturemakers; US1: (2) Corbis/Holmes; (3,4) Avenue Images GmbH/Rubberball; S.3: DigitalVision; S.8: (1) Getty Images/stone/Loewenherz; (2) Corbis/Stockwell; (3) Corbis/Sayer; (4) Corbis/ Sharmin; (5) Getty Images/stone/Enderbee; (6) www.britainonview.com; S.9: (1) Corbis/London Aerial Photo Library; (2) Corbis/Oksanen; (3) www.britainonview.com; (4) Getty Images RF/ Photodisc; S.10: Getty Images/ Photographers Choice/Pritchard; S.11: Corbis/ Wheeler; S.12: (1) Corbis/ Hellestad; (2) Getty Images/taxi/Campbell; S.16: Klett-Archiv/Dekelver; S.17: Song: © Wintrup Musikverlag Walter Holzbauer, Detmold; S. 17: (1,3) Mirror Syndication Internat.; (2) Corbis/Peterson; S.18: (1) Alamy Images/Headline Pictures; (2) Image 100/RF; S.19: Corbis/Firefly Productions; S.21: Corbis/Dagli Orti; S.22: (1,2) Alamy Images/Morgan; (3) Corbis/Ward; (4) www.britainonview.com; (5) Corbis/Boys; S.23: (1,2) www.britainonview.com; S.23: (3) Corbis/Conger; S.25: www.britainonview.com; S.26: (1) Alamy Images/The Photolibrary Wales; (2) PhotoAlto; (3) Corbis/Estall; S.27: Song: © by NIGHT GARDEN MUSIC/WARNER TAMERLANE PUBL. NEUE WELT MUSIKVERLAG GmbH, Hamburg. WARNER/CHAPPELL MUSIC GERMANY GmbH & Co.; S. 27: (1) Corbis/Kaufmann; S.28: Picture-Alliance/dpa; S.31: Picture-Alliance/akg-images; S.32: CartoonStock Ltd/Hagen; S.35: Getty Images/PhotoDisc RF; S.38: (1,3) Corbis/Lenars; (2,5) Internet/Screenshot/Fjordside; (4) Siddorn; S.39: (1) Siddorn; (2) Corbis/Lenars; (3,4) Internet/ Screenshot/ Fjordside; (5) Ashby; S.40: (1) Furor Normannicus/Borgwardt; S.46: MEV; S.48: defd; S.49: (1) www.cartoonstock.com/Schwadron; S.50: (1) Stockfood Photo Stock Agency/Golden Goose Prod.; (2) Stockfood Photo Stock Agency/Schieren; (3) Corbis/Fukuhara Inc.; (4) MEV Verlag GmbH; S.51: (1) Stockfood Photo Stock Agency/Prost; (2) Stockfood Photo Stock Agency/Carlott; S.52: (1) Corbis/Ressmeyer; (2) Corbis/Colton; (3) Corbis/Rotman; S.53: (1) Corbis/Hamilton; (2) Picture-Alliance/ Zucchi; (3) Vario-Press; S.56: Fotoagentur Version; S.57: Corbis/Klee; S.62: Song: © Boneless-Skeletor OY/Grotto Entertainment OY/ Sony/ATV Music Publishing (Germany GmbH), Berlin; S. 62: (1) MEV Verlag GmbH; S.63: ZEFA/masterfile/Knox; S.68: (1) Corbis/ Mauzy; (2) AP/Warren; (3) Corbis/Rogers; (4) MEV Verlag GmbH; S.69: (1) Corbis/Weatherly; (2) Corbis/Westmorland; (3) Corbis/ Mooney Photography; (4) MEV Verlag GmbH; S.70: (1) Corbis/Rogers; (2) Corbis/DiMaggio/Kalish; S. 71; Song: © Screen Gems EMI Music Inc., EMI Music Publishing (Germany GmbH), Hamburg; S.74: Corbis/Braasch; S.76: (1) Fotofinder/Schapowalow; (2) The Cartoon Bank/Steiner/Ferry; S.79: plainpicture; S.80: (1) Corbis; (2) Corbis/Aurness; (3) Corbis/Smith; (4) Corbis/Ury; S. 81: Song: © by Ludlow Music, Ltd. D/A/CH: Essex Musikvertrieb GmbH, Hamburg; S.81: (1) Corbis/Muench; (2,3) Corbis; S.82: (1) Corbis/Image Source RF; (2) Corbis/Morsch; (3) Corbis/Faris; (4,6-8) Getty Images RF/PhotoDisc; (5,9-11) MEV Verlag GmbH; S.83: (1,6) Getty Images RF/ PhotoDisc; (2) IMAGO/City Press; (3) Corbis/Roberts; (4) Corbis/Mirer; (5) Corbis/Holmes; (7) MEV Verlag GmbH; S.84: Picture-Alliance/epa Niedringhaus; S.85: (1) Corbis/RF; (2) PhotoAlto; (3) Bananastock RF/Watlington/Oxon; S.86: (1) ZEFA/Emely; (2) Getty Images/stone/Darell; S.87: Getty Images/Image Bank/Erlanson; S.88: Corbis/RF; S. 90: Song: (c) Oakfield Avenue Music Ltd. EMI Music Publishing, Hamburg; S.91: (1) Corbis/Henley; (2) Fotosearch RF/Photodisc RF; S.92: Corbis/ Souders; S.93: www.cartoonstock.com/Therien; S.94: (1) Fotosearch Stock Photography/PhotoDisc; (2) MEV VERLAG GmbH; S.95: Fotosearch RF/Brand X Pictures; S.96: PhotoDisc/RF; S.98: (1) MTV Networks Europe/AKUD/Elsesser/Reimann; (2) MEV Verlag GmbH; S.99: (1) Cinetext; (2) Picture-Alliance/Abc Television Network; (3) Universal Press Syndicate; S.100: (1-9) Klett-Archiv/Smith; S.101: (1,2,4) Klett-Archiv/Smith; (3) Corbis/ Ball; S.102: (1,3) Fotosearch RF/Image 100 RF; (2) Bananastock RF/RF; (4) Creativ Collection Verlag GmbH; (5) MEV; (6) Corbis UK Limited/RF; S.103: (1) Global Pictures/Superbild/Agence Phanie; (2,3) MEV Verlag GmbH; (4) Fotosearch RF/ RF; S.105: Getty Images/Eyewire RF; S.106: Alamy Images/Kase; S.107: AKG/Cook; S.108: (1) Corbis/Sayer; (2) Getty Images/Photodisc; S. 109: Klett-Archiv; S.110: MEV Verlag GmbH; S.111: Picture-Alliance/Michel; S.112: Corbis/Morris; S.113: Fotosearch Stock Photography/Stockbyte; S.114: Global Pictures/defd; S.115: Fotosearch Stock Photography/Stockbyte; S.119: (1) Corbis/Hellier; (2) Alamy Images/geophotos; S.122: Modular/Steinle; S.129: Picture-Alliance/Gacad.
Textquellen: S.105: DeBella World Industries; S.108: www.aboutbritain.com; S.110/111: www.neuschwanstein.de

revision 1–3
Test yourself solutions

Erklärung: Test yourself!

Und so wird's gemacht:

1. Ermittle anhand der Lösungen, in welchem Bereich du die meisten Fehler gemacht hast (A, B, C oder D), am besten mit Hilfe einer Strichliste.

2. Schau dir dann im Workbook die zugehörigen Doctor-G-Seiten an. Dort ist bei jeder Übung angegeben, welchen Bereich (A, B, C oder D) du damit üben kannst.

3. Wähle anhand deiner Strichliste die diesem Bereich zugeordneten Übungen aus, um gezielt deine Schwachstellen zu verbessern. Doctor G hält zu jedem Bereich einen Grammatiktipp bereit, mit dem du dir den Stoff wieder ins Gedächtnis rufen kannst, den du für die einzelnen Übungen brauchst.

revision 1

3 The mouse and the cheese (Seite 35)

1. was 2. lived 3. woke 4. noticed 5. was coming 6. thought 7. smells 8. am beginning 9. ran 10. thought 11. is ('s) 12. warned 13. do I know 14. are 15. don't like 16. knows 17. didn't want 18. sat 19. waited 20. was sitting 21. heard 22. is waiting 23. thought 24. didn't go 25. got 26. smelt / smelled 27. is sitting 28. thought 29. never know 30. lay 31. as listening 32. heard 33. said 34. chased 35. was sleeping 36. don't think 37. leave 38. went 39. ran 40. was starting 41. jumped 42. killed 43. ate 44. happened 45. didn't have 46. said 47. doesn't get 48. did 49. told 50. learnt / learned 51. found

Welcher Bereich ist verbesserungsbedürftig?

- **A** Falsche Zeitebene: Gegenwart oder Vergangenheit?
- **B** Verwendung der *simple*-Form statt *progressive*-Form oder umgekehrt: Abfolge von Handlungen *(simple)* oder Hintergrundhandlungen *(progressive)*?
- **C** Falsche Bildung oder Schreibung der Verbform.

➜ **Workbook, S. 24–25**

4 Before a trip to London

1. Are you going to, we're going to 2. It won't be, there'll be 3. It'll, we're, He's going to, we'll probably go 4. I'll 5. don't, we'll miss, we're going to miss 6. Are you going to, I'll take 7. Will you, you're, I'll, I won't

Welcher Bereich ist verbesserungsbedürftig?

- **A** Verwendung von *will-future* statt *going-to-future* oder umgekehrt: Voraussage oder Plan?
- **B** Falsche Verbform in Sätzen mit *when* oder *if*.

➜ **Workbook, S. 26**

revision 2

3 An e-mail from Denver (Seite 65)

1. have just arrived 2. landed 3. have already found 4. Did you get 5. haven't answered 6. spent 7. have ever visited 8. have ever met 9. didn't get 10. didn't want 11. persuaded 12. was 13. Have you ever flown 14. had 15. have never seen 16. haven't had 17. Did Forest win 18. haven't lost 19. have always been 20. Did I tell 21. went 22. didn't think 23. was 24. didn't say 25. haven't organized 26. haven't forgotten

Welcher Bereich ist verbesserungsbedürftig?

- **A** Falsche Zeitebene: *present perfect* oder *simple past*?
- **B** Falsche Bildung oder Schreibung der Verbform.

➜ **Workbook, S. 49–50**

4 Parents and kids (Seite 65)

a) 1. needn't 2. can 3. mustn't 4. can't 5. mustn't 6. can 7. can 8. must 9. must 10. needn't

b) 1. will be allowed to 2. won't be able to 3. had to 4. were allowed to 5. was able to 6. didn't have to 7. wasn't allowed to 8. wasn't able to 9. will have to 10. will be able to 11. won't be allowed to 12. won't have to.

Welcher Bereich ist verbesserungsbedürftig?

a) A Wahl des Modalverbs mit der falschen Bedeutung.
b) B Falsche Zeitebene: *Past* oder *future*?
C Falsche Bildung oder Schreibung der Verbform.
D Verwechslung der beiden Bedeutungen von *can:* dürfen oder können?

➜ **Workbook, S. 50–51**

3 Telephones (Seite 95)

1. most important, hard, useful 2. terrible, wrong, well, more clearly, better 3. regularly, best (better), long, more expensive, normal 4. longer, safe.

Welcher Bereich ist verbesserungsbedürftig?

A Verwendung eines Adjektivs statt eines Adverbs *(-ly)* oder umgekehrt.
B Falsche Bildung oder Schreibung der Adjektiv- oder Adverbform.

➜ **Workbook, S. 74–75**

4 Add the adverbs

1. I **usually** switch the radio on when I get up **in the morning.** 2. Do you **often** listen to music **in the car?** 3. Sally bought a new CD **at Martins Media yesterday.** 4. Tim plays the piano **well.** He practises **regularly,** of course. 5. Did you watch that programme **on TV last night?** 6. The best films are **always** on TV **late at night.**

Welcher Bereich ist verbesserungsbedürftig?

A Falsche Platzierung eines Adverbs der Häufigkeit *(usually, always etc.)*.
B Nichtbeachtung der Regel Ort vor Zeit.
C Trennung von Verb und Objekt durch ein Adverb.

➜ **Workbook, S. 75**

5 A long way home

1. was enjoying 2. broke down 3. were not (weren't) able to 4. needed 5. had to 6. was 7. did not (didn't) speak 8. felt 9. met 10. don't know 11. told 12. will be 13. has broken down 14. don't get 15. will miss 16. will be 17. miss 18. will be 19. don't appear 20. offered 21. will ('ll) take 22. will ('ll) get 23. will ('ll) be able to 24. don't want 25. protested 26. laughed 27. am going to spend 28. took 29. got 30. went 31. asked 32. was waiting 33. arrived 34. cried 35. will ('ll) never forget 36. 've given/gave 37. was just leaving 38. noticed 39. were.

Welcher Bereich ist verbesserungsbedürftig?

A Falsche Zeitebene: Gegenwart oder Vergangenheit?
B Falsche Zeitform (z. B. in einem *if*-Satz; Verwechslung von *will* und *going to* oder von *simple past* und *present perfect).*
C Verwendung der *simple*-Form statt *progressive*-Form oder umgekehrt: Abfolge von Handlungen *(simple)* oder Hintergrundhandlungen *(progressive)*?
D Falsche Bildung oder Schreibung der Verbform.

➜ **Workbook, S. 76**

Talking to the teacher

Can you help me, please?	Können Sie mir bitte helfen?
I don't understand this.	Ich verstehe das nicht.
Can you explain that again, please?	Können Sie das bitte noch einmal erklären?
What do we have to do?	Was müssen wir denn machen?
What's that in English / German?	Was heißt das auf Englisch / Deutsch?
Can I say: …? / What does … mean?	Kann ich sagen: …? / Was bedeutet …?
How do you do this exercise?	Wie macht man diese Übung?
Is this right? I'm not sure.	Ist das richtig? Ich bin nicht sicher.
Sorry, I don't know.	Tut mir Leid, das weiß ich nicht.
Can you write it on the board, please?	Können Sie das bitte an die Tafel schreiben?
Can I ask a question, please?	Kann ich bitte eine Frage stellen?
Pardon? Can you repeat the question / sentence, please?	Wie bitte? Können Sie die Frage / den Satz bitte wiederholen?
Can you play the CD again, please?	Können Sie die CD bitte nochmal abspielen?
Can we do another example, please?	Können wir noch ein Beispiel machen?
Whose turn is it?	Wer ist dran?
What's for homework, please?	Was haben wir als Hausaufgabe auf?
I'm not feeling well.	Ich fühle mich nicht gut.
I've got a headache.	Ich habe Kopfweh.
Can I open the window, please?	Darf ich bitte das Fenster öffnen?
Can I go to the toilet, please?	Darf ich bitte auf die Toilette gehen?

Understanding the teacher

Open your books at page … .	Schlagt Seite … auf.
Turn to page … .	Blättert auf Seite … um.
Read the text on page … .	Lest den Text auf Seite …
Who would like to write on the transparency?	Wer möchte auf die Folie schreiben?
Come to the board, please.	Komm bitte an die Tafel.
Who would like to play the CD?	Wer möchte die CD abspielen?
You're going to hear the CD twice.	Ihr werdet die CD zweimal hören.
Please play track 5 again.	Spiel bitte den Track Nr. 5 noch einmal.
Who would like to play the part of …?	Wer möchte die Rolle von … spielen?
Write the answers in your exercise book.	Schreibt die Antworten in eure Übungshefte.
Would you collect the exercise books / worksheets, please?	Würdest du bitte die Übungshefte / Arbeitsblätter einsammeln?
Do this exercise for homework.	Macht diese Übung als Hausaufgabe.
Be quiet. Sit down, please.	Seid ruhig. Setz dich / Setzt euch, bitte.
Please speak up.	Sprich / Sprecht bitte lauter.
No prompting, please.	Nicht vorsagen, bitte.
Excellent!	Prima!
You can do better. Try again.	Das kannst du besser. Versuch es noch einmal.
That's it. Well done.	So ist es richtig. Gut gemacht.

Talking about stories, poems, songs, …

I like/don't like this story.	Diese Geschichte gefällt mir/gefällt mir nicht.
I think it's good, interesting, brilliant, funny, really exciting.	Ich finde sie gut, interessant, toll, witzig, wirklich spannend.
I think it's sad, terrible, boring.	Ich finde sie traurig, schrecklich, langweilig.
It was OK, but I've read better ones.	Sie ist ganz nett, aber ich habe schon bessere gelesen.

Talking about diagrams and numbers

As you can see in this diagram …	Wie man in diesem Diagramm sehen kann, …
The results show that …	Die Ergebnisse zeigen, dass …
More than half/a third/20 percent …	Mehr als die Hälfte/ein Drittel/20 Prozent …
Less than half/a third/20 percent …	Weniger als die Hälfte/ein Drittel/20 Prozent …
It's surprising that …	Es ist erstaunlich, dass …

Discussion phrases

What do you think?/What's your opinion?	Was meinst du?
Would you like to comment on …?	Würdest du gerne etwas zu … sagen?
In my opinion …	Meiner Meinung nach …
As far as I know …	Soweit ich weiß …
According to … it's …	Laut … ist es …
It's a fact that …	Tatsache ist, dass …
Actually, …	Tatsächlich/Eigentlich …
Basically, …	Im Grunde …
I think you are right/wrong.	Ich denke, du hast Recht/Unrecht.
I agree. / I disagree.	Ich stimme zu. / Ich bin anderer Meinung.
Well, it's true that …, but …	… ist zwar richtig, aber …
Well, I must admit that …, but …	Ich muss zwar zugeben, dass …, aber …
However, …	Jedoch …
On the one hand …, on the other hand …	Einerseits …, anderseits …

Presentation phrases

I'm going to talk about …	Ich werde über … sprechen.
My topic is …	Mein Thema ist …
I'd like to begin with …	Ich würde gerne mit … anfangen.
I wanted to find out …	Ich wollte herausfinden, …
The aim of my presentation is …	Das Ziel meines Vortrags ist …
First of all, …	Zuallererst …
Secondly, …	Zweitens …
Now let's turn to …	Nun lasst uns zu … kommen.
Another important point is …	Ein weiterer wichtiger Punkt ist …
Apart from that, …	Außerdem …
Here you can see …	Hier könnt ihr … sehen.
This is the reason why …	Dies ist der Grund, warum …

List of irregular verbs

infinitive	simple past	past participle	German
to **be** [bi:]	**was/were** [wɒz; wɜ:]	**been** [bi:n]	sein
to **beat** [bi:t]	**beat** [bi:t]	**beaten** ['bi:tn]	besiegen, schlagen
to **become** [bɪ'kʌm]	**became** [bɪ'keɪm]	**become** [bɪ'kʌm]	werden
to **begin** [bɪ'gɪn]	**began** [bɪ'gæn]	**begun** [bɪ'gʌn]	beginnen
to **bend** [bend]	**bent** [bent]	**bent** [bent]	beugen
to **bet** [bet]	**bet** [bet]	**bet** [bet]	wetten
to **blow** [bləʊ]	**blew** [blu:]	**blown** [bləʊn]	blasen
to **break** [breɪk]	**broke** [brəʊk]	**broken** ['brəʊkn]	brechen
to **bring** [brɪŋ]	**brought** [brɔ:t]	**brought** [brɔ:t]	bringen
to **build** [bɪld]	**built** [bɪlt]	**built** [bɪlt]	bauen
to **burn** [bɜ:n]	**burned/burnt** [bɜ:nd; bɜ:nt]	**burned/burnt** [bɜ:nd; bɜ:nt]	brennen
to **buy** [baɪ]	**bought** [bɔ:t]	**bought** [bɔ:t]	kaufen
to **catch** [kætʃ]	**caught** [kɔ:t]	**caught** [kɔ:t]	fangen
to **choose** [tʃu:z]	**chose** [tʃəʊz]	**chosen** ['tʃəʊzn]	(aus)wählen
to **cling** [klɪŋ]	**clung** [klʌŋ]	**clung** [klʌŋ]	(sich) festhalten
to **come** [kʌm]	**came** [keɪm]	**come** [kʌm]	kommen
to **cost** [kɒst]	**cost** [kɒst]	**cost** [kɒst]	kosten
to **creep** [kri:p]	**crept** [krept]	**crept** [krept]	schleichen; kriechen
to **cut** [kʌt]	**cut** [kʌt]	**cut** [kʌt]	schneiden
to **deal (with)** [di:l]	**dealt** [delt]	**dealt** [delt]	(be)handeln
to **do** [du:]	**did** [dɪd]	**done** [dʌn]	tun, machen
to **draw** [drɔ:]	**drew** [dru:]	**drawn** [drɔ:n]	zeichnen
to **dream** [dri:m]	**dreamed/dreamt** [dri:md; dremt]	**dreamed/dreamt** [dri:md; dremt]	träumen
to **drink** [drɪŋk]	**drank** [dræŋk]	**drunk** [drʌŋk]	trinken
to **drive** [draɪv]	**drove** [drəʊv]	**driven** ['drɪvn]	fahren
to **eat** [i:t]	**ate** [et; eɪt]	**eaten** ['i:tn]	essen
to **fall** [fɔ:l]	**fell** [fel]	**fallen** ['fɔ:lən]	fallen
to **feed** [fi:d]	**fed** [fed]	**fed** [fed]	füttern
to **feel** [fi:l]	**felt** [felt]	**felt** [felt]	(sich) fühlen
to **fight** [faɪt]	**fought** [fɔ:t]	**fought** [fɔ:t]	streiten, kämpfen
to **find** [faɪnd]	**found** [faʊnd]	**found** [faʊnd]	finden
to **fly** [flaɪ]	**flew** [flu:]	**flown** [fləʊn]	fliegen
to **forget** [fə'get]	**forgot** [fə'gɒt]	**forgotten** [fə'gɒtn]	vergessen
to **get** [get]	**got** [gɒt]	**got** [gɒt] *(BE)* **gotten** [gɒtn] *(AE)*	(be)kommen; werden
to **give** [gɪv]	**gave** [geɪv]	**given** ['gɪvn]	geben
to **go** [gəʊ]	**went** [went]	**gone** [gɒn]	gehen
to **grow** [grəʊ]	**grew** [gru:]	**grown** [grəʊn]	wachsen; anbauen
to **hang** [hæŋ]	**hung** [hʌŋ]	**hung** [hʌŋ]	hängen
to **have** [hæv]	**had** [hæd]	**had** [hæd]	haben
to **hear** [hɪə]	**heard** [hɜ:d]	**heard** [hɜ:d]	hören
to **hide** [haɪd]	**hid** [hɪd]	**hidden** ['hɪdn]	(sich) verstecken
to **hit** [hɪt]	**hit** [hɪt]	**hit** [hɪt]	schlagen; treffen
to **hold** [həʊld]	**held** [held]	**held** [held]	halten
to **hurt** [hɜ:t]	**hurt** [hɜ:t]	**hurt** [hɜ:t]	verletzen, weh tun
to **keep** [ki:p]	**kept** [kept]	**kept** [kept]	behalten; weitermachen
to **know** [nəʊ]	**knew** [nju:]	**known** [nəʊn]	wissen

infinitive	simple past	past participle	German
to **learn** [lɜ:n]	**learned/learnt** [lɜ:nd; lɜ:nt]	**learned/learnt** [lɜ:nd; lɜ:nt]	lernen
to **leave** [li:v]	**left** [left]	**left** [left]	(ver)lassen
to **lend** [lend]	**lent** [lent]	**lent** [lent]	leihen
to **let** [let]	**let** [let]	**let** [let]	lassen
to **lie** [laɪ]	**lay** [leɪ]	**lain** [leɪn]	liegen
to **lose** [lu:z]	**lost** [lɒst]	**lost** [lɒst]	verlieren
to **make** [meɪk]	**made** [meɪd]	**made** [meɪd]	machen
to **mean** [mi:n]	**meant** [ment]	**meant** [ment]	bedeuten; meinen
to **meet** [mi:t]	**met** [met]	**met** [met]	(sich) treffen
to **pay** [peɪ]	**paid** [peɪd]	**paid** [peɪd]	zahlen
to **put** [pʊt]	**put** [pʊt]	**put** [pʊt]	stellen, legen, setzen
to **read** [ri:d]	**read** [red]	**read** [red]	lesen
to **ride** [raɪd]	**rode** [rəʊd]	**ridden** ['rɪdn]	reiten; fahren
to **ring** [rɪŋ]	**rang** [ræŋ]	**rung** [rʌŋ]	klingeln; anrufen
to **run** [rʌn]	**ran** [ræn]	**run** [rʌn]	rennen, laufen
to **say** [seɪ]	**said** [sed]	**said** [sed]	sagen
to **see** [si:]	**saw** [sɔ:]	**seen** [si:n]	sehen
to **sell** [sel]	**sold** [səʊld]	**sold** [səʊld]	verkaufen
to **send** [send]	**sent** [sent]	**sent** [sent]	schicken
to **set** [set]	**set** [set]	**set** [set]	setzen, legen, stellen
to **shake** [ʃeɪk]	**shook** [ʃʊk]	**shaken** ['ʃeɪkn]	schütteln
to **shine** [ʃaɪn]	**shone** [ʃɒn]	**shone** [ʃɒn]	scheinen, glänzen
to **shoot** [ʃu:t]	**shot** [ʃɒt]	**shot** [ʃɒt]	schießen
to **show** [ʃəʊ]	**showed** [ʃəʊd]	**shown** [ʃəʊn]	zeigen
to **shut** [ʃʌt]	**shut** [ʃʌt]	**shut** [ʃʌt]	schließen
to **sing** [sɪŋ]	**sang** [sæŋ]	**sung** [sʌŋ]	singen
to **sit** [sɪt]	**sat** [sæt]	**sat** [sæt]	sitzen
to **sleep** [sli:p]	**slept** [slept]	**slept** [slept]	schlafen
to **smell** [smel]	**smelled/smelt** [smeld; smelt]	**smelled/smelt** [smeld; smelt]	riechen
to **speak** [spi:k]	**spoke** [spəʊk]	**spoken** ['spəʊkn]	sprechen
to **spell** [spel]	**spelled/spelt** [speld; spelt]	**spelled/spelt** [speld; spelt]	buchstabieren
to **spend** [spend]	**spent** [spent]	**spent** [spent]	ausgeben; verbringen
to **spill** [spɪl]	**spilled/spilt** [spɪld; spɪlt]	**spilled/spilt** [spɪld; spɪlt]	verschütten
to **stand** [stænd]	**stood** [stʊd]	**stood** [stʊd]	stehen
to **steal** [sti:l]	**stole** [stəʊl]	**stolen** ['stəʊlən]	stehlen
to **stick** [stɪk]	**stuck** [stʌk]	**stuck** [stʌk]	kleben; stecken
to **swim** [swɪm]	**swam** [swæm]	**swum** [swʌm]	schwimmen
to **take** [teɪk]	**took** [tʊk]	**taken** ['teɪkn]	nehmen
to **teach** [ti:tʃ]	**taught** [tɔ:t]	**taught** [tɔ:t]	lehren
to **tell** [tel]	**told** [təʊld]	**told** [təʊld]	sagen, erzählen
to **think** [θɪŋk]	**thought** [θɔ:t]	**thought** [θɔ:t]	denken
to **throw** [θrəʊ]	**threw** [θru:]	**thrown** [θrəʊn]	werfen
to **understand** [ˌʌndə'stænd]	**understood** [ˌʌndə'stʊd]	**understood** [ˌʌndə'stʊd]	verstehen
to **wake** [weɪk]	**woke** [wəʊk]	**woken** ['wəʊkn]	aufwachen; wecken
to **wear** [weə]	**wore** [wɔ:]	**worn** [wɔ:n]	tragen, anhaben
to **win** [wɪn]	**won** [wʌn]	**won** [wʌn]	gewinnen
to **write** [raɪt]	**wrote** [rəʊt]	**written** ['rɪtn]	schreiben

The London Underground
Bakerloo
Central
Circle
District
East London
Hammersmith & City
Jubilee
Metropolitan
Northern
Piccadilly
Victoria
Waterloo & City
DLR
Under construction
National Rail
UNDERGROUND
River Thames
Preston Road
Northwick Park
Wembley Park
South Kenton
Harlesden
Neasden
Dollis Hill
Willesden Green
Kilburn
West Hampstead 200m
Brondesbury Park
Kensal Rise
Brondesbury
Kensal Green
Queen's Park
Finchley Road
Swiss Cottage
St. John's Wood
Maida Vale
Kilburn Park
Warwick Avenue
Royal Oak
Westbourne Park
Paddington
Edgware Road
Marylebone
Baker Street
Golders Green
Hampstead
Finchley Road & Frognal
Belsize Park
Hampstead Heath
Gospel Oak
Kentish Town West
Chalk Farm
Camden Town
Mornington Crescent
Great Portland Street
Euston
Euston Square
Euston 200m
Warren Street
Archway
Tufnell Park
Kentish Town
Camden Road
Holloway Road
Caledonian Road
Caledonian Road & Barnsbury
King's Cross St. Pancras
Manor House
Arsenal
Finsbury Park
Tottenham Hale
Walthamstow Central
Canonbury
Hackney Central
Highbury & Islington
Dalston Kingsland
Homerton
Angel
Old Street
Farringdon
Barbican
Moorgate
Liverpool Street
Bethnal Green
Mile End
Bow Road
Shoreditch
Ladbroke Grove
Latimer Road
White City
Holland Park
Bayswater
Queensway
Lancaster Gate
Bond Street
Regent's Park
Oxford Circus
Goodge Street
Russell Square
Holborn
East Acton
Shepherd's Bush
Notting Hill Gate
Marble Arch
Tottenham Court Road
Chancery Lane
St. Paul's
Bank
Aldgate
Aldgate East
Stepney Green
Whitechapel
All Saints
High Street Kensington
Hyde Park Corner
Green Park
Covent Garden
Cannon Street
Shadwell
Westferry
Kensington (Olympia)
Goldhawk Road
Piccadilly Circus
Leicester Square
Mansion House
Monument
Tower Hill
Tower Gateway
Fenchurch Street 150m
Limehouse
Knightsbridge
Charing Cross
Blackfriars
Wapping
West India Quay
Hammersmith
Barons Court
Gloucester Road
Sloane Square
St. James's Park
Temple
London Bridge
Rotherhithe
Canary Wharf
West Kensington
Earl's Court
South Kensington
Victoria
Westminster
Embankment
Charing Cross 100m
Bermondsey
Canada Water
Heron Quays
South Quay
Crossharbour & London Arena
Mudchute
Island Gardens
West Brompton
Fulham Broadway
Parsons Green
Putney Bridge
East Putney
Waterloo
Pimlico
Southwark
Waterloo East
Lambeth North
Vauxhall
Elephant & Castle
100m

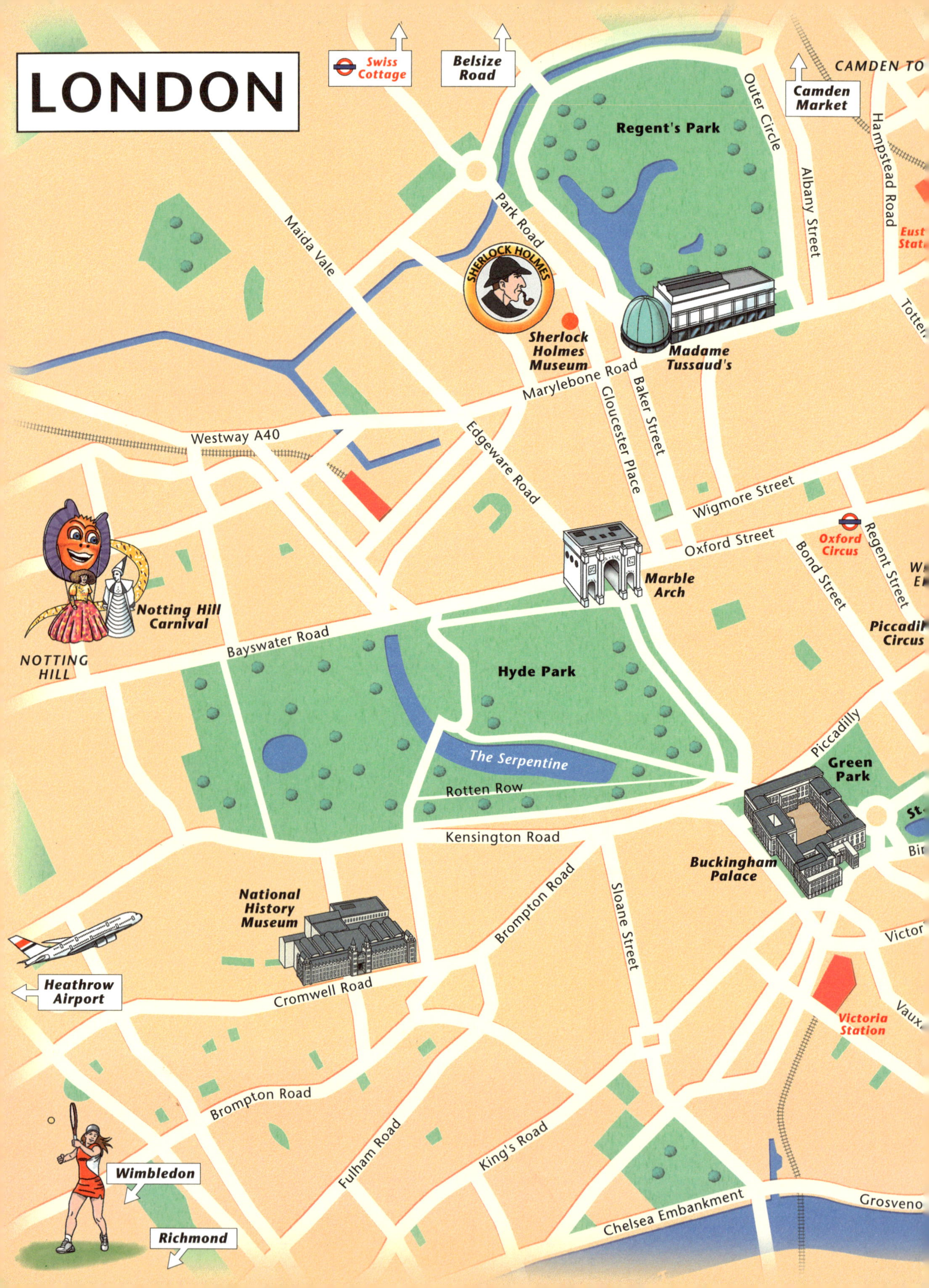
LONDON
Swiss Cottage
Belsize Road
CAMDEN TO
Camden Market
Regent's Park
Outer Circle
Albany Street
Hampstead Road
Eust Stat
Park Road
Maida Vale
Sherlock Holmes Museum
Madame Tussaud's
Totten
Marylebone Road
Gloucester Place
Baker Street
Westway A40
Edgeware Road
Wigmore Street
Oxford Street
Oxford Circus
Regent Street
Bond Street
Marble Arch
Notting Hill Carnival
NOTTING HILL
Bayswater Road
Hyde Park
Piccadil Circus
Piccadilly
Green Park
The Serpentine
Rotten Row
Kensington Road
Buckingham Palace
St
Bir
National History Museum
Brompton Road
Sloane Street
Victor
Heathrow Airport
Cromwell Road
Victoria Station
Vaux
Brompton Road
Fulham Road
King's Road
Wimbledon
Richmond
Chelsea Embankment
Grosveno